Standing at Sinai: Sermons and Writings

Fred N. Reiner

Published by Temple Sinai, Washington, D.C.
to mark the retirement of Fred N. Reiner
Senior Rabbi, 1985-2010

authorHOUSE®

AuthorHouse™
1663 Liberty Drive
Bloomington, IN 47403
www.authorhouse.com
Phone: 1-800-839-8640

First published by AuthorHouse 6/23/2011

ISBN: 978-1-4567-6506-4 (sc)
ISBN: 978-1-4567-6507-1 (e)

Library of Congress Control Number: 2011908012

Printed in the United States of America

This book is printed on acid-free paper.

Table of Contents

Foreword

Some rabbis pontificate. Others re-tell the events of their times through a glossy Jewish veneer. Still others attempt to project a self-defined charismatic persona through personal anecdotes and stories.

Fred Reiner, my colleague and friend for 25 years at Temple Sinai, instead taught the Torah of social justice, Reform Jewish theology, and ethical practice, through his wise, insightful, and caring sermons and writings.

Fred is a scholar who also knew how to be a rabbi, able to translate his erudition into words that could help define and enrich the lives of his congregants. He did not need to be "showy" to be effective; he simply needed to say what was true in carefully thought out and precise language.

Fred rarely (ever?) raised his voice in anger or criticism. So when he spoke in a loud voice at a High Holiday service, or preached on a difficult or controversial topic, people listened. Congregants who were accustomed to listening to or being politically powerful individuals counted on Rabbi Reiner to direct their thoughts and actions to the transcendent, the lasting, the just. They respected his words and valued his character.

Washington, D.C. is not such an easy place to be a rabbi. We are a city of words, of speechwriters, of the press. Everyone has something to say and the means to say it. Over the years of Fred's career, those means became more universally available with the advance of technology. At the same time, there are many orators here who rely on others to write their words for them. Sometimes, especially after a major crisis or historic event, we rabbis ask ourselves: What is left for me to say? And will I know how to say it?

Fred Reiner always managed to find an answer, always grounded in Torah and Jewish tradition, always poised between the power of the past and the exigencies of the present.

Social justice advocacy was a foundation of Rabbi Fred Reiner's rabbinate, and as we can see from this collection of outstanding sermons, a focal point of his preaching. But he is also a God-centered person, consistently identifying Jewish theology as the catalyst for his social justice concerns. We were expected to be activists as Jews, Jews as activists; Torah was to be a constant challenge, not just a comfort. We always had more to do.

Fred had his lighter side, too. His Purim messages were amazingly creative. Combining scholarship and wit, he managed to invent a new commentary every year. These Purim pieces deserve a much wider audience than they have previously received, and I am especially pleased that he has included them in this collection.

And then there's Christian David Ginsburg and the Masorah about which Fred wrote his rabbinical school thesis and continued to study for almost four decades (and counting). Very few congregational rabbis continue their academic studies in such a serious way. Fred, in contrast, published papers on Ginsburg and Masorah and spoke at meetings of the Society of Biblical Literature and other scholarly groups. This was truly *Torah lishma*—study for the pure sake of it, which he will continue in his retirement. Masoretic literature, though of great interest academically and intellectually, was not a "jazzy" topic for a congregational rabbi—unlike Midrash or contemporary theology or literature "useful" for sermons or teaching. It was simply what Fred loved to study—and in doing so, he became an even better rabbi.

I know how much his congregants miss him—this volume will bring back fond memories and inspire continuing thought and action. It will also be a great gift to those who never had the chance to hear Fred in person.

It was my privilege to be his colleague for 25 years, and it is also my privilege to introduce this collection.

We read in *Pirkei Avot*: "Seek out a rabbi; and acquire a friend."

In Fred Reiner, I found both. If you haven't already, you will too in this volume. It is a treasure.

Rabbi Mindy Avra Portnoy

Introduction

More than anything else, rabbis are communicators. We speak from the pulpit. We write letters, messages in our bulletins, and e-mails. We teach and tutor. We counsel and guide. We supervise and lead. We shape our congregations, our leaders, our students. We represent our congregations in our communities. We observe and capture the trends in our society, the challenges our people face, and we try to bring Jewish values to bear upon them. At weddings and funerals, at bar and bat mitzvah services and baby namings, we try to capture the essence of the person or family and share that insight with those who have gathered. We convey our vision of what it means to be a good Jew so effectively that others will share it and be inspired.

No less should rabbis seek and create new knowledge. We do research and share our findings in the classroom, from the pulpit, and sometimes in academic settings. Sometimes we need to lead others with humor, as on Purim.

I believe that our words also shape our history. They can give us a window to the events we see and confront. They can help us understand the changes that swirl about us. Preserving our words is a way to preserve our history, to record the events and trends of our lives and our communities.

This book is published as I retire from twenty-five years of service to Temple Sinai in Washington, D.C. In preparation for this transition, our Archives Committee asked me to undertake an oral history interview. We expanded the concept to include this volume, which reflects not just my history but the history of the congregation and this Jewish community.

Certainly they were years of expansion and growth—of the congregation, its schools and building, its programs and activities. They were years of challenge, as well. Can our Jewish community maintain its integrity as it continues to assimilate? What role does Israel play in our lives? What form does social action take in our day? What are the beliefs and values that help to shape us as post-modern American Jews? How do Judaism's timeless principles stand up to the values in our American society?

As we communicate, we articulate what we stand for. We take our stands in the pulpit; we stand with our congregants at peak moments; we stand proudly as preservers and transmitters of Jewish texts and values; we stand as religious leaders in the community.

This volume, *Standing at Sinai*, captures some of the trends and the struggles of these twenty-five years at Temple Sinai in the nation's capital. Our congregation is well educated and sophisticated. They appreciate nuance, and many seek Jewish answers for issues in their lives or in the world around them. They seek to reconcile the quest for social justice with what they understand from our sacred Jewish texts.

In planning this book we decided to include a variety of writings: sermons from across the twenty-five year span; Purim messages in the tradition of Purim-Torah, finding our sense of humor as we prepare for the early spring holiday; a few of the scholarly papers I published or delivered; some samples of writings from historic moments.

I have been privileged to work with many outstanding colleagues these twenty-five years. Rabbi Mindy Portnoy and I have worked side by side for most of them, so I am particularly pleased that she is setting the stage for this collection through her foreword. Christine Intagliata, a woman of remarkable and varied talents, serves as the editor. Marilyn Goldhammer and Carole Brand, each a leader in our congregation, have guided this project from conception to delivery, along with the assistance of Nina Borwick. The project is supported by the Harris History Fund of Temple Sinai, established by Ruth Harris in memory of her husband, Isadore. Ruth, a professional historian, is passionate about preserving the history of our community, and I hope this volume is a fitting contribution to that endeavor. Above all, I thank Sherry Levy-Reiner, my wife and faithful editor. Her skill and acumen is reflected in each sermon, and in other writings, as well. She sharpens ideas and makes the awkward felicitous.

Fred N. Reiner
Washington, D.C.
1 August 2010

Sermons

Renewal in the New Year

Rosh Hashanah Eve 5746
September 15, 1985

The year I went to Israel in my second year of rabbinical school, my suitcase was lost on the way. I knew that lost bags usually turn up right away and make it to the correct destination on the next flight. But this time El Al lost it, Swiss Air found it in Europe, cabled my parents in Chicago, and sent, at long last, the wrong bag to Jerusalem. They searched all over again, and several weeks later, the suitcase and I were reunited. The clothes had been missing so long it was if they were new. As I opened my suitcase in my room, now rediscovering the clothes I had packed for the year, my Israeli landlady smiled and said, "*Titchadesh*," may you be renewed. This is the Hebrew word we say when someone purchases a new article of clothing, as we might say in English, "wear it in good health" or "wear it well." But the Hebrew has a way of saying it—"may you be renewed"—as if the garment might renew our inner lives, strengthen our inner selves. We say *titchadesh* because the clothes were as if pre-worn, and my evident excitement at having recovered them was like one getting a whole new wardrobe. *Titchadesh*, may you be renewed. Here we are today, some of us wearing new clothes, all of us needing to be renewed. All of us needing to find our spiritual baggage again. All of us needing to wrap ourselves in our best Jewish garments, sometimes forgotten or lost of tradition, and stand these days before God. Rosh Hashanah is a time of renewal.

We live in a time of technology and information and change, as pointed out by many commentators. Literary critic Clint Brooks says, "We are living in an age of information in which we seek not information but meaning and wisdom."

Sociologist Robert Bellah points out that we live in a culture of success and freedom and justice where we need values and coherence. Business critic John Nesbitt calls it a time of technology where we need the warmth of human response. There are anomalies in these observations. With all the information we acquire, our children seem to know less. Studies point out a decline in test scores and in educational skills. With all the technology that we have gained, we have less time for family. We feel more rushed and frenzied. And with all the personal freedom we enjoy, we feel more acutely a sense of loneliness.

Clearly we cannot live by technology and information alone. For with instantaneous worldwide communications it took a month to find my suitcase. All of us need meaning and wisdom and warmth. Rosh Hashanah comes to help us find them.

Dr. Harry Harlow at the University of Wisconsin performed a famous experiment with infant monkeys. Two surrogate mothers were placed in a cage with an infant monkey—one of them consisting of a wire frame, the other one covered with terry cloth. The twist was that the wire mother was the one that nursed; the cloth mother didn't. The infant would cling to the cloth mother for warmth and softness and affection, then run over to the wire mother to nurse, and then run back to the cloth mother. The infant monkey was able to compensate for the shortcomings of each. Harlow summarized this experiment by saying, "Man cannot live by milk alone."[1] We all need food and warmth, information and wisdom, freedom and a sense of belonging.

All year long we are caught up in careers and urgency and pressure to succeed and win and make our contribution, but today we pause and seek renewal. We look inside ourselves and examine our shortcomings and our direction. We seek to find our spiritual garments that have gone astray and put them on and be renewed.

Today we also seek continuity in a time of change. The pre-Socratic philosopher Heraclitus said, "The essence of the universe is change." You cannot step into the same river twice, for it is constantly changing. We see changes swirling about us in our own lives. In this age of technology and information, words and ideas are instantly transmitted; we realize that there are changes that we cannot observe. Biologists tell us that we change all the cells in our bodies every seven years. Physically we are never the same person; we hope we can grow and continue to change spiritually as well. We see our bodies change. We see our children and our grandchildren and our parents changing, all of us growing older. We know that all of life changes before us.

This day of Rosh Hashanah comes to help us manage that change. To mark time. To help us scoop up some of river of life constantly flowing underneath us and capture some of its life-giving waters. Rosh Hashanah comes to tell us that there is continuity as well as change.

Once again this year Rosh Hashanah returns full of memories

—laden with our sense of inadequacy amid all the rush in our lives. Here is Rosh Hashanah to bring us renewal. But how? How do we find the continuity that we need? How do we find the time with ourselves, the warmth we crave, the renewal we seek? Our liturgy on these Days of Awe speaks of turning. *Teshuvah* is the Hebrew word for "turning," and the same word is for repentance. We are commanded to turn, or at least to begin to turn, on the New Year. To turn from carelessness to caring. To turn from ourselves to others. To turn from a life of consumption to a life of concern. To turn from the common to the commandments. It is a motif and a reference we recognize from our weekly prayer book, for as we turn to place the Torah in the Ark each Shabbat, we read the words of Lamentations: "Help us to return to You, O God, then truly shall we return. Renew our days as in the past." This is the part of the message of Rosh Hashanah, too. To turn to God. To return to our childhood sense of wonder and religion. Seeing flowers for the first time, marveling at the world around us. To return to our personal Jewish past, our sense of who we are, the memories of our Jewish lives, of Rosh Hashanahs past, of family gatherings and long services. To renew our days as in the past. We must return to renew our sense of values and purpose as well. To remind ourselves that there is meaning and order in the world and in our lives. And to renew our dedication to values that lead us to caring and to God: providing for those in need, honoring parents, respecting age, being honest with one another. These are values that need renewal in our lives today, and Rosh Hashanah is the time to begin to renew.

Our ancestors used to wear white robes—*kittels*—to worship on the holydays. White was the symbol of purity and still is. Our prayer book quotes Isaiah: "though your sins be as scarlet they shall be white as snow." So even today we change pulpit robes and torah mantles to white each year. But more than wearing white, everyone in those days wore the same garment. There was equality and simplicity and dignity and purity and continuity.

Once we Jews used to get new clothes twice a year: on Rosh Hashanah and on Pesach. Two times a year we would say to one another *titchadesh*. But on these two occasions, ironically enough, the men would wear *kittels*, which would cover their new clothes, the same *kittels* year after year, on the High Holidays and at Seder. The *kittel*, moreover, was a reminder of mortality. The *kittel* was to be the shroud in which one would be buried. So the entire male congregation would come before God on the Days of Awe angel-like, wrapped in garments of purity, reminding them of their equality before God and their trust in God's forgiveness, reminding them of their ultimate mortality.

Today we no longer wear *kittels*. These garments are lost to us. Yet we seek what that generation sought—forgiveness and purity and renewal. We seek to be cleansed and made whole. We seek our own garments of renewal. We seek warmth and continuity and values and tradition in the fabric of our lives. We who have lost touch with our spiritual selves, we who have lost our Jewish baggage, we who have lost our sense of purpose—we come here for strength and direction and healing and repentance. To wrap ourselves in the holiness of this day. May we find it here. *Titchadesh.* May we be renewed.

---

1. Harry F. Harlow, "The Nature of Love," *American Psychologist, 13,* 673-685.

Say Hineni

Rosh Hashanah Morning 5746
September 16, 1985

Not long ago I saw a bumper sticker that said "Say Hineni to God." As bumper stickers go, it was a bit esoteric, containing the Hebrew word *hineni*, meaning "here I am." It's a fascinating, simple word that most Hebrew students learn early. I remember answering *hineni* in Hebrew School, an elegant way of saying "present" when the teacher took attendance.

Hineni is a composite of *hiney* and *ani*. It means literally "here I am," but it is an expression indicating readiness: In English we might say "at your service." Saying it makes the speaker conspicuous. It is a word of acceptance, an acknowledgment of readiness and willingness to accept responsibility whether in Hebrew class or when uttered by Abraham in response to God's call.

Sociologist Thorstein Veblen pointed out over 75 years ago that one of the guiding principles of our society and economy was what he called "conspicuous consumption." So much of what we do in America—from the clothes we wear to the cars we drive—is guided by our desire to demonstrate our background, our affluence.

But if we take conspicuous consumption for granted, we do not take conspicuous Judaism for granted. We are conditioned, rather, to make our Judaism inconspicuous—perhaps because we have felt the sting of anti-Semitism, perhaps because we simply don't want to be too visible. We all have had the experience of being in a room with strangers and sensing who is Jewish. As Jews, most of us know dozens of ways to hide and dozens of ways to discover one another. While our tradition teaches us to be anonymous when giving charity and to serve others because, it is our responsibility and not a path to glory, all of us need pride in being Jewish.

Rosh Hashanah evokes that pride in us; it summons us to say *hineni*, to affirm the importance of Judaism in our lives, to accept our responsibilities.

There are many definitions of Judaism and who is a Jew. There is the Halachic definition: someone born of a Jewish mother or who converts. There is the practicing Jew who keeps 613 mitzvot. There is the contributing Jew who gives to Jewish charities. There is the praying Jew who attends services. There is the gastronomic Jew who eats Jewish food. There is the cardiac Jew who says "I feel it in my heart." There is the pediatric Jew who is Jewish "for the sake of the children." There are "rock Jews," who are perpetually in hiding, and there are "crisis Jews," who emerge only in times of personal or public crises. What we need are participating and committed Jews willing to say *"Hineni*—here I am! I am ready! Ask me."

It's a hard word for us to say today: *hineni*. We live in what Robert Bellah calls "a culture of separation," apart from one another in mind and body; we look out for ourselves. Yet is a time when it is more important than ever to say *hineni*.

Not once but three times does Abraham say *hineni* in the Akedah story. First to God, at the beginning of the story; next to Isaac, as they ascend the mountain; and a third time to the angel, who has just halted the attempted sacrifice. So do we need to respond three times: to God, to families, and to those who serve.

God doesn't call to us with tests as God did to Abraham, as a disembodied voice commanding us to take strange journeys. But here we are today because God calls to us in a different way. God calls to us through the message of this day, through the call of the shofar, through the words of the prayers we read. God calls to each of us on Rosh Hashanah to examine our ways in turn, to plumb the depths of our Jewish lives, to seek strength and comfort in the rhythm of Jewish life, to know who we are and before Whom we stand. And God does not just call to us on Rosh Hashanah and Yom Kippur, but throughout the year and throughout our lives. And while it is easy for us to ignore God's call, to ignore the prayers and avoid the rituals in all the busyness of our lives, still God calls out to us and like Abraham we must answer with humility and trust: *hineni*.

The second *hineni* comes in the middle of the story, as Abraham and Isaac are going up the mountain together. Isaac notices that there is no animal for the sacrifice and says, "Father." Abraham answers *hineni*.

How often do the members of our family call out to us and we fail to respond, *"Hineni*, here I am"? Be it our parents or children, spouses, brothers, sisters – we need to be ready to reassure, to put first those people who are most important to us and whom we so often take for granted.

Most of our lives lack the drama of Abraham's journey to Mount Moriah. The demands that are made upon us are real but less pressing than those we read about on Rosh Hashanah. Yet the issues and struggles are the same, and when our families and friends cry out to us, we need to listen and respond *hineni*. Rosh Hashanah comes to give us a fresh start, to turn us to those who are closest to us as we turn to God and to say "*Hineni*, I am ready."

The third *hineni* is Abraham's response to the angel. When Abraham picks up the knife to slay Isaac, the angel calls to him with urgency and concern: "Abraham, Abraham." Unlike Abraham, we are not alone with an angel. Today we are gathered as a congregation. If we need to hear ourselves say *hineni*, so we need to hear one another say it too. (You realize, of course, that God may call once, but our congregation calls twice, even three times and more. For we recognize that synagogues and congregations need to ask and ask and need a great deal of attention.) We need to say and hear *hineni* more from ourselves and from one another. We need to strengthen our own commitment and thus strengthen one another. Instead of saying "I don't have time," we should say "I'll make the time." Instead of saying "I can't accept such a responsibility," we should say "This will be quite a challenge." Instead of saying "I've done my part for years," we should say "I know how much this needs to be done." Instead of saying "I don't feel like I belong here," we need to say "This is my place and I want to help." We need to say "*Hineni*. Here I am. Ask me."

You and I are far removed from Abraham's world. We live in a society where people are searching for values. What are we committed to that is worthwhile? Where in our lives are our spiritual values, or have they disappeared? Where is our ability to love, to pray, to sacrifice, to pledge commitment to something beyond ourselves? In an age of self-commitment, in times such as these, how do we meet our spiritual needs, needs that are an essential part of us? We need to make a personal statement of commitment to remind ourselves of who we are, where we are, and where we are going. We need to strengthen ourselves spiritually, to sustain and direct the guiding principles of our lives. We need to hear ourselves say *hineni*.

Think of Abraham journeying three days, without a guide or path, in the wilderness, to a place he didn't know, to do something he couldn't understand, leaving everything behind, and still his response was *hineni*. We need to put aside our misgivings and make ourselves proud and supporting, to continue the road that has been marked and laid out for us, to feel that it is our road, not just a pathless wilderness. We need to know that others have been committed before us and marked the way, and we need to follow and keep the road maintained. Like Abraham, we need to be ready to set out on our journey, to be committed for ourselves and one another, to say with everything that is within us—*hineni*.

Mixed Marriages:
What Do We Do For Them?

Yom Kippur Morning 5749
September 21, 1988

I remember the call well. The woman wasn't Jewish, and she didn't really have any Jewish friends. But now her daughter had just told her that she was engaged—to somebody Jewish! The woman was at a loss as how to respond and what to do. So she got out the Yellow Pages, looked up "synagogue," and found me. She ended her introduction with the question: "What do we do for them?"

Her other, unspoken questions were probably not too different from the questions on the minds of the Jewish parents in a similar situation: How will the ceremony work? What religion will there be in their house? Will I have Jewish grandchildren? And perhaps some of the same questions that I hear from Jewish callers: Why did this happen? Where did I go wrong?

I did my best to reassure the woman on the phone that Jews are people not unlike those she knew. "What do you do for them?" I said. "They are in love, and it's a happy time. You congratulate them and wish them well and plan a wedding with sensitivity. Perhaps you can get the couple to explore the religious issues in their relationship, and perhaps let them know your feelings. Then stand back."

There is no topic more on our minds as Jews than mixed marriage. Some in our community perceive it as a threat to Jewish survival, and others view it as a reality with which we must come to grips. We cannot help but view it personally as well, for chances are that mixed marriage will come into your family as it has come into mine, with all the mixed feelings, all the discomfort, and all the concerns that go along with it.

For today, 35-40 percent of Jews who marry will choose spouses not born Jewish. That figure compares with 6 percent in 1950, when Jewish mixed marriages were a curiosity, and it compares with 70 percent in some cities in our nation today. That means that one-third to one-half of the children in our religious school—our b'nai mitzvah, our confirmands, youth groupers, and college students—will marry someone not born Jewish.

I don't believe there is much you or I can do to reverse these trends today in our society. One fourth of these marriages lead to a conversion and a Jewish marriage, and these are not my concern. But two-thirds of these couples do nothing about religion in their family. For me that is the most alarming statistic, that two-thirds of these interfaith couples neither convert nor make a decision about religion in their home or for their children. These figures, cited by Egon Mayer of Brooklyn College and quoted by Paul and Rachel Cowan in their recent book *Mixed Blessings,*[1] spell out the departure from meaningful Jewish life of 25 percent of the Jews who marry.

What could be more on our minds today? On this day of introspection and consideration of past and future, on this day when we think of the bonds that unite us as Jews with ages past, with endangered Jewish communities, with the martyrs of our people, what could be more pressing than the disappearance of one-quarter of our children from the Jewish community?

Our Torah reading this morning gives us an insight about this situation. We read from Deuteronomy the powerful words of Moses' oration: "You stand here today—all of you—before Adonai your God, everyone in Israel: men, women, children, the strangers in your camp, to enter into the sworn covenant with God" (Deut. 29:9-11). Read it carefully and the text says: "not just Jews, but the ones who live with you, as well; not just your family of birth, but those close to you also."

It is a message of open doors: Open doors for all who enter, including those men and women who are married to Jews but are not Jewish themselves. Many of these people have no other religion. Some of them, at least, want to be a part of the Jewish community. We need to open our doors. We need to tell them the doors are open. We need to get these families through the doors, or we will lose them. And this is why we need to reach out to the interfaith couples in our midst.

We don't say Kaddish or sit shiva for our children who marry out. We cannot think for a moment of writing these children off, or of keeping them cloistered, or of ruling their adult lives. Yet we cannot honestly deny the differences between Jews and non-Jews, between Jewish and interfaith marriages. The challenge that mixed marriage brings to us is how to deepen our own commitment—for all of us—to the covenant Moses proclaimed at Sinai.

Sometimes people ask me, "What is the blessing for a mixed marriage?" After all, Judaism has blessings for so many things: hearing thunder, seeing a rainbow, receiving good news and bad news alike. The rabbi in Anatevka devised a blessing for the anti-Semitic czar. So surely, rabbi, there must be a blessing for a mixed marriage.

There is! Every marriage, of course, should be blessed with love and satisfaction and companionship. But a mixed marriage must be especially blessed with openness and clarity. It must have openness to understanding, to building a religious life, to reaching reasonable decisions, and openness to commitment. It must have clarity to appreciate differences, to understand ourselves and our religion; it must also have clarity to acknowledge that Judaism is a system of practice and belief and not just a culture. We need to be honest with ourselves and with others and recognize that Jews believe in one God, that we do not accept Jesus as divine, that we do not celebrate holidays of other religions, that we have a strong tradition of practice and belief that is unique to us and different from Christianity, Islam, and other religions, even though we share much in common. We need to say clearly that Judaism is important to us, that Jewish survival is important to us. We should be showing our children and our parents that we want Judaism to be important to them, an integral part of the life of every Jew, as we stand symbolically today—with all other Jews—before God.

Here is the most difficult question of all. It is harder than "What can we do for them?" and "Is there a blessing for this marriage?" The hardest question is: "What can we do to insure Jewish survival?" We ask this in a time when many Jews do not marry and of those who do marry, at least one-third marry non-Jews.

Here is the answer: Judaism can survive only if Jews care enough about it to make it survive. We take our Judaism too much for granted. Except for a few days each year, most of us are indifferent. For many of us, Judaism is like a special garment we put on from time to time, at peak moments in our lives. It is an important part of our identity, but not the motivating force in our lives. We are uncomfortable with belief in general, unwilling to be guided strictly by Jewish practice, and unknowing about Jewish spirituality. We have translated our Judaism into Jewish culture: bagels and an occasional Jewish word, a quaint custom here, a Jewish contribution there. We have satisfied ourselves—most of us—with this cultural definition of what it means to be Jewish. So our children—or our fiancé—come to ask us: "If Judaism is so important, why don't you do more?" Or, "How can I as a non-Jew be part of a culture I wasn't born into?" Or, "Where is the substance? I need a religion that satisfies my need for God and guidance." When we hear these questions, we find ourselves too often unable to answer.

The adult child of one mixed marriage finds his religious life centered in the Hindu tradition of Yoga. It is a spiritual discipline to achieve union with the "Universal Soul." "It is ecumenical," he says. It involves no rejection. "I can comfortably say I am both Jew and Christian." Unable to choose, he has opted out of both.

We must remind ourselves that Judaism has a remarkable richness to draw upon, a richness of practice and prayers and ceremony and belief and study. It is the result of the spiritual quest of five millennia, centered in a covenant between God and our people, the covenant described in our Torah reading, the covenant entered into with those who stood at Sinai and equally with future generations. It is a covenant with open doors, a covenant that faces the future, a covenant that cares about survival.

No less today we must be concerned about our own covenant, our own survival, our own relationships. No less must we keep our own doors open, for the real concern about mixed marriage and survival should be concern about these families, and this is why our interfaith couples group and our study programs are so important.

It is not a problem of wedding ceremonies that last fifteen minutes but of marriages that last many years. It is not a problem of "compatible cultures" but of ultimate commitments. It is not a problem of achieving success or failure but of reestablishing Jewish life for vast numbers of our people. I see many mixed married couples stuck on trying to reconcile their religious differences and others flourishing as a Jewish family. I see many where each goes his and her own religious way or non-religious way. I have rejoiced that many do choose Judaism, motivated by a commitment to build a family dedicated to Jewish life. I see many families where Judaism is deeply important to the Jewish partner and something simply not shared at home.

There are, after all, many Jewish life styles and many ways to practice Judaism. Some of them are easier, some are more difficult, and some are indeed problematic. The question is not which Jewish life style to select, but "How soon can you start?" The threat of our day is not mixed marriage but apathy—apathy whether there is in the family one Jewish person or two or three or four.

So where is the key to Jewish survival in our day, when mixed marriage is so common? My answer comes from Deuteronomy—from our Torah portion this morning: "It is not in heaven that we need someone to go and fetch it for us. It is not on the other side of the sea that we need to go there and get it" (Deut. 30:11-14). It is not in the sociological studies of marriage trends. It is not in the doomsday prophecies. It is not distant from us nor hard for us to understand. No, it is very near to us: in our mouths, in our hearts, and in our minds, if only we would *do* it, before it is too late.

---

1. Paul Cowan with Rachel Cowan, *Mixed Blessings: Marriage Between Jews and Christians*, (New York: Doubleday, 1987).

Homosexuality, Holiness, and Sin

Kol Nidre 5750
October 8, 1989

I have always been intrigued by the choice of the traditional Torah reading on Yom Kippur afternoon. The traditional Torah reading is not the magnificent Holiness Code from Leviticus 19 that we read at Temple Sinai, as do Reform congregations everywhere. Rather, it is the simple list of the forbidden marriages and sexual immoralities listed in Leviticus 18. I often have asked myself, as others have before me, "Why has our people read a passage from the Torah dealing with the laws against incest and sexual immorality on the holiest day of our year?"

The answer is not clear. Different authorities have offered explanations over the years: Max Arzt in his classic work, *Justice and Mercy*, offers the explanation that it is a warning to young men against selecting the wrong mate. Israel is warned, he says, to shun the licentious ways of the heathen. Abraham Epstein suggests a connection with other cultures. He points out that to primitive cultures the New Year brought a sense of abandon; we have here a warning to counter the earlier excesses. J. D. Eisenstein, writing in 1919, points out that on Yom Kippur even the greatest sinners come to the synagogue—those who do not come again for another year; therefore, the largest number of people must be warned against illicit sexual relations. In the sixteenth century, the Italian commentator Sforno said that it was the intention behind both the warning against sexual prohibitions and stating our ethical obligations that we be led to holiness, a theme of Yom Kippur. Thus, in the minds of the rabbis selecting the Torah readings, the issues of sexual morality and Yom Kippur—sin and atonement—were linked.

We would hope that this list of *arayot*, or forbidden relationships, was largely irrelevant for most of the congregation. This was the conclusion of the Reform Movement in rejecting this traditional Torah reading in favor of the chapter that follows it. Despite the irrelevancy, however, the sexual lives, the Jewish lives, the sin, and the atonement of the congregations all were linked. Most of these thirty verses do not speak to us today. We would not think of uncovering the nakedness of our aunts or uncles, nor of committing bestiality. But one verse in this chapter stands out and troubles us as modern liberal Jews: "Do not lie with a man as one lies with a woman; it is an abhorrence" (Lev. 18:22).

Should we understand this clear and unequivocal prohibition against homosexual behavior as it is written? Is this law—chosen as part of the traditional Yom Kippur afternoon Torah reading—part of the timeless verities of our tradition, equal to "do not murder" or "honor your parents"? Or is it a law to be interpreted and changed and possibly disregarded in subsequent ages, along with laws such as: "Do not boil a kid in its mother's milk," and "Do not mix wool and linen," or the laws limiting women in Jewish religious life or prescribing the ordeal for accusing a wife of infidelity? How do we understand homosexuality in Reform Judaism today? Do we see it as a sin or a lifestyle? Do we regard it as a choice or a disease? Should our attitude be understanding, condemnation, sympathy, or openness?

As I see it, our attitude about homosexuality is the most troubling moral issue confronting the Reform Movement today. For the past twenty years, our movement has been dealing—indeed struggling—with this question. In 1969, and again in 1973, Rabbi Solomon B. Freehof, the leading Reform authority on Jewish practice, upheld the view of Jewish law that homosexuality is sinful. In 1973, however, our Union of American Hebrew Congregations accepted the membership of Beth Chayim Chadashim, the first gay and lesbian synagogue, despite Rabbi Freehof's rabbinic opinion to the contrary. In 1975 and 1976, the UAHC and the Central Conference of American Rabbis (CCAR) passed resolutions affirming the civil rights of homosexuals in the secular sphere.

While the UAHC passed an even stronger resolution in 1987 that called upon member congregations to develop educational programs and to employ without discrimination, the CCAR remains deadlocked over a stronger stand. In 1986, a resolution was offered at the CCAR convention and referred to a new ad hoc Committee on Homosexuality in the Rabbinate. For a year, the committee studied and argued and researched the topic to determine what moral leadership the Reform rabbinate should offer. Given the profound differences of opinion among rabbis and within the congregations and organizations they serve, and given the conflict between *halacha* (as confirmed and interpreted by many of Reform's leading voices), and given the direction of the movement, a conclusion was difficult to reach. In 1987, the committee reached no conclusion and instead of issuing a report, simply sponsored a late-night session at the convention. Two years later—this past June—there still was no resolution. Instead, four papers were distributed to colleagues, and a discussion was held at the convention. This unresolved issue confounds the Reform rabbinate.

AIDS, on the other hand, is an issue we can deal with as a movement. As Reform Jews, we all agree that AIDS is a devastating and tragic disease. Those of us who witnessed the moving presentation of the AIDS Memorial Quilt in our city cannot help but share in the sorrow that AIDS has brought to so many. The quilt, with its 10,800 individual panels covering fourteen acres, represents only 18 percent of the AIDS deaths in the United States.

We can relate to AIDS sufferers as we can relate to all who suffer: with caring, empathy, and outreach. No one has contracted AIDS on purpose, and we can deal with their suffering without being judgmental. We Reform Jews can afford to be liberal on AIDS, to make it a major issue for us, because in some ways it is safe.

I applaud our Reform Movement for its important work through its Task Force on AIDS and its excellent materials. Its courageous advocacy and its excellent educational efforts demonstrate our commitment in this area. I applaud our own Social Action Committee here at Temple Sinai for its forum on AIDS and its important work in developing an AIDS policy for our own congregation. The policy, currently in draft, is carefully wrought, grounded in Jewish concerns, and enlightened on medical issues. As we work on it and pass it, it will continue to place our congregation in the leadership role of our movement and in our city on this crucial and important issue.

But AIDS is not really the entire issue. AIDS is a touchstone for a larger issue, for our attitude as Reform Jews towards homosexuality. AIDS is a catalyst to help us begin discussing the moral issues and to help us with our anxieties, frustrations, and fears on many levels. But I am frankly concerned that AIDS has also led us to focus on a side issue, for our attitude toward AIDS and toward people with AIDS may be very different from our attitude and our moral conclusions about homosexuality.

The great problem is how we reconcile a liberal, accepting position with the clear prohibition in the Torah, in Jewish law, and among Reform interpreters. Or, on the other hand, how do we resolve a condemnatory position with our historical Reform position that all people are children of God, created in God's image?

Part of our problem is that we don't understand the nature of homosexuality. Medical scientists do not agree. Human behaviorists do not agree. Jewish sources and authorities do not agree. Even the homosexual community does not fully understand all the factors that go into the development of sexual orientation. The old questions still go unanswered: Are the determinants a matter of disorder or lifestyle? Of genetics or of character development? We do not know. In the Reform Movement I can't even tell you that the disagreement falls along the lines of traditionalists versus classical Reform advocates or conservatives versus liberals. The only insight I have to offer is that the issue divides among rabbis along generational lines.

Where, then, can we find models to help our understanding? How can we sort out conflicting viewpoints and work toward reaching a Reform ethic?

In his article in the journal *Judaism,* Rabbi Robert Kirschner of Congregation Emanu-El in San Francisco offers a model of how *halacha* is capable of changing.[1] He points out how modern rabbinic opinion recognizes the limits of ancient rabbinic knowledge in his model of the *heresh* or deaf-mute. In the Talmud, a *heresh* is deemed incompetent and is classed with minors, the mentally deficient, and others who cannot serve as witnesses. The *heresh* cannot be counted in a *minyan*, nor can he be married. The rabbis assumed that those who could not hear nor speak could not possibly know what they were doing.

This is a view we could hardly support. We now know better than to exclude from Jewish life individuals with any kind of disability. We now know so much more about deafness and communication that even Orthodox halachic authorities, beginning in the nineteenth century, came to understand that deaf mutes could communicate and were mentally competent. So, albeit hesitantly, they included them in Jewish life.

This is an apt analogy, especially considering the fact that we support congregations for the deaf and hearing impaired, and almost every liberal Jew would support the rights of the deaf to lead the fullest possible Jewish life.

But I have a problem with this model, for I do not think of

homosexuality as a disability. I suggest a different model, and to begin I must tell you about my Uncle Joe.

My Uncle Joe and I – as different as we were in age and background – shared one special trait: We were both left-handed. Uncle Joe used to tell me how his left-handedness would get him into trouble as he grew up. He grew up in a generation when people didn't understand left-handedness. They thought it was inferior, unnatural, a lifelong trouble to be endured. So they went to great lengths to suppress the natural instincts and inclinations of left-handed children. Uncle Joe used to tell me horrible stories of how teachers would wrap his left hand in bandages so he couldn't use it to write. He told me how they would strike his left hand when he used it to pick up a pencil. All of these acts were meant to guide him to use his right hand, to develop an imposed right-handedness for writing and doing other tasks. So Uncle Joe wrote with his right hand and ate with his left hand.

Uncle Joe's teachers were participating in a well-established anti-left-handed tradition spanning many cultures and generations. In many places, it is considered an insult to extend one's left hand in greeting or to be placed at someone's left side. Left-handed people are thought of as "sinister" (hence the word), evil, wicked. We Jews also have participated in this tradition: Our Bible calls the right hand (of both God and people) the hand of strength. Left-handedness is seen as a sign of weakness, even a malady. As Jacob blesses his two grandsons, Ephraim and Manasseh, his right hand clearly confers the greater blessing. The Talmud states that the right hand controls all *mitzvot* except *tefillin*, and that is only because *tefillin* are wrapped on the right arm and hand. The Midrash says that in heaven there is only the right side. So for Uncle Joe's sake, they bound and hit his left hand and forced him into conformity.

By the time I was growing up, most people knew better. I learned that left-handedness is a recessive genetic trait, transmitted at conception. Certainly it was no more connected with good or evil than the color of one's eyes or hair. Today, a generation later, scientists are even less certain: Some authorities believe left-handedness is inherited; others believe that it is learned; still others believe it is determined during pregnancy. And it is possible that all three theories are in some way correct! New parents still eagerly await the day when they can tell which hand their child seems to favor and make the appropriate entry in the baby book. But we still do not understand left-handedness entirely.

Some people are able to use both hands, and we certainly know that genetic determination either can be encouraged or discouraged. Those of us who are left-handed have learned early to look for the left-handed corner of the table, to be careful in selecting scissors, and that it is easier and neater to write Hebrew than English.

But would we say for a moment that this left-handed five or ten percent of the population is inferior, unnatural, evil? This is what people have said in one way or another for centuries and still do say in many countries. Not for a moment. We would read or reconstruct biblical stories and Talmudic law that have an anti-left-handed bias to be sure that our religion includes all Jews, regardless of hand-persuasion.

As Reform Jews, we know how to recognize the ethical laws in the Torah and how to distinguish between the ethical and ritual precepts. When the Torah says, "a woman must not wear a man's clothing" (Deut. 22:5), how do we understand this? Orthodox law prohibits women from wearing pants, but we Reform Jews do not for a moment forbid it, even though the Torah calls it *toevah* – an abomination – the same word used to describe homosexual relations. We say instead that the law against women wearing men's clothes was a carry-over from ancient cultic practices. We are not troubled to see a woman wearing slacks or a suit, and we certainly do not view this as an issue of sexual ethics.

The Torah also tells us what parents should do in dealing with a wayward and defiant son they cannot discipline (Deut. 21:18). They are to take him to the town square and tell the elders of the community of their problem. Then all the men will stone this young man to death, and all Israel will hear and be afraid. Not only would we never consider doing this, we are greatly relieved that one Talmudic rabbi said this never happened and never will. Similarly when we read in Leviticus 20:13 that homosexual acts are capital offenses because they are abhorrent, I do not think we have any trouble rereading "abhorrent" as belonging to another place and time.

Our problem is in acceptance: of the different, of the threatening, of the unfamiliar, of people we don't quite understand. And our sin is in excluding and ostracizing and oppressing them.

I submit we find it easier to deal with black people, because we know we're not black, and we can see the differences between us. We find it easier to deal with handicapped people because we know and understand those differences. We find it easier to press for equality of women and men because we know of the years of oppression, and we can understand this as a movement to unleash human potential.

But even we find it very hard to deal with the homosexuals among us – that ten percent, we think – because we do not understand and we cannot quite figure it out. Nor can we understand if we should respond to this problem with compassion (as with AIDS), or with caring, or with righteous indignation. I find it troubling that the movement that has pressed for equal treatment and openness – for all races, all immigrants, men and women, everyone with disabilities – finds itself stuck on the issue of sexual orientation. But I believe that this issue is too close to home for many people and therefore too dangerous.

Let us understand that homosexuals are no longer "over there," on the other side of the sea. They are here: in our city, in our neighborhoods, in our families, in our midst. We cannot for a moment oppress nor segregate nor victimize these people, for they are creatures of God just as surely as you and I are. And just as we have been a movement concerned about all people – black and white, rich and poor, and especially the downtrodden and powerless and wanderer in exile—let us be concerned about these people, too. As we read tomorrow morning that the Jewish people stand side by side before God—from the heads of tribes to the strangers in our midst—let us be concerned about all Jews standing in *our* midst.

I am not condoning promiscuity among homosexuals any more than among heterosexuals. I know better than to think that individuals of one sexual bent will be more inclined to wantonness or loose morals or "recruiting" others.

Rather, I recognize that each of us must learn to deal with our own sexuality individually, as part of our maturation and growth. While there are many commonalities among people, this work is different for each person, part of the uniqueness within each of us, an expression of an important part of our lives. It must be guided by our Jewish tradition and by an ethical system.

So let our message this Yom Kippur be one of openness and honesty and understanding of people who may be different from us. As we appreciate people with different color skin and hair, of different backgrounds and abilities, of different languages and cultures, of differences in self-expression, let us appreciate the spark of divinity that is in each of us. Each of us is a creature of God; each of us is struggling

21

in our own way to be our own self; each of us is developing throughout our lives.

Let our sin this Yom Kippur be that there are many in our midst whom we have rejected, shunned, and denied. There are many whom we have feared without reason. When the time has come for honesty, we have been dishonest. When the time has come for welcoming, we have rejected. When the time has come for understanding, we have failed to listen.

Let us push our sin aside and do the introspection we need to do. Let us consider our responsibilities to others: to accept one another in openness, to welcome the stranger, to recognize that all of us are creatures of God. Let us bring these values to our homes, to our neighborhoods, to our congregation, to our families. In this way, let us seek holiness and find it within one another and within ourselves.

---

1. Robert Kirschner, "Halakhah and Homosexuality: A Reappraisal," *Judaism* vol. 37, no. 4, Fall 1988.

Jewish Survival and Open Doors

Yom Kippur Morning 5752
September 18, 1991

Three years ago this morning, I spoke to you about the issues of mixed marriage and Jewish survival. My message was one of open doors for Jews and for non-Jews married to Jews—a message of caring enough about Judaism for it to survive and for us to survive as a people.

Based on the studies available at that time, I reported that more than 30 percent of Jews who married chose non-Jewish spouses and that two-thirds of these couples did nothing about religion in their families.

We often have hoped that for most of these couples conversion to Judaism is a possibility, and that even if no conversion takes place, most of these families opt for Judaism in some way. After all, we have thought, Judaism is at least as important to our children as any other religion is to their spouses. And Jews are a minority with strong roots and an ethnic heritage. Somehow, we would preserve our people from generation to generation. If these couples did anything in their religious lives, so we assumed, it would likely be Jewish.

I stand here today to tell you that I was wrong. In the spirit of Yom Kippur, I tell you that three years ago, I sinned a sin of too much hope. For as troubling as my message was three years ago, the most recent information we have is far grimmer for the future of Judaism and the Jewish people.

The first national study of the Jewish community in twenty years was released this summer.[1] Here is what the researchers found:

- The core Jewish population in the U.S.—people who consider themselves Jewish in some way—is 5½ million.
- In addition to this group, another 1.3 million people were born to Jewish parents but have converted out or are being raised in another religion. More people have converted out of Judaism than have converted into Judaism.
- Whom are our children marrying? Today more than half of the born Jews who marry will marry someone not Jewish

(either by birth or conversion). Compare these rates of intermarriage:

- 50 percent today
- 25 percent in the late 1960s
- 10 percent before 1965

Even more alarming is what happens religiously to the children in these families:

- Only about one-quarter of the children in the surveyed mixed-married households are being raised as Jews.
- More than 40 percent are being raised in another religion.
- Thirty percent are being raised with no religion at all.

How can this be? More than half of our children are marrying out of our faith, and less than one-third of their children are being reared as Jews. Why does Judaism mean so little to so many? And what can we do to reverse these trends and to ensure our survival, our vitality, our continued strength?

One answer to the question of "How can this be?" is the growing integration of Jews into our American society. Once a sequestered people, our children now study, work, and socialize with people of many religious backgrounds. As sociologist Egon Mayer points out in the current issue of *Moment* magazine: "We Jews are successful as a favorite American minority. As the Jews secured the tolerance and amiability of their gentile neighbors, they became less distinctive in their religious beliefs and life-style. ... Since the end of the 1950s [Jews] have found less reason to filter their gentile friends as potential marriage mates."[2]

A second answer is intellectual and theological. Our generation has redefined Judaism in our own minds. Once Judaism was only a set of laws prescribing a way of life; or it was a religion, with beliefs and practices; or it was a covenant with God, embracing both these aspects. But for the past half-century, we Jews have viewed ourselves increasingly as an ethnic and cultural group. Mordecai Kaplan realized this and founded Reconstructionism. Our Jewish Community Centers build their programs around this reality. Our Jewish Federations and many secular Jewish organizations recognize the great strength of cultural and ethnic ties and appeal to us as one people with links of history, tradition, and culture. And we have come to believe that it is this part of Judaism that is dominant.

This trait of the American Jewish community came through clearly in the 1990 survey. When asked what it means to be a Jew in America, our people responded:

- First: being part of a cultural group
- Second: being part of an ethnic group
- A distant third: being part of a religious group

Certainly we all recognize that Judaism is partly an ethnic and cultural system, but we may not realize how important this distinction is. We are born into an ethnic group, and it is easy to opt out of it—to leave it behind—in our melting pot or salad bowl society. An ethnic or cultural identity is not demanding, threatening, or challenging. It's just who you are, or were. In our country, we understand and even expect that ethnicity gives way to Americanism. Ethnicity you can take or leave, and it easily becomes irrelevant to basic life decisions.

Religion, on the other hand, can and does make demands. We don't feel guilty if we don't make *taiglach* on Rosh Hashanah, the way our grandmothers did. We do feel guilty if we don't fast on Yom Kippur. While we recognize differences among Jews on issues of belief and practice, religion always demands loyalty. Our religion has hundreds of mitzvot for us to encounter, to accept, to modify, to reject, but in some way to take seriously if we are religious Jews. But we have redefined Judaism in our generation, turning away from religion and toward "peoplehood" so that we see ourselves as just one culture among many in our multicultural society, no more important to us than our hometown and for many even less so. And that is one reason that so many Jews feel that Judaism is irrelevant and unimportant in their lives.

A third reason that Judaism means so little to so many is that we have convinced ourselves of the primacy of the ethic of universalism: that Judaism reduces to a belief in the equality of all people. This ethic worked well for Jews as we fought religious and racial prejudice and as we taught our children to love their neighbors as themselves. This universal ethic worked well as we learned to live in an open society and led us to social action: trying to repair our troubled world, dealing bread to the hungry, giving clothes to the needy, supporting the fallen and downtrodden. We believe in this at Temple Sinai, and we do it well! And I expect that this year, too, we will involve scores of our congregants in these vital efforts.

But what is distinctively Jewish about this ethic, as we believe and practice it? Do we perform these deeds as Jews or as ethical human beings? Especially if we really believe that Judaism is reducible to a universal ethic, then what difference does it make if our homes, our families, and our children are Jewish so long as they are ethical? We have misled ourselves into thinking that Judaism is no more than universal ethics, no more than ethnic and cultural folkways. And now we are paying a fearful price.

For Judaism is more than a culture and an ethic. Above all, it is a covenant. It is a cultural covenant that leads us to appreciate the unity of the Jewish people across generations. It is an ethical covenant that guides us to see all people as God's children, requiring ethical conduct. Above all, it is a covenant of life that demands loyalty and observance—not just tradition, but obligation. Only through accepting these obligations can we reverse these trends.

I say to you this Yom Kippur that open doors are not enough. We need to bring the people in. We need to stand up for that covenant, as our ancestors stood before God. We need to assert that Judaism is important to us and our children. We need to find a way to include our own mixed-married families in our midst.

Our sin this Yom Kippur is the sin of apathy. Most of us care so little about Judaism. We may feel a nostalgic identification, but we redefine it in our lives, in our families, in our homes. Or we may care, but feel powerless to make a difference, as I hear so often, in so many families, including my own. We are afraid to say, "Judaism is important to me." We are so eager to be even-handed in our families that we cannot say to ourselves (or anybody else) what Judaism means to us. And we are afraid to teach our children that Judaism must be important to them.

I want our synagogue to be a place of caring: a place of caring about Judaism and a place of caring for Jews and their families. I want this building to be a place of comfort for parents who think they have failed. And I want this building to be a place to welcome these mixed-married families, to teach them what questions to ask, to guide them as best we can. I want this building to be a place of growth, where individuals and families can grow in Jewish commitment and in religious sensitivity and in speaking our piece about the Judaism that is important to us. So much psychological energy goes into planning a wedding filled with symbolism and nuance; I want at least that much energy to go into planning a marriage.

I don't apologize for my own decision not to officiate at mixed-marriage ceremonies, for I officiate within a context of Jewish law and practice that guides me to that decision. But I do apologize for the mistaken impression that we reject or do not care about these families. We must be a synagogue of open doors, as challenging, threatening, or uncertain as that might be.

And even if our doors are open, that is still not enough. The commitment must be there. We must remind ourselves that Judaism is far more than Jewish culture and ethnicity. For if it is only that, then no one new can enter. We must affirm that Judaism is instead a sacred covenant between God and the people Israel; a covenant with religious practices and ethical guideposts; a covenant that can make demands upon us; a covenant that will speak to our minds and hearts if only we will let it.

The Torah portion we read this morning speaks to our situation: Moses calls the people together in the waning days of his career and life to enter into the covenant with God. It is a covenant of choices: life or death, good or evil. It is a covenant for all people: men and women, officials and ordinary folks, even the non-Jews who lived among them. It is a covenant of responsibilities.

Our religion is not based solely on the clan you are from, nor on the way you treat other people. It is based on your relationship with God and with the people that Moses describes. The doors to that covenant must be open, as the doors to the synagogue must be open, and our Torah text tells us just how open the doors must be.

For Moses tells the people that even the non-Jews in their midst are part of this covenant. The *ger*—the stranger in the midst of the people— must be included in the covenant. The word *ger* comes from the root "to dwell" and means "sojourner," although some might say "stranger" or "resident alien." A *ger* is a person not *of* the clan, but living *with* it, like the non-Jewish spouses in our mixed-married households. The *ger* in the Bible had some of the responsibilities and some of the privileges of the Jewish community. For example, in the Ten Commandments, the *ger* was specifically supposed to share in Sabbath rest. Recognizing human nature, the Israelites were prohibited from oppressing the *ger* or taking advantage of these co-dwellers, having themselves been *gerim* in the land of Egypt. Later, in Rabbinic times, *ger* came to mean a "convert" or "proselyte," as it means today in modern Hebrew.

The rabbis distinguished among different types of *gerim*. One was a *ger toshav*, or partial proselyte, a person who lived among the Jews, but did not formally convert. Such a person was considered "one of the family," an honest seeker of truth who enjoyed many rights in the Jewish community. If our doors are open, we thus have the precedent for bringing these sojourners into our midst.

They are not temporary, nor aliens, nor simply residing in our midst. No, they are our husbands and wives, our daughters and sons. They are our family, and we must make a place for them in the covenant we share with God. But even that is not enough. We Jews first must want to make a place for them and be certain that this covenant is important to us.

Indeed, many of these partial proselytes are part of our congregation already, part of our community, part of the Jewish life we are building with our families and with one another. For many, being a partial proselyte is a point along the way. Some will want to convert to Judaism later in their marriage; others will not, for a wide variety of personal and religious reasons. Still, we must welcome them into our congregation, provide programs for these families, educate their children, explain to them how they fit in, or can fit in to the Jewish world.

But we must do this with husband and wife together, and both partners must share in this commitment. We first must remind ourselves and our children how important Judaism must be to us, and our families, and then we must be prepared to find a place for the many non-Jews in our midst.

I remember well a letter I received many years ago from a woman I had prepared for conversion. After she and her husband were married a short time, she decided that it was best to have one religion in her family, and she lovingly decided to explore Judaism. She did this at some considerable inconvenience, traveling many miles for many weeks to attend the Introduction to Judaism course I was teaching and to meet with me, for there was no rabbi in her city. She studied and found the material inviting and decided to convert, a decision she did not take lightly. Soon afterwards, she and her husband had their first child. But now, she wrote, she had decided to convert back to her former religion because she found the Judaism in their home dry and meaningless. The support she needed from her husband was not there. Her spiritual and religious needs were unmet. Ultimately, she cared deeply about her religion and her religious life, and her husband did not care about Judaism at all. So instead of a shared religion in their home, she simply had discovered more religious loneliness than she had known before. Judaism is a religion of choices: Adam and Eve chose the forbidden fruit; Abraham chose the one God; Moses chose to return to Egypt and confront Pharaoh; this woman's husband chose to ignore the Judaism that was his and was potentially so precious to her.

And our Torah portion today tells us that the Jewish people must choose. We must choose between life and death, blessing and curse. And we must choose life: life for our spirit, life for our people, life for our families.

And we must reach out to others in our midst to choose life with us, to be part of this covenant of life, so that we and our families and our offspring may live and long endure.

---

1. The 1990 National Jewish Population Survey was conducted by Dr. Barry Kosmin, Research Director for the Council of Jewish Federations.
2. Egon Mayer, "Why Not Judaism," *Moment*, October 1991, 41.

Opening Our Eyes and Seeing God

Rosh Hashanah Morning 5753
September 29, 1992

Perhaps you wonder where the story of the Akedah—or the binding of Isaac—takes place. The Bible itself tells us, but the explanation raises more questions than it answers. Just after Abraham's hand has been held back—and he sacrifices the ram instead of Isaac—we read (as we did this morning):

> Abraham named that place *Adonai-Yireh*, or "God sees" as it is said to this day: *B'har Adonai Yeraeh*, "On the mountain of God there is vision."

What does this mean? What is that vision? Does the phrase *Behar Adonai Yeraeh* mean, "On the mountain God appears," as the early Greek Septuagint version translates it? Or does it refer back to Verse 8 of the story, when Abraham tells Isaac that God will see (*Yireh*) to the sheep for the sacrifice, so that this verse means, "God will see to the sheep"? Or does the verse mean, "On the mountain God will see" what kind of a person or what kind of a Jew Abraham is? Or does it mean, "On the mountain [Abraham] had a vision of God?" Or did the two words *Yireh* and *Yeraeh* get reversed in copying, so that the verse originally meant (as in another translation):

> Abraham named that place "God will be seen"; hence the present saying, "He will see on God's mountain."

This kind of a verse is called an "etiology." It concludes or interrupts a story to explain the origins of a name or a tradition. For example, Jacob's name is changed to Israel (*Yisrael*), as the Torah explains, "Because he wrestled with God." Abraham and Abimelech took an oath at a well, and therefore, the Bible tells us, the place was called *Beersheva*—"the well of the oath."

But this etiology has problems. First, there is no place named *Adonai-Yireh*. Jewish tradition places the Mount Moriah in this story in the center of Jerusalem, the Temple Mount. Second, to the author of

30

our verse, the saying "On the mountain, God is seen" apparently was a common proverb. But it has been lost to us, and theologically we believe that God is invisible. So why does the text say "God is seen"?

There are many ways to understand this verse, but clearly it is telling us that Abraham and God had a visual encounter. On this first day of the New Year, how can we do the same? How can we see God or be seen by God? How can we acquire such vision and visibility? How can our worship on this hill lead us to a life-changing encounter with God?

Judaism teaches that God is invisible, that we cannot see God. But we can see toward God, and this first day of the New Year is a time to begin.

Let us begin to create our own vision of God today, for this is a day to see and to be seen. We gather on Rosh Hashanah to see where we are, and who we are, and how we fit in, and before Whom we stand.

We begin by seeing one another and surely feel—in this seeing—part of a congregation and a community of Jews. We find in this annual gathering a message of hope and of continuity.

I remember so well the strong feeling of belonging I had when I was growing up and saw all the people I knew from the congregation all together on these days each year. I feel that today—as I do every year—seeing all the people I know and have worked with through the year: in joy and in sadness, on committees and boards, teaching and studying and praying as one congregation, all here together. To me, the ability to see you all together reassures me of the continuity and the strength and vitality of our people and our congregation.

As we come to see one another (*Yireh*), we also come to be seen (*Yeraeh*). Not that we are on display for one another, but we want so much to be seen by God. For on these days each year, we know, God examines each of us as we examine our own lives, seeking out a new vision for ourselves. And we try, out of this seeing and being seen, to find some glimpse of God, some vision of the divine, as we look toward our Judge.

We Jews don't believe that we can see God with our eyes. It is not our way to gather, as many did this summer, to see a vision of God in Kentucky or a vision of Mary in New Jersey. Something similar happened in our own sanctuary not too many months ago: A non-Jewish visitor told me after the service that when the ark was closed, she had seen God come down from the ceiling and rest upon the ark.

While she was clearly ready for this religious experience in the light of her tradition, my own background leads me away from it.

God is invisible to us Jews, but on this day we can look toward God. I, too, have felt God's presence here in this sanctuary. I have experienced the presence of something beyond us—something that cannot be seen—with families in moments of great joy linking generations when we name a baby or mark the transition from childhood to maturity, and in moments of sorrow, seeking comfort in the face of illness or death that we have shared together.

I have seen, too, how some people's eyes and ears are open to God, while others' are shut. Indeed, I have seen how God can be sought and welcomed here in our sanctuary or how God can be excluded. For some of us truly seek God in these life experiences, while others only try to "get through it." I have seen some families search for meaning and depth and God's presence in a ceremony, while others seek to just get on with the celebration. The prophet Jeremiah speaks to this idea of readiness for spiritual encounters when he says that the people of his day "have eyes but do not see; they have ears but do not hear."

How, then, can we open our eyes and ears to see what lies before us this Rosh Hashanah?

It is revealing that Hebrew has a special word for opening one's eyes or ears: *Pakach.* Thus the eyes of Adam and Eve were opened when they ate of the forbidden fruit; thus the eyes of Hagar were opened so she could see the well and give Ishmael, her son, something to drink.

What will it take for us to open our eyes this New Year to one another, to our people, to God?

One way that we can open our eyes, as I learned this summer, is through encountering our past. In June, Sherry, David, and I visited the Pinkas Synagogue in Prague. It is from this synagogue, with its long and proud history, that Temple Sinai's Holocaust Torah scroll comes. The synagogue itself was first mentioned in 1492, five hundred years ago. It was named for a Rabbi Pinkas, who had a dispute with some of the leaders of the Old-New Synagogue, the Altneuschul, and in 1479 founded a private synagogue down the street. In 1519, the synagogue passed to Rabbi Pinkas's grandnephew, Aaron Meshulam Horowitz, who later had the synagogue restored and reconstructed (a familiar story). This was the first of many changes to this synagogue building that borders the famous Prague Jewish Cemetery.

The most important change to the Pinkas Synagogue began in 1955, with the Prague post-war Jewish community's decision to inscribe on the walls of this synagogue the names of all of the Jews in Bohemia and Moravia (the Czech part of Czechoslovakia) who had been killed in the Holocaust. Researchers were able to recover 77,297 names from transport records, one-third more names than are on the Vietnam Veterans Memorial. The names in the Pinkas Synagogue were organized by cities and arranged alphabetically; each listing included the person's date of birth and the date of transport—the date they were last officially seen. In 1960, after five years of painstaking work, the world's largest epitaph was completed and opened in the Pinkas Synagogue.

But only eight years later, just after the "Prague Spring," the synagogue was closed by the Communist government. And while it was closed, the government painted over the walls so that the names could not be seen and the memory of the deceased would thus be obliterated. Only this past spring was the Pinkas Synagogue reopened and the process of putting back the 77,297 names begun again. With its magnificent vaulted ceiling and galleries, the Pinkas Synagogue is an architectural gem.

What a moving experience it is to be in that synagogue on a site that is five hundred years old, just rededicated last *Yom HaShoah*, Holocaust Day! Although most of the names are still covered up, in that place my eyes were opened. If you look carefully in some spots, you can see the original names through the whitewash, and throughout the synagogue you can feel the names and memories and souls of the departed that surround you in that empty building: among them, the names of my own family that I had just discovered had perished in Bohemia during the Shoah.

How much all of these names are with us today, as we read from Torah scroll Number 56, written in 1780. It is one of the 1,564 scrolls rescued from Bohemia, Moravia, and Slovakia—lovingly cared for and restored and sent to synagogues around the world to keep the words and the memories alive and in our sight for future generations.

Our tradition calls Rosh Hashanah *Yom Hazikaron*, the Day of Remembrance. We Jews are commanded to remember, and we pray that God will remember us. I urge each of you to remember and to begin your search, if you have not already. It is so important, in our days of Jewish amnesia, to find your own personal connections to our history and our places and our people. Today is the day to begin that search and thus to be led to new vision.

Rabbi Lawrence Kushner in his new book, *God Was In This Place and I, I Did Not Know*, points out that Abraham and Isaac "initiated history when they decided to follow God's command." They stood atop the mountain and they "stepped up to the plate," as the saying goes. They did not simply do what they heard God say. They trusted where God had put them and in what God put before them. They chose to step forward into their destinies. They saw; they were seen; and we see them still.

Each of us stands on the mountain today. Each of us can trust or not trust, see or not see, choose or avoid choosing, inscribe our names or not. We are here, on this day, filled with opportunities to make a difference: to see toward God—if only we are ready, if our eyes are open.

One way we see toward God is with our eyes; one way we see is through our memories; and a third way is through envisioning a better world. The medieval commentator Rashi quotes a Midrash on the verse, "Abraham named that place, 'Adonai-Sees.'" Rashi says that as God sees us each year reading the story of the binding of Isaac, God forgives us and redeems us from our suffering.

There is so much suffering in our world—so many children bound to sorrow, so many that we see starving in Somalia or war-torn Bosnia, as in our own country, and in our own city: all of them God's children. We pray that they be relieved from their suffering; we pray for a vision of a world at peace; we see instead God's creatures at war.

Here today, however, we can begin to create our own vision; we can begin to give of ourselves and our resources to make the world a better place, to realize our vision.

The New Year comes, with its opportunities for a fresh beginning and a renewed vision, to tell us to dedicate ourselves to achieve our image of a repaired world. There are many ways we can do this: with our time and skills through any of the ten projects developed by our Social Action Committee; through our creativity and sensitivity in reaching out to others in need; through our checkbooks as Temple Sinai's Fund for the Needy reaches out at this season and again and again during the year.

But first, our eyes must be open to see and our ears must be open to hear. Our eyes must be open to see the suffering and our ears to hear the plight of the downtrodden; we must see and hear toward God, as Abraham saw and heard that fateful day on Mount Moriah.

We do so much as individuals and as a congregation, yet we must do still more. Rosh Hashanah comes to tell us that Abraham's vision must be our vision: a vision of hope, of life, of peace. Abraham's vision is a vision that can be achieved and in its achieving will enable us to see toward God and enable God to see us.

Rabbi Zalman Schachter-Shalomi tells a story about God and two members of a congregation. One Shabbat morning, the richest man in town was asleep in the synagogue, as was often the case. But this week, he awoke during the Torah reading just long enough to hear the verses commanding Israel to place twelve loaves of hallah in the tabernacle. The rich man did not know that he had awakened, and so at the end of the service he didn't realize that he had heard the Torah being read. He thought that God had spoken to him in his sleep with specific instructions. He felt honored and immediately went home and baked the twelve loaves of bread and brought them back to the synagogue. Where to put them? Certainly the best place—since this was God's command—was in the ark. So he put them there, closed the ark, and went home.

Not long after, the poorest Jew in town, the janitor of the synagogue, came to present his case to God. As he walked up to the ark to polish the ornaments, he appealed to God: "Unless you perform a miracle, we will all starve, my family and me." When the janitor opened the ark he found, of course, the twelve loaves of bread, and—overjoyed—he took them all home.

When the rich man, who had been eager to know what happened to those loaves of bread, came back to the synagogue, he found them gone! And so it continued for many years: Each Friday the rich man would bring twelve loaves of hallah and deposit them in the ark, and each Friday the janitor would find them and take them home. He kept one loaf for Shabbat, fed his family for the week with six more, sold four, and gave one to charity, week in and week out.

One Friday, however, the rabbi saw what was happening. He called both men into his study and opened their eyes to the truth about this weekly ritual. Both were disappointed. The rich man said, "Do you mean God doesn't really eat the hallah I leave each week?" And the poor man said, "Do you mean God hasn't been baking hallah each week after all?"

So the rabbi told them to look at their hands. To the rich man he said, "Your hands are the hands of God, giving food to the poor." To the poor man he said, "Your hands are also the hands of God, receiving gifts from others."

So can our hands be the hands of God, doing God's work. And so can our eyes be the eyes of God, filled with insight, with visions of our life and history, with remembering our place in creation, with our hope for a better world.

Let us use this day to look toward God, to see and to be seen. And may our eyes and our hands work together; may our eyes see visions and the work of our hands be strengthened.

Building on a Foundation of Justice

Kol Nidre 5753
October 6, 1992

This year one verse from the Yom Kippur Haftarah we read tomorrow morning especially speaks to me:

> You shall raise up foundations
> of many generations,
> and you shall be called
> "Repairer of Fallen Walls,
> Restorer of Streets To Dwell In" (Is. 58:12).

For just beyond this sanctuary, our new Bet Am—our chapel—is taking shape: the foundation is finished, the steel framework has just been put in place, and soon the walls will begin to rise. These words— "raise up the foundations... Repairer of Fallen Walls"—resonate in our building this Yom Kippur as we live with many fallen walls and breaches, many of them already repaired and made whole again.

Some people have told me that they cannot bear to look at the construction; it is too disconcerting, too messy, too worrisome. Yet look we must, and as we look, we must ask:

- What are the real groundings, the foundations of our synagogue, our congregation, our Jewish life?
- Upon what are we building, as a Jewish congregation, for ourselves, for one another, for future generations?
- How can we build a synagogue that is grounded in the core Jewish values of righteousness and the preservation of Jewish life?
- How can we lay the foundations of our synagogue in empathy and caring?

Now that we have laid the foundation, now that we have done our planning and fundraising and negotiating, now that the architects and the contractors and the consultants have done their work, we still must ask, "Upon what does the foundation of our congregation rest?" How can we build and repair and restore our house with empathy, as well as efficiency, economy, and foresight?

Many times on this Day of Atonement we recite the *Al Het* confession, and we include in it not only our failures as individuals but also as a congregation and as a community. We ask forgiveness for the sins that we have committed by hardening our hearts, and with our thoughts and words and deeds. We ask forgiveness for the sin of silence and indifference, for failing to support our people, for exploiting the weak. On this day each year, we ask:

- How can we break out of our pattern of indifference?
- How can we care more and feel more the plight of others?

Our failures of empathy nag at us always and especially on Yom Kippur. On this Yom Kippur, we see them in the context of the synagogue we are building. When you build a synagogue, you must make many difficult choices. When Temple Sinai was first built, for instance, the leadership needed to decide whether or not to keep the Kohler plumbing fixtures that had been installed, since Kohler was in the midst of a protracted strike and thought by many to be unfair in its labor practices.

We have found many different kinds of difficult ethical choices involved in building a synagogue. There are issues of planning and equality and fiscal responsibility. And there are issues of accessibility.

As we worked on the plans for our building, we were particularly conscious of something else Isaiah said: "My house shall be called a house of prayer for all peoples" (Is. 56:7). Not just people with strong legs or a steady gait, not just people with good vision and hearing, but all of us created in God's image. God's creation is remarkable diverse, and our congregation is remarkably diverse, and out of this diversity we must find the sensitivity we need to make ethical decisions.

We have been faced with many difficult choices in planning our building project, but none has been more complex than the decisions on handicapped accessibility. How much is enough? Is meeting the code requirements sufficient? Is it enough to meet the new federal standards (although we are largely exempt)? Is it enough to do simply what other synagogues do?

I see many people in our building each month with less than perfect mobility or sight or hearing, people of all ages whom we must welcome with sensitivity and caring. But how easy it is to listen to their repeated requests and gradually to grow deaf to their pleas and their needs, which are really our needs.

Instead, we must be able to see the larger ethical issue: that all people must feel welcome in this house of God. When we realized that the real question was, "What is right?," we concluded that we could do no less than everything.

As a result, Temple Sinai will have new wider doors to all our rooms, ramps, an elevator, four new fully accessible restrooms, lift and railings to the sanctuary bimah, and a ramp to the bimah in the new chapel so that all of us can worship and study and participate fully. Now, when I see someone having difficulty coming up the bimah steps or struggling on a steep ramp, I can count the days until we have railings and lifts and security for all who are here.

Most of my research time in Oxford this summer was spent at the New Bodleian Library, built in the 1950's. The New Bodleian is accessible only if one climbs five steps and goes through a revolving door. Ironically, there is a small sign at the *top* of those five steps, next to the revolving door: "Handicapped readers ring here for assistance." How often do we do the same thing: We put up barriers and then invite people to fail!

That is one message of Yom Kippur: that all of us appear before God today with all our imperfections—our failures, our falling short, our faithlessness in ourselves and in one another. For some of us, our legs don't work the way we would like. For others, it is our hands, and with so many of us it is our tongues, our minds, our hearts.

All of us miss the mark; we all carry our imperfections; we all wish we were otherwise. Yom Kippur comes to tell us to do our human best and leave the rest to God.

But sometimes God's work must be our own, and it is our responsibility to improve what we can in this world of ours. So as we build our synagogue, we build for ourselves a communal house of empathy and caring, a house of God for all people, a house with foundations set in righteousness and sensitivity.

And we at Temple Sinai know that we cannot stop there, for we are aware of so many in our city who have no house at all. We could not build a new house for ourselves without creating a new home for those without one. This is just as Isaiah said in virtually the same breath (in our Haftarah tomorrow morning):

This is the fast I desire:
To unlock the fetters of wickedness ...
to let the oppressed go free;
to break off every yoke.
It is to share your bread with the hungry
And to make a home for the poor ...
(Is. 58:6-7).

So many yokes and fetters restrain us. Some of them are physical; others are psychological; and for many people they are economic. Every night at least 100,000 American children go to sleep homeless. They are not guilty of anything. They are not discharged from hospitals, nor using drugs, nor from somewhere else. They are just too poor to have a place to live. Their families are among the more than ten million low-income households in America competing for six million affordable apartments and houses.

The story in Washington is particularly bleak: Housing costs are far too high, and government grants and help are far too low. The District of Columbia has lost 120,000 inexpensive apartments since 1977, and this is one reason that more than five hundred families with children need a place to sleep every night. Can you believe that there are one thousand homeless children each night in our city—the city with the most highly educated population, the city with the highest family income of any city in our nation? Surely Isaiah's complaint rings true to us today!

And it is so easy to look the other way, to avert your glance at the Metro station, to look down at the sidewalk, to move on to the next story in the paper. But as we read Isaiah's words today, we must not look away, nor forget, nor ignore the poor within our midst.

Because today is a day for looking: looking at ourselves, at our shortcomings, at our responsibilities as Jews—and because today is a day for looking at the needs of others.

I am very pleased that for the past year, a number of members of Temple Sinai's Social Action Committee have been laboring on behalf of our congregation to continue in our tradition of helping and reaching out to homeless families. They were as troubled as Isaiah was, and they did the research, studied the need, developed the plan, presented the case, drafted the documents, and brought the plan forward for Sinai

House. The plan was adopted by our Social Action Committee, by our Board of Trustees, and by our entire congregation. Now, we are hard at work enlisting volunteers and contributions to save three or four of those families from homelessness and to give them a fresh start. They need our help, our caring, our resources, in so many ways.

As I see our congregation's history evolving, we could not possibly build a new house for ourselves without creating a new home for others. Both houses are built on foundations of righteousness; both recognize what we must do as Jews.

This year, then, let our *Al Het* be different. This year let us feel more keenly how we have silently excluded others and failed to recognize our own shortcomings and those in the people around us. This year let us feel more keenly how we have ignored the plight of the needy and turned our faces from their outstretched hands. This year let us capture the opportunity to create and build two new houses together.

One of the Talmudic rabbis asked the question, "What happened to the tablets of the Ten Commandments that Moses shattered?"[1] The answer was that they were kept in the Ark with the second, unbroken, tablets. These fragments did not lose their sanctity just because they were broken. So it is with people, the rabbi continued. They do not lose their sanctity if they are broken. They need to have the same place of honor, for they, too, are created in the image of God.

And today we can add: All of us are broken; all of us are less than we could be. All of us are incomplete and need to be restored and repaired: some of us with our bodies; some of us with our homes; some of us with our souls. We come here today to make ourselves as whole and complete as we can be—we and the people around us, as well as our neighbors in the streets.

Let us raise up our foundations and build our houses with righteousness; let us become the ones who repair the fallen walls and who restore the places to dwell in. In that way we will restore ourselves and restore one another, we who are broken and need to be made whole again.

---

1. Hayim Nahman Bialik and Yehoshua Hana Ravnitzky, eds., *The Book of Legends (Sefer Ha-aggadah): Legends from the Talmud and Midrash*, translated by William G. Braude (New York: Schocken Books, 1992), 89:83.

Our Presence and God's Presence

Rosh Hashanah Eve 5754
September 15, 1993

Once there was a man named Max who lived in St. Petersburg. When Max lived there—at the time this Chasidic story was told—most Jews could not live in the Russian capital, but Max's father qualified, so Max grew up there in an assimilated home.

Shortly before Max's father died, he called his son to him and said, "Maxele, it is almost time for me to leave this world. Before I die, I want you to swear to me that you will always remember that you are a Jew."

Max said to his father, "Of course I will swear that to you; I will always remember that I am a Jew. But please tell me: What is a Jew supposed to do?"

Max's father responded, "I wish I knew. But when I was twelve years old, I was kidnapped to serve in the Czar's army. For twenty-five years I was never permitted to see my family or practice my religion. By the time I was released, I had forgotten my Jewish heritage entirely. I only know two things: I was born a Jew, and on Rosh Hashanah a Jew goes to the synagogue."

Max's father died soon thereafter, and on the following Rosh Hashanah Max found a synagogue in order to fulfill the oath he had made. He did not know what to do, but he went in and sat in the back. He was unable to read the prayers, because he did not know the words or even the letters, but he sat and prayed as best he could. In that place, on this day, he reached beyond himself. He turned to God in his father's memory and with his people.

That is the power of this day: Rosh Hashanah helps us to reach beyond ourselves, giving us transcendent moments that renew our lives and our Jewish lives, year in and year out.

Each of us is a little like Max of St. Petersburg. We do what is expected of us: We remember that we are Jews, and we have come here today! But now that we are here, what are we, as Jews, supposed to do? What is expected of us as Jews on this day? What do we really need and want, as Jews and as people?

I believe that we come here today seeking to reach beyond ourselves, to find some transcendent moments in our overburdened lives. Most of us know more than Max and his father, but do we know how to put meaning into this day we spend in the synagogue? How can we ensure that we do more than simply read the words?

Please do not misunderstand: If you are here tonight, but you are not sure why, that is all right. Indeed, I would hope that every Jew knows that he or she ought to be in the synagogue on Rosh Hashanah.

But we must not stop there. Now that we are here, what do we do—tonight, tomorrow, on Yom Kippur?

The answer is: We come here to seek and to find transcendent moments, time that reaches beyond itself.

Such a moment is part of what we all felt on Monday, as we watched the signing on the White House lawn.[1] It was not just two leaders signing a document or another event in the politics of the Middle East, as significant as the diplomatic breakthrough was.

When we use terms like "historic" and "watershed," what we are really saying is that this is an event that reaches beyond itself. Moments like these remind us of a past that reaches back for centuries; moments like these fill us with hopeful anticipation of many future decades of peace. The enormous power of Monday morning for most of us was that it was a time that looked beyond itself, a transcendent moment.

Seeking such transcendent moments in our own lives brings us to the synagogue. Such moments are what Max of St. Petersburg sought, and that is what we seek here tonight as we welcome this promising New Year.

Max was guided to reach beyond himself through worship, as we do this evening. Certainly our renewed sanctuary provides an enhanced setting in which we do that. Our sanctuary has undergone many changes—many subtle, all for the good—since last Rosh Hashanah. Some changes are for our comfort: better seats, better sound. But there are more important changes: By developing our courtyards and removing the draperies, we perceive the sanctuary as larger. The openness lifts our spirits and encourages us to feel a new sense of God's presence. Our sense of the expansiveness of the sanctuary has evoked smiles and tears in the past few weeks as congregants have seen and experienced our new *bet tefillah*—our new house of worship.

As marvelous as our sanctuary is, of course, it is not an end in itself, but a means to help us worship. Even as we rejoice in it, what we most need, as individuals and as a congregation, is for this new sanctuary to help us to achieve those transcendent moments when we reach beyond ourselves.

Sociologist Wade Clark Roof describes how some are searching for such transcendent moments in his recent book, *A Generation of Seekers: The Spiritual Journeys of the Baby Boom Generation*. Roof describes our generation as more individualistic than previous generations. He calls us "seekers"—not joiners—seeking, especially, spiritual growth. He suggests that our generation may be less likely to seek organized religion in churches and synagogues and more likely to seek spiritual growth privately.

Some people come to me and say, "I want to become more Jewish, but I am not sure how." Like Max, they know what they are supposed to do, but they want it to have personal meaning. They are confronted by an emptiness in their lives. They want to pray with meaning.

While Roof sees this as the quest of the baby-boomers, I see it as the quest of each one of us here tonight. We don't want to say formulaic prayers by rote; we don't want to be here because of obscure obligations.

We come here tonight in search of a transcendent moment, seeking an experience that will bring us comfort and strength and renewal. We come here tonight because we want to be moved—to feel God's presence in the same way that we felt it when our son was born, or when our mother died, or at our nephew's bar mitzvah, or when we first saw Jerusalem, or when we became engaged, or when we witnessed the peace accord being signed on Monday.

We want to feel God's presence brush past us as it sometimes does on Pesach when we open the door and our children watch for Elijah to enter.

Perhaps most of all we want to be able to arouse that feeling in ourselves with no external prompt, no special occasion, no earthshaking event.

The more we can recognize this—our very own—human need within ourselves, the more we can talk about it, the closer we can come to feeling God's presence.

Fortunately for us, our calendar and the wisdom of our ancestors provide these Days of Awe to help us. They mark a specific time for us to search our souls for signs of life, to look inside ourselves, to probe the yearnings of our hearts.

Just as we see doctors about our physical health and accountants about our financial health, today we come to the synagogue to examine our spiritual and Jewish health. This is what we all really need and want, even though we may not know it.

Certainly we do not need sociologists to tell us that we yearn to comprehend and draw upon the religious vein inside each of us. The question we bring today is: How? How can we begin to tap the riches of our Jewish spiritual lives?

As Roof points out, it is not easy to create a congregation of individualists, for a congregation grows out of a shared experience and a shared commitment.

We need to think tonight about what makes us a congregation. What is our common quest? What are our shared values? And how, as a congregation, do we provide opportunities for ourselves as individuals to grow in our spirituality—to feel God's presence?

At Temple Sinai we build upon a shared history of over forty years, yet we are constantly changing. Our prayer book describes God as continually renewing, each day, the work of creation. So it is with our congregation, for it is alive and evolving and changing and never static.

I should have said "our congregation*s*," for there are many congregations within Temple Sinai: our Friday evening and Saturday regulars, our lay leaders and our affiliates, our adult education regulars, our Tot Shabbat and school families, those who sing in our choir, those who are helping to create Sinai House.

There is much overlapping, of course. And at the same time, each of us has a primary way in which we relate to our synagogue, to Judaism, and to God.

Over and over I ask myself: "What unites all these different congregations? And what links these congregations to those who simply say they are the 'paying/praying/playing' Jews?"

Our goals are so diffuse, unlike the goals of other places: You go to a hospital, and you come away diagnosed or treated and hopefully healthier. You go to a school or a college, and you come away educated. You go to a health club, and you come away trim and fit. But when you go to your synagogue, what happens? Do you come away more Jewish? More fulfilled? Better educated? More spiritually attuned?

We come here for many reasons: out of blind obligation, for a quick Jewish fix, for a life-cycle event. What matters most, though, is what happens while we are here: Can we reach beyond ourselves? Can we experience a transcendent moment? Can we find a place for God in our lives? Can we find the strength to reach beyond ourselves?

I think it is particularly important to consider these questions now when we are rejoicing in our renewed building because we know well that our building does not take the place of the congregation. While this congregation does not worship buildings, we need to remind ourselves of the values that fill this building with life. Plus, these past several months have seen more than a little acrimony.[2] Yes, this is just the right moment to remind ourselves of what holds us together as a congregation and how, through participating in our life as a congregation, we can move toward feeling God's presence.

I want Temple Sinai to be a congregation dedicated to mitzvot of the spirit. Three particular mitzvot have been central to our congregation's life since its beginnings two generations ago:

- Worship
- Study
- Responsibilities to others.

I single out these mitzvot because they unite us as a congregation and because they have the potential to ennoble our lives. These mitzvot, especially, lead us to look beyond ourselves. They are the windows into our Jewish lives and the windows through which we see our world.

Our tradition tells us—and we know—that one way to feel God's presence is through worship. The prayer book helps some people find their way: some through the words; others through the music. The goal is the same: to deepen our Jewish spiritual experience. We come together as a congregation today and indeed every week to join in worship, and this moves our spirits. We must examine what goes on within our *bet tefillah*, our house of prayer. Can we reach beyond ourselves? Can we feel the presence of God?

I didn't tell you the ending of the story about Max of St. Petersburg. After sitting and watching the service for some time, Max stood up in his place. He looked up and prayed: "God in Heaven! Until this moment, I had forgotten that I am a Jew. I never had the chance to study, so I do not even know how to read the words. But I always have known how Your glory fills the whole world. I love You with all my heart, so please don't forget me, Max from St. Petersburg."

As the Chasidic rabbi told this story, his voice trailed off, and his disciples noticed that he was crying. He said, "You wanted me to teach you the secret of prayer. Once in my life I would like to be able to pray like Max from St. Petersburg."

A second mitzvah through which we can deepen our spiritual lives and feel the presence of God is study. We come together at Temple Sinai to teach and to study at many times: on Monday evenings, on Sunday mornings, on Shabbat, and during the week.

We come for many reasons: to learn what we have forgotten or have never known, to open new doors to our tradition. What is of primary importance is the magic of the classroom: seeing people engaged in texts and ideas; watching them reach beyond themselves for new concepts. If we are successful in our study, then we can achieve that transcendent moment that ennobles and enriches our lives and pushes us beyond.

Finally, our tradition shows us a third path toward the presence of God: through *mitzvot* that serve others in a Jewish context and make the world a better place. Worship and study in themselves are both mitzvot, but they are just for us. We also have a responsibility to serve others. As we do so in a Jewish context, we address another set of our spiritual needs, another side of our lives.

Unfortunately, we tend to make two mistakes in thinking about mitzvot. First, we think of them as doing a favor for someone else, rather than fulfilling a Jewish responsibility. We think along the lines of the Yiddish meaning of "mitzvah"—a good deed—rather than understanding the basic Hebrew meaning, a commandment. And second, we tend to focus on the good that these mitzvot will do other people rather than the good they can do for us.

A perfect example is the meal of comfort that our Sisterhood has provided for many years for families returning home after a funeral. Through the meal of comfort, we reach out to one another, providing support and nourishment, often to people we don't know. Finding an adequate number of willing hands has become increasingly difficult in recent years; now this valuable service is suspended until additional volunteers come forward.

At a funeral, furthermore, we rely upon ushers from our congregation who honor the memory of the deceased and support our grieving families by welcoming and seating worshippers. At present, we have to make more and more phone calls to recruit the minimum number of ushers.

I know that these calls come without advance notice. But I hope you will recognize that when we call upon you to help, what we actually are offering is a chance for you to do a mitzvah, an opportunity for you to grow in your own spirituality. For such true caring acts as these can expect no recompense.

I know how caring we want to be, based on the hundreds of responses we received for the work of the Mitzvot Without Measure Committee. Our challenge is to tap these enormous resources to meet the needs of our congregation and give others the opportunity to do these mitzvot.

Two thousand years ago, Rabbi Hillel said about studying what we should say about all these mitzvot: "Do not say, 'When I have leisure, then I will study.' Perhaps you will never have leisure." We must not say, "When I have a free afternoon, I will help with the meal of comfort." Those kinds of free afternoons never come. We need to understand these mitzvot not as "good deeds," but as responsibilities, commandments of the first order.

So let our congregation be bound together—united—by our worship and our study and the mitzvot that we do with one another. All of us today are a bit like Max of St. Petersburg—coming out of a sense of obligation, holding the books in our hands, not quite sure of what to do with them. How can we use the words and music to transcend our daily lives and make us into better Jews? How can we feel God's presence in our time, in this place, on this day?

The words and the music and the books alone will not be enough. Let us seek and find transcendent moments together. Let us use this year, so filled with promise, to reach beyond ourselves, to let our spirits rise up, to let our congregation grow in mitzvot, and to feel God's presence in our lives.

---

1. On September 12, 1993, Israeli Prime Minister Itzhak Rabin and Palestinian Liberation Organization Chairman Yassir Arafat famously shook hands after the signing of the first peace agreement between Israelis and Palestinians. The

accord constituted a Declaration of Principles on Palestinian self-government in Gaza and the West Bank.

2. The decision of the Temple Sinai Board in spring 1993 to seek an invested cantor rather than retain our cantorial soloist generated controversy. Ultimately, a vote at a special meeting of the congregation confirmed the Board's decision.

Day of Judgment – Day of Hope

Yom Kippur Morning 5754
September 25, 1993

I shall never forget this Yom Kippur day twenty years ago. I was a newly ordained rabbi, conducting Yom Kippur services. Near the end of the morning service, word reached us that Israel had been attacked.

We were overwhelmed with emotions—fear, anger, anxiety for Israel—and our feelings of belonging to the Jewish people. Our prayers turned from ourselves to concern for our people. Was this going to be the Day of Judgment for Israel and the Jewish people? How our prayers were filled with foreboding and apprehension that Yom Kippur afternoon!

Ever since that Yom Kippur of 1973, this day has never been the same for me—or for any of us. Yom Kippur now bears the stamp of that war: It holds reminders of our vulnerability as a people and as a nation; it reminds us of our links with Jews in Israel and throughout our world; it reminds us of our place in Jewish history.

Just as we cannot open the door for Elijah on Passover without thinking how our grandparents feared a pogrom at that moment, so we cannot confront Yom Kippur without remembering the year it brought us war. This day forces us to remember the vulnerability of Israel, the fragility of its peace, and it forces us to remember that these last 45 years have held more war than peace. We think about the many ways in which the true promise of the Jewish state—the flourishing of our homeland—has been held back by the inexorable concerns of security and fear of terrorism. Even in times of peace those shadows are always there.

It's no wonder that this year, then, we approach the peace accord and recognition of the PLO with mixed feelings.[1] We are elated, and yet . . . .

It's not easy, as Prime Minister Rabin said, to put aside the pain and the hatred we have felt. We are filled with hope that *shalom* will come to Israel's borders, yet we are cautious because we have been deceived before. To be a Jew, after all, is to remember our history, as painful as it might be. But to be a Jew is also to have hope in the future.

This day brings a history of its own: a history of somber memories and reflections of where we stand as a people before God. One question we ask this Yom Kippur, as we ask every Yom Kippur, is: "With whom do we stand? Do we stand only with one another, as a people? Are we prepared to stand with the strangers in our midst? Can we stand even with our enemies, with those who hate us?"

We have just read this morning in the Torah the parameters of our responsibilities as Jews: "You stand this day, all of you, before God ... everyone in Israel, to enter into a covenant: men, women, children ... even the strangers in your camp" (Deut. 29:9).

Who are these strangers? A *ger* is someone who lives with you but is not part of your family. There are many interpretations of this word, but on this Yom Kippur the word takes on yet another new meaning. This year, we see that these *gerim*—the strangers in our midst—are the descendants of Ishmael, the son of Abraham and Hagar, sent out to the desert (as we read on Rosh Hashanah) by Abraham: our Arab cousins.

Our relationship with these "strangers" is problematic indeed. Like us, they are descendants of Abraham, yet they are not our family. They have shared the same land for centuries, yet they compete for space. They are our cousins, yet they have been a threat to us.

Last week, as Sherry and I were attending a reception in honor of the peace accord, I felt a little uncomfortable: Here we were, amid Jews and Arabs, wondering if Yasser Arafat would show up as rumored. We were standing *among* our cousins, the Arab-Americans, but not really *with* them.

Our challenge this Yom Kippur is: Can we stand with the Arabs we have mistrusted? Can we join hands? Can we help them in their troubles? Can we treat them as neighbors? Can we forgive them? Will they forgive us?

One link between the Torah portions that we read this morning and that we will read this afternoon is that they both talk about strangers. Deuteronomy instructs us to include the stranger. Leviticus, we will hear this afternoon, tells us, "When a stranger lives with you in your land, you must not oppress him. You shall love him like yourself."

Thus we are commanded by God to overcome our human instinct, for it is so easy to oppress strangers. And how well we know that, having been strangers ourselves in Egypt and so many other places. Yet we are told: Do not wrong the stranger, but include him. And further: You shall not take vengeance nor bear a grudge.

Today is the day we are commanded to overcome our human instincts, to put aside past wrongs and reach out to our past enemies. This may well be the most difficult task we face on Yom Kippur. Our human side leads us to bear grudges and seek vengeance and nurse our hatred. Yom Kippur tells us to put these feelings aside and to treat the stranger as one of us, loving our neighbors as ourselves.

Prime Minister Rabin pointed out that we do not make peace with friends. Only with enemies do we make peace, and enemies are different from strangers or kin or neighbors. The natural antipathy we feel toward enemies is so hard to push aside. And certainly we have viewed Arafat and the PLO as enemies for more than a generation.

As Leon Wieseltier notes in *The New Republic*, Arafat to many of us is but the latest in a long line of enemies of our people.[2] This line begins with Amalek and Haman, continues through Chmelnitsky and Hitler, and in our own day, Arafat. These feelings lead us inevitably toward caution, even fear, that this peace will backfire, that the situation will be worse than before.

All of us are wary, even as we are elated. I am comforted in my feelings of wariness by the insights of Leonard Fein:

> It is but for the Israeli government to make the choice, for it is the Israeli people that bear the burden, it is they who must live with the risk. For now, they have made their choice. They have chosen the path of peace. . . . Until now we have prayed for victory in war, so now must we pray for victory in peace, and praise those who have chosen to walk this unfamiliar road. They know the risk of this new journey better than we. They will not walk it blindly, nor naively. They will walk it carefully, step by step. Of that we may be certain. We could be certain of that with any Israeli government—the more so with a government headed by a man whose entire lifetime has been devoted to protecting Israel's security.

Still, we ask this Yom Kippur: Can we reach out to our past enemies? Can we forgive and be forgiven? Can we overcome the human within us? This is the message of Yom Kippur. Our human instinct is to recoil from those who hate us, but Yom Kippur comes to tell us to make peace with our enemies. This is the day to begin to include the stranger, to turn away from hatred, to seek reconciliation in our own lives and in the life of our people.

There have been many enemies of our people since Amalek and Haman: enemies from without and enemies from within. How should we deal with our enemies, beginning on this day of reconciliation?

The answer comes from Exodus: "When you encounter your enemy's animal wandering, you must take it back to him. When you see your enemy's animal lying under its burden and would refrain from helping it, you must nevertheless raise it with him" (Exod. 23:4-5).

An early twentieth century Bible commentator, Benno Jacob, explains that our first thought when we see an enemy in trouble is to ignore him and to refuse to extend a helping hand. When we instinctively say to ourselves, "Shall I do a good turn to someone who has treated me so badly?," the Torah calls on us to do everything to help him.[3]

An earlier commentator, Malbim, points out that the very fact that this passage mentions an enemy demonstrates the imperfection in the world and in ourselves. We live in an imperfect world: There are enemies. We hate others. We have not succeeded in conquering our own evil instincts.

Another verse in Deuteronomy is very similar: "If you see the animal of your kin fallen on the road, do not ignore it. You must help him raise it" (Deut. 22:4). Here is the same rule. In Exodus, it refers to your enemy, and in Deuteronomy, it refers to your relative. We are commanded to help the fallen animal, regardless of whose it is.

But what would happen if you came upon two fallen animals and both needed your help? (The rabbis of the Talmud loved hypothetical situations!) The answer is, "Our first duty is to attend to the animal of our enemy in order to discipline our instincts" (Baba Metzia 32b).

How well the rabbis knew our instincts to turn away from responsibility, to hide from assisting, to seek excuses, to ignore those who hate us. How well they lead us to responsibility to help not only our family and our neighbor, but also our enemy and all that belongs to him.

This is a powerful message for us today as we stand before God united with our people here, in Israel, and around the world. And today we stand across the generations, reaching back twenty years, twenty generations, twenty centuries, and more. It is a message for those of us for whom Israel means so much. For Israel is our homeland, a place of promise, a sanctuary for our people.

But Israel is more than a chapter in Jewish history, a distant symbol of Jewish promise. It can—and should—be a part of our own lives. For those of us who have visited Israel, we know that is far more than a vacation or a tour; it is an encounter with ourselves: our people, our history, and—often in ways we do not recognize for years—it is a life-changing experience.

This was true of the group we led there last January, and it is true on a larger scale. One recent study of the American Jewish population has demonstrated that a visit to Israel is the best way to ensure Jewish continuity and involvement among our young people. As a result, Temple Sinai is participating with other area congregations in a new program to encourage and assist our high school students to visit Israel through a variety of programs. May our young people be filled with the spirit of our Jewish homeland, and may their experiences there enrich them and indeed all of us.

Even when we are not there—even from this distance, we expect so much of Israel: We want it to have peace and flourish; we want it to be guided by the best of Jewish values; we want it to be a center of Jewish life, an inspiration for Jews around the world; and we want Israel to be a center of social justice. I am pleased that so many in our congregation have supported and continue to support the work of ARZA to help build in the Jewish state a society of religious pluralism and opportunity.

As American Jews, we have so much to give to Israel and so much to get. We need to share not only our resources, but also our insights and values. We want Israel to meet *all* of our dreams: We want it to be our Jewish homeland, a source of our spiritual energy, and a shining example of justice and freedom and peace, as envisioned by the Prophets and developed by the Zionist builders.

The prophets knew well of our obligations to others, even to our enemies. And many of the early Zionists knew that only with peaceful borders could Israel flourish. Both prophets and pioneers knew that we need to join hands and make peace with our Arab cousins, if we could ever create a Jewish homeland that would represent the best of Jewish values for our people and for all peoples.

So how with these lofty ideals do we deal with our enemies? We help them; we do not oppress them; we do not take vengeance; we treat them as we would treat our own kin. We do this even when it is difficult, and especially *because* it is difficult. We do this even on this day of Jewish unity as we remember all those who died for our people and all those who suffered because they were Jews.

And we do this especially on this day when we are commanded to forgive others and reach out to those who hate us. We do this even on this anniversary of war and especially on this day when we must overcome our instincts to hate and know that to be a Jew we must care even for our enemies.

Our tradition calls Yom Kippur the Day of Judgment, for each of us is judged before God today. Why, then, do we wear white, when the mood is solemn and black would seem more appropriate? Because the Jew is never without hope. We come before God on this holiest day of our year ready to be judged, yet filled with hope.

May this Day of Judgment become a Day of Hope for all of us and for our people. May this day, this season, this year be a time of new beginnings for us, for our people, and for the land of Israel.

---

1. Earlier that month, Israel and the PLO had signed their first accord, a Declaration of Principles on Palestinian self-government in Gaza and the West Bank.
2. Leon Wieseltier, "Letting Go," The New Republic, 10/4/93, Vol. 209 Issue 14, 27-29.
3. Nehama Leibowitz, *Studies in Exodus* (Elinor Library, 1986), 428, 431.

Prayers of Our Hearts

Rosh Hashanah Morning 5755
September 6, 1994

Last spring, during a discussion of prayer in the public schools, a minister said something that surprised me. "In my religious tradition," he said, "we must pray. It is a necessary part of our lives."

I realized then and there that he and I were speaking different languages on the use and purpose of prayer: that we were coming from entirely different cultures in terms of our deeply rooted habits of thinking and ways of acting. For while most of us Jews might feel a need to pray from time to time, very few Jews I know consider prayer a necessary part of their lives.

These Days of Awe are a time to tell the truth. If truth be told, we Jews must say that we pray rarely, irregularly, and with difficulty. As Rabbi Portnoy pointed out last evening, prayer is the path to spirituality that we are least likely to take and the part of Jewish life we are least comfortable with. We do many things in our synagogues: We study, socialize, work, teach, cook, stuff envelopes. But we do not pray, at least not often.

Even when we do come to pray—for a service, to say Kaddish—we are just as likely to focus our energy on the non-praying aspects of our experience. We might come for the service, but what attracts our interest is an idea in the Torah reading, an insight in the sermon, a beautiful melody, the food at the oneg shabbat, and (especially) who is there. As Rabbi Lawrence Hoffman points out, though the prayer book is the text in our hands, the various sideshows attract our attention.[1]

I know that—unlike my Protestant colleague—I do not come from a people that must pray. I come from a people that is not quite comfortable praying, does not quite know *how* to pray anymore; a people that probably rather would be doing something else.

So this morning is filled with contradictions. Here we are: a people unaccustomed to praying, more than a little uncomfortable in praying, gathered together ... to pray! On this morning and on Yom Kippur, in fact, there are more Jews praying than doing anything else, or at least there should be. Here we all are, gathered together, to do something we don't particularly like doing, something we don't quite know how to do.

Indeed, we are not unlike Abraham in this morning's Torah reading. Did you ever notice that in his moment of great trial and testing, Abraham does not pray? All Abraham seems capable of uttering is "*Hineni*," "Here I am." Abraham speaks no more than this single word to God or to the angel. He gives an order to his servant and says only a few words to Isaac, "God will see to the lamb for the burnt offering, my son." This man of faith, who argues so well with God, does not pray at this crucial moment in his life.

Where is Abraham's prayer in this morning's portion? Was he too stunned to speak? Was he afraid? Or was he, perhaps, like us, incapable of praying?

No doubt it has occurred to you by now that teaching Jews how to pray is a task for synagogues and rabbis.

We do teach our children the prayer book, or liturgy, the prayers themselves. When I was in religious school, we had a textbook, *Teach Me to Pray,* that taught the Hebrew prayers much as we teach them to our children today. Historically Jews have prayed in Hebrew, so we want our children to know how to read the Hebrew prayers and what they mean.

When we study and teach our children liturgy, however, we teach the *what*. We don't teach the *how*. *Teach Me to Pray* taught me the Hebrew words and their meaning and some of the concepts, but it did not teach me how to pray.

As an adult, I have both taken and taught courses in liturgy, and most center on the words in the prayer book: the language, the themes, the metaphors, the theology. Similarly, we confuse the *what* of our prayers with the *how* of praying. It's easier to teach the words than to describe the feelings they are meant to summon.

Do not think that I am opposed to teaching the language and content of our liturgy. To the contrary, I believe strongly that as Jews we must know more about our prayers. But we must not stop there. As Rabbi Harold Shulweis points out in his latest book, too much of our "religious education turns ... the majesty of prayer into mechanical mumbling."[2] He observes we "have been taught the prayer book without anticipating the questions about the efficacy of prayer and its pertinence to living." Learning the words is important, but it is never enough.

Not making an effort to learn how to pray is negligent. It leads us to devalue our worship and potentially makes our central religious experiences, such as our High Holy Day services, exercises in hypocrisy. For what we are supposed to do in the synagogue on these High Holy Days—pray—and what we in fact do—read words, listen, look around—are very different activities. The fact is that we are not prepared to do what we are supposed to do. We do not know how to pray.

And why do we continue to avoid the *how*? The answers are deeply personal and different for each of us.

One reason, I think, is that prayer is the service of the heart, not of the mind. Most of us are trained to be guided by our rational side. We are taught, through our graduate and professional education, to work with our minds, unencumbered by our feelings.

Just as, in the rest of our lives, we may find ourselves unable to "get in touch with our feelings," so it is in our spiritual lives. By comparison, it is easy to learn the words; it is easy to learn the language; it is easy to learn the history; it is easy to learn the philosophy. But it is not so easy to feel humble and in need of support, to yield to a sense of awe; not so easy to experience the fervor of prayer.

The Haftarah we read this morning, in contrast to the Torah portion, offers us a model. Tormented by her inability to bear children, Hannah turned in her grief to God. In the Temple, "weeping copious tears," she prayed to God and uttered a vow. Eli the priest looked at her mouth, and the text tells us, "Hannah was praying silently; though her lips were moving, she made no sound, so that Eli took her for a drunkard" and chastised her.

Hannah prayed with her heart but not with her voice. On this day we pray with our voices, but how many of us are praying with our hearts? What can Hannah teach us about the importance of individual prayer? Is she the one who can show us *how*?

Rabbis in the Talmud certainly considered her an example. From the verses of this story, Rabbi Hamnuna deduced a methodology of worship, a recipe for *how* to pray:

- The text says, "Hannah spoke in her heart," so Rabbi Hamnuna said that one who prays must direct one's heart.
- The text says "only her lips moved," so Rabbi Hamnuna said that one who prays must frame the words distinctly with his or her lips.

- The text says, "but her voice could not be heard," so Rabbi Hamnuna said that it is forbidden to raise one's voice during worship.
- The text says, "Eli thought she was drunk," so Rabbi Hamnuna said that anyone who is inebriated is forbidden from leading prayers.

Thus, from these verses we have a series of regulations governing the conduct of public worship.[3]

Rabbi Eleazar, though, noted the most crucial point for us this morning: "The verse 'Hannah spoke in her heart' means that *she spoke concerning her heart*."[4]

Hannah's prayer, in other words, was not just silent. Hannah's prayer came from inside her. Hannah knew the longings of her heart: She wanted a child. How many of us come here today knowing what we want in our lives, knowing the longings of our hearts? How many of us can feel those longings, and how many of us can express them?

How rare are these prayers, these spiritual moments, these prayers of the heart! How prone we are to putting aside these prayerful moments! How easy it is to misunderstand them, as Eli did when he thought Hannah was drunk!

I empathize with Eli the priest, sitting at the entrance of the Temple at Shiloh, concerned about the well-being of his Jewish community, no less concerned about the sacredness of God's shrine. I share with Eli the "view from the bimah" of our congregation. Week after week, year after year, I observe.

I see on Shabbat evening the people who come frequently, obviously finding meaning and strength in our worship. I see those who come primarily to say Kaddish out of a sense of duty and often leave having found purpose in the prayers we say together. I see those who come for special occasions only, to rejoice or celebrate or learn with the congregation.

I also see those who are here in body, but not in spirit. Maybe they know the parents of the baby being named, or they've been invited to the bar mitzvah. Some Jews come only to observe, not to worship. From the bimah, I see those who don't bother to take prayer books, and I see those who take them but don't bother to read them. I hear those who read, those who read with meaning, those who read mechanically, and those who talk incessantly. I see those who almost defy us to make this a meaningful spiritual experience. Certainly if they (or anyone else) are not ready to encounter God, there is little we can do for them, or to them, or with them.

No matter what brings us here, every heart has longings, even if we do not think we feel them, even if we do not want to feel them, even if we cannot express them. How can we learn to move beyond the liturgy—beyond the words of the prayers—to the spiritual meaning we seek in coming here today and throughout the year?

We Jews, over the years, have had many ways of reaching beyond the text of our prayer books. We have davened and shuckled and moved our bodies to the rhythm of the prayers. We have chanted the words and made them come alive. As Reform Jews, we have prayed in our own language, building upon the meaning as well as the sound. We have brought new poetry and the beauty of instrumental music into our worship. We have strengthened the prayers of one another by singing them together. These various ways have worked for our people as different generations have sought to reach beyond the words of the prayer book and address the prayers of their hearts.

What way works for us? How can we reach beyond the text to pray the prayer of our hearts?

Rabbi Lawrence Hoffman, whom you may remember as our scholar-in-residence a few years ago, points out that we need to develop worship that heals. Hoffman writes:

> People want ritual that heals, heals their broken selves, heals the wound of broken communal connection both through time and across space, and promises healing in a world that can prove shattering. *The transformation from rote to rite should be our worship agenda for the 1990s.*[5]

Hannah came to the Temple because there she found sanctuary, a place that offered healing. Hannah had no prayer book; Jewish prayer books didn't appear until the Middle Ages. What Hannah did have were the yearnings of her heart, and she knew where to take them. Today we have prayer books, but we're not sure how to use them, and we have lost touch with the yearnings of our hearts. We separate the "spiritual" from the emotional in our lives; we don't know what to take to the synagogue and what to take to our therapists. Like Eli the priest, we confuse the spirit of prayer with the presence of spirits.

To heal ourselves, we need to bring our feelings with us as we pray. This is how to release our spiritual longings, to help us to pray with all our hearts. This is how our synagogue must become a place of healing, a place of rejoicing, a place of comfort, as temples and synagogues have been since the time of Hannah and Eli.

We must reach out in rejoicing and comfort and healing to those whose lives have been enriched or rent asunder: the mourners and all who suffer pain. Too often these sorrows are experienced in private, without the healing that a congregation can offer.

We need to welcome those who have recovered or returned or been restored to life and peace. Our tradition has a specific prayer for those who have been saved from danger or recovered from illness: "*Baruch attah adonai eloheinu melech ha-olam she-g'malani kol tov.* We praise God, Ruler of the universe, who bestows great goodness upon me." This prayer can be said privately, of course, but it can also be said at a congregational service because then the congregation can respond, "May the One who has been gracious to you continue to favor you with all that is good."[6]

How sweet it would be for all of us to recite these words often as a congregation, to share our joy and healing with others. How much more, then, would we be making our synagogue a sanctuary. Our shared joy and our healing would help bind us together as a congregation.

To say these words with meaning, of course, we need to believe them. We need to believe that we are capable of turning to God; we need to believe that the wellsprings of Jewish prayer are capable of offering us strength and comfort. We need to feel that healing goes on within this building. We need to feel that worship can heal us and help us, as Hannah was helped. We need to feel that we are part of a congregation and a community that cares for one another—as our people have felt for centuries—and we need to know that we can experience these feelings as we worship together.

This already happens here from time to time but not often enough. I see new parents or grandparents coming to the synagogue in thanksgiving just after the birth of a child. I see a spouse or a child or a parent coming to worship as their loved one lies in the hospital or struggles through a crisis. I see mourners recovering from the shock of loss, seeking the comfort of our tradition and the support of our community.

There is more, though, that we as a congregation can do to respond to all the different emotions that people bring to our worship services. I am concerned by the increasing privatization of our life cycle celebrations. We need to encourage our members to share their simchas with the congregation. We need to share birthdays, anniversaries, births, and marriages. We need to understand, for example, that as a young person becomes a bar or bat mitzvah, this is cause for rejoicing for the congregation, and not an "invitation only" service.

These rituals are all significant Jewish markers of the milestones in our shared life as a congregation. They remind us in the most public way that our lives are blessed and that our joy has a direct bearing on how we live our lives in daily contact with our community.

We must not be satisfied, moreover, with simply bringing these celebrations into the synagogue. The simchas and sorrows of one another must become our own. For being a congregation means caring for one another. Elie Wiesel tells a story about the Gerer Rabbi, who asked one of his disciples about someone in the community: "How is Moshe Yaakov doing?" The disciple did not know. "What!" exclaimed the Gerer Rabbi. "You don't know? You pray under the same roof? You read the same book? You worship the same God, and you tell me you don't know how Moshe Yaakov is, whether he needs help, or advice, or comforting. How can that be?"[7]

We, too, need to know how Moshe Yaakov is doing. We, too, need to connect ourselves to one another and approach that sense of caring. We, too, need to feel that we share in the joys and sorrows that people bring to our sanctuary. And when it is our turn to come to the sanctuary in joy or sorrow, we need to know that others will be here to share with us and strengthen us. As Jews seeking spiritual meaning, we must direct our hearts as Hannah directed her heart.

In studying liturgy, we distinguish between the fixed words of the prayer book, *keva*, and the feelings we bring to them, *kavanah*. Though we are comfortable with the words, we need to be more accepting of our feelings.

The words are on paper; we can read them, study them, learn to understand them. Yet the words are only the instrument of our prayer: the means, and not the end.

What is crucial, and overlooked, is how we read or sing the words: Do we read mechanically, or do we approach the words as a gateway that will lead us to the prayer of our hearts?

Sometimes the prayer of our heart is without words, as was Hannah's prayer. Sometimes we find it in the music, sometimes in our surroundings. And sometimes the prayer of our heart is a pure spiritual experience, attainable through the feelings we bring.

We need to understand that the spiritual experience itself is our goal, even if we feel it only occasionally—to pray, as Hannah did, with all our hearts. We can approach those sanctified moments of prayer by knowing our prayer book better, by praying more frequently, by being more open to our feelings as well as to the words and music of our prayers, by sharing in the joys and sorrows of others in our congregation.

As Israel Baal Shem Tov, the founder of Hasidism, once was about to enter a synagogue, he stopped at the door and refused to go in. When his followers asked him why he didn't enter, he responded:

> This synagogue is too full of prayers and words. The people have been saying their prayers, but they are just words, not prayers from the heart. The words take up a lot of space, and there is no room for me. Prayers that come from the heart ascend to Heaven, but these prayers are trapped in the synagogue; they need the heart in order to be released to God. And until that happens, there is no room for me.[8]

In our synagogue, there must be room: room for each of us and for the prayers of our hearts. No less than anyone else, we Jews need to pray: to pray from our hearts, to pray not only the words, but the feelings. No less than anyone else, we Jews need healing. And no less than anyone else, we Jews need a community, a community of prayer and sustenance and support. On these Days of Awe and prayer, these days of ingathering for our people, let us begin together.

---

1. Lawrence Hoffman, "From Common Cold to Uncommon Healing," *CCAR Journal*, Spring 1994, 5ff. See also "How to Cure the Synagogue and Satisfy the Soul," *Reform Judaism*, Summer 1994, 32-34.
2. Harold Shulweis, "For Those Who Can't Believe." *Sh'ma* offprint, 2-3.

3. Berachot 31a, Soncino, 191.
4. Berachot 31b, Soncino, 194.
5. Hoffman, 19.
6. *Gates of the House*, 22.
7. Jack Riemer, *The World of the High Holy Days*, Vol. II., 61.
8. Martin Buber, *Tales of the Chasidim: The Early Masters*, translated by Olga Max. (New York: Schocken Books, 1957), 73.

I Believe With Perfect Faith

Rosh Hashanah Eve 5756
September 24, 1995

Ani maamin be-emunah shleimah b'viat hamashiach
v'af al pi she-yitmahmei-a
im kol zeh ani ma-amin.

"I believe with perfect faith in the coming of the Messiah; and even though He is delayed, still I believe."[1]

These are strange words for us—as Reform Jews—to say, yet we sing them often. They are in *Gates of Prayer*, in the liturgy for Yom Hashoah, the Holocaust Remembrance Day service. They remind us of the faith of the millions who perished with these words on their lips and in their hearts.

Why are these words important to us—we who are more cerebral than faithful, we who are accustomed to thinking, but not necessarily to believing? Why do *we* repeat them and teach them to our children? What gives these words sufficient meaning that they move us still?

These words were written by Moses Maimonides in the twelfth century; they were part of his thirteen principles of the Jewish faith. They were later included in the traditional prayer book as a creedal statement and remain there. Within our century they took on a new and amplified meaning, becoming a source of hope for many Jews during the Shoah.

This past summer, as I stood with thirty members of our congregation at the Terezin concentration camp, I reflected on what these words must have meant to those who lived—and died—there. For the inmates of this and the other concentration camps, there was no reasonable hope. They knew—as their friends and members of their families were selected or died or disappeared—how utterly hopeless life was for them.

Yet as Jews, we are commanded to hope. This is part of what Rabbi Leo Baeck taught them, in the years he was in Terezin, and what he and they continue to teach us today: our need and our responsibility to hope, even in life's darkest hours.

All of us face crises and need to move beyond our rational side to our spiritual. We need to be able to say, "I've done everything I can; now the future is in God's hands." We who love to control, we who use our minds more than our hearts, we who are more in touch with our creature comforts than our creatureliness, we need to hear what Rabbi Baeck taught: "You must hope."

Hearing these words, "I believe with perfect faith," gives us a sense of the spiritual as others experienced it. For we come here today seeking the spiritual, seeking to hope, seeking the side of our lives we too often ignore.

They who were so spiritually pure can give us so much. They did nothing wrong, save that they were Jewish. Yet when everything material in their lives was taken from them, they maintained their hope. We who know better how to keep than how to let go must follow their example. It is a miracle that despite Nazi attempts to break their spirits, so many emerged with their minds and their spirits. And from their spirits, our own spirits are renewed.

Why were these words so important? Because of all the articles of Jewish faith, only these had a direct effect on people's lives. Lacking the power to control their own lives, they believed that only the Messiah would release them from their misery. For them, belief in a Messiah symbolized their hope and faith; as we repeat their words today, they have become a symbol of their martyrdom.

It is ironic that these words appear in our Reform prayer book or that I should begin a sermon with them. For more than any other tenet of Jewish faith, this belief in the Messiah was rejected by the founders of Reform Judaism in the 19th century.

At the first Reform congregation in the United States, in Charleston, South Carolina, the rabbi rewrote this principle of faith to read, "We believe that the Messiah announced by the Prophets is *not* come," thus turning it into an anti-Christian statement.[2] When the Messiah came, so it was believed, he would regather the Jewish people as a nation in Palestine.

The early Reformers, however, saw their Jewish lives in the context of the countries in which they lived, as we do today. They reinterpreted the Jewish belief in the Messiah as a belief in a messianic era, a time of universal peace. This is no accident: the rise of Reform Judaism coincided with great political and social revolutions in Europe, and in many countries, the emancipation of the Jews. The times were times of hope and promise.

The 19th century Reform leaders asserted that in action—in social action—they could help to bring about the messianic era.

What do *we* believe, we 20th century Reform Jews? We who are post-Depression, post-Holocaust, post-Zionism, post-death of God, post-A-bomb; we who lack the faith of both the inmates of Terezin and the early Reform Jews: Can we find such hope in our lives? Can we find such optimism amidst our cynicism? Can we find spiritual satisfaction in the midst of the materialism of our age?

Have no doubt that we desperately need to feel that hope and optimism. For we, too, are confronted with disappointment and despair, with frustration and futility. We, too, hear the bad diagnosis; we, too, see the life of someone dear to us slipping away; we, too, know the pain of a child not fulfilling her aspirations.

But we do not let ourselves feel the faith of previous generations. We feel that faith is anti-intellectual and see ourselves as dedicated to the life of the mind. We are well educated, read a lot, and respond better to evidence and carefully reasoned proofs than to the yearnings of our hearts. We think that listening to our heart is done with a stethoscope rather than with spiritual sensitivity. It is no wonder, then, that our spiritual capacity has declined, for most of us, and we are simply not in touch with this part of our lives.

We confuse our own spiritual needs with the mindless faith of Fundamentalists, with the messianic expectations of the Branch Davidians or the Lubavitcher Chasidim. We smile indulgently at the Lubavitchers, who believed that the late Rabbi Menachem Schneerson was the Messiah.

The Lubavitcher Rebbe was not the Messiah, although many faithful and pious Jews looked to him as such. They believed (in our day) with perfect faith in the coming of the Messiah.

A large part of our skepticism comes from our history of false messiahs. Many proclaimed themselves to be the Messiah, or others did it for them. They attracted followers for a time and gave a troubled people some cause for hope. Today they give us cause for cynicism.

The most celebrated among them was Shabbetai Z'vi, who lived from 1626 to 1676, a time of great persecution of the Jews. In addition to Inquisitions in Spain and Portugal, the Chmelnitzki Pogroms in

Russia were instilling fear for Jews everywhere. In Smyrna, in Turkey, life looked black. As Shabbetai studied Jewish mystical texts and traveled to Jerusalem, he decided that he was the Messiah. He sent letters to Europe, to Asia, to North Africa, and people believed him! There was rejoicing throughout the Jewish world.

Though Shabbetai Z'vi was imprisoned by the Sultan's police, people still believed in him. After all, they said, did it not say that the Messiah would suffer tribulation? In prison, he occupied a special cell, continued his religious teaching, and made pronouncements, including overturning the fast of Tisha B'Av.

Finally the Turkish authorities could stand it no longer. He was offered the choice of converting to Islam or dying. Since he was neither brave nor committed, he chose to convert.

And here is the interesting part: even his apostasy did not dissuade his followers. Despite his conversion, many still proclaimed him the Messiah, and the Sabbatean movement continued (with new leaders) for centuries.

This is because the people needed hope; they needed belief; they needed a spiritual grounding.

We need these no less than they did, and this day of spiritual renewal is a time to begin. That is our challenge on these Days of Awe.

How can we approach belief? How can we get in touch with the yearnings of our hearts? How can we move from the cognitive to the evocative in our lives? How can we find our spiritual selves?

For many centuries our people have wondered when the Messiah would come. They have wondered out of pietistic curiosity. They have wondered out of hope for release from their suffering. They have wondered out of their faith in the future.

The Talmud[3] relates the story of Rabbi Joshua ben Levi who was visiting a grave when he encountered Elijah the prophet, the forerunner of the Messiah.

Joshua asked Elijah, "When will the Messiah come?" and Elijah answered, "Go and ask him yourself."

When Joshua asked, "Where will I find him?" Elijah replied, "At the main gate of Rome."

And when Joshua asked, "How will I recognize him?" Elijah said, "He is sitting among the beggars and tends to their wounds. He changes their bandages one by one. He thinks to himself, 'I might be called at any moment, so I must waste no time.'"

So Rabbi Joshua went to Rome and found the Messiah in the gate, just as Elijah had described him. He greeted the Messiah and asked him, "When will the Messiah come?" And much to his surprise, the Messiah answered, "Today."

Rabbi Joshua hurried back home. The next day he again met Elijah, and he complained, "The Messiah spoke untruthfully. He said he would come today, and he has not come."

This time Elijah responded, "The Messiah meant, 'Today, if you would only listen to my voice.'"

The same is true for us, of course. The Messiah will come, even today, if we would only listen to God's voice.

But how do we know God's voice? How can we hear it, with so many other voices around us?

In commenting on this story, Gershom Scholem points out that this story was written in the Second Century Common Era, just after the Roman armies had conquered Jerusalem, destroyed the Temple, and driven the Jewish people into exile. What place could be more unlikely for the Messiah to be than in the gate of Rome? Rome was hardly a place of Jewish hope, but even there, hope resided.

How can *we* find hope? How can *we* hear the Messiah in the din of our own day?

The answer to these questions also is in the story. The Messiah sits among the beggars and changes their bandages one by one. He cares for all God's creatures. Until he is called, he spends his time alleviating suffering. We have the chance to do the same.

I have thought for some years that we need to do more as members of the congregation to reach out to those who need our help. We do a lot already: we serve meals and deliver meals, tutor students, and collect food and coats. Sisterhood members volunteer; Brotherhood volunteers. Our congregation has established Sinai House, creating new hope for four families.

Truth be told, however, very few members of Temple Sinai participate in the combination of all these programs.

We can do a lot more, and we can do a lot better.

When the Social Action Committee discussed how to get more people involved, someone suggested setting aside one day each year to volunteer. While that is tempting and works in other places, I have a higher standard for Temple Sinai. I think we should volunteer more than one day a year. I think that if the Messiah can spend her time changing bandages one by one, then we should be able to prepare several meals *and* help someone repair their house *and* drive someone to services.

I know you will support our food drive this year as you have in the past, and that we will have thousands of pounds of food to take to the D.C. Central Kitchen. But our city needs more than an extra few items from each of us. Our city is filled with people who need their bandages changed, people who are hungry, people who need our help.

And we need to help them. We need to help till the soil and weed at the Rabbi Lipman garden; we need to look in our closets and ask our neighbors for coats; we need to have so many volunteers to cook dinner for the homeless women that we add a few days each month for Temple Sinai.

And we need to serve one another better: We need to call the people in our neighborhoods to ask them if they'd like a ride to services; we need to support the bereaved by ushering at a funeral or shopping for the meal of comfort.

We need to put these mitzvot first, rather than fitting them in when we have time. A few weeks ago we discovered that we needed an usher for a service. The person we enlisted said that her list for Saturday morning was no shorter than anyone else's but that nothing on it was more important.

Saving the world is all about changing bandages until you are called. It is about helping the hopeless and serving people one at a time and alleviating suffering in your corner of the world. Some of us may do a lot, but none of us does enough.

For this is the way we can find hope. We find hope for ourselves by sharing it with others. Reaching out to others not only gives them hope but puts our own lives into perspective. Reaching out to others helps to bring about the messianic time of truth, justice, and peace. As we help others, we benefit.

Our congregation always has been involved and committed, and it must be no less so today. I want you to complete the green social action commitment cards and place them in the boxes on the tables. I want those boxes to overflow with commitment, and I want us to have to struggle to find tasks for the hundreds who will volunteer to help bring about the messianic era. I know that when this congregation knows it is needed, it always answers the call. It is part of my belief, and I hope it is part of yours.

I want to close with a Rosh Hashanah story from the Holocaust. Wolf Fischelberg and his 12-year old son were walking among the barracks in the Bergen-Belsen concentration camp when suddenly a stone came flying over their heads and landed at their feet.

"What does it mean?" Wolf asked his son.

"Just an angry Jew hurling stones," replied the son.

But Wolf said, "Angry Jews do not cast stones; it is not part of our tradition." So he bent down to pick up the stone and discovered a small note wrapped around it. The note was written in Hebrew by a Dutch Jew who said he had a shofar. If the Hasidic Jews wanted to use the shofar for Rosh Hashanah services, they could smuggle it in one of the coffee cauldrons, he suggested.

So Wolf said yes and threw the stone back across the electrified barbed wire, saying to his son, "You see, Jews never throw stones in vain."

They smuggled the shofar successfully, only to encounter the next problem: It was clearly dangerous to sound the shofar loudly, but could they fulfill the commandment by sounding it softly? They debated in good Jewish fashion and decided that God surely would accept the muffled sounds of the shofar just as God had accepted so many different kinds of prayers over the centuries.

Wolf's little daughter Miriam listened to the shofar, hoping that it would bring down the barbed-wire fences of Bergen-Belsen. The fences did not come down, but the shofar gave the people who heard it new hope, in spite of their suffering.[4]

So may the shofar this Rosh Hashanah give us new hope. May its sounds tear away at the suffering in our communities and in this world. May it remind us of the sounding of the Great Shofar our people have hoped for. May it carry us closer to the messianic era and bring us renewal, new commitment, and hope in the New Year.

---

1. *Gates of Prayer*, 575, 753.
2. Michael A. Meyer, *Response to Modernity: A History of the Reform Movement in Judaism*, (Oxford University Press, NY and Oxford, 1988), 234.
3. Sanhedrin 98a.
4. Yaffa Eliach, *Hasidic Tales of the Holocaust*, 49-51.

Truth and Faith

Rosh Hashanah Morning 5757
September 14, 1996

One of the more troubling verses in the troubling Akeda story we have just read is Abraham's response to Isaac. As they walk together up Mount Moriah, Isaac notices that they have all that is necessary for a sacrifice except the animal! "Father," he says, "here are the firestone and the wood, but where is the sheep for the burnt offering?"

Abraham answers with more than a little evasiveness, "God will see to the sheep of the burnt offering, my son." And then, according to Genesis, "the two of them walked on together" (Gen. 22:7-8).

If we are uncomfortable when we hear the Akeda story, we are particularly troubled by Abraham's answer because he lies to his son. He does not say, for instance, "Perhaps we will find an animal along the way," or "There is not supposed to be a sheep," or "I am only doing what God commanded me to do: to place you on the altar," or even "I do not understand this mission."

No, Abraham misleads his son and is less than truthful under trying circumstances. Abraham may pass this test as a person of faith, but how does he measure up as a person of truth?

Today we value truth above faith. We value honesty. We value honesty in dealing with our children, whom we would not want to mislead even in such a life-and-death situation; we value honesty in all our human relationships. On Yom Kippur we will read from the Torah, "You shall not defraud your neighbor ... [and] ... You shall not falsify measures, but you shall have an honest balance and honest weights" (Lev. 19:13, 35). In the Ten Commandments, we are bidden not to swear falsely in God's name, nor to bear false witness against our neighbor.

While these commandments relate to specific circumstances, they lead us clearly and explicitly to a Jewish moral position: We value truth and honesty. As Jews, as Americans, as human beings, we value truth. We want our doctors to tell us exactly what's wrong; we want our friends to tell us what's on their minds. We expect ourselves and others to be honest in our business and personal dealings.

Our ethical dilemmas emerge only when the truth might hurt or harm others. Not so long ago, for instance, some parents would protect their children from the reality of death by telling them, "Grandpa went on a long trip." Today, we are more likely to aim to be truthful in such difficult moments because we know that honesty engenders trust and because we believe in the validity of the truth. We don't want to have to tell our children that we lied to them because we didn't think they were old enough to handle the truth.

We avoid euphemisms and talk about people who have died (not "passed away"), who have cancer or AIDS or depression or a disability. Once we talked about the "C-word" or dodged the questions or made excuses, but today we are candid, open, and honest. It is a sign of our coming to grips with our situation, of our acceptance of what life has dealt us.

So we are especially disappointed when we see that Abraham has been less than honest with his own son at such a critical moment in their lifetimes. We want total disclosure, openness, candor.

In fairness, we need to say that the story of the Akeda *is* about faith, not honesty. As Reform Jews today, however, we may find ourselves valuing honesty but not being so sure about how faith fits into our lives. We train ourselves to accept the truth, but how do we come to accept faith? We are skeptical about those who proclaim their faith; and as Jews, in particular, we may have grown up with a greater emphasis on practice than belief. We may know more about what we should do (even if we don't do it) than about what we should believe.

Faith is a set of beliefs that strengthen us and give us hope and comfort in times of crisis. I cannot tell you what *your* faith should be, for each of us must develop our own faith, our own set of beliefs. Some of us believe in a caring God, who gives us support in crises. Some of us believe in the strength of the Jewish people, providing us with a sense of community, history, and continuity, telling us we are not alone. Some of us believe in the power of prayer: prayer that can sustain and comfort us; words from our tradition and our heart that can nourish and soothe our spirits.

But faith is not just what we believe. Faith also must lead us—move us—to commitment, and make a difference in our lives. Faith is not a garment we can put on or take off, but a deep and lasting commitment that for most of us will dictate our actions. Faith is *beyond* our cognitive and rational side. It addresses our hearts *and* our minds; it speaks to our feelings and guides how we conduct our lives. Faith should not oppose truth or honesty but should complement it.

Some years ago I served as a chaplain at a large hospital, where I encountered a family in crisis. The patient was a young man in his twenties, who had been born with a physical disability. Now he was in the hospital because he had developed cancer that was in its final stages. His parents, who visited him each day, denied the gravity of his illness; they had faith that he soon would begin to get better.

The hospital staff—doctors, nurses, social workers—all wanted to tell this young man how sick he was, so that he could begin to prepare himself and talk about his feelings. His parents adamantly refused. "We have cared for him every day of his life," they said, "and we will not hurt him more with this news. Moreover, we have faith that he will get better." So they would weep in the hallway but always smile in his room. I would see them, and him, on my rounds, and I, too, tried to move the parents to accept the situation, to call in the special social work team for death and dying. I utterly failed to convince the parents that truth was better than deception.

Sometimes, truth and faith do *seem* to conflict: the truth of the diagnosis versus our faith that everything will be all right; the truth of science versus a belief that we have been created by God; the reality of Abraham's mission versus our conviction—our belief—that God would not really demand that Abraham sacrifice his own son.

But truth and faith need *not* conflict.

Often when I tell children a story, they ask me, "Is it true?" Usually I say, "No, but it's a story worth remembering." As adults, we should concern ourselves instead with the question, "What does it mean?"

We study our Torah to absorb its values and learn what it can teach us about the way we should live, not to explain the natural world. We are liberal Jews, not Jewish fundamentalists; we do not believe that the Torah must be the truthful word of God to make it worthy of our study. We seek to understand in the words of Torah who we are and before Whom we stand, to discover how we should lead our lives, to learn what we should value, to find meaning in the covenant our people made with God. We read Scripture for answers about "how" and "why," but not "what."

We come to the synagogue on Rosh Hashanah looking for answers to the same questions: "How do I relate to God?" "How do I relate to the Jewish people?" "Why do the good sometimes suffer?" "How can I become a better Jew?"

We come to the synagogue on Rosh Hashanah to strengthen the links that unite us with one another, with our people over the centuries, and with our God. We come here today not to determine whether the stories we read in the Torah are true, but to learn their message. We come here valuing candor and openness, and seeking meaning.

Most of us have trials in our lives, as Abraham did, though we hope and pray neither so severe nor so intense. When we are tried, we naturally seek knowledge and truth and meaning. If we hear a bad diagnosis, we head immediately to the medical library to learn as much as we can about this pernicious disease. No matter what decision we face, we do our research: selecting the right college, the right house, the right job, even the right toaster. We want *all* the information, all the *truth* we can get our hands on.

Unfortunately, we often are so busy seeking information that we forget to seek meaning. We skip over a deeper look into our search; we fail to probe the issues of faith or belief that also may guide us. Will this house become the "small sanctuary" our tradition describes? How will an education enrich this person's life? What does this change mean to us? What will we gain? What will we lose?

We would want *our* Abraham to be guided by truth *and* faith. We would want him to be able to share his doubts and frustrations with Isaac, with Sarah, with God, with the angel; and still be guided by his belief in a beneficent God and his hope for future generations.

Alas, he does none of this in the biblical story, and we are left to wonder how our patriarch—who argues with God about the justice of killing "sort of" innocent people in Sodom and Gomorrah—can be silent about God's demand that he kill his own innocent son.

Abraham's journey toward truth and faith is a midrash that *we* must write: we must imagine his innermost thoughts as he wonders what God means, what God wants. Should he share the purpose of the mission with Sarah? How much can he tell Isaac, without scaring him so that he runs away? The Abraham of our story, who dissembles by saying to Isaac, "God will see to the sheep for the burnt offering, my son," leaves us cold.

In these words, we do not feel Abraham's struggle. We hear his faith, but we cannot hear him asking, "Why does God demand this of me?" We say with Kierkegaard, "Though Abraham arouses my admiration, at the same time [he] appalls me."[1]

Even if we read the Akeda as a story of faith, we insist that our faith cannot be blind; it cannot deceive others nor obscure the truth, and it must help us to understand our lives. This we intuit. But also: Our faith must make demands upon us, in order to be complete.

Michael Goldberg, in his recent book, *Why Should Jews Survive?*,[2] claims that the tacit communal faith of American Jewry is based on our commitment to survival. He identifies "survival" as the lens through which we see every element of Jewish life: the motivation for ritual and education and every activity of this congregation and all others.

Goldberg says that this Jewish faith, or worldview, results when the Holocaust is considered the central event in Jewish life. To support his argument, he notes that a cult has developed around the Holocaust: a cult with its own sanctified places, holidays, rituals, and language.

Without minimizing or trivializing the horror of the Holocaust nor its meaning to us, I must agree with him that for many Jews today the Holocaust has pushed aside other facets of Judaism. The Holocaust has been appropriated by Jewish federations, Zionist organizations, and many Jewish communal agencies as their (and our) reason for existing. This worldview presents all Jews as survivors, whether we actually experienced the Holocaust ourselves or are simply among the surviving people.

But for *what* did we survive? Where *does* our survival lead us? Is there nothing to our Judaism beside mourning our dead and honoring their martyrdom?

Survival, says Goldberg, is not an end in itself but a means to an end. He compellingly argues that the central story of Jewish life instead should be the Exodus story. The narrative we read on Pesach is the central story of the Torah. Most importantly, the story of our exodus leads to the covenant at Sinai. For the Jews who wrote that story and for the Jews who have read that story from generation to generation, surviving life-threatening danger was never an end in itself; survival was but the means to living a redemptive way of life, a way of life prescribed by God's covenant with our people at Sinai.[3]

The goal of Judaism, Goldberg points out, is not merely to survive, but to enter into the covenant with God, to find the faith of previous generations to enter into the covenant that began with Abraham that is our covenant. It is a covenant that leads us to a consecrated life. Surely *that* is a truth that we can learn this Rosh Hashanah.

Isaac survived, and Abraham survived. And we are survivors, too: survivors with a faith in the future. But the key to survival in the Akeda story is a covenantal promise of hope in the future, a renewed promise of blessing.

So it is with us. We, too, are tested in our faith; we too face trials that shake us to our core: trials with our health, with our families, with our futures and our pasts, with life and with death. Instinctively, we seek knowledge and truth to help us survive these trials: to know what to do, to know how to decide. But information is not enough; we also need faith.

For after our research, after the therapy, after the comprehension, the physician or the therapist turns to us and says, "You know all the facts, and I have done all that I can do. To face the future, you will need inner strength, or faith."

In serious crises or losses, we need faith as well as truth to succeed. We need a faith that gives us courage and strength. We need a faith that goes beyond knowledge and leads us to find our own inner resources. We need a faith that leads us to commitment. We need a force that can motivate us and guide us through life: faith.

Rosh Hashanah demands that we seek truth as well as faith: truth in our introspection, truth in our relationship with God and with others, truth in our quest for the future. Rosh Hashanah comes to tell us that we must do more than survive. Rosh Hashanah comes to tell us we must not take the easy way and follow a comfortable Judaism that makes no demands on us. Rosh Hashanah comes to tell us that we must search for the way to faith and hope and commitment in the coming year. Rosh Hashanah comes, at last, to tell us that we must have faith and hope that God will see to all the offerings in *our* lives, to all that *we* must do and believe and hope for in the future.

---

1. Soren Kierkegaard, *Fear and Trembling* (Penguin, 1985),, xvi, 89-90.
2. Michael Goldberg, *Why Should Jews Survive?: Looking Past the Holocaust Toward a Jewish Future* (Oxford University Press, 1995).
3. Goldberg, 162.

Are Reform Jews Nothing?

Kol Nidre 5757
September 22, 1996

Perhaps you remember the story of the rabbi who was overcome with remorse one Yom Kippur. Suddenly during the service she threw herself down on the bimah before the ark and began to appeal to God: "Source of forgiveness, I know how inadequate I am. I am here to lead this congregation, but I am not doing it well. I am supposed to set an example for them, but it is so difficult. I am filled with feelings of hypocrisy. Today I know my shortcomings, and I throw myself down before You, for I know that I am a nothing."

Seeing this display of humility, the cantor, too, walked in front of the ark, threw himself down on the bimah and began to wail: "Creator of the universe, I, too, am a nothing. I am supposed to lead this congregation in prayer, but it is such a difficult task, and I fear I am not up to it. I know the words, I know the music, but I cannot direct my heart to You. And without that, I am not authentic, and I have failed. Source of mercy, I am a nothing."

Now from the back of the sanctuary, the shammes was watching the rabbi and cantor in this spontaneous outburst of humility. He, too, ran up onto the bimah, threw himself down before the ark, and began his plea: "God of all generations, I come here deeply humbled. I am supposed to serve You and Your people, but I cannot. I am supposed to be a model Jew, but truly I am only a pretender. I feel so inadequate to the task of leading the people and serving this holy congregation. Source of mercies, I am a nothing."

Here were the three of them lying on the bimah before the ark, when the rabbi turned to the cantor, pointed to the shammes, and said, "Look at him. Look who thinks he's a nothing!"

Yom Kippur is supposed to lead all of us to feelings of remorse and inadequacy. Yom Kippur is supposed to lead us to question the depth of our Jewish feelings and our Jewish authenticity. At the same time that we feel the most connected to our people and our Jewishness, we are commanded to examine our shortcomings, to see where we have missed the mark, where we have fallen short, where we have failed in our Jewish lives. We, too, are pretenders. We, too, know too little. We, too, feel inauthentic.

People are always confiding to me that they don't *feel* sufficiently Jewish; they feel like they are not "real Jews." They feel guilty because they didn't have a bar mitzvah; or they weren't confirmed; or that they never went to Hillel; or that they can't read Hebrew, or that they can read Hebrew but can't understand it. They feel remorseful that they do not or cannot observe Shabbat each week, or as often as they would like. They feel guilty because they haven't read a Jewish book or studied anything Jewish this year. They feel inauthentic because their parents didn't belong to a synagogue, and they never went to services. They feel hypocritical because they believe in social action, but they never really *do* anything about it. They feel ashamed because Judaism means something to them, and they wish they could do more, but they are so busy, and there are so many other demands on them. They know there are people who seem to be able to lead more Jewish lives; they even know some of them personally, and that makes them feel even worse.

We come here tonight—or we are supposed to come here tonight—with our pockets full of unkept promises, our hearts full of regrets, knowing that there is so much more we could or should be doing. We are not the Jews we should be, not the authentic, complete, practicing, committed Jews we should be.

This time, even as we grapple with these issues of our personal authenticity, we also have to confront the fact that we have been told by some of our non-Jewish neighbors that Judaism is less than an authentic religion, and we are being told by other Jews that Reform is less than authentic Judaism.

Last June, the Southern Baptist Convention adopted a resolution calling for efforts to convert Jews to Christianity. For the first time in decades, they appointed a missionary to the Jews, reinstituting a policy they had allowed to lie dormant for many years. This is truly a setback for Baptist-Jewish relations and for Jewish-Christian relations in general. In recent years, several Protestant denominations—including the Presbyterians and the United Methodists—have encouraged dialogue with the Jewish community and stopped trying to convert us.

These breakthroughs in interreligious relations have sent the message that God can relate to different religions equally. In other words, these religious bodies have altered their beliefs to conceive of a God who can maintain a covenant with the Jewish people even though Jews do not accept Jesus as the Messiah.

These unheralded efforts are significant because they confirm the religious authenticity of Judaism. We take this for granted, of course, but much of Christianity does not.

We need to recognize that for many Christians, missionary work is central to their religious practices and beliefs. Converting the Jews—that is, convincing us to accept Jesus as our savior—has been an important aspect of Christianity since its inception, based on the assumption that Judaism is an incomplete religion. Many Christians believe that Jews must accept Jesus as their personal Messiah in order to be saved and go to heaven; they maintain, moreover, that the second coming of Jesus will be hastened when all the Jews do accept him as the Messiah. That is why our conversion is so vital to them.

Many people have tried to convert the Jews. Even Theodor Herzl, whom we are studying this year, developed a plan for the mass conversion of Austrian Jewry to Christianity! In his brief, flamboyant life, Herzl came up with several outlandish ideas, and this one stands out. In the 1890s Herzl saw anti-Semitism as the greatest threat to Jewish survival. If all the Jews converted to Christianity, Herzl believed, that would be the end of anti-Semitism. Herzl even proposed a mass conversion ceremony. The Jewish community would gather "in broad daylight ... with festive processions" in front of St. Stephen's Cathedral in Vienna. All the Jews, except their leaders and Herzl, would be baptized in the Cathedral. Then, thought Herzl, he could strike an alliance with the Pope that would bind the Roman Catholic Church to eradicate anti-Semitism.[1]

Fortunately for us, Herzl had some other ideas as well!

It's often hard to distinguish between anti-Semitism and attempts to convert Jews. In 1980, the president of the Southern Baptists declared that "God doesn't hear the prayers of Jews." And there are the gratuitous comments of Louis Farrakhan that Judaism is a "gutter religion."

These comments remind us that there are those who question the religious authenticity of Judaism and our authenticity as religious people. They make us angry, especially—perhaps—*because* we feel we work so hard as a community to teach that there are many paths to God. In our integrated and assimilated Jewish community, we see Judaism as one religion among many, one path to God among many: different paths toward the same destination.

If we are distressed by the actions of the Southern Baptists, how much more do we feel challenged as Reform Jews by recent religious events in Israel. One month after the Southern Baptist convention, Israel's Sephardic Chief Rabbi Eliyahu Bakshi Doron gratuitously denigrated Reform Judaism. Speaking about the biblical Pinchas, who killed an Israelite named Zimri because Zimri was engaging in illicit sex with a Midianite woman, the rabbi labeled Zimri "the first Reform Jew" and implied that his followers should emulate the zealous bravery of Pinchas.

Rabbi Bakshi Doron was speaking about intermarriage, the preservation of Judaism, and the need for Jewish zealotry in Israel, the Jewish state that grew out of Herzl's Zionist dream.

The same Herzl who saw Austrian Jews leaving Judaism in vast numbers, as we know, acted upon his later vision of Jews leaving Austria instead, founding their own state in a proud act of self-assertion. Herzl was not motivated by a desire to develop Jewish culture, nor was he motivated by a desire to encourage Jewish religious life. Herzl simply saw the Jewish State as the best way to rescue Jews from anti-Semitism and statelessness and provide them with a respectable place in world society. The establishment of a Jewish State was a dream in which all Jews—religious and non-religious alike—could take part and take pride.[2]

So where is the government of Israel today on the matter of religion? For me, the effect of the election of Benjamin Netanyahu as Prime Minister on the role of the religious parties in Israel is just as alarming as his election's effect on the peace process. The religious parties are stronger today than at any time in the history of the State of Israel. The number of Knesset seats they control has jumped almost fifty percent, from 16 to 23, and their impact has been felt immediately: in the Ministries of Education and Interior, in local religious councils, in the increasing violence against women and secular Jews, in the statements and actions of Prime Minister Netanyahu.

Have no doubt that amendments to the Law of Return will be once again on the Orthodox agenda, and have no doubt that government support for Reform and Conservative congregations and institutions in Israel—of which there already is precious little—will come under renewed attack. And this is because the Orthodox parties clearly feel that we Reform Jews are not authentic. In the wake of Rabbi Bakshi Doron's outrageous comments, his assistant stated plainly that Reform Judaism is not Judaism. He said, "It's not a question of whether or not it's true Judaism. It's simply not Judaism. For 2,500 years, Judaism has survived the Orthodox way. There is no need for any reforms."

Certainly ARZA—the Association of Reform Zionists of America— and the World Union for Progressive Judaism have their hands full! They represent the Reform Movement in Israel, through the legal system and by helping individual Israelis in their conflicts with the Orthodox authorities or the government. They work to build an indigenous Reform, or Progressive, movement in Israel despite tremendous odds. They responded to the Sephardic chief rabbi immediately, with other Reform organizations, calling for a retraction and a reprimand.

Yet we can see that many of the small victories of recent years now will be lost; the future for Jewish religious liberty and pluralism in Israel is bleak. Our responsibility continues to be the support of these efforts through individual memberships in ARZA, through support of institutions such as the Israel Religious Action Center, and through our continuing readiness to speak and act on their behalf.

A larger issue, however, is our own authenticity as Reform Jews. Surely, the stance of the Southern Baptists will affect Jewish-Christian relations and our ability to live together in tranquility. Once again, we will have to increase our vigilance.

And we must have no doubt that our Reform expression of Judaism is authentic. The attacks from the Orthodox rabbinate in Israel—from verbal maligning to political maneuvering—threaten to destroy the very fabric of the Jewish people. They claim to be "religious" as though we are not.

The way to withstand these threats—these charges against our authenticity as religious people—from the outside and from the inside is to ensure that our beliefs and practices are solid and substantive and sincere.

We come here tonight to plumb the depths of our Jewish feelings, to determine where we stand, and with whom we stand, as Jews. We come here to examine our Jewish beliefs and practices, and our introspection is no less authentic than that of any other Jewish congregation. For me—and I hope for you—Reform Judaism is not the lazy person's alternative; Reform Judaism is not a minimalist approach to Jewish life.

Reform Judaism is authentic Judaism. It is equal to Conservative, Orthodox, and Reconstructionist Judaism. It is modern Judaism, and it has appealed to more Jews in the United States and Canada than any other Jewish stream.

Reform Judaism tells us that as individuals and as congregations we have the right and responsibility to make educated individual religious decisions in the context of the society in which we live:

- We need to be *educated*. We must know enough of Jewish history and practice to decide in an informed way.
- As *individuals*, we have the right—and the responsibility—to make these decisions for ourselves.
- Our *religion* is based on Torah and other ancient texts, but it is interpreted anew in each generation.

So we must make our own decisions about which mitzvot we will accept and practice, and how we will perform them. Reform Judaism tells us that we must determine how we will conduct our Jewish lives.

Reform Judaism is defined by other principles as well: complete religious equality of all Jews, the legitimacy of Jewish religious differences. These are the principles that guide our movement and guide us as individuals.

But how many of us lead Jewish lives to the fullest, according to the principles of Reform Judaism, or any other Jewish interpretation, for that matter? How many of us do all that we can to educate ourselves in our religion? How many of us have studied what it means to be a Jew since we left Sunday School—either just before or just after our bar and bat mitzvah? How many of us nourish our religious and spiritual lives, worshipping, observing Shabbat, celebrating holidays? How many of us embrace the life of a righteous person, involving ourselves in our community, giving *tzedakah*, and supporting Jewish institutions? How many of us consciously choose to be and act as Jews? How many of us stop to think about what Judaism says about this or that? How many of us know? How many of us care?

How many of these choices does it take to make us an authentic Jew? On this day of introspection, when we evaluate our *Jewish* lives, these are the questions we must ask ourselves.

We stand here today, as our ancestors stood before God, in the

Torah portion we read tomorrow morning: "This commandment which I command you this day is not too hard for you, nor too remote. It is not in heaven ... nor is it beyond the sea. No, it is very near to you, in your mouth and in your heart, and you can do it."

But we do not "do it" enough, not by any definition of authentic Judaism.

Orthodox Jews have it easier on this point. For them, authenticity is based on the fulfillment of mitzvot, or commandments. The more mitzvot you do, the more authentic you are as an Orthodox Jew. What you eat, what you wear, how you observe Shabbat, how much you study: all add up in "authenticity points." Orthodox Jews also are concerned with who supervises these mitzvot, and who apportions the points, and sometimes, as a result, they're never satisfied. There is a story of an Orthodox Jew who went to heaven and was met by the angel Gabriel. "Welcome," said Gabriel, "we're just about to eat lunch." "Lunch?" asked the Orthodox Jew, "what are you eating?" Gabriel answered, "Leviathan. We just caught it today." "And who supervised the preparation?" asked the Orthodox Jew. "Why, Moses himself. Moses, our rabbi, supervises all the cooking here in heaven," Gabriel answered. "Thank you, but I'll just have a glass of water and a straw, please." For some people, even Moses himself would not be authentic enough.

We Reform Jews cannot add up authenticity points for our mitzvot; nor can we simply add up all our Jewish observance. For it is incumbent on us as Reform Jews to examine mitzvot and test whether they make a difference in our lives, and evaluate them for ourselves. This means we are free to reject mitzvot without sacrificing our authenticity; it also means that we must think about every decision we make, everything we do.

How do we get to that point? How do we begin to move toward Reform Jewish authenticity? We need a foundation of knowledge, practice, and commitment. We need to study Jewish texts, history, culture. We need to study about Jewish practice as we might practice Judaism. We need to know *why* we do what we do, so that we can know why we don't do something else. We need to find a path of Jewish practice for ourselves, a path that we can follow. We need to find Jewish motivation and commitment that will guide us on our Jewish journey.

On Yom Kippur, we stand before God and before the Jewish people across the generations. We stand here knowing that we are far from perfect, far from complete, far from authentic. But we do not stand before the Southern Baptists, nor before Rabbi Bakshi Doron. We stand proudly as Reform Jews, knowing that our religion and our expression of Judaism hold the promise of sanctity for us and our children. We stand in this place as part of a continuum of many generations and many interpretations.

Yom Kippur is the day on which we do *cheshbon hanefesh*, the examination of our souls. Yom Kippur is the day on which we look at our shortcomings, our misdeeds, our unkept promises. Yom Kippur is the day when we feel the least authentic and the most authentic, the day on which we deepen our Jewish roots and the day on which we recognize that our Jewish roots are so shallow. Yom Kippur is the day on which we resolve to seek authenticity in our Jewish lives. Yom Kippur is the day on which we suddenly recognize that we are a nothing, with the promise to become an everything, or at least the best Jews we can be.

---

1. Jacques Kornberg, *Theodor Herzl: From Assimilation to Zionism* (Indiana University Press, 1993), 116-121.
2. Kornberg, 175-77.

Legitimate Judaism and the Western Wall

Rosh Hashanah Eve 5758
October 1, 1997

Each year on the High Holy Days I try to speak about an issue that confronts us as Jews, as Reform Jews, or as a congregation. This year I want to speak about the fractures within the Jewish community, the threats to *Klal Yisrael*, and the baseless antagonism of one Jew against another.

I literally grew up with this issue. The neighborhood and elementary school of my childhood in Chicago were predominantly Jewish, and most of the students attended the nearby Conservative congregation. My family attended a Reform synagogue. Over and over again, I was questioned by my friends about my "other" version of Judaism, about whether or not it was really Judaism, about whether I was as Jewish as they were. I eventually learned how to answer these challenges in one way or another ("Our services are shorter because we delete the repetitions, and everyone comes at the beginning."). Later, of course, I studied exactly how Reform Judaism differs. In the four decades since, Reform and Conservative Judaism have grown closer, and Orthodox perhaps has moved further away. The questions of authenticity remain, nevertheless, and they are being asked with increasing ferocity today.

According to a proposed conversion law now before the Israeli Knesset, Reform converts in Israel are not really Jewish, and Reform rabbis in Israel are not really qualified to perform conversions. And after two delays in seeking a compromise on this issue in Israel, still the matter is unsettled. The current conversion bill is only the latest of a string of such legislation that the Orthodox parties have attempted over the past several decades. It represents only the legal challenges to Reform and Conservative Judaism, and not the most vitriolic affronts that tear even more profoundly at the fabric of *Klal Yisrael*, the community of Israel.

In June and August, Jews around the world celebrated Shavuot and Tisha B'Av, respectively. Both of these holidays emphasize the theme of the unity of the Jewish people. Shavuot celebrates the giving of the Torah on Mount Sinai and the response of the people: "We will do and we will listen." Tisha B'Av commemorates the destruction of the

First and Second Temples; it is a national day of Jewish mourning that focuses our attention on the sorrow and persecution our people has endured.

But in our day—in 1997—these holidays were marked by attacks on Reform and Conservative Jews who were trying to pray near the Western Wall in Jerusalem. In this sacred place of Jewish unity, on these holy days, men and women wanted to pray together, as is their custom, and they were attacked for doing so.

On Shavuot, a group of 100 non-Orthodox men and women worshipers was attacked by a crowd of aggressive Orthodox Jews. Violence erupted when the non-Orthodox men and women took out their Torah and began to read it. Name calling—Jew against Jew—descended quickly into shouting and spitting at the worshipers. As police escorted the Reform and Conservative Jews away, Orthodox seminary students threw rocks and garbage on them from windows above.

On Tisha B'Av, when 200 Reform and Conservative men and women worshiped in a specially designated area near the Western Wall, an Orthodox crowd disrupted the group's prayers with shouting. The police, eager to avoid another confrontation, broke up the non-Orthodox prayer group and forced them away from the Kotel Plaza and out of the walls of the Old City.

Rabbi Uri Regev, of the ARZA-sponsored Israel Religious Action Center, said, "They are … driving us out of the gates of Jerusalem." The group concluded its worship outside the walls of the Old City with a statement on hatred and sang *Hatikvah*. Wrote Rabbi Andrew Sacks, our Conservative colleague who organized the service, "As we sang *Hatikvah*, I felt my deepest shock of the evening. The *Haredim* (or aggressive Orthodox), looking down on us, jeered and hissed. Was our presence a provocation? We came to pray. We will not give over the Kotel to hooligans."

The Western Wall, or Kotel, is a sacred place of Jewish unity, a place of collective memory for our people, a place that should hold the most precious of memories and values for our people. Instead it is fast becoming the place that reminds us most vividly of the fractures within our people. Just listen, for example, to Haim Miller, the Deputy Mayor of Jerusalem: "The very fact that the Conservative Jews who symbolize the destruction of the Jewish people came to the place that is holiest to the Jewish people is itself a provocation. They have no reason to be in this place. Whoever holds the integrity of the Jewish people dear to heart will fight to the end so that Conservative Judaism will not have a place in the State."

I hope you are as outraged by this statement as I am! Who owns the Western Wall? The Orthodox politicians? The Orthodox Rabbinate or the yeshivot that surround it?

The Western Wall belongs to the Jewish people—all the Jewish people—and the State of Israel and its representatives who have jurisdiction over the Wall are merely the keepers and stewards of those stones that belong to the ages and have carried the hopes and prayers of our people for centuries.

For many Jews, a visit to the Western Wall is a highlight of their trips to Israel, even of their lifetimes. I know, too, that for many others, their visit to the Kotel only reminds them of the stranglehold that the Orthodox Rabbinate has on Jewish religious life in Israel. Rather than being moved, they find themselves angry that men and women are separated, that while praying they are approached and harassed by Orthodox proselytizers and beggars, that they are made to feel that *they* are not doing enough, not feeling enough. What could and should be a peak emotional experience often ends in bitterness and disappointment.

When Rabbi Rabinowitz, the rabbi of the Kotel and other holy Jewish sites in Jerusalem, visited Washington this summer, I attended a meeting with him and several of my Reform, Conservative, and Reconstructionist colleagues. We told him of the pain and disappointment felt by many when they visit the Wall in congregational groups and are asked to leave the area or disperse, in his name. The rabbi was polite and sympathetic and said he disapproved of violence, but he refused to publicly denounce these actions or to sign a statement condemning violence at the Wall.

Just as the Wall is a symbol of Jewish history and hope and aspirations, these continuing incidents at the Wall remind us of who controls the Wall, and they tell us who is left out of official Jewish life in Israel. They nag at us about the struggle to be Jewish and about the struggle to be Reform Jews in the Jewish state.

Is Judaism static and unchanging, or can it grow and develop, evolving with the times? Do we think of our services here today—with musical instruments, electricity, men and women praying together, reading prayers in English—as an affront to Jewish life and survival? Do we see ourselves taking steps down the path to the destruction of the Jewish people? Of course not.

What is at work here is not Jewish law so much as it is Jewish power. What is at stake is the unity and future of the Jewish people. The real threat to Jewish survival comes from those who think that only their Jewish way is correct, from those who spit on other Jews.

Judaism never has been static, although there always have been those who claim that their particular interpretation was given to Moses on Mount Sinai. In a famous story in the Talmud, Moses asks God to allow him to see the great Rabbi Akiva, who lived in the second century, C.E. God grants his wish, and Moses enters Akiva's academy. The students are discussing a passage of Torah with Akiva, but Moses is not able to follow the discussion. Moses becomes so distressed by being unable to follow the discussion that he grows faint. Then one student asks Akiva where he learned this interpretation, and Akiva replies, "It is a law given to Moses at Sinai."[1]

But how could Akiva's understanding have come from Moses, when Moses himself did not understand it? Surely Akiva was mistaken: The interpretation was not given by God to Moses on Sinai, but came from Akiva's genius and insight. Perhaps he was being modest; perhaps he knew this was the only way it would be accepted.

In every generation we Jews have claimed authenticity of the highest order: going back to Mt. Sinai. For centuries we rabbis have claimed that our interpretations—or at least our right to interpret—go back to Sinai. To lend credence to their decision, the ancient rabbis taught that on Mount Sinai God gave Moses the Written Law, or the Torah, *and* the Oral Law, the post-biblical *Halacha* that began with the Mishnah and extended through the Talmud and beyond.

Today, far too many people still believe that their interpretation of Judaism was given by God to Moses on Mount Sinai. In fact, for example, the laws that prohibit men and women from praying together grew out of a cultural sense of propriety and modesty in Jewish life and men's fear that women would distract them from their prayers. There is no reference in the Bible to men and women praying separately. In last week's Torah portion, in a passage contained in our prayer book, Moses instructs the Israelites: "Assemble the people—men, *women*, and children—and the strangers in your communities, that they may hear and so learn to revere Adonai your God and to observe faithfully every word of this teaching." The women explicitly are included. The law of a separate women's section developed in the Talmudic period, centuries later. As late as the early twentieth century, men and women prayed together at the Western Wall, as a photograph distributed by the New Israel Fund shows; even at the Kotel there was once more inclusiveness than there is today.

Those Jews who condemn the practices of other Jews in the name of preserving Jewish life deserve our censure. Is the opposite of "Torah-true Judaism" only "Torah-false Judaism"? If you are not a "Religious Jew," does that mean you are an "Irreligious Jew"?

We need to stop thinking of our own Jewish path as being less authentic, or less genuine, than others. We need to stop thinking of Reform Judaism as a watered-down version of Judaism, a compromise of belief and practice and ritual that endangers our Judaism.

We hear this statement in various forms: "You're not authentically Jewish." We hear, "Your rabbis aren't really rabbis," and "Your worship services aren't really worship."

Some may say this in the name of "Orthodoxy," but I want to be very clear that not all Orthodox Jews are guilty of such narrow thinking. Many of them believe, as I do, that all Jews are religiously equal, that we may agree with some and not with others.

But we must not condone Jewish anti-Semitism, the baseless hatred of Jew against Jew, the denial of Jewish authenticity, the empty accusation that other forms of Judaism are leading to Jewish destruction. The violence at the Western Wall was perpetrated only because Jews wanted to pray in a Jewishly sacred place.

Certainly we Jews have argued before. Argument is our "tradition," and we have permanently enshrined that tradition in the Talmud. And it is in the Talmud that we read of an argument between two rabbis, Eliezer and Joshua. Finally, Rabbi Eliezer lost his patience and said, "If the law is according to me, let this carob tree move." And it moved. Still the majority sided with Rabbi Joshua. So Rabbi Eliezer said, "If the law is as I said, let the river reverse itself." And it did. But the other rabbis still sided with Rabbi Joshua. Then Rabbi Eliezer said, "If the law is as I interpreted, let the walls of this yeshiva bend inward." And they did. And still the other rabbis sided with Rabbi Joshua.

Finally Rabbi Eliezer said, "If the law is according to me, let a voice be heard from heaven." And a voice from heaven was heard saying, "Why do you argue with Rabbi Eliezer? The law is according to his opinion." But Rabbi Joshua responded to the heavenly voice: "The Torah is not in heaven. We pay no attention to a heavenly voice. The rabbis must decide the law." According to the story, God then responded: "My children have defeated me."[2]

Indeed, God has been defeated this past summer, on Shavuot and on Tisha B'Av. God has been defeated by small-minded, power-hungry, and self-righteous Jews who claim to be God's sole legitimate Jewish representatives.

We must renew our fight for legitimacy and recognition, our fight for *Klal Yisrael*. We have registered in large numbers for the World Zionist Congress elections; we have voted for the ARZA slate; we have supported the cause of Jewish religious pluralism and religious freedom in the Jewish state. And we must continue to raise our voices in the name of Jewish pluralism and to support ARZA and the other groups fighting for religious freedom in Israel. We must continue our fight for recognition and for preserving *Klal Yisrael*, understanding that our style of Judaism is no less legitimate than any other.

At the same time, we need to deepen our own Jewish commitment, accept our responsibilities, and strengthen our resolve to grow in our Jewish knowledge as Jews over the coming year. Our quest for legitimacy also must be consistent with what we do as Jews.

As a community, we Reform Jews must not only fight for our rights, but also build a Jewish life for ourselves that is genuine and nourishing. We are not denying nor unknowing Jews, nor have we drifted away. We are the accepting Jews, the ones who show up—at least on the High Holy Days. We are the ones who remind ourselves of who we are, and to whom we are related, and before Whom we stand.

We must continue to create a Judaism that values worship and study and the performance of acts of kindness. And we must work to strengthen the fabric of our people, the shared sense of *Klal Yisrael*, the community of Israel.

During these Days of Awe we must ask ourselves what we have done as Jews. We must acknowledge that we have fallen short, that we can do more—individually and collectively—that our Judaism can and should mean more to us, and that we must never isolate ourselves from the Jewish community. We must find the discipline to participate in worship, in study, in Jewish communal life.

Though the stones of the Western Wall are massive, they are held together without any mortar. They are notched and ridged so that they fit together, and so they have remained for two millennia. It is an engineering marvel that these enormous stones were put into place without machinery, forming a wall without mortar.

What has kept them in place, so that they do not shift or move? The prayers of our people. What preserves the Wall is the Jewish tradition of writing a prayer on a small piece of paper, or *pitkah*, and placing it into the cracks between the stones of the Wall.

When the teenagers from our congregation went to Israel this past summer, each one carried an envelope stuffed with *pitkaot* written by the children of our religious school. The spaces between the stones are open to all Jews, open to anyone. No one asked our teenagers which kind of Judaism they practiced as they placed the prayers in the Wall.

These *pitkaot* have held the stones of the wall together all these centuries. The accumulated prayers and hopes of all Jews—our ancestors, our parents, our grandparents, coming together in their *shtetlach* in Poland, and their grand synagogue in Budapest, on the Lower East Side and in Galveston, uttering in Hebrew and Yiddish and German and English the same prayers we say tonight, singing the same beautiful melodies, remembering the past year and wondering what the coming year will bring—these are what have bound our people and brought us to this day and this place.

May they continue to grant us strength in the coming New Year. May we all fit together like the stones of the Western Wall, each different, each treasured, each forming a part of a sacred whole. May this year be a year of unity and not hatred, a year of fitting together and not falling apart, a year of acceptance and not abuse, a year of understanding and not polemics, a year of building upon our own commitment and not tearing down.

We must be accepting Jews, proud Jews, committed Jews, and strong Jews. And we must strengthen one another.

---

1. Babylonian Talmud, Men. 29b.
2. Baba Metzia, 59b.

Is Judaism True?

Rosh Hashanah Morning 5759
September 21, 1998

In *The Spiritual Life of Children*, psychiatrist Robert Coles writes about eleven-year-old Avram of Brookline, Massachusetts. Avram speaks to God, and God answers him. Avram's parents have told him to talk "special" when he speaks to God, so Avram says he tries to do that: "I bow my head; I lower my voice; I close my eyes. I say my prayers [in Hebrew]. I wait a while; then I ask [God] for help. ... I hear [God] saying that I should work hard, and do my share. I guess [God will] do His share if we do ours."[1]

This morning we read about a different Avram who also spoke to God and heard God's voice. In the terrifying story of the Akeda that we read each fall as the year turns, we read that God spoke to Abraham three times: commanding him to sacrifice his son, then telling him to save his son, and finally promising Abraham greatness.

What about us, Abraham's descendants, the heirs of that covenant, we who hear and read this story each year? Can we hear God's voice? Can we speak to God? Can we feel God's presence in our lives? As we come here as our year turns, as our lives turn, can we feel the closeness to God that defines "spirituality"?

Unlike Avram and unlike Abraham, many of us do not communicate routinely with God; the idea, in itself, is somewhat alien to us. We are suspicious of those who say they speak to God, those who say they hear the voice of God, those who talk about the active role that God plays in their lives.

In fact, each of us is Abraham; each of us needs to know that God is with us; each of us needs to feel God's presence soothing the stresses of our lives; each of us needs the guidance of something beyond our selves when we are called upon to make sacrifices, when we encounter crises, and when we are alone, as Abraham was alone on Mount Moriah.

Unlike Abraham, we base our lives mostly on the facts. We presume that faith and intellectual rigor are opposites. Consider, for example, the traditional "conflict" between science and religion. I am always surprised to hear Confirmation students say modern science keeps them from believing in God: "If the world wasn't created in six days," they ask, "How can we believe anything the Bible says?"

When did we Reform Jews teach that the Bible is literally true? When did we teach a kind of Fundamentalism that conflicts with the Theory of Evolution? When did we believe that one must choose between religion and science? We Reform Jews do not, and we never have.

Our liberal stream of Judaism always has welcomed scientific inquiry, distinguishing between the science that explains our universe and the values that help us live our lives. For us, there is no conflict. Our understanding of our world does not depend on miracles.

Other religions and other Jews do foster belief in miracles, insisting that faith would be shattered if the Bible were disproved. They flock to religious statues that cry tears, paintings that bleed; they visit shrines to be healed of disease or visit Rachel's Tomb to reverse their infertility.

Most of us scoff at such stories of mysterious cures or miracles; we consider those who believe in them to be superstitious and naive. This type of faith is easy for us to reject: a faith that requires, first, complete devotion; second, a willing suspension of disbelief; and third, rejection of modern science and objective reality.

Let us not deceive ourselves into thinking, however, that faith has no place in our Reform Jewish lives. To the contrary, Reform Judaism developed a theological system that was consistent, informed, enlightened by philosophy and humanities, and still pious. The earlier generations of Reform Jews created a set of beliefs that depended on an appreciation of the scientific study of Judaism and an understanding of God's role in their lives. Our Reform Jewish forebears were blessed with a sense of God's presence in their lives. They turned to God in dark moments, and they could feel God turning to them.

This view was reflected in the theology of the nineteenth and early twentieth century Reform leaders. Kaufmann Kohler, the primary architect of Reform theology, wrote:

> Prayer is the expression of [our] longing and yearning for God in times of dire need and of overflowing joy, an outflow of the emotions of the soul in its dependence on God, the ever-present Helper, the eternal Source of its existence.[2]

Young Avram feels the same way: "God has nothing more important to do than to speak to us, to anyone who really and truly wants to speak to Him. He's there, watching and hoping for us. ... [God] really takes an interest in us, and ... really hopes for the best—that our lives will work out well. God ... gave us our freedom. It's up to us!"[3]

We Reform Jews do not pray for miracles. We do pray for strength to encounter adversity, for compassionate caregivers, for a sense of God's presence in our lives that will make a difference in dark moments.

Our challenge, as we begin this new year, is to be able to pray the words of the prayer book and the words of our hearts. Our challenge is to open our ears to the voices of our spirits. Our challenge is to hear God's voice speaking through us.

When Abraham hears God commanding him to sacrifice Isaac, he obeys without question. Soren Kierkegaard points out that "Abraham represents faith,"[4] but that Abraham also appalls us because we never see him struggle with God's command, as all of us surely would.

Do we struggle with this story, or do we simply reject it as "quaint," "troubling," or "irrelevant"?

Our sin is that we close our ears to God's voice altogether, that we reject any possibility of belief, that we suppress our spiritual side and do not permit our souls to aspire to God, in Kaufmann Kohler's words. Unlike Abraham, we cannot hear God's voice, and we cannot hear—we cannot recognize—the voice of our own spiritual longing. How much we need to open our ears and hear the voice of our own spirits!

How much we need to hear God's voice, to feel God's presence in our lives today. We suffer no less than our ancestors: we feel powerless in the face of disease or death; we despair when confronted by loss; we are confused about the direction we want our lives to take. We need strength and support no less than did Abraham or Sarah, Job, Jeremiah, or Ruth and Naomi.

The details of our stories may be different, but our questions are the same. Only they had the relationship with God that we lack. Their ears were open to God's voice; our ears are closed. We are skeptical. Sometimes.

Robert Coles, skeptical about Avram's story, writes:

I wondered: Exactly whose voice does he hear when he tells me it is God's 'voice' that addresses him during his time of praying? . . . "Avram, is it your dad's voice you hear, or the rabbi's, or your own? Do you actually hear God's voice?" Avram answered, "When I pray to God, it's not like I'm talking with my friends. No, it's not the same as being with my dad or mom. ... It's not [God's] voice—I mean, [God] doesn't speak to us when we pray; we speak to ourselves. But it's [God] telling us what to say—to tell ourselves. Do you see what I mean?"

Robert Coles did understand, as do I. The Hebrew word "to pray" is reflexive, *l'hitpalel*, telling us that praying is speaking to ourselves and at the same time speaking to God.

The second time Abraham hears God's voice in the Akeda story, the angel is telling Abraham to save Isaac's life. For us, hearing God's voice can save our lives from the pettiness of our existence, from the meaninglessness of our routine, from the spiritual emptiness we feel.

I am convinced that a growing number of Jews yearn to hear God's voice calling to us. One of our sins that we must acknowledge during these Days of Awe is our dismissal of God's presence in our lives, our failure to reach into our spiritual selves and to reach beyond our selves to God.

Many of you have been to a Shabbat evening service when we sing the *Mi Shebeyrach* prayer for healing, adapted from the liturgy and composed by Debbie Friedman. Sometimes we mention the names of our congregants, our family and friends, who are confronting illness or suffering. Sometimes we simply sing the prayer without names. Either way, it is an extraordinarily transcendent moment, as it was this morning. What happens at Temple Sinai is mirrored in scores of other congregations. This prayer has struck a chord in contemporary American Jewish life. I ask myself, "Why?" Is it because we think that this prayer will make a difference? Will it bring healing? Miraculous cures to the incurable? Will it work wonders?

Without doubt, this prayer has great power but not to alter the course of disease. Its power is to give strength and courage to those who are living with illness and those close to them.

I believe this *Mi Shebeyrach* is so enormously popular because, through its words and music, it speaks to our spiritual selves. It brings a message of comfort and hope to people who need it. We do not need this prayer instead of medical treatment; we need it in addition.

We live our lives by the numbers: Our medical diagnosis depends on our blood count; our professional success on our billable hours; our financial success on our money in the bank; our scholastic success by our SAT scores. Everything we do, it seems, is quantified and measured.

But when all the measures are tabulated, what is the value of our lives? Have we succeeded or failed? Where does our strength come from? Where do we turn for the answers to these questions, questions that go to the very heart of our existence? Can we turn to God?

Abraham heard the voice of God calling to him to save the life of his son. Can we hear the voice that will save our spiritual lives? Only if we listen very carefully, only if our ears are open to hear the yearnings of our hearts.

Finally, Abraham heard God's voice calling to him a third time, through the angel who describes to Abraham God's covenant. To reward Abraham for his faith, God will bestow blessings upon Abraham so that "all the nations of the earth shall bless themselves by your descendants" (Gen. 22:17-18). This is the covenant that we still observe today, as Avram described to Robert Coles:

> I hear [God] saying that we should obey the Commandments and live good lives. I hear [God] saying that one day He will bring all of us Jews back together. God made a pact with us, and God will help us, but we have to show God we are deserving, we are ready for God's help. God's voice is in you when you are making choices—it turns you towards the right direction.[5]

We hope that God's voice can put our lives into context and help to restore our perspective. This is part of what we seek here today: a context and a perspective.

Context and perspective are themes in the recent film, *The Truman Show*. The movie is about Truman Burbank, the unknowing star of the world's "longest-running documentary soap opera in history." In the film, Truman is real, as his name suggests, but everything around him is contrived. He lives in a beautiful town, actually a huge set for a real-time television program beamed around the world. Every person with whom he interacts is an actor or actress; his actions and reactions are the only ones not scripted. Everything he does is recorded by thousands of hidden cameras transmitting his life to millions of viewers. Everyone but Truman is in on the "secret." The realization dawns sooner for us than for Truman that Truman's life is invented and produced by someone who controls even the weather and the rising and setting of the sun. Eventually, Truman begins to understand his situation, and at the end of the movie, we see him taking charge of his own life.

We, who struggle to take charge of our own lives, need to relinquish some of our control to God. We need to see where we fit in God's creation. It is a new year, and Rosh Hashanah comes to help us to focus ourselves, to put our lives in perspective, to repair our relationships with one another and with God, to seek our spiritual resources, to escape the pettiness of our existence.

In her book, *Kitchen Table Wisdom*, Rachel Naomi Remen points out that competence and expertise are two of the most highly respected qualities in our society and—I believe—so much the more so in Washington. As Remen points out, however, "they are not sufficient to fully sustain us."[6] She retells a parable by an Italian psychiatrist, about interviewing three stonecutters building a cathedral in the fourteenth century.

When asked what he is doing, the first stonecutter replies bitterly that he is cutting stones into blocks, over and over, knowing that he will continue to do this until he dies. The second stonecutter, doing exactly the same work, tells the interviewer instead that he is earning a living for his beloved family, creating a home filled with love. The third stonecutter, who also does the same work, gives us pause with his response. With joy, "he tells us of the privilege of participating in the building of this great cathedral, so strong that it will stand as a holy lighthouse for a thousand years."[7] He alone is able to place his life and work into perspective, to find a context and a meaning beyond cutting stone.

How much we all need to move beyond competence and expertise, to experience a deep sense of joy and gratitude in our work and in our lives. We need to put our lives into context, to renew our relationship with God, to feel God's presence in our lives, to hear God's voice.

We are an auditory people. Our first and last prayer is *Shema Yisrael*: "Hear, O Israel." Yet we are a people that has failed, again and again, to hear God's voice. How much we need to listen: to one another, to our spiritual selves, to the sound of the shofar calling us to justice, to the words of our prayers, to God's voice as it speaks to us in this New Year.

It is a still, small voice, so we must listen carefully. But it will change our lives, as it changed Abraham's life on Mount Moriah so long ago.

1. Robert Coles, *The Spiritual Life of Children* (Boston: Houghton-Mifflin, 1990), 76.
2. Kaufmann Kohler, *Jewish Theology, Systematically and Historically Considered* (New York: Ktav, 1968), 270.
3. Coles, 78.
4. Soren Kierkegaard, *Fear and Trembling* (Penguin, 1985), 85ff.
5. Coles, 75.
6. Rachel Naomi Remen, *Kitchen Table Wisdom* (New York: Riverhead Books, 1996), 161.
7. Remen, 161.

Sin and Morality

Kol Nidre 5759
September 29, 1998

I cannot remember a time when sin and morality have been more on the mind of our nation. All summer long—and especially during Elul, our month of preparation for the High Holy Days—all America has considered the issues of sin and repentance, morality and ethics, with increasing intensity and feeling.[1]

And tonight we gather as a holy congregation to look at our own deeds for the past year: to perform *heshbon hanefesh*, the stock-taking of our souls; to stand with one another before God, to seek repentance, to ask forgiveness for our sins, to make amends, to strengthen our obligations for the coming year, to recommit ourselves to the values we know are most important in our lives.

This year, these issues have been thrust before the nation with inexorable force, focusing our collective attention on the spiritual tasks we Jews are obligated to perform—year in and year out—as we approach this night of forgiveness and Day of Atonement.

Out of these months of anguish for so many comes one benefit for us Jews this year: our attention has been directed to the same issues of morality that we are supposed to consider these past weeks, weighing our deeds of the past year.

What are the sins in our lives? How do we find repentance? How can we move past our shortcomings to build a renewed life, to purify ourselves, to atone for our sins? Can we find a path, as we must, from sin to repentance, from frailty to forgiveness?

Certainly it is easier to flee from acknowledging our shortcomings, as Jonah fled when God called him. We will read tomorrow afternoon that the word of the Eternal came to Jonah:

> Go at once to Nineveh, that great city, and proclaim judgment upon it; for their wickedness has come before Me. Jonah, however, started out to flee to Tarshish, from the service of the Eternal (Jonah 1:1-3).

All of us flee, as well, from responsibility for our actions, from accepting the simple truth of what we have done or not done. We may be subtler than Jonah: We don't get on a ship and head the other way, but we do use language to remove ourselves from the path of responsibility. We define our terms and explain our actions in ways that absolve us of wrongdoing. We manipulate language in a hundred different ways in order to avoid telling the difficult truth. We speak in the passive voice to avoid accepting responsibility for our actions: "It has been decided that … " instead of "I decided." We teach our children to say on the telephone that we're not home when we are or that we are home when we're not. We ask our assistant to protect us from interruption by saying "She's with someone," when we're really alone.

All of us bend the truth from time to time, and none of us can tell the whole truth all of the time. We tell white lies to avoid hurting another person. We use formulas and code words to avoid confrontation with others. We are less than candid much of the time, disingenuous some of the time, and deceitful part of the time. In our attempts to shelter and protect the people we live and work with, we too often have failed to distinguish between truth and falsehood, and we have fled from the truth too often.

We are dishonest about one thing, and it leads us on the path to being dishonest about another. In the Hebrew expression *aveirah goreret aveirah*, one misdeed leads to another. We lie to protect ourselves and sometimes to protect those around us. We fail to teach our children and our community the value of telling the truth.

In his book, *What Ever Became of Sin?*, Karl Menninger laments the fact that sin has been redefined as symptom, confession redefined as psychotherapy, and that "the crying needs of millions of people … go untended."[2]

How many of us have redefined our sins? How many of us have separated ourselves from one another, from our own true self, from our God? Certainly we are more likely to view our world in legal or medical terms, defining sin as pathology, considering morality by whether or not a law was violated.

We do not seek moral certitude in most of our lives, but we have sunk into a time of moral relativism, when we feel that issues of morality are fluid and fungible, that no one can really know what is moral or immoral because there are so many competing definitions. We think we can only judge legality, because the law is fixed (though we know, of course, that law also changes). We don't presume we can judge morality, because that is "subjective"; it varies from person to person, from community to community.

Where, then, can we turn for moral authority? We cry out for moral direction, and Yom Kippur comes to show us the way. We come here today—and throughout the year—to hear the words of Torah: "You must not act deceitfully, nor lie to one another." We will hear tomorrow how Moses sets before the people good and evil, life and death. Moses tells our people and tells us today that we have free will, that it is our challenge and our responsibility to distinguish between right and wrong, to make moral and ethical decisions and choices.

Like Jonah, all of us have fled from responsibility and sought instead to protect what is ours. We, too, are more concerned with getting caught in our misdeeds than in doing the right thing. We, too, use other people and deceive ourselves and those around us. We, too, put more energy into redefining sin than we put into avoiding it. We, too, want to be moral, but our human frailty keeps us from becoming the best people we could be.

Tonight we stand together with the gift of Yom Kippur, the opportunity to acknowledge once again our shortcomings and purge them. Once again we say the words of repentance. Once again we are called to recognize our human frailty. Once again we must strip away pretense and seek forgiveness. How do we understand sin and repentance from our own Jewish perspective?

In the version of Jonah we read tomorrow afternoon, we skip the prayer that Jonah speaks while he is in the fish. He says:

> In my trouble I called to God,
> Who answered me ... and heard my voice.
> The waters closed in over me. . . .
> I sank to the base of the mountains. . . .
> Yet you brought my life up from the pit. . . .
> When my life was ebbing away,
> I called God to mind;
> And my prayer came before You (Jon. 2:3-8).

If we undertake the introspection this day demands of us, we, too, will turn to God from our own depths, our own troubles, and we, too, will feel the same release and rescue that Jonah felt. How can we begin such introspection? How can we find the path to repentance?

The great Orthodox Rabbi Joseph Soloveitchik analyzes the structure of the act of repentance. He points out two distinct ways in which Yom Kippur purges us of our sin: The first is *kapparah*, the removal of our sin, "acquittal" in Soloveitchik's term. To begin the process of repentance, we must turn to other people and God—those whom we may have hurt or injured—to release us from our sins and forgive us.

This is not enough, however, Soloveitchik points out. The second aspect of Yom Kippur repentance is *taharah*, or purification. For through our sins we have become polluted, and now we must be cleansed.[3]

Kapparah requires that we personally accept our wrongdoing and feel remorse. We do this both collectively, as a congregation, and privately, as individuals. Most importantly, we are personally responsible for this difficult work. At a time when we are represented by others in so many aspects of our lives, here is one area where we must appear ourselves. We can have no mediators for our sins; we must assume total responsibility. And we must refrain from blaming others, a human tendency since Adam blamed Eve for leading him to eat the apple in the Garden of Eden, and Eve blamed the serpent for tricking her.

We must accept responsibility, Soloveitchik emphasizes, in order to repent and return to wholeness. We must feel our own remorse.

Yet even remorse is not enough. We also must purify ourselves through *taharah*. How do we do that? Confession, although a necessary first step, is not enough. Again Soloveitchik gives us guidance. The Talmud, he says, lists professional gamblers as one group of individuals who are disqualified to serve as witnesses. What if an individual decides to stop gambling? When will he be permitted to serve as a witness? Only when he discards his dice and undergoes a complete reformation, so that he will not even gamble for fun. Purification requires not only repentance, but also a complete break from everything that led us to sin in the first place.

We need acquittal and repentance—*kapparah* and *taharah*—removal of our sin and purification; we need the resolution to change, and the removal of everything that would lead us to sin again.[4]

Jonah got a fresh start and a second chance. God called to him a second time to "Go at once to Nineveh ... and proclaim to it what I tell you." Jonah did what God told him to do; everyone in Nineveh mourned their misdeeds; and they were forgiven (Jon. 3:1-6).

Was Jonah satisfied? His life had been saved; he had a second chance to do God's work; he was fabulously successful in bringing God's word to the people of Nineveh. You would think Jonah would be pleased. What more could he ask for?

But Jonah was not pleased. He was angry that God forgave the people; he complained to God for renouncing their punishment; and he begged to die. Why would Jonah, the successful prophet, be so angry and miserable? Because he did not care about the people he saved; he only cared about himself, and he felt manipulated by God.

It is easy for us to fall into Jonah's trap: to care only for ourselves, to care little for others, and to feel manipulated. In order to use this day well, we must not only accept our sin, seek forgiveness, and purify ourselves; we also must work to repair our relationships with one another.

We know we must do this with our families, those about whom we care the most. We must do this with our colleagues and co-workers; we must do this with our neighbors and friends. And to find the path to purification, we must even do this with the strangers in our midst.

We must find our way back to civility, to courteous and caring relationships with the people around us and in our community. I am very concerned about the loss of *derech eretz*, or civility, that I have observed in our congregation and schools. *Derech eretz* literally means "the way of the land"; it is best understood as courtesy, good manners, politeness, respect for others.

Derech eretz is not just a quaint Hebrew term. It is a significant Jewish value. It was so important to the ancient rabbis that they developed two tractates of the Talmud to describe how we should govern our lives by the principles of *derech eretz*:

> Let the honor of another person be as dear to you as your own. Show respect to all persons. ... It is better that you be ashamed of yourself than be put to shame by others. Let not your teeth bring shame upon you, nor your mouth bring you to abuse (*Derech Eretz Zuta* 2:8).

How often do we demonstrate that we do not respect one another in our parking lot or even in our sanctuary? Should we need to be reminded that our congregation is a group of individuals who must demonstrate politeness and courtesy to one another, that our schools must be a model for mutual respect, that our sanctuary a place of respect before God? We must set this building apart and know here, at least, that there is some of the divine in each of us, and that this fact must govern how we treat one another.

In his recent book, *Civility: Manners, Morals, and the Etiquette of Democracy*, Stephen Carter points out that in the reconstruction of civility, we need "religions willing to challenge the faithful to adopt values different from those of the larger political and market cultures."[5]

On this day of challenge, consider yourself challenged. Carter could have been writing for the Talmudic tractates when he composed some of his fifteen rules to guide us in reconstructing civility:

> Our duty to be civil toward others does not depend on whether we like [one another] or not. Civility requires that we sacrifice for strangers, not just for people we happen to know. Civility has two parts: generosity, even when it is costly, and trust, even when there is risk. We must come into the presence of our fellow human beings with a sense of awe and gratitude. Civility requires that we listen to others with knowledge of the possibility that they are right and we are wrong. Civility requires that we express ourselves in ways that demonstrate our respect for others. Religions do their greatest service to civility when they preach not only love of neighbor but resistance to wrong.[6]

How often we violate these principles in our interpersonal relationships, just doing our "daily business." While we certainly want what is best for our family, we also must respect the needs of others who are part of this congregation. For just as we stand before God this night as individuals, burdened by our sins, we also stand together as a congregation, forgiving one another, recognizing our mutual dependence on each other.

We can do better than Jonah, I am sure. We can put aside our anger, respect one another's shortcomings, and care for each other, as Jonah could not, but as a congregation should and must. I see this every week, as our members work to help one another in times of sickness and crisis, reaching out to one another through our Member-to-Member Committee, caring for one another through our Sisterhood and our school communities. I know how caring we can be, so I am always distressed when I see that we have forgotten about the *derech eretz* that also should guide us as we seek purification.

For our moral imperatives in Judaism are based in part on the Holiness Code that we will read from the Torah tomorrow afternoon. In the majestic verses from Leviticus we find the guidance and the challenge we seek this Yom Kippur:

> You must not act deceitfully nor lie to one another. . . .
> You must not oppress your neighbor. . . .
> You shall not hate your brother or sister in your heart. Rather, you must reason with your kin. . .
> You shall love your neighbor as yourself (Lev. 19:11, 13, 17, 18).

We are commanded to respect and to love the people we might oppress or mistreat: the stranger, the aged, the disabled, the powerless. For we must always remember that once we, too, were powerless; we, too, were strangers; we, too, are disabled—morally, if not physically—imperfect, flawed. We, too, lack the strength we might have, the moral strength, the empathic strength, the strength to care for others as we should.

How can we find the way to repentance on this Yom Kippur? The prophet Isaiah provides us with a classic answer:

> Wash yourself clean; put away your evil doings from My sight; cease to do evil. Learn to do good. Devote yourself to justice. Aid the oppressed. Uphold the rights of the orphan; defend the cause of the widow. ... If your sins are like crimson, they can become white as snow (Is. 1:16-18).

Let us cleanse ourselves this day. Let us turn to goodness. Let us renew our commitment to justice. Let us be kind to one another. Let us begin our journey with civility and continue by recommitting ourselves to the moral precepts of seeking truth and respecting others. Let us purge ourselves of sin and cleanse ourselves and find our way back to caring. May it be the way of the land, *derech eretz*, and may it be the way of honesty, the way of moral rectitude, the way of caring for one another.

1. During the summer of 1998, national attention was focused on allegations of sexual impropriety between President Bill Clinton and White House intern Monica Lewisnky. In August, Clinton admitted to an "improper physical relationship" with Lewinsky.
2. Karl Menninger, *What Ever Became of Sin?* (New York: Hawthorn, 1973) 218.
3. Pinchas Peli, *Soloveitchik on Repentance* (New York: Paulist Press, 1984), 49-50.
4. Peli, 55-57.
5. Stephen Carter, *Civility: Manners, Morals, and the Etiquette of Democracy* (New York: Basic Books, 1998), 275.
6. Carter, 279-285.

The Wake-up Call

Rosh Hashanah Eve 5760
September 10, 1999

"It was a wake-up call to America to kill Jews."

These were the words of Buford Furrow after his shooting spree in California: "A wake-up call to America to kill Jews." These words and the indelible image of children being led out of a Jewish community center hand-in-hand by the police are our memories of the summer of '99.[1]

These images are now part of our memories, too: arson in Sacramento synagogues; hit lists of prominent members of the Sacramento Jewish community; attacks on Jews returning home from synagogue in Chicago; a murdered letter carrier, a murdered football coach, and a murdered graduate student, all members of minority groups.

We Jews feel vulnerable. We know there are hate groups at work in our land. We know there are demented individuals who are filled with hatred and racism. We know that in the wake of these isolated violent acts, we must respond. We lock our doors when we want to be welcoming. We suspect packages and people we do not know when we want to be trusting. Like other synagogues and Jewish institutions, Temple Sinai has tried to react thoughtfully, carefully, and prudently in the last few weeks when we wish we could only be preparing in positive ways for these Days of Awe.

These troubling events have been a wake-up call: a wake-up call *for* the Jews. And today we are commanded to wake up.

Rosh Hashanah is our "wake-up" holiday. The single mitzvah, or commandment, unique to Rosh Hashanah is to hear the sound of the shofar, as we will do tomorrow morning.

What is the message of the shofar? Moses Maimonides used these words: "Awake, you sleepers, from your sleep! Awake … from your slumber!"

The shofar is our spiritual alarm clock, and Rosh Hashanah is our annual wake-up holy day.

Maimonides characterized this awakening as an opportunity to search our deeds and turn in repentance. We are commanded to remember our Creator, to look to our souls, to better our ways, to abandon the evil and turn to the good in our lives.[2] The sound of the shofar is not an end in itself, but a means to our repentance and renewal.

One Chasidic rabbi, the Magid of Dubno, related a story about fire alarms and Rosh Hashanah. Once a man from an isolated village visited the city for the first time. He was awakened by the sound of beating drums. When he asked what it was, he was told that the sound was a community fire alarm. The man returned to his village and told his neighbors about this wonderful system: When a fire breaks out, all the people beat drums, and before long the fire burns out. They ordered a supply of drums for the village and distributed them. When the next fire broke out, everyone beat on their drums. They made a lot of noise, but the fire spread and threatened the entire town. A visitor from the city derided them, saying, "Do you think a fire can be put out by beating drums? The drums only sound an alarm for the people to wake up and extinguish the fire."[3]

The shofar is only an alarm, a warning to wake up and turn to *heshbon hanefesh*, the soul-searching that these days demand of us.

The shofar also reminds us, particularly this year, of the unity of the Jewish people. The sounds of the shofar are the most ancient voice of our people, the call that reverberated in the wilderness and on the mountains of Sinai, the blast that summoned together the Jewish people, the cry of alarm or warning in the camp, the wordless proclamation of the giving of the Torah, the announcement of the new month and the new year. The shofar has been our people's call to gather and to pray, to confront ourselves and our God. The shofar is the oldest voice of our people, and it inevitably reminds us (as Saadya Gaon pointed out more than one thousand years ago) of the unity of the Jewish people over space and over time. The shofar has sounded the note of alarm and fear, of unity and hope, of our ancient covenant with God. It is our wake-up call to being Jewish.

The events of this past summer should awaken us to a heightened sense of Jewish identity. For many years, Reform Jews justifiably have been concerned about divisions within the Jewish community and particularly Orthodox attacks on the legitimacy of Reform and Conservative Jews. We all have been deeply concerned and frustrated and angry about incidents in Israel challenging the rights of Reform and Conservative rabbis and congregations.

Yet even as we distinguish among ourselves, the anti-Semite does not distinguish between Orthodox, Conservative, Reform, or Reconstructionist. The anti-Semite does not distinguish between Jews who belong to synagogues and Jews who do not, between practicing Jews and Jews who do nothing. The anti-Semite hates all Jews, without thinking and without discriminating.

While I am not saying that we should let the anti-Semite define us, anti-Semitic acts are powerful reminders that come from outside to help us remember that the words "Reform," "Orthodox," or "Conservative" are only adjectives describing where we belong, or how we practice. At the core, we are all Jews.

One message of the incidents this summer has been that all of us Jews must stand together when it comes to fighting the hatred that is too often directed against us and other minorities.

We feel our ties to one another when we read a newspaper story and pick out the Jewish names. When Israeli doctors care for Turkish earthquake victims, we take pride. When a Jew commits a heinous crime and flees to Israel, we cringe. This summer we have identified with the Jews of Sacramento and the Jews of Granada Hills and the Jews of Skokie. They are our people, and if we walked into their synagogues or JCCs, we would feel at home. Surely anyone who hates them will hate us.

What other lesson can we take from the events of this past summer? Now we know anti-Semitism in a different way.

We have studied anti-Semitism and taught it. We know the suffering our people has endured; some of us have endured it ourselves. We have studied the images at the Holocaust Museum. We have felt vicarious terror and experienced profound sorrow. We have heard stories and empathized with those who came before us, those with names we know and those we do not know, across centuries.

We have felt far removed, safe, we who always have lived in the Land of the Free, the *goldene medinah* for our people. We feel a sense of distance from the historical terror of anti-Semitism. We are intellectually aware of those before us who could not feel this same sense of security, and we are grateful for their efforts that made it possible for us to be here.

But now ... now we can have no doubt that the Jews of Granada Hills and Sacramento and Chicago were attacked only because they were Jews. They did nothing to provoke these senseless acts—nothing but identify themselves with the Jewish community: participating in synagogue life, attending Shabbat services, attending a Jewish day camp.

And so, now, as we come together as individuals linking ourselves tonight to a congregation, participating in a worshipping community, bringing our children to the synagogue, this Shabbat evening, this Erev Rosh Hashanah, we cannot help but feel, too, a special shared vulnerability. We, too, are hated just because we are Jews.

What is our response to this vulnerability? As modern Americans, we want to analyze the problem and solve it. We will enlist our sociologists and psychologists, our educators and communal workers to study the roots of hatred. We know it comes from ignorance, so we promote educational programs and better understanding. We know it comes from paranoia, so we promote better community mental health programs. We know that violence springs from the unspeakable availability of guns, so we push for better gun control legislation. We know that this hatred is spread through the internet, so we investigate stronger controls on public hatred and hate crimes, without sacrificing our commitment to free speech.

We have developed highly effective communal organizations whose sole purpose is to work against such hatred and the violence it spawns. They remind us that we are not defenseless even as they constructively and convincingly educate and communicate.

Our tradition cuts through all our modern analysis and problem-solving, however, and calls this kind of anti-Semitism *sinat chinam*, baseless hatred, hatred with no cause.

Rabbi Amnon of Mayence confronted baseless hatred at the end of the eleventh century. According to a legend, Rabbi Amnon was given the choice of converting to Christianity or being put to death. He asked for a few days to consider his fate. Overcome with remorse for having suggested that he might convert, he did not appear before the authorities with his response. He was arrested and tortured cruelly. As he was about to die, on Rosh Hashanah, he asked to be carried to the synagogue and there, with his last breath, uttered our famous *Unetaneh Tokef* prayer.[4]

Being at risk is part of the message of the High Holy Days. Our tradition calls these days "the Days of Awe" because we stand powerless before God, mindful of our shortcomings, fearful of our fate. The *Unetaneh Tokef* prayer of Rabbi Amnon tells us that on Rosh Hashanah it is written and on Yom Kippur it is sealed: who shall live—and how they shall live—and who shall die—and how they shall die. "Who shall be secure and who shall be driven; who shall be tranquil and who shall be troubled."[5] This is the day when "the great Shofar is sounded, the still small voice is heard; the angels, gripped by fear and trembling, declare in awe: This is the Day of Judgment! For even the hosts of heaven are judged, as all who dwell on earth stand arrayed before You."[6]

As Jews we respond to this message of vulnerability by reinforcing our relationship with God, our Judge. We take upon ourselves the responsibility of introspection: examining our deeds, counting our shortcomings, probing our lives, and seeking ways to strengthen ourselves.

Fear, then, is not the end, the ultimate message of these days. Fear is only a means to an end, an impetus that should move us to greater piety, challenge us to acknowledge our shortcomings, force us to renew our relationship with God, to find our way back to commitment and piety.

How can our sense of vulnerability lead to good?

How can this time of awakening benefit us?

It is not enough to wake up; you have to get out of bed and start a new day.

I have a confession to make: I work hard not to obsess about the level of private Jewish observance in our congregation. I know that Temple Sinai is filled with deeply committed individuals who cherish many different definitions of Jewish commitment: some are committed to social justice, some to study, some to worship, some to involvement in other worthy Jewish causes. Each and every one of these commitments is fundamental and positive.

And even though I know all this, it is tempting for a rabbi to wonder about and even judge what people do and don't do in their own homes. (Our rabbinic ordination empowers us both to teach and to judge!) How many of us observe Shabbat by setting it apart from the rest of the week? How many of us read two Jewish books a year? How many of us celebrate Jewish holidays other than Rosh Hashanah, Yom Kippur, and Chanukah? I try very hard not to focus on what people don't do; I try very hard to build upon and enhance what they do.

And yet ...

Tonight is not only Rosh Hashanah but also Shabbat, the most important Jewish holiday, so I'll use it as an example. Here is how I could challenge you; I could say:

- How much effort do you expend on Shabbat observance?

- How many weeks during the year do you gather with other Jews and, if possible, your family on Friday evening and "make Shabbos," do something special to set it apart?
- How many weeks do you plead that you are too tired, or too busy, or too committed to mark Shabbat?

We are all of these: too busy, too committed—to some of the wrong things—and not committed enough to Shabbat. Sometimes Judaism seems like just one more activity that we try to fit in as best we can. "This week I'll do Shabbat, next week I'll do Kennedy Center, or a movie, or soccer." Shabbat and even Judaism are just choices on our menu of life rather than the ultimate commitment they should be.

How do we break out of this mind-set of the "optionality" of Judaism, of the sense that Shabbat is one of many choices arrayed before us on Friday evening or Saturday?

You gather the people together, tell them who they are and what must be important in their lives. You tell them that they are vulnerable, that their safety and very lives are at stake. You tell them that they are far too caught up with today and tomorrow, and this week and next week, and that they need to see themselves in context: the context of centuries and a people that is older than anything they know. You tell them with words and with music, with memories and with symbols, with emotions and with chastisements. You tell them that they have been given a gift—being part of the Jewish people—and they don't even know it. You gather them all together, you scare them a little, and you sound an ancient instrument that touches them to the core of their existence, that reminds them of who they are and what God expects them to be.

And then you pray that they will wake up and hear, that they will understand who they are and where they fit in and before Whom they stand. You pray that their hearts will be moved and their actions will be changed, even just a little. You pray that they will do more to enrich their lives, which is what you really wanted for them all along. And you hope that this is the year they will hear the wake-up call.

---

1. In August 1999, a disciple of Aryan Nations attacked a daycare center in the North Valley Jewish Community Center in Los Angeles, injuring three children

and a staff member. In addition, the shooter killed a postal carrier who was Filipino-American.

2. Maimonides, Hilkhot Teshuvah III. 4; cited in S. Y. Agnon, *Days of Awe*, 72-73.
3. Alexander Alan Steinbach, in Philip Goodman, *The Rosh Hashanah Anthology* (Jewish Publication Society of America, 1970), 125-26.
4. Lawrence A. Hoffman, *Gates of Understanding, vol. 2*, 75-76.
5. *Gates of Repentance*, 108.
6. *Gates of Repentance*, 107-8.

It's Only a Test

Rosh Hashanah Morning 5760
September 11, 1999

I remember the tests of the emergency broadcast system on television when I was growing up. "This is a test," the announcer would state dramatically. Then a new picture would appear and a tone would sound. Eventually the announcer would repeat, "This has been a test," and explain what would have happened, "had it been a true emergency." When the "regularly scheduled programming" would resume, we watchers and listeners felt well prepared for whatever emergency might come our way, and we felt relieved that it had only been a test.

Yes, we were well prepared!

What if God were speaking to us, asking us to do something impossible?

That is, after all, what happens in the Torah portion we read this morning. The terror we share with Abraham as we read this chapter is softened only by the fact that we know from the beginning that "This is a test." Even our prayer book is reassuring, translating the first verse, "There came a time when God put Abraham to the test."[1]

Immediately we know that God's command to sacrifice Isaac is not meant to be carried out. It is only a test.

Abraham, on the other hand, does not know and must suffer the agony of deciding what to do. The rabbis of the Midrash taught that this was one of many tests of Abraham's faith ... but it was the greatest test.

From the beginning, God had pushed Abraham further and then further, until now, the final demand, the ultimate test.

Introducing the story in this way creates a tension in the narrative: we know that this is only a test; Abraham does not. How will Abraham react to God's command? How will Isaac react? Where will this assignment take them? Will they ever be the same? We want to cry out, "It's only a test," but we cannot reach them.

On Rosh Hashanah, each of us stands—like Abraham before God, our Judge. Like Abraham, each of us is tested all year long, and Rosh Hashanah comes each year as our Jewish examination. This is the day we are commanded to test ourselves, to see where we have done well and where we have fallen short. This is the day we examine our deeds to assess how we have done on our test.

Many times, as we look at how we have conducted our lives, we may be tempted to say, "It's only a test." In a real situation, we think, we would act differently. We would say the comforting and conciliatory words. We would make the moral choices. We would do the right thing.

Judaism teaches us that we have free will, that we can make moral choices … and that we can make mistakes.

The problem is that, also like Abraham, we may not know at the time if it's a test or for real. We may not recognize a test of our moral courage, our spiritual strength, our ethical will, our loyalty to God, our caring for others.

How are we tested? How are we challenged as individuals, and as a community? What can we learn from looking at how Abraham met God's challenges?

Before God told him to take Isaac up Mount Moriah, Abraham already had been tested many times.

One day, Abraham saw three men approaching his tent. Inviting them in, he said, "Let me get you something to eat and drink, so that you can refresh yourselves." These strangers were not ordinary men, as we learn, but angels, and Abraham's hospitality is rewarded by the birth of Isaac. We will never know if Sarah would have given birth to Isaac had Abraham turned away or ignored the strangers. The lesson for us is that Abraham's tent was open to all.

Abraham's example teaches us to welcome others into our midst. While we might not personally exclude others from our neighborhoods or congregation, our society and culture lead us to distrust and reject the stranger in our midst.

The incident at Columbine High School has opened our eyes to the cruelty with which some young people treat one another.[2] No amount of being ridiculed or shoved justifies murder. Analyses of the tragedy, however, have brought to our attention how much pain some of the students at that school and some of our own children live with day in and day out, just beneath the surface.

How often do we neglect to make the right decisions! We are guided instead by the cliques in our schools, by the politics in our offices, by the reputations of others, rather than by our sense of how we should relate to the human beings with whom we study, work, and live.

The reality for most of us at school, at work, in our neighborhoods, is that there is too much gossip, too much cruelty, too much rejection of those who are not just like us.

Our excuse is that it is human nature to be tough, that we want to be with people who are like us, who share our values and our background.

And so are we tested: how do we react to the strangers in our midst? With Abraham as our example, we should welcome them and reach out to them, bring them into our tents, if not making them our friends, then at least being kind. We should each be a mensch. For we, like Abraham, will never know if "this is a test" or not.

Abraham was tested when he argued for the people of Sodom and Gomorrah. "What if there are fifty innocent people in the city?" Abraham cries out to God. "Will you bring death upon the innocent as well as the guilty? ... Far be it from You! Shall not the Judge of all the earth deal justly?" (Gen. 18:24-25).

Reading this story, we are impressed with Abraham's chutzpah as well as his negotiating skills. What should impress us particularly, however, is Abraham's sense of justice. What did Abraham risk to confront God? What risks are we willing to take on behalf of justice? Are we willing to stand up for the ignored and forgotten? Are we willing to defend the kid in our class who is being picked on? Are we willing to risk anything on behalf of the innocent who might be swept away with the guilty? And most importantly, will we know when we are being tested and when it's "for real"?

Not everybody passes a test like this, of course. When God created Adam and Eve, God said, "You are free to eat from every tree in the garden except for the Tree of the Knowledge of Good and Bad. You must not eat of that tree" (Gen. 2:16-17). No sooner were those words spoken than Eve reached out, took the fruit, and the two of them ate. They failed the first test.

Later, when God encountered Adam in the Garden, God asked, "Where are you?" Surely God knew the answer, since God knows everything. The rabbis of the Midrash point out that God was giving Adam and Eve the opportunity to acknowledge their sin, to accept responsibility, to confess. But Adam answered instead, "I heard you walking in the Garden, and I was afraid ... so I hid" (Gen. 3:9-10). Adam failed the second test, too.

God asked, "What's happened here? Did you eat of the tree from which I had forbidden you to eat?" Again God gave Adam and Eve the chance to accept responsibility for their wrongdoing. But Adam said, "The woman You put at my side, she gave me the fruit, and I ate." And Eve said, "The serpent duped me, and I ate" (Gen. 3:11-13). Adam and Eve failed the third test.

When we are tested, we must look to Abraham to show us the way: accepting responsibility, pursuing justice, taking risks, being concerned about others.

And when Abraham was tested in a society where might made right, he rejected violence. Early in his story, Abraham traveled with his nephew Lot, semi-nomads moving their sheep and cattle from here to there in the Land of Canaan. As time went on, their flocks and herds increased so much, the Bible tells us, "that the land could not support them staying together" (Gen. 13:6). Their herdsmen began to quarrel over whose animals could graze where.

Abraham, we see in Genesis, rejects the violence that is the standard of the culture. He says to Lot, "Let there be no strife between you and me, between my herdsmen and yours, for we are kin. Is not the whole land before you?" (Gen. 13:8-9). You go one way and I will go the other, he says, so that peace will prevail in the land—and in our family. Lot journeyed eastward across the Jordan, and both groups were satisfied.

How different from the test of Cain, just after he had killed his brother Abel. God said to Cain, "Where is your brother Abel?" You know that God knows the answer. It's the same kind of testing question that God asked Adam and Eve. The question gave Cain the opportunity to accept responsibility for his deed, to confess his sin, to acknowledge that he did the wrong thing.

Cain failed the test. He said, "I do not know. Am I my brother's keeper?" As we hear this story, we want to shout out, "Yes! You are your brother's keeper. We are all our brother's and sister's keepers."

Even though we know we must be responsible for one another, we are reminded instead of the description of Noah's time, when "the earth became corrupt before God ... and was filled with lawlessness." It grieves us all, I know, to see metal detectors and security guards at the entrances of our schools. Instead of being a place of refuge, too many of our schools have become a place of violence. Instead of learning about our great world, children must learn how to protect themselves. I don't for a moment think that we should compromise the safety of our children; but I grieve at the loss of the sense of community our schools once represented.

Our challenge is to recreate and restore that sense of shared values and mission that we once found in our schools, our workplaces, and our neighborhoods. Most of us live in safe neighborhoods and study and work in places of relative safety.

That wasn't always the case for our people. We Jews have lived in poverty and in danger. We have lived in fear and in suffering. We have lived with many tests and trials that seem distant to our lives here today. What has kept our people alive was not our comfort nor our success in life, but what we stood for and what we stand for: the values that shape our lives, our ability to recognize sin, our willingness to acknowledge our shortcomings, our understanding of the difference between right and wrong, our choice from day to day and hour to hour of good over evil.

You and I face the same tests today: the tests faced by Abraham, by Adam and Eve, by Cain. We are challenged to care for others, to follow our beliefs, to make the right choices. And we never know if it is a test or a real challenge.

When our people suffered the most—whether from poverty, from hatred, or from oppression—they prayed for the Messiah, who would bring an end to their suffering. They wondered, "How will we recognize the Messiah? How will he appear to us? What will she look like? How can we be sure to welcome her properly, for we must not risk turning her away." There were many answers to these questions, many theories about the Messiah.

One of my favorites is that the Messiah will come disguised as a beggar. A beggar would be the least likely person to bring a time of peace and plenty. You might want to overlook the person begging in the street, but that very person might be the Messiah, God's messenger. So, this story teaches, we must reach out to everyone, just in case, for you never know if the time of deliverance is the very next moment. Every encounter is a test; every person has the potential for greatness.

Our own tests come all the time, not just at critical moments. Today—on Rosh Hashanah—we are commanded to examine our deeds and our lives, to see where we have done well and where we have failed. We have the power to choose and the will to do better in the New Year. We are tested and challenged, like Abraham. Let us have the strength and the will to prevail.

1. *Gates of Repentance*, 125.
2. In April 1999, at Columbine High School near Denver, Colorado, twelve students and one teacher were shot to death by two students at the school, who also killed themselves. Because the two shooters had allegedly been tormented by fellow students, the incident brought national attention to the issue of bullying in schools.

The Torah We Believe

Yom Kippur Morning 5760
September 20, 1999

The Israelites are gathered at the foot of Mount Sinai, waiting for Moses to come down the mountain. It has been such a long time, and they are worried that he will never return. Suddenly they see him descending the mountain with a second set of tablets in his hands. As they rejoice, they notice a strange look on his face. When he gets close enough, Moses addresses the people: "Children of Israel, I have good news and bad news for you. The good news is: I bargained down to Ten Commandments. The bad news is that 'You shall not covet' is still one of them."

This humorous story raises serious theological issues. Do we believe that God spoke to Moses on Mount Sinai? Do we believe that the Ten Commandments—or any other part of the Torah—are the words of God? How free are we to interpret these words, to alter or change their meaning, to say, for example, that they no longer apply to us? What do we, as Jews and as Reform Jews, believe about divine revelation?

Traditional Judaism has taught for many centuries that God dictated the Torah to Moses on Mount Sinai; that the words of the Torah are true, perfect, and unchanging. Each time we read from the Torah, we raise it and sing the traditional words, "*V'zot hatorah. . .*This is the Torah that Moses placed before the people of Israel to fulfill the word of God." Even our Reform liturgy is replete with reminders that Torah is God's gift to the Jews.

Each time we read from the Torah, we avow that the words we are hearing and seeing are the words of God. Do we really believe this? Do we really think that the Torah is God's revealed word?

Most of us probably do not. We may think of the Torah as very old, very important, very venerated, but not God's word.

As Reform Jews, we are far less concerned with the question of the truth of Torah than with the relevance of Torah.

As Reform Jews, however, we *should* be concerned with the truth of Torah.

I believe that the Torah is God's word. That's not to say that God wrote it. Yet the Torah is more than a grand old book containing great wisdom for all. When I fast on Yom Kippur, or observe the Sabbath, or make an ethical decision to give *tzedakah*, I don't do so for nostalgia or tradition. I do it because I believe it is a divine imperative: God commands me to do it.

It is far more comfortable for us to attribute what we do as Jews to "tradition": we light Shabbat candles because our bubby did it; we come to the synagogue on Yom Kippur because we know our dad would want us to come. It is acceptable—it is politically correct—to seek your roots these days, to get in touch with where you came from, to find a place to fit in.

On the other hand, we are not comfortable with the idea that the Bible is something more than a very old and venerated book. It may be interesting; it may be significant; but God's word? For most of us, I think, it is great literature with a message. It's the Jewish epic, our own version of the *Iliad* and *Odyssey*, or *Gilgamesh*, or the *Code of Hammurabi*. It is our contribution to the world, so it had better be important to us as well. We may study its words, especially its stories. But do we really believe it is God's revealed word?

Most of us, I suspect, would say "no."

Today, this Yom Kippur, I want to challenge you. I want to tell you that when we deny that God wrote the Torah, we take the sanctity out of the Torah, and we take God out of Judaism.

God has given us a guide to live our lives: Torah. The Torah is our link, as Jews, to God.

Years ago, when I was touring the Sinai desert, our guide pointed out that several mountains in the area could be "the" Mount Sinai. He added, "*if* there was a Mount Sinai, and *if* there was a Moses."

It was at that moment that I realized what I believed in. I was quite prepared to say that God did not create the world in six days, that the flood didn't happen, that the Sea did not part to save the escaping Israelites. But I did believe that Moses had lived and that the Israelites had stood at the foot of Mount Sinai and accepted the covenant from God.

What do we do, as Jews, because God expects us to?

What do we do, as Jews, for religious reasons?

How do we know what God expects of us?

How do we know what we should do as Jews?

The Torah tells us. The Torah contains 613 mitzvot, or

commandments, not just the ten Moses was able to whittle them down to. Keeping these 613 mitzvot is the essence of what it means to be a traditional Jew. They are in the Torah, and the Torah comes from God. Have no doubt that traditional Jews consider observing Shabbat and fasting on Yom Kippur as fulfilling God's commandments.

If this is what traditional Jews believe, what do Reform Jews believe? Where do we differ? If traditional Jews accept all 613 commandments, what basis do Reform Jews have for picking and choosing?

At the core of Reform Jewish belief, since the founding of the movement in the nineteenth century, is the imperative that individual Jews have the ability and the responsibility to interpret Torah for themselves.

As Reform Jews, then, we believe that we can interpret Torah and mitzvot for ourselves and for our own day. That does not take God out of Torah. That was not the original intent of Reform Judaism either, despite what some people think.

Reform Judaism was born when scholars first began to study religion critically. As they analyzed the Hebrew Bible, they discovered sources, such as J, E, D, and P, and used this source analysis to study the text. But these early Reformers never took God out of the Bible.

Isaac Mayer Wise, the founder of American Reform Judaism, said that God dictated the Ten Commandments, but people wrote the rest of the Torah.[1]

In an 1885 statement of principles, the Pittsburgh Platform, Reform rabbis declared "We hold that Judaism presents the highest conception of the God-idea as taught in our Holy Scriptures."[2]

In 1937, Reform rabbis expanded on the origin of the Torah by saying that "revelation is a continuous process, confined to no one group and to no one age." They saw the Torah as the culmination of "historical processes," and they still believed that some of the laws had "lost their binding force." The rabbis of 1937 distinguished between these outdated laws and the "permanent spiritual ideals" through which "the Torah remains the dynamic source of the life of Israel."

The rabbis' 1976 Centenary Perspective reflects yet another shift; now, even more clearly, "Torah results from the relationship between God and the Jewish people," a covenant. The rabbis of 1976 describe the Torah as a "heritage whose study is a religious imperative and whose practice is our chief means to holiness." For the first time in the history of Reform Judaism, Torah was described as the document of the encounter between God and the Jewish people.

Does this mean Reform rabbis believe God wrote the Torah? Do they believe God dictated it to Moses? Not really, and the process of revelation that they describe is vague. They were not ready, any more than I am now, to describe exactly how this encounter between God and the Jewish people, called revelation, occurred. They believed, as I do, that God's word is in the Torah, that it is more than a social document, that it is the product of revelation.

This idea of revelation was affirmed in the new Statement of Principles adopted last May in Pittsburgh by the Central Conference of American Rabbis.

At the core of these principles, and at the core of Reform Jewish belief, is this statement on Torah: "We affirm that Torah is the foundation of Jewish life. We cherish the truths revealed in Torah, God's ongoing revelation to our people and the record of our people's ongoing relationship with God."

What is key here are the words "ongoing revelation." In other words, Reform rabbis are saying that revelation did not stop with the Torah. Revelation continues today with our constantly changing interpretation of the word of God. It is our understanding, subject to many variables, of what God is telling us to do.

I would have preferred the adoption of the preamble language submitted by Rabbi W. Gunther Plaut, editor of our Torah commentary. He emphasized that one aspect of what makes Reform Judaism distinct is that "rather than considering the written Torah to have been dictated by God to Moses, Reform believes it to be a result of our people's search for and meeting with God, a process that lasted for many centuries."[3]

Thus all four statements of Reform Jewish belief—from 1885 to 1999—assert that God's word is present in Torah; that we have both the ability and the responsibility to interpret Torah for our own day; and that Torah (at least some part of it) is central to what it means to be Jewish.

This is not an easy position to take, and it is under attack from both sides. Many modern Jews believe that people wrote the Torah and that it is not the product of divine revelation. Orthodox Jews, on the other hand, believe that God dictated the Torah to Moses on Mount Sinai, as my joke implies. They believe that the Torah is true, perfect, and cannot be interpreted loosely. Among some Christians who agree with

Orthodox Jews, the question of the truth of the Bible, or "inerrancy," divides denominations, churches, and seminaries.

A firm belief in the truth of the Bible is at the center of the controversy over teaching "Creationism" and suppressing the teaching of evolution in Kansas schools. Fundamentalists who believe in the God-given truth of the Bible and Orthodox Jews who believe in "Torah-true Judaism" share a passionate intensity about the correctness of their beliefs. They feel they must shut out any scientific information that might conflict with it.

We Reform Jews disagree with the fundamentalists. We are committed to a style of Jewish belief and practice that is modern and enlightened. We believe that science is not to be contradicted nor suppressed, but that science has inherent limits on what it can state. The scientist can describe the universe, but she is not qualified (nor willing) to draw moral conclusions from these descriptions. The scientist is in the realm of *is*, not *ought*.

Most of us thought we had moved beyond the Scopes trial. For many years, I have used the play *Inherit the Wind* in Confirmation class to illuminate the Reform Jewish belief that there is no conflict between religion and science. Reform Jewish belief is that science teaches us about our world and Judaism teaches us how to lead our lives.

Confronted with modern Scriptural criticism, Orthodox Jewish belief, and Christian fundamentalism, why did four generations of Reform leaders feel compelled to state their belief in progressive revelation? Because they recognized that we need for our Judaism to be more than a quaint collection of stories, customs, and ceremonies; more than just cultural curiosities; more than literature with a message. They recognized that we have a deep need for our religion—our Judaism—to sanctify our lives, to lead us to God, to be our path to eternal truths. We need to believe that the Judaism we practice is what God expects of us, not just a quaint set of customs our grandparents followed. We need to ground our Judaism in expectations deeper than doing what we think is right, or comfortable, or meaningful, or relevant. We need to believe that God does make very specific demands on us and for that reason and that reason alone we have the responsibility to fulfill them.

We read this morning that Moses tells the people that the Instruction he is giving them is not beyond their reach. "It is not in the heavens or beyond the sea. ... No, it is very close to you, in your mouth and in your heart, to observe it" (Deut. 30:12-14).

Our primary sin this Yom Kippur, and every Yom Kippur, is that we do not take Torah seriously enough.

We sin by keeping Torah at arm's length, if we even keep it at all.

We sin by dismissing the words of Torah in so many ways.

We sin by expecting the words of Torah to be interesting and educational and relevant.

We sin by not keeping the words of Torah in our mouth and in our heart, and by not observing them, as Reform Judaism teaches.

The new Statement of Principles affirms that we "are called by Torah to lifelong study ... [and that] through Torah study we are called to mitzvot, the means by which we make our lives holy."

In countless ways, Reform Judaism represents the ability and the responsibility to choose.

- Which of the stories in the Bible are "real" and which are there to teach us a lesson?
- Which commandments should we make part of our lives?
- How should we live our lives and make the right choices?
- How do we know what God expects of us?
- How do we know what we should do as Jews?

These are the questions we must each answer for ourselves.

The ancient rabbis told many stories, or *midrashim*, about how they thought the Torah was given. One of the stories tells that the Torah was not given in the loud thundering, described in Exodus, but in silence.

At the moment that God gave the Torah, no bird chirped, no lion roared, the sea waves made no sound, all the people stopped talking, everything was silent. The whole world was hushed into silence, so that the still small voice of God could be heard.

You and I can hear that voice, as well, if we will stop and listen. We can hear the voice of God speaking to us out of the Torah when we study, out of our prayers, out of the good we do in the world. We can hear that voice, and it can guide us and transform us and awaken our souls.

---

1. Michael A. Meyer, *Response to Modernity* (Oxford University Press, 1988), 240.
2. This statement, as well as later ones cited in this sermon, may be found on the website of the Central Conference of American Rabbis, www.ccarnet.org.
3. Gunther Plaut, "Draft Statement of Principles," May 1999, 3:33-36.

Pride and Sacrifice

Rosh Hashanah Morning 5761
September 30, 2000

One summer while I was in high school, I came home from a youth group program at camp with a sweatshirt. The sweatshirt had the insignia of NFTY, the National Federation of Temple Youth, and a biblical quotation in Hebrew.

I was very pleased with my new sweatshirt, but my parents were nervous about my wearing it. They said it was okay for me to wear it around the house, but not when I went out.

We don't advertise our religion, they told me. They told me this even though I had gone to an elementary school that was 90 percent Jewish. In those days—the early 1960s—my parents were so intent on not *advertising* their religion that we did not even have a mezuzah at our front door.

My parents divided their world between Jewish and Gentile. You could trust Jews to do you no harm (most of the time), but non-Jews you might be concerned about. You never knew when anti-Semitism might raise its ugly head, they said.

My parents felt vulnerable as Jews living in America, and their feelings of vulnerability made them cautious. After all, when I was growing up, many neighborhoods and suburbs kept Jews from buying houses or renting apartments or opening businesses; many colleges and universities only accepted a certain quota—or limit—of Jews; and many businesses and professional firms hired gentiles only.

We Jews more or less knew our place: with other Jews. Our place was in a Jewish neighborhood or suburb, where we could feel comfortable and protected. The last thing we wanted to do under these circumstances was advertise our religion.

Beginning with the great waves of Jewish immigration in the nineteenth century, many American Jews kept their Jewishness private. Rather than call our institutions "Jewish," we would call them the "Hebrew Home" or "Hebrew Union College." People called themselves—or encouraged others to call them—"Israelites" or individuals "of the Mosaic persuasion." Some people changed their names to make them sound less Jewish (or more American), and many Jews even denied they were Jewish.

So I find myself wondering, as Jews wonder, WWPT: What would my parents think about the first Jewish candidate for Vice President of the United States?[1] What would they think about a vice presidential candidate who proudly proclaims that he is a traditional Jew? Would his candidacy make them proud to be Jewish? Would they be uncomfortable that he is *advertising* his Judaism? What would be their reaction to knowing that Joseph Lieberman's Judaism was quite different from their Judaism? How do we feel about that?

I also ask myself—since we are studying the life of Rabbi Stephen Wise this year—What would Stephen Wise think about the Lieberman candidacy? Wise was a friend of Presidents Woodrow Wilson and Franklin Roosevelt and Supreme Court Justice Louis Brandeis. He supported the Catholic—and therefore much feared—Al Smith for Governor of New York and President. Wise knew better than most Americans of his day the nuances of mixing minority religion and national politics.

In my lifetime—and not just in the past few weeks—I have seen the attitude of many Jews change from privacy to pride, from being an American Marrano to being a proclaimer of their Judaism, from being a Jew-in-hiding to being a Jew whose life and destiny are shaped by their active participation in a community of Jews.

Today, we can look to Abraham in our Torah reading as our model: Abraham, whose loyalty to God and whose devotion to Judaism led him to say, "*Hineni*; I am here, I am ready, send me."

We cannot imagine the dismay and conflict Abraham must have felt in this story. How could God make such a demand on me? With Ishmael gone, how could God ask me to sacrifice my other son? What about God's promise of greatness for Isaac and his descendants? What does this covenant mean now, this sacred agreement with God: I will be devoted to God, and God will grant me many descendants? If Abraham follows God's command, the promise will be broken.

Despite his conflict, despite his misgivings, despite his anguish, Abraham says, "*Hineni*; here I am, I am ready, send me."

The ancient rabbis of the Midrash thought of Abraham as a person who advertised his Judaism, who reached out to others in God's name. They said that Abraham's tent was open on all four sides, so that he and

Sarah could welcome travelers coming from all four directions. They were models of hospitality, as the custom still continues in Israel and the Near East today.

The rabbis went on to say, furthermore, that Sarah and Abraham shared with their many guests their experience of God, their personal faith, their participation in the Jewish covenant. Abraham and Sarah, the rabbis taught, had followers for their new religion, Judaism.

When God calls to Abraham to leave his native land of Haran and head for Canaan, the Bible tells us that Abraham and Sarah took their little family, all their possessions, and "the persons that they had acquired in Haran" (Gen. 12:5). While we might think that these persons were slaves or servants, the rabbis understood that these were the earliest followers of Judaism, converts who were attracted to this family and this new religion because of the hospitality of Abraham and Sarah and their ability to reach out to others. These people were loyal to God, devoted to Judaism, unafraid to say "*Hineni*; here I am, I am ready, send me."

How many of us have a similar sense of pride in our own Jewish lives? How many of us instead shy away from Jewish commitment? How many of us view our Judaism as another extra activity competing for our time and attention, rather than an integral part—in fact the essence—of who we are?

We lead incredibly busy and demanding lives. We have work and school and family, our neighborhood and community, our interests and our sports and hobbies, the issues we follow, and our volunteer activities. How often are we torn between these competing demands that make claims on us. We learn the hard way that the god of soccer is a jealous god (as one colleague has put it), and so are the gods of work and success. Our failure is that we see Judaism as just one more thing to do, one more activity to squeeze into our crowded lives.

We must rather understand Judaism as the way of life we follow, a foundation for everything else we do, all that we are, every decision and choice we make.

Today we come here to renew our relationship with the one God of our life and our people. We need to give our attention to God not just today, but every day throughout the year. We need to understand that the demands that Judaism makes upon us are part of who we are and that Judaism provides the ultimate values that should guide our lives.

We need to renew our relationship with God and the Jewish people, and be proud and caring Jews. We are here today to look again and this time to find a way to commit ourselves in the New Year and say, for once and for all, "*Hineni*; here I am, I am ready, send me."

Joseph Lieberman is a proud Jew. And while his way of practicing Judaism may not be our way—and while we may not agree with him on all issues—we cannot fault his commitment to Judaism and to Jewish life. He is not afraid to wear a Jewish sweatshirt, or put up a mezuzah; he is not afraid to proclaim his Jewishness and tell us—and all Americans—about the difference Judaism has made in his life. He has been able to reconcile Jewish practice with a demanding workload and lifestyle, leading a Jewish life with caring and integrity.

His candidacy and all the talk surrounding it have taught us much. We each have had to confront and determine our individual comfort level in speaking publicly about our religion, our practice, our view of God. We may have been called upon to explain to our friends, neighbors, and co-workers the differences between Orthodox, Traditional, and Reform Judaism.

We have been asked how we feel about a Jewish candidate for Vice President: Do we give the same answer to Jew and non-Jew? What do we say to ourselves about public Judaism and Jewish practice? How does our Jewish life compare?

A significant part of our task on this Rosh Hashanah and during these High Holy Days—as it is every year—is to renew our commitment to be proud and caring Jews.

Clearly, there is more than one way to practice Judaism. We Jews thrive on diversity, right down to the shipwrecked Jewish man. When he was found years after his boat went down, he gave a tour of his little island to his rescuers, who noticed two synagogues. His rescuers asked him, "Why are there two synagogues if you are the only Jew here?" He replied, "This one is the one where I belong, and that one over there, I would never set foot in!"

We, as Reform Jews, must be no less committed to synagogue life or proud of it.

Reform Judaism has taught us that we could adapt Jewish practice to the modern world, that there were additional values that Judaism taught us that stood side-by-side with ritual life. Reform Judaism taught us that Judaism could be reshaped, reformed in the modern period, if we did it carefully, thoughtfully, conscientiously. If we studied the mitzvot—the commandments—of Jewish life, we were capable of interpreting, accepting, or rejecting them in our own way and for our own day.

Reform Judaism reminds us that the Bible did not end with the Torah but continued with the majestic statements of the prophets, whose call to social justice especially spoke to us. Reform Judaism teaches us that Judaism did not end with the Bible, nor with the Talmud, but that it has been a vital and changing religion over many centuries, that it has adapted to many ages and cultures, and that we have the right to adapt it to our own time and place. Reform Judaism shows us that other values we hold dear can be integrated into our Judaism: the equality of all Jews, of men and women; the dignity of religious worship; that all people are creatures of one God; that we must work for better understanding between religions and cultures; that we are called to work for justice in our communities, in our nation, and in the world.

One message that I want you to take home today is that Reform Judaism is committed Judaism. It is not a Judaism of convenience, or indifference, or carelessness.

Reform Judaism is responsive Judaism: responsive to our own lives and situations, responsive to our communities, responsive to the best of Jewish sources.

Reform Judaism, like every other Jewish interpretation, makes demands upon us. We need to confront these demands and integrate them into our lives. Like Abraham, we need to be ready to say: "*Hineni*; here I am." Like Abraham, we need to be ready for sacrifice, no matter what our sacrifices may be. For Abraham, sacrifice meant giving up what was most precious in his life. For us, it is just an hour here or there, some time that has its own rewards, a few moments that will enrich our lives.

Are we willing to give anything up for Judaism, for God, for Jewish commitment? Of course we are. Scores of our members sacrifice their time and energy to work for our congregation, our committees, and our affiliates. Hundreds of our members sacrifice their means to support the Temple's financial needs. Dozens of our adults and young people sacrifice their Sunday mornings and evenings and Wednesday afternoons to teach the next generation of Jewish students about Jewish texts and Jewish life.

But what about the rest of us? What are we willing to give up for Judaism? In the balancing act of our lives, where do Jewish practice and Jewish commitment fit in? In order to participate in the Shabbat dinner and service with your class, you need to leave sports practice early, so your coach is not pleased. If you stay to the end of the practice, however, your teacher or rabbi is not pleased. How do you balance the commitments of sports and music and family time with Jewish life? We see this week after week, as we work through—and negotiate—with family after family in our congregation and religious school. How can I get to the service *and* the basketball game? How can I participate in the tennis match *and* religious school? How can she be part of the class social action project and still make it to her music recital?

You saw this next sentence coming!

If Abraham is willing to sacrifice his son, if Senator Lieberman is willing to sacrifice a day of campaigning each week, what are you willing to sacrifice?

Compared to those sacrifices (not to mention the sacrifices of our people over the centuries), the sacrifices we are asked to make seem very small indeed.

Judaism demands that we make sacrifices, and Reform Judaism demands that we make decisions and that we be prepared for the sacrifices that follow.

I am worried that we no longer understand the idea of sacrifice for Judaism, as our people once did. I am even more worried that we no longer appreciate the joy of Jewish observance and the warmth of Jewish practice.

A religious school parent tells me she is pleased because there is a Shabbat dinner before the service conducted by her son's class. Otherwise, she says, they would have to pick up something on the way and eat on the run.

How can we help this Jewish family—and each of our families— comprehend the beauty of Shabbat dinner: a time for family rituals, hospitality to others, connecting with one another and with the values that make us what we are and the choices that determine the course of our lives?

Are we running too fast, trying to do so much, that we cannot stop to appreciate the joy and beauty of life in general and Jewish family life in particular? Are we working and playing so hard that we seek a Judaism of convenience rather than a Judaism of meaning? On the calendars that govern our lives—work, school, sports, music—do we leave space for Jewish time? For it is the Jewish calendar that defines a time for work and a time to stop. It is the Jewish calendar that teaches us to treasure each day and to treasure each other, our families and our friends.

Here we are at the beginning of a New Year with a new set of opportunities and a new chance for commitment. Here we are, given an opportunity to say, "*Hineni*; here I am, I am ready, send me." Here we are, given a fresh start for our lives, new energy for the struggle to balance. Here we are, challenged anew to care about what is important, to put Judaism first, to say no to distraction, to find our way to caring, to renew our relationship to God and the Jewish people.

So today is the day for parents to say, "This is what is really important," or "You must complete your religious education," or "Shabbat is a priority in our family." Today is the day to focus on values and make them our own. Today is the day to understand that Judaism, like anything important, demands sacrifice.

Then we will wear our Judaism proudly, unafraid to be a caring Jew, seeking a Jewish commitment that will enrich and ennoble our lives far more than we can imagine.

---

1. In the summer of 2000, Democratic presidential candidate Al Gore chose Connecticut Senator Joseph Lieberman to be his vice presidential running mate.

Justice, Mercy, Humility

Erev Rosh Hashanah 5762
September 17, 2001

We enter this New Year with many mixed feelings, but there is no taste of sweetness in our mouths. We feel sadness, anger, fear, and grief as our disbelief gives way to empathy and concern for survivors and family members. All of these emotions have washed over us this past week, and we have watched and listened in stunned silence as we attempt to grasp the enormity of this tragedy.

One of our tasks on this Rosh Hashanah is to sort out these feelings, to find new strength for the new year as well as the days ahead, to put the events and emotions of these past days into perspective, to find hope and direction for the year we enter.

Another task this Rosh Hashanah is to reaffirm our core values. What do we really believe? What do we hold sacred? What are the fundamental principles that guide our lives as American Jews?

Each fall, as our year turns, we gather here to affirm what we believe as Jews, the values that guide our lives. This year our need is more urgent, more basic, more elemental, as we reach beyond this tragedy to affirm our beliefs, to reconnect with what is fundamental in our lives. Today we are here to learn nothing less than how to pull ourselves back together again.

There is a Chasidic tale of a man who often forgot where he put his clothes when he got undressed at night. So he devised a plan: as he took off each article of clothing, he wrote on a slip of paper where he put it, and he placed the slips of paper next to his bed.

When he awakened the next morning, he would know that his pants were in the closet, his shirt was on the hook, his shoes were under the bed. His system worked well until one morning. There he stood with his slips of paper in his hand, and suddenly he began to weep. "I know where my shirt and pants and shoes are, but where am I?"

Each year Rosh Hashanah comes to ask us that question, and especially this year: Where am I? Where do I fit in? Where do I stand with my family, with my community, with my nation, with my people? Where do I stand before my God? What are the values I can validate and live by? What are the goals I can set for myself in the year ahead? How can I escape the triviality of the rest of the year and look at my life?

These are the questions that we ask every Rosh Hashanah, and today they are more poignant and pressing than ever before, as we encounter this New Year amid the tragedies of a week ago. We feel the stamp of history on these days, and we seek to put these events into historical perspective. To help us do this, we join together this year to mark the fiftieth anniversary of our congregation.

It was on Rosh Hashanah 51 years ago that three members of Washington Hebrew Congregation spoke to one another about the need for another Reform congregation in Washington. Our history says that they were looking for "a new form of Reform Jewish worship—a service warm in human and spiritual quality."

They gathered a few other families and by December of that year, they held their first service. They organized a Ladies Auxiliary, established a religious school, and in March 1951 held their first congregational meeting, where they adopted a constitution and by-laws, and elected officers. Thus Temple Sinai was born.

On Rosh Hashanah 1951—the first High Holy Days for the new congregation—more than 800 people attended Temple Sinai's services. The great promise of Washington's second Reform congregation had become apparent to a Jewish community that had more than doubled following World War II to 45,000 in 1951.

Our founders were motivated by more than growth and numbers. They wanted to build a different congregation: a Jewish home for themselves and their families; they wanted a Jewish home for themselves as we seek a Jewish home tonight. They wanted to pray, as we have come to pray. They wanted to seek justice, as we seek justice. They wanted to reaffirm sacred principles, as we seek to do on these Days of Awe.

There are many ways to articulate what Temple Sinai's founders envisioned, but the words of the prophet Micah say it all: "It has been told you what is good and what God requires of you: only to do justly and to love mercy, and to walk humbly with your God" (Mic. 6:8).

What does God require of us? What do we require of ourselves?

We need prayer. We need to pray as a congregation, supporting one another, strengthening our words, letting our voices rise together, addressing our spiritual yearnings. That is one reason we are here today.

Over this past week, I myself have come to a new understanding of the spiritual and religious needs of our congregation. This past Wednesday morning we decided we would have a service that evening. With only a few hours' notice, and using mostly incomplete e-mail lists, we notified boards and committees and religious school families. By seven that evening, our sanctuary was filled with people of all ages: all stunned, all hurting, all turning to one another in the context of a congregation, all yearning for a way to understand, a way to respond, a word of solace, a sense of peace. On Friday evening, our Sanctuary was filled to overflowing as we gathered once again seeking strength and understanding of events we cannot yet fully comprehend.

On those evenings, I could see clearly how we were dazed and stunned, filled with grief and anger and fear, grappling with disbelief, in need of help. And I also could see, as never before, how we found comfort together in worship, reading and singing the words of our prayers, being part of a congregation. People were profoundly grateful for the opportunity to come together at both services; many said there was no other place they could imagine being on Friday evening.

As I looked at your faces, as I heard you praying, and as I listened to your voices and your silences, I felt your profound spiritual need. We experience many poignant moments in our Sanctuary—times of rejoicing and times of deep sadness—but I have never felt moments like these.

This week must teach us that even the busiest and most sophisticated among us must listen to our hearts and seek comfort from one another. This week must teach us that even the people we rarely see at our synagogue have deep yearnings to understand the profound issues that Judaism addresses. This week must teach us that our feelings of sorrow, doubt, and hunger for human contact are *religious* needs. This week must teach us that those among us who declare they are not "praying Jews" need to pray—or at least to seek comfort and strength in a worshiping congregation—when confronted by the fragility and mystery of life and death.

The founders of our congregation instinctively understood these religious needs. They left a congregation where they felt the ritual was too austere, and they created a place of welcoming and participatory worship.

How can we apply the values of our congregation to help us understand what is happening in our world today? How can we use the tools that were lovingly handed down to us—not just from the founders of Temple Sinai but from our parents and our parents' parents and all the generations of our people—to find our personal and our public way to respond to the events of this week?

Our founders heard the prophet Micah's voice commanding them to do justice and love mercy. More than ever do we need to hear that voice today.

We have heard so many voices this week: calling for war, calling for revenge, calling for love, calling for retribution. There is almost panic in our land as we compulsively watch the television, listen to the radio, surf the Internet, exchange e-mails, tease out the details, share our personal experiences. This communication is vital at this time of hurt and fear and anguish.

Yet we also need to sort out these voices. To help us, we can listen to the voice of our own congregational tradition. We know, as did the founders of Temple Sinai, that the role of a synagogue and a congregation is not limited to sanctuary and classroom— prayer and education—but must touch and affect our community and our world. Our congregation must seek justice.

One of the first groups formed within the new Temple Sinai was a social action committee. In the 1950s, the committee and their rabbi, Balfour Brickner, spoke out against segregation. They spoke out against capital punishment in the District of Columbia, and they worked for equal housing and schooling.

This commitment to social action—a vital part of our inheritance today—was not self-evident then. In 1955, the Reform Commission on Social Action, led at that time by my predecessor Rabbi Eugene J. Lipman, affirmed, "Some people challenge the idea that the synagogue should go beyond prayer and ritual and the religious school. The Reform Movement [has] stated categorically that the synagogue must be concerned with the moral issues of society, even though controversy may result."

This new/old tradition of seeking justice involved Temple Sinai in issues such as draft counseling, opposing the war in Vietnam, helping

Asian refugees, providing sanctuary for Central American refugees, seeking peace and justice in Israel, and addressing homelessness in our city.

Now, as always, we must do justly.

But seeking justice is not enough. We also must love mercy, the quality that makes us human. The mercy or kindness that God demands of us—*hesed* is Micah's word—is what leads us to reach out to others in our congregation and community, what leads us to feel enormous empathy with those affected directly and indirectly by the great tragedies of the past few days.

This week we all have been looking for answers to life's hardest questions: Where does evil come from? Why do innocent people suffer and die? Why is goodness eclipsed and evil unleashed? We come here today—to our synagogue—to seek Jewish answers to these questions.

Jerry Falwell's answer is not the Jewish response; he said that it was "God's will that the enemies of America gave us what we deserve."[1] We must say that such "theology" is repulsive, destructive, and loathsome. I do not believe in a God who kills innocent people, and I abhor those who use these tragedies to promote their sectarian agendas.

Micah would tell us we must love mercy. Our God is not a God of vengeance, but a God of mercy and caring, a Source of comfort and strength. Our God is the God of Isaiah who says, "When you pass through fire and water, I will be with you; they shall not overwhelm you. … Fear not, for I will redeem you. … Comfort, oh comfort my people, says your God." Like the prophet Micah and our founders, we must value mercy, embrace it, be comforted by it.

Today we need to ensure that *our* voices are heard in the land because our voices call for the pursuit of justice, our voices call for mercy for all the afflicted.

Micah's third imperative is to walk humbly with our God, to respect each other as individuals endowed with sacredness. We always have been—and remain—a congregation of equals: our High Holy Day seating does not depend on how much we pay; our services are led by men and women, girls and boys; our building is accessible to all, our doors open wide to welcome Jews from many backgrounds, non-Jews who choose to join us, gays and lesbians. Temple Sinai values all people as children of God.

In these troubled days, we have heard whispers of anti-Semitism and fear that it may erupt again. In these troubled days, we hear voices of prejudice who threaten the safety of Arab-Americans who love our country and our freedom as much as we do.

We must heed Micah's words and the values of our founders and say clearly that just as terrorism must be eradicated, so must the evils of racial and ethnic prejudice. All of us must be equal in our land of freedom and before God, our Creator.

This evening we read a prayer that we will read many times during these Days of Awe: *Uvechen*, attributed to Rabbi Jochanan Ben Nuri, who lived almost 2,000 years ago, when the Romans were persecuting the Jews of Palestine. Most of us will find these words familiar, but this Rosh Hashanah, they carry a special significance:

> Eternal God, cause all Your works to stand in awe before You. Let them all become a single family, doing Your will with a perfect heart. … Grant hope to those who seek You, courage to those who trust You, and cause the light of redemption to dawn for all who dwell on earth. Then the just shall see and exult, the upright be glad, and the faithful sing for joy. Violence shall rage no more, and evil shall vanish like smoke; the rule of tyranny shall pass away from the earth.[2]

How much we need this prayer this year! How much we need hope and courage and the light of redemption. How much we need to pray that violence will end, that evil will vanish, that tyranny will disappear.

This is a year already laden with pain, worry, and concern. Let it also be a year filled with hope and courage. Let it be a year of reaffirmation, a year of reconsecration to the values of our congregation. Let it be a year when we support one another, a year of strengthening ourselves and our families and our neighbors, a year when we feel God's presence in our midst, a year in which our shofar proclaims what God requires of us: to seek justice, to love mercy, to walk humbly with our God.

1. Jerry Fallwell, Sr. was a Christian fundamentalist pastor, televangelist, and conservative commentator. He was quoted by John F. Harris in "God Gave U.S. 'What We Deserve,' Falwell Says," *Washington Post*, September 14, 2001, C3.
2. *Gates of Repentance*, 32.

Who is a (Good) Jew?

Rosh Hashanah Morning 5762
September 18, 2001

I always had thought that Katharine Graham was Jewish.[1] Her father, Eugene Meyer, was not only Jewish but descended from a family of rabbis. In recent years she had been honored by several Washington Jewish organizations as if she were a member of the Jewish community. Participating in a memorial service at which I officiated, she seemed quite comfortable in a Jewish service.

So when the announcement was made that her funeral was to be at the Washington National Cathedral, I was surprised. A few people called me with the same reaction. She was, after all, a patrilineal Jew who seemed to take pleasure in her ties to the Washington Jewish community.

This is a game that we Jews play all the time: Was so-and-so Jewish, or *really* Jewish? Does the fact that they had Jewish parents count, if they never acknowledged their own Jewish identity? Do we count self-denying Jews? Does it matter that they converted to another religion or were baptized? Does it matter that they experienced anti-Semitism? Does it matter what they thought about their own religious identity? Or was the common perception of the community enough? There are so many marginal Jews—from Heinrich Heine to Benjamin Disraeli to Gustav Mahler to Hank Greenberg to Fiorello LaGuardia (his mother was an Italian Jew)—that some people make this their full-time hobby!

As for Katharine Graham: I was wrong. While it is true that her father, Eugene Meyer, was Jewish, his Jewishness was a subject that was not only sensitive, but taboo—never discussed by anyone in the family. Katharine Graham tells us in her autobiography, *Personal History*, that "remarkably, the fact that we were half Jewish was never mentioned. I was totally—incredibly—unaware of anti-Semitism, let alone of my father's being Jewish. I don't think this was deliberate. But there was enough sensitivity so that it was never explained or taken pride in."[2]

Indeed, the family had a pew in St. John's Episcopal Church on Lafayette Square, and all of the children in the family were baptized at home when Katharine was about ten years old to satisfy her devout

Lutheran maternal grandmother. Despite these rituals, Katharine Graham reports, "For the most part, religion was not part of our lives."[3]

Were there any Jewish experiences in young Katharine Meyer's life that might have shaped her identity or enriched her life? She describes three Jewish memories, all negative.

In school, her class was reading *The Merchant of Venice* aloud, and one of her classmates suggested that Katharine should be Shylock the Jew because she was Jewish. She asked her mother if she was Jewish and what that meant, but her mother avoided the subject, [and Graham did not remember the answer].[4]

Second, at the University of Chicago, she was kept out of a couple of clubs on campus because she was "considered Jewish," as Graham puts it.[5]

Third, Katharine and her husband were about to purchase a house in Washington during World War II when they learned it was in a restricted area, zoned against sales either to Jews or Negroes. While it was illegal, the Grahams backed away from the fight. Katharine reports, "It took me totally by surprise."[6]

Katharine Graham noted that her father had supported Jewish organizations because they were good for the community, not because they were Jewish, and that she followed in her father's philanthropic footsteps. Clearly, she was a woman of remarkable commitment to her city and a host of worthy causes, and she gave generously of herself and her resources. Yet she did so as a caring human being, not as a Jew.

How sad for her that she missed out on learning about anything Jewish, that she was untouched by Jewish rituals or holidays, that the Jewish line in her father's family stopped with her. Katharine Graham was denied by her parents the opportunity to learn about her father's Jewish heritage because *he* did not care about it and wished to distance himself from Judaism.

Eugene Meyer had grown up in a Reform congregation in San Francisco where he had learned Jewish history and Hebrew, "but when the time came for his bar mitzvah, he declined."[7] His relationship with Judaism was to flee from it, to deny it, and to make sure it was never discussed in his family. As a result, his daughter Katharine grew up with absolutely no sense of what Judaism meant nor how it related to her. It took only one generation for this "distinguished Jewish family" (as

Katharine Graham calls it) to lose all personal connection with Judaism and Jewish life.

And so, this year, when you hear the sound of the shofar, I want you to hear Rosh Hashanah calling to us—this year, as every year—asking: What is *our* relationship with Judaism? Where is *our* connection to Jewish life? What is *our* commitment to Jewish values? Where is *our* Jewish identity grounded? How can we as a family ensure that our children will value their religion and that specifically Jewish values will be sustained through future generations?

I ask these questions in light of the latest survey of the Jewish community, the *2000 Annual Survey of American Jewish Opinion*, conducted a year ago for the American Jewish Committee. In that study, 80 percent of the Jewish individuals surveyed said that intermarriage is inevitable in an open society such as ours. Half said that it is racist to oppose Jewish-Gentile marriages, and fewer than half said that it would pain them if their child married a Gentile. The respondents to this survey think that intermarriage is inevitable (and I would agree), but they also do not see this as a problem for Jewish survival (here, I disagree).

It has been ten years since I have spoken on the issues of mixed marriage and Jewish survival on the High Holy Days, and it is time to do so again. The New Year we welcome today also will bring us the results of the 2000 *Population Study of the American Jewish Community*, results we should await with some trepidation. The last study (released in 1991) revealed that the rate of intermarriage already had risen to about 50 percent from nearly zero in the 1950s.

The recent opinion study by the American Jewish Committee tells us that most American Jews surveyed think that intermarriage was inevitable, and that most are neutral about it. In fact, more people think that marriages between Jews and gentiles are a positive good (16%) than those who strongly disapprove of these marriages (12%).

We see the truth of these statistics here at Temple Sinai:

- in the growing number of mixed married couples joining the congregation,
- in our nursery and religious school communities,
- as we plan bar and bat mitzvah services,
- and when the young people of our congregation become engaged.

The larger Jewish community deals with these trends, predictably, by studying them, by wailing and blaming, and by writing books. Every year one or two books appear about this subject: *Embracing the Stranger, Opening the Gates, Rabbis Talk about Intermarriage, Imagining the Jewish Future, Strangers to the Tribe.* The books are written by sociologists such as Egon Mayer and Gary Tobin, journalists, or writers with a personal story to tell.

Have no doubt that we Jews love to talk about, write about, and read about the elusive and changing nature of Jewish identity. Some of the books and articles sound a panic alarm, while others calmly reassure that there is no cause for panic.

As for me, I find the statistics alarming. Without wailing and blaming, I must say that the crisis is not imaginary.

I do not doubt that the rate of intermarriage now exceeds 50 percent, nor do I doubt that a large and growing number of Jews accept intermarriage as an inevitable part of American Jewish life in the 21st century. We have welcomed non-Jewish spouses into almost all of our families, including my own, even as we wonder what it means and what to do about it.

We are too polite to ask the difficult questions, even in our own family: Has she thought about conversion? What religion will you practice in your home? In what religion will you raise the children? Will they even know that one parent is Jewish? What will it mean to them? What does it mean to you?

We are afraid to ask these questions because we don't want to hurt or offend. Surely, we do not want to push this couple away. And perhaps most importantly: The core value today that we embrace is not Jewish survival but universal human values. We are liberal in our minds and liberal in our hearts. The worst thing we could do is judge someone by their religion or race or ethnic background; that would violate our deeply held belief that all people are the children of God. That is our ethic.

We work, live, and study among more non-Jews than Jews; they are our friends and neighbors. How can we think of ourselves as better than they are? How could we not welcome them into our homes, our lives, our families? We scorn narrow-mindedness of previous generations of Jews and rejoice in the security of our Jewish community in America.

We have stopped telling our children to have Jewish friends, date only Jews, marry a Jew.

In Washington, and at Temple Sinai, I believe we are on the cutting edge of an integrated Jewish community. We do not live in Jewish neighborhoods; we are not part of a strong multi-generational Jewish community; we believe deeply in those liberal and universal human values such as the pursuit of justice for all and the equality of all people. Our young people are surrounded by intermarried couples who are doing just fine. And we, of course, are only the Jews who care enough to join a congregation, educate our children, and come to services today.

All in all, I am pessimistic about the chances for Jewish survival unless we heed the sound of the shofar, unless we ask ourselves the question today and begin today to answer it as well: What is *our* relationship with Judaism? Where is *our* connection to Jewish life? What is *our* commitment to Jewish values? Where is *our* Jewish identity grounded? How can we as a family ensure that our children will value their religion and that specifically Jewish values will be sustained through future generations?

Each year I discuss this with my Confirmation class. As we explore their identities, their expectations, their hopes and desires, I have learned something very interesting. Almost all of them feel good and comfortable about being Jewish. Most of them see themselves continuing to participate in a Jewish community, in ways much like their parents: joining a congregation, sending their children to religious school. Most of them see Judaism having a role—not a big role, they might add—in their adult lives.

To my surprise, my students often minimize the role Judaism plays in their family; they have what we used to call an "inferiority complex" about their Judaism. They assume that already they are not "good" Jews, because good Jews go to the synagogue every Friday—or every day. Many have internalized the notion that Orthodox Jews are "better" than Reform Jews; hence, as Reform Jews, they are not good enough. Often, I point out that their parents may have taken on a major responsibility in the congregation, or that they themselves have been coming to the synagogue at least weekly for many years (we call it religious school), and that this has been a significant and meaningful part of their lives. But I know they go off unconvinced.

And when I ask about marrying someone Jewish, most say that

while they want to be Jewish, have a Jewish home, and probably raise Jewish children, they can't possibly say whom they might marry. If they can see themselves as married, they assume they will marry the person with whom they fall in love. I point out that they are more in control of whom they might fall in love with and marry than they think. I point out that the more you have in common with your spouse, the fewer basic conflicts you have. I point out that if you really want to establish a Jewish home, it is a lot easier if both partners are Jewish. Usually they agree—out of logic, politeness, or respect for the rabbi (another important value).

These conversations with class after class of students each year have led me to the conclusion that the Jewish community studies are asking the wrong questions.

Instead of focusing on the rate of mixed marriages, we should be focusing on the extent to which our young people—single, married, living together—are making Judaism and specifically Jewish values an integral part of their young adult lives. Instead of putting all our attention on the fifteen-minute wedding ceremony, we should direct our attention to the role Judaism will play in this new family.

In interpreting the Torah portion we read this morning, the rabbis of the Midrash invented a dialogue between God and Abraham at the beginning of the story. In Genesis, God says, "Take your son, your only one, whom you love, Isaac" (Gen 22:2).

The rabbis asked, "Why did God have to use four expressions to tell Abraham to take Isaac?" They invented this dialogue between God and Abraham:

God: Take your son.

Abraham: Which one? I have two sons, Ishmael and Isaac.

God: Your only one.

Abraham: They are both only sons from their mothers.

God: The one whom you love.

Abraham: I love both of them.

God: I mean Isaac.[8]

This invented conversation shows us more than a little reluctance—and chutzpah—on the part of Abraham; it contains echoes of Abraham bargaining with God for the inhabitants of Sodom and Gomorrah. Reading the Akeda, we wonder why Abraham followed God's command so quickly, without argument. Why is Abraham, once so argumentative, now almost silent? He speaks a word to the angel, he speaks to God, he speaks to the servants, and during the entire three-day journey, he speaks not a word to Isaac. Only when Isaac asks about the sheep for the burnt offering does Abraham reply, "God will see to the sheep" (Gen. 22:7-8). Part of the power of this story is that it is a story about life and death and yet it is told with so few details. Isaac not only is Abraham's favorite son; Isaac is Abraham's hope for creating a people and the fulfillment of God's promise and covenant with him. Isaac is the first link to Jewish survival, yet on their three-day journey, Abraham is silent.

How often are we silent with *our* children—not just about Jewish survival but about *their* survival as Jews? How often do we fail both to tell them and to show them what is most important to us in our Jewish lives? How often do the most important questions go unasked? How often are we—like Abraham—afraid to discuss issues of deepest importance to us?

Today is a day to discuss these issues of deepest importance, a time to consider our Jewish lives and futures, a time to think about where we stand as Jews, a day to commit ourselves to the strength and survival of our people, a time to measure the successes and failures of our own Jewish lives.

Katharine Graham was not a patrilineal Jew after all—because her parents simply chose not to rear her as Jewish. They chose instead to expunge Judaism from their family's conversations. We may find that attitude deplorable or threatening, but it is actually far more widespread than we might think. Ten years ago, the Jewish population study identified 5.2 million people in the United States who consider themselves to be Jews. They also discovered another 1-1/3 million people born to Jewish parents who have converted out of Judaism or who are following another religion.

The belief that mixed married couples are most likely to follow Judaism turned out to be a myth. Today we know better. Some partners in a mixed marriage convert to other religions, some follow other faiths, and many follow no religion at all.

I certainly understand the need for all to respect the religious and cultural differences among us. I, too, believe that we are all children of God; all legitimate believers; all equal in the eyes of our country. In America, we have grown from prejudice to tolerance to celebrating our diversity and distinctiveness as members of diverse religions and cultures.

There is no shame, however, in feeling pride in your own people, your own heritage, your own history. I fear we are not giving our children at home the knowledge and understanding of what it means to be a Jew, what it means to follow Jewish practices, celebrate Jewish holidays, and—perhaps most importantly—embrace Jewish values. The synagogue cannot do it alone. *Sending* your children to religious school is not enough. *Teaching* them the blessing for the Shabbat candles is not enough. Setting aside every Friday night for quiet family time, a special meal, and/or communal worship—demonstrating the value of Shabbat—is quite another story altogether.

I want our children to be committed Jewish adults. If they choose to marry, I would want them to marry Jews by birth or conversion, as you would expect me to. I know that many of them will not. What is primary, however, is that I want all of our children to understand and feel that Judaism is a significant part of their lives. I want them to establish Jewish families (recognizing that what we mean by "family" changes). I want them to lead Jewish lives, to observe Jewish holidays, to pray Jewish prayers, to read Jewish books, to study Jewish topics, to give *tzedakah*, to rear Jewish children (if they choose to rear children), to strengthen the Jewish community, to belong to a synagogue.

I want our children to be committed Jewish adults not just because I believe in Jewish survival. I want our children to be committed Jewish adults because we as Jews have a message to bring to the world. The world needs our Jewish perspective on justice and mercy. The world needs to understand—as we do—the strength and power of community. I want our children to be committed Jewish adults because I believe that we are part of an eternal people that calls to each of us and can strengthen each of our lives. I believe that the world needs our Jewish message of the unity of all people and our Jewish responsibility to work to repair our world.

How can we ensure that our children become committed Jewish adults—or at least work toward it? We can do it by caring about Judaism ourselves and letting our children and students know how much we care. We can do it by speaking openly and thoughtfully—with respect and sensitivity—about our Jewish future, in our families, our community, within our people.

Our biggest struggle at Temple Sinai and in our schools is not with people who want the best, but with those who want the least. When you are ten years old, it may seem that every extra activity is of equal importance, though some may be more fun than others. As parents, however, we need to teach our children that Judaism, soccer, tap dancing, and Tae Kwon Do are not of equal importance in the long run. Yes, each activity teaches values and skills. Only Judaism teaches you who you really are; only Judaism teaches you what is ultimately important; only Judaism gives you a path to follow from the moment you are born until the moment you die—indeed, a path that is vital to those who came before you, all-important to those who come after you—a path to a way of life that is intellectually satisfying and emotionally fulfilling.

None of us here can even imagine Judaism being a "forbidden" topic at our dinner tables. None of us here deny our Jewishness to the extent that our children do not know what being Jewish means.

At the same time, all of us here must work to integrate Judaism and Jewish values into every facet of our lives: to place Judaism in our hearts and on our minds, that we may live it with all our strength and being.

1. Katharine Graham was long-time publisher and chairman of *The Washington Post*.
2. Katharine Graham, *Personal History*, (Vintage 1997), 51-2.
3. Graham, 52.
4. Graham, 52-53.
5. Graham, 81.
6. Graham, 158.
7. Graham, 6.
8. Hayim Nachman Bialik and Yehoshua Hana Ravnitzky, *The Book of Legends, Sefer Ha-Aggadah* (New York: Schocken Books, 1992), 40, and the midrashic sources cited there.

Looking Towards Israel From Afar

Rosh Hashanah Morning 5763
September 7, 2002
Yom Kippur Morning 5763
September 16, 2002

Have you ever wondered how Abraham knew *where* to take Isaac to be sacrificed?

In the Torah portion we read this morning, God first commands Abraham to take Isaac to "one of the heights that I will point out to you" (Gen. 22:2). Two verses later, we read, "On the third day Abraham looked up and saw the place from afar" (Gen. 22:4). How did Abraham know the place? Did God point it out to him? Why is this detail in the story?

In eleventh century France, Rashi speculated that Abraham saw a cloud over the mountain, a sign that this was the place. A century later, Nachmanides, writing in Spain, surmised that Abraham saw the land of Moriah. Almost three hundred years later, the Italian commentator Sforno wrote that Abraham saw a place for sacrifices on Mount Moriah, and Sforno added that Abraham was able to see it from afar because God granted him the vision to perceive the appointed place.

Today, we understand Mount Moriah to be the Temple Mount in the Old City of Jerusalem. The ancient Rabbis connected the name Moriah with the Hebrew word *mora*, meaning "awe," for this is a place inspiring great fear and awe. Atop the mount today you see the Dome of the Rock, or Mosque of Omar, built in 691 C.E. Inside the Mosque is a huge rock, the very site—according to tradition—of the attempted sacrifice of Isaac, and the very same rock from which Muhammad ascended to heaven. Abraham, after all, is the common ancestor of Jews and Muslims alike, and this place is sacred to both religions.

Today we would all recognize Mount Moriah, or the Temple Mount, from afar, with its distinctive gold and silver domes just above the Western Wall, the highest point in the Old City of Jerusalem. Abraham, however, saw only a hill with a cloud over it, or smoke rising from its top. Perhaps the text tells us that Abraham saw the place from afar to heighten the suspense. As Bible scholar Nahum Sarna points out, "The sight of [the place] from afar immediately stirs consciousness of the actuality of the impending horror."[1]

As Abraham saw from afar the place that would come to be so emblematic, so pivotal, so critical, so do we see the Land of Israel from afar, from a distance that is partly geographic, partly psychological, partly in our hearts.

My grandmother looked upon Israel from her native Poland, just outside Warsaw. While she and my grandfather chose to emigrate with their son to the United States in 1907, my grandmother was a deeply committed Zionist. She kept a copy of the Israeli Declaration of Independence in her home, countless tree certificates, and on the wall, recognition of her many years of volunteer work for Pioneer Women. Much as she loved and believed in the idea of the State of Israel, she never traveled there, and she did not pass on her Zionist commitment to subsequent generations. While she took great pride that all of her eight grandchildren graduated from college, most of them have never been to Israel.

Rachel Lapidot looked upon Israel from Russia. Not long after the Revolution, she and her husband left Moscow to settle in the land of Israel. Her husband became a bank manager, providing them with a comfortable living with which to raise their five children. They built a home in Jerusalem, a home I stayed in during my second year of rabbinical school more than thirty years ago. Rachel Lapidot taught herself to read Modern Hebrew—Eliezer ben Yehuda had said that if you are Jewish you must learn Hebrew—and she read every word of the Hebrew newspaper each day. She listened to each hourly news broadcast on radio or television from early in the morning until bedtime and mourned every loss and rejoiced in every victory as if it were her own family. In fact, it was her own family, for the sense of *nachat* (pride) and closeness in Israel is remarkable. From Mrs. Lapidot, I absorbed the sense of destiny that she and her generation of Israelis felt. She taught me something of the suffering they must endure, something of their yearning for peace and security, something of what it was to survive riots, wars, and bombings. She showed me the promise of Israel, and she taught me to respect Jewish practice and tradition in all its variety.

I always had looked upon Israel from the distance and safety of America. While I bought trees in religious school each year for Tu Bishevat, my grandmother's love of Zion got lost between the generations. The Reform Judaism of the 1950s—when I was growing up—was ambivalent at best about the importance of Israel to Jews. Prime Minister David Ben Gurion told my generation that to be a fulfilled Jew, one must live in Israel. Others told us not to take him seriously, but it was more than a little troubling to be told that our type of Judaism was not authentic. It was troubling because more than anything, as American Jews, we wanted to be accepted and authentic.

We Jews wanted to be accepted where Jews never had been accepted in the United States: in neighborhoods, colleges, and the workplace. As Reform Jews, moreover, we wanted to be accepted as a legitimate stream of Judaism. We Jews wanted to be accepted as an authentic religion, albeit a small minority, in American religious life and culture. Our life—and our Jewish life—was in America. I couldn't get my grandmother to tell me much at all about what she called "The Old Country," and we never discussed Israel.

Israel, for much of my family, was a distant place of Jewish importance, with the emphasis on "distant." It was a tourist destination for a very special, perhaps once-in-a-lifetime trip, which would be filled (of course) with great meaning. It was not a part of our daily lives. We had no family in Israel; we knew no one who lived there.

And so I went to study for a year at the Hebrew Union College in Jerusalem, the first in my family to make the trip of my grandmother's dreams.

Not surprisingly, it was far more than a special trip. It was an encounter with myself and my Judaism that I never could have anticipated. Israel taught me about Jewish life and Jewish suffering and Jewish history. Israel taught me about Jewish values I had taken for granted or ignored. Israel taught me about Jewish acceptance and the power of Jewish peoplehood.

After that year, I no longer saw Israel from a distance, for now I was part of Israel, and Israel was part of me. After that year, I understood that Israel was my country, in a different way from the United States, and that part of me belonged there. Now I understood that what bound me to *Eretz Yisrael* was that it was the center of Judaism, that its destiny was my destiny.

At the end of my year in Israel, I told each of the various merchants in my neighborhood—the bank clerk, the launderer, the corner grocer—that I would be leaving soon and returning to the United

States. Uniformly, their response was, "What, you're not staying? Why do you have to leave? When will you return?" While they understood that I needed to finish rabbinical school, they spoke as one speaks to a close friend. They made me feel as if I were deserting them and the Jewish people. I still hear their voices reaching out to me.

"On the third day, Abraham looked up and saw the place from afar."

How do *we* look upon Israel? Israel is far more than just another country. Israel is the Jewish homeland. Some of us have family or friends there, and they are in our thoughts constantly these days. Many children of this congregation have made *aliyah* and some still live in Israel. Many of us have visited Israel, and we remember some of the power that Israel has over our souls. Others still look forward to their first visit and regret that visits to Israel have become so tough.

Some of us read the headlines from afar and weep; we think of the fear Israelis live with each day, how their lives are disrupted, how they are grieving: the deaths and injuries of so many, a broken economy and profound isolation in these trying times. Some of us read the same headlines through a lens of universal social justice. Some feel the plight of Palestinians, who hate the oppression they feel and who long for the freedom that an independent state will bring. Some are troubled by the harsh treatment of Palestinians and wonder at Israel's ability to continue—as it has in the past—being a light to the nations.

These are contentious and confusing times. How can the Jewish state—a nation that is part of our lives as Jews—seemingly oppress people living within its borders? On Yom Kippur we will read, "When a stranger resides with you in your land, you shall not wrong him ... you shall love him as yourself, for you were strangers in the land of Egypt" (Lev. 19:33-34). How can Israel reconcile this commandment to love the stranger with the treatment of so many Palestinian strangers? On the other hand, for those of us who love Israel, how can we not do everything in our power to preserve the safety and security of the Jewish homeland? These are the questions we must ask ourselves this Rosh Hashanah, as we look at Israel from afar, from this distant land.

Before September 11, I would have said, "from this distant land of safety and security," for we Americans felt powerful, invulnerable, and removed from the kinds of fear with which our Israeli sisters and brothers live every day. As some people said in the wake of the September 11 attacks, "Now we are all Israelis."

This sea change in America helps us better to understand the questions before us in this New Year. The fear and horror are fresh in our minds, and though the fears may have lessened, they are always with us now. At times we felt like hostages to our fears, taking precautions with our mail, searching for medicines we never heard of for diseases we prayed would never be inflicted upon us.

September 11, and the events that followed it, demonstrated first that we are vulnerable, and second, that out of our fear can come ugliness and hatred. We have been forced to confront deeply held feelings and determine which values are most precious to us as Americans. Almost a year later, we still do not have all—or even many—of the answers. We do know there are many uncharged prisoners sitting in detention, but we do not know how many, or who they are, or where they are. We have tightened some of our security and found ways to make ourselves feel safer and able to resume our lives, but we will never feel entirely secure again. Now we know what it is like to feel like captives: afraid to open our mail, afraid to ride the Metro, afraid to take a plane.

Over the centuries, we Jews have learned how to deal with fear and how to reach out to captives. We have a long—and often overlooked—history of freeing and ransoming captives. You may hear an echo of it in the *Gevurot* prayer we read in the *Amidah* at every service. This morning we prayed, "Your power is in the help that comes to the falling, in the healing that comes to the sick, in the freedom You bring to the captive..."[2] Freeing the captive was not just the subject of prayer, but the work of Jewish communities who sought to do God's work themselves.

We know from the Mishnah, written two thousand years ago, that Jewish captives were ransomed by their communities. We know from the Talmud, completed a few centuries later, that the Romans routinely arrested Jews, who were then freed with funds from their community. In the Middle Ages, Jews were held hostage by pirates as well as by the emperor or other civil authorities, and Jewish congregations and communities had communal funds specifically set aside for the ransom of captives.

Just as we collect *tzedakah* funds today for the needy in our community, for resettlement of Jews in Israel, for direct support of Jews in Argentina, for flood victims in Prague, so for centuries did Jews have a specific fund for *pidyon shevuyim*, or the ransom of captives. Medieval *tzedakah* boxes sometimes had multiple compartments so that coins could be directed to different causes, and this was an important one.

In one particularly harsh instance of oppression, Emperor Rudolph of Habsburg enacted cruel laws against the Jews in the Rhine and Main valleys in the thirteenth century. He forbade them to leave their houses during Holy Week and disqualified Jews from public service. At the same time, he sought loans from the wealthier Jewish families. Many of these families decided to leave Germany for the Land of Israel, led by their rabbi, Meir of Rothenberg, who was a great Talmudic authority known throughout Europe as Maharam. As he was leading his families across Europe toward Palestine, Rabbi Meir was recognized, seized, and imprisoned by the Bishop, acting on behalf of the Emperor. The Jewish community offered 20,000 marks for the release of their rabbi, but Rabbi Meir declined to be ransomed for such a large sum, fearing that other rulers would try to extort money from a Jewish community by arresting their rabbi. So Rabbi Meir died in prison in 1293. Even then the Emperor refused to release his body for burial for fourteen years, until a hefty ransom was paid.

In our own day, Jews were ransomed from Nazi Germany, some by individuals of means who were able to obtain the release of their family members, some by institutions such as the Hebrew Union College, which paid for students and teachers at the Berlin Hochschule to come to America. It was a privilege to be able to ransom and rescue Jews, to free our people from captivity.

Today, the Jewish community of Israel is in captivity. They are captives of terrorism. They are captives of an ongoing Intifada that has paralyzed daily life. They need our help and support. You have heard and read about the essential emergency campaigns, that I support, but now I am referring instead to the other kinds of support we must also give our sisters and brothers in Israel. Now it is our turn to ransom the captives, to do our part to support them because they are our people, and we are all responsible for one another.

When I first learned about *pidyon shivuyim*, the ransom of captives, I never imagined that it would be relevant in my own lifetime.

Unfortunately, we now can imagine the unimaginable: Daniel Pearl held hostage and murdered because he was Jewish; Israeli Olympic athletes held hostage 30 years ago; a government (even our own) arresting and detaining hundreds of people because they are of a different religion. In the face of the unimaginable, then, our responsibility extends beyond money to other kinds of support we must give to our people in the State of Israel. We must understand that these are days when the most basic human instincts are at work: ensuring our safety, protecting our children, preserving the freedom to live our lives without fear. As they are for us, so much more so are they for Israel. These are times of great fear, times of difficult decisions, times of distrust. The poisonous fear that so many Israelis feel has not only made them hostages but also has led them—justifiably in some cases, unfortunately—to distrust their neighbors. The fear has driven such a wedge between Jew and Arab that many of the Israelis most eager for peace no longer can speak to their potential partners for peace.

Listen to the words of Rabbi Michael Boyden, writing last week from Hod Hasharon, near Tel Aviv:

> "We approach the New Year with more than a little uncertainty about the future. ... Two years of Intifada have taken a serious toll on our society. Hundreds have been murdered and thousands have been injured and maimed in a bloody war against Israel that has not distinguished between soldier and civilian and in which men, women, and children have been murdered as they went about their daily lives. No society could undergo what we have suffered daily without being scarred by the effects of terrorism. If 9/11 has changed America, then how much more so the almost daily assaults against our citizens. . . .
>
> "It has served to increase the level of antagonism and distrust between Israelis and Palestinians. ... the delicate relationship between Israeli Jews and Arabs [is threatened].
>
> "The damage to Israel's economy in a time of world recession has been particularly harmful. Tourism is dead. ... Businesses are cutting back. ... The average wage has declined a full 5% since last year.
>
> "A nation cannot undergo what we have sustained over the past two years ... without there being casualties."

It is a chilling report from Rabbi Boyden, who will speak at our congregation this fall.

At this time of crisis, as our people are held captives of terror, we must not distance ourselves from the people of Israel. We must not look at their plight as from afar.

We must, for the moment, put aside our criticisms, letting the Israelis criticize themselves. From this distance, we cannot know the fear they feel, the risks they must take, the vulnerability that pervades their lives.

What can we do? What should we do? We can educate ourselves, studying the history of Israel and the Zionist movement to help us understand better what the Israelis call *hamatzav*, the situation. We are beginning our year of study about Israel on Sunday, September 29, from 10 until 1, with a teach-in on Israel. We are following up with a fall adult education class beginning in November. We are developing new materials on Israel for students and parents throughout our religious school. We are welcoming two leading Israeli Reform rabbis to speak to our congregation in November. I am organizing a February study mission to Israel from our congregation. In April our music committee is planning a special program to celebrate the ever-flourishing cultural life of Israel. Our ARZA committee is planning additional programs and activities to enable us to reach out to our people in Israel and show them our support.

We need to reach out in tangible ways, as well. I propose that we adopt at least one family that is suffering from the effects of terrorism. We can do much more to support the Israeli economy by purchasing Israeli products and asking that they be carried in our local stores. We can create in our congregation a community of support and caring for Israel.

I am not suggesting for a moment that we abandon our hope for peace. Nor must we forget the plight of millions of innocent Palestinians who also suffer. This summer on our vacation in Italy, Sherry and I were explaining to our hotel waiter that we did not eat pork or shellfish. He nodded knowingly and said, "So you're Jewish. I understand. I am Palestinian." His comment took us aback, but then he told us his story: that he was born in Bethlehem, educated in Cyprus, and now hoped for a successful career in Italy. The tragic bombing at Hebrew University occurred a few days later, and this same waiter expressed to me his sadness that such a thing could happen and that Palestinians and Israelis cannot live together in peace.

I have long been an advocate of better Arab-Israeli understanding and a supporter of the many efforts for peace. I continue to hope and pray for peace, that new partners for peace will be found among the Palestinian people, that the climate will change from distrust to cooperation, from bitterness to caring. May those days of hopeful anticipation for peace return soon, and may the promise of *shalom* be fulfilled.

We enter this year with so many feelings. We feel profound sadness at the lost hope of peace. We feel dismay at the suffering of our people in Israel. We feel empathy for their plight and concern for their future because we are part of *K'lal Yisrael*, the Jewish people, and Israel is the soul of our people. We look from afar; we see the place; we must understand their sacrifice; we can only imagine their struggle. We face the new year with hope for better days. This is a difficult time to be Jewish. It is an even more difficult time to be Israeli. We must stand together.

1. Nahum Sarna, *Jewish Publication Society Torah Commentary*, Genesis, 152 (note on Gen. 22:4).
2. *Gates of Repentance*, 105.

To Tell the Truth

Kol Nidre 5763
September 15, 2002

When I was a student in college, my parents' automobile insurance company introduced a new premium discount for young male drivers. To qualify, I had to take a supervised test. We jumped at the opportunity, and I signed up for the examination.

I expected a test of my driving knowledge with perhaps a few questions thrown in to see if I was a wild young man, likely to drive recklessly. Instead, the true-false test began by explaining that it was to determine whether or not I told the truth. After a couple of introductory questions came this one: "I always tell the truth."

I stopped and pondered. This was, after all, a test of whether or not I told the truth. But, to be honest, there were circumstances under which I did not tell the truth. Like anyone else, I told white lies to be polite, to get out of awkward situations, to save embarrassment, to avoid hurting someone else's feelings. I might say, "I had a really nice time," when in fact I had a terrible time.

I considered my options on the test and decided that I did not always tell the truth, so I checked "false." The same question appeared many more times on the test, in many different variations. Each time I had to stop and think about the line between telling the truth and lying and the philosophical nature of automobile insurance premiums in those days.

The good news is that I passed the test, and my parents and I received the discount!

From time to time I think about that test: about how hard I puzzled over it, the questions it raised about the limits of truth and falsehood, and the meaning and implications of telling a lie.

Yom Kippur is a day of such testing for all of us, a day for us to examine the truths and lies we live by. Having asked forgiveness from our spouses, our children, our parents, our friends, and our colleagues—as we all have done in the last few days since Rosh Hashanah—we now search our own hearts and souls for the ultimate truths so that we may encounter and speak directly to God.

The Jewish New Year—our New Year—begins with days of heightened moral consciousness, a week-and-a-half when we are commanded to consider the essential truth of our words and deeds. We are given this gift of time: time to examine our lives over the past year, time to recall when we have fallen short of truthfulness, when we have dissembled, evaded, prevaricated, or misrepresented.

The Kol Nidre service begins with a legal formula releasing us from all vows, obligations, or promises we make that we cannot fulfill. While we understand these as religious promises, why is the highlight of our most sacred service in the entire year not a prayer, but a formal legal statement? Why do we focus on vows rather than deeds? At a time when we are most spiritual, why begin our holiest day of the year with a legal formula?

We begin Yom Kippur with Kol Nidre because the rabbis understood—as we ourselves know still to be true—that we are human, that we miss the mark, that we make promises we cannot keep, that what we intend and what we do are far apart. We begin Yom Kippur with Kol Nidre because we dedicate this day to renewing our lives, our words, our obligations. We begin Yom Kippur with Kol Nidre because we know that we evade the truth, speak words we do not mean, and make oaths we do not fulfill.

While this formula dates back at least to the eighth century Common Era, its words and theme especially ring true this year.

We live in dishonest times. In the year just past, we saw leading corporations such as Enron and WorldCom fall under the weight of the lies they told; we saw the decline of accounting firm Arthur Andersen, which certified some of the falsehoods. The Roman Catholic Church concealed the misdeeds of scores of priests and developed a conspiracy of silence to hide its truth. As the weeks rolled by this past spring and summer, we all were stunned at the level of deceit in the business and religious communities.

The corporate culture that thrives in many companies, we learned, is one of deception. The motivating factor for this deception is simple greed. Greed and greed alone have encouraged people to conceal financial truths, inflate stock prices, and destroy the financial futures of thousands of loyal employees. What is lost, ultimately, is more than money; what is lost is confidence in our fellow human beings.

As Sissela Bok points out in her insightful book, *Lying, Moral Choice in Public and Private Life*, "…veracity [is]…a *foundation* of relations [ships] among human beings; when this trust shatters or wears away, institutions collapse."[1]

So public confidence has collapsed, and the stock market has collapsed with it. The government's response—requiring chief executive officers personally to attest to their company's financial filings—only begs the real questions: Where is our commitment to truth? Can we not expect honesty?

The concepts of truth and truthfulness, deception and lying that Professor Bok explores are complicated moral issues that all of us face in our professional and personal lives.

- Should physicians withhold the truth from dying patients to alleviate their fear or anxiety?
- Should professors exaggerate the accomplishments of their students as they recommend them for jobs or schools?
- Should journalists lie to sources if it is for a story to expose corruption?[2]

There are many ways that we are misinformed, Bok points out, but a lie occurs when the speaker intends his or her statement to mislead.[3] There are many types of lies, some of which may be justified: lying to protect colleagues or clients, lying for the public good, lying for the sake of sociological or psychological research, or lying at a time of danger or crisis.

The executives at Enron, however, lied to fill their own pockets. The Arthur Andersen executives lied to protect themselves and their pockets. And while some of the Roman Catholic bishops surely lied to protect priests, they did so at the expense of the individuals whose lives had been damaged. In situation after situation, many of those who lied were the very people who were trusted to certify and stand for the truth.

Yes, it is only human to lie. That is exactly why we Jews have Yom Kippur: to bring us back to the truth. In the *Ashamnu* prayer we sing and read several times, we admit:

- *dibarnu dofi*, we have defamed;
- *tafalnu shaker*, we have spoken falsely;
- *yaatznu ra*, we have given bad counsel;
- *kizavnu*, we have lied.

Today we will confess to many sins that we have not committed, but most of us are guilty of stretching the truth with the intention to deceive.

Nevertheless, as Professor Bok points out, one lie leads to another, and soon we are trapped in a web of lies. We make up our own justification and our own rules about the truth, and we lose touch with the truth itself. We lie even to ourselves. Yom Kippur comes to make us break that cycle: to confront our lies and our shortcomings.

In some religious systems, lying is always wrong. The fourth century church father St. Augustine declared that God forbids all lies and that anyone who lies is guilty of sin. St. Augustine identified eight levels of lies, but stated that all eight were wrong.[4] Over the centuries, Aquinas, Pascal, and others continued to develop this theological position.

Within Judaism, on the other hand, there is more flexibility.

Abraham and Sarah, for example, clearly lied to protect their lives. As they journey from one place to another, Abraham tells Sarah to say that she is his sister, not his wife. Abraham's explanation is that Sarah is so beautiful that the king will kill Abraham in order to marry Sarah. This story, repeated three times in Genesis, obviously was a favorite of the biblical authors.

Later, when Abraham and Sarah are visited by three divine messengers, Sarah laughs at the prediction that she will have a child. One of the angels asks why Sarah is laughing, saying, "Is anything too wondrous for God?" (Gen. 18:14-15). Suddenly the tone of the encounter has changed, and Sarah is frightened. Realizing that she is speaking directly to God, she lies and says, "I did not laugh"; but the angel messenger, wanting to make it clear that Sarah must acknowledge her lie, responds, "You did laugh."

While the rabbis of the Talmud assumed their colleagues would tell the truth, they listed specific exceptions. They said, for example, that rabbis might lie to avoid being boastful or to avoid embarrassment for themselves or others.[5] For the rabbis of the Talmud, truth telling was assumed, but it could be put aside to preserve other important values.

The truth of our words is linked to the biblical concept of justice. We read tomorrow afternoon in Leviticus: "You must not act deceitfully nor lie to one another...You must have honest scales and weights" (Lev. 19:11, 36). Our translation says "honest scales and weights," but the Hebrew, *moznei tzedek* and *avnei tzedek*, refers to weights and balances that are *just*, not honest. For the author of Leviticus, truth is not just a matter of transparent honesty, but of justice.

What is the difference between "honesty" and "justice"? Justice relies on honesty and the assumption that the people seeking justice are telling the truth.

In a famous Talmudic case, two persons appear before a court, and each is holding a part of the same garment. Each of them says, "I found it," and each of them says, "It belongs to me." What is the court to do? Rather than being asked to bring evidence to substantiate their conflicting claims, each is required to swear that his share in the garment is not less than half. Then the garment is kept by the court, and its value is divided between the two claimants.[6]

Why do the rabbis ask for a sworn statement rather than witnesses or other evidence? Because the rabbis placed such a high value on telling the truth that they could imagine no better evidence than a sworn statement. They could not conceive of lying. Why do the rabbis have the claimants swear that *at least half* of it is theirs, rather than the entire garment? Because if both men had found the garment and taken hold of it at the same moment, their claims would be identical and each only would be entitled to half. Although each one claims that he is entitled to the entire garment, the court does not want to require them to make a sworn statement that might be false. The Talmudic rabbis reasoned that while it was possible that someone might cheat in financial matters, it was impossible that someone would swear falsely. Testifying in a court or making a sworn statement is a precious privilege in Jewish law, not an obligation to be evaded.

Jewish law is based on the assumption that we speak truthfully, that we do not bear false witness against our neighbor. It is the bedrock of Jewish ethics and all social ethics, and central to our Jewish concept of justice.

How much we need to remember these values on Yom Kippur: the day our tradition calls *Yom Hadin*, the day of judgment, the day that gives us no choice but to be truthful. We live in a time when greed overpowers truth. We live in a time when so many bend and distort truth for their own purposes, a time when the question is not, "How can we preserve the truth?" but "How much of the truth can we conceal?" We live in a world that needs to hear our commitment to truth and to justice. Our responsibility, as Jews, is to proclaim these values, to be a light to our nation.

On Yom Kippur, we have no choice but to be true to ourselves and true before God, for our soul-searching and our prayers are a charade if they are not grounded in the truth. This is our one day of the year for painful introspection, *heshbon hanefesh*, the scrutiny of our souls. This is difficult and demanding work, for all of us have been less than honest: first with ourselves, then with one another, and ultimately with God. All of us have deceived and dissembled and covered up our lies with other lies.

Yom Kippur is a day to be released from our lies, to turn toward the truth, even though the truth can be painful.

In the fourth century Common Era, a Talmudic rabbi named Rava told a story about a town called Kushta.[7] He began, "I used to think that there was no such thing as truth in the world until I heard this story about a place called Kushta," where everyone always told the truth and no one ever broke their word. Kushta also was a place where no one ever grew old.

In one retelling of the story, a king heard about this place where no one grew old and, like many other people, did not want to grow old himself. So he went to Kushta with a huge bag of gold. He stepped out of his carriage in the town square and shouted to the crowd, "I have a handsome reward for anyone who will tell me what I want to know!"

"What do you want to know?" asked one of the townspeople.

"Tell me," said the king, "why the people of Kushta never grow old."

The people looked at one another. It never had occurred to them that no one grew old because they had no comparison, so they couldn't answer the king's question.

The king, however, thought they were silent because they did not trust him, so he held up the bag of gold, raised his right hand, and said, "I am a king, and you can take my word for it. I swear to you I will reward you handsomely if you tell me your secret."

"It's no secret," one of the men said. "This is a town of trust. In our language 'Kushta' means truth. As long as we live, we always tell the truth. I guess that's why we live so long." Everyone in the town square nodded, and some of them held out their hands for the gold.

But the secret didn't sound like anything of much value to the king, and he pushed them back. They looked surprised and shouted, "What about the gold? You promised to give us the bag of gold!"

The king was no fool. Why should he give them his gold for nothing? He took his bag of gold, jumped into the carriage, and sped off. By the time his carriage reached the palace, however, the king who had broken his word had died.

And in Kushta, something even stranger happened. The people who had never grown old suddenly began growing older. When the king broke his promise in the town of truth, the trust of the town was broken, too. The people of Kushta didn't trust one another any more.

And today, the story concludes, if a traveler should happen to stop at the town called Kushta, she would find it hardly different from any other place.[8]

Today we live in a time of broken trust, a time when truth is dispensable. We live in a time when we cannot believe the word of others, when we suspect even the words of our leaders. We live in an age when the truth is manipulated and massaged and masked, a time of secret truths and public falsehoods. We live in a time when truth is spun by spinmeisters, when truth is "packaged," when truth is "timed" to be "leaked," and when truth is evaluated by focus groups.

In our time of broken trust and broken words and broken truth, Yom Kippur comes to return us to the truth, to return us to trust, to return us to the golden value of our word and our words. As people of unclean lips, as people who have fallen short, as people who have gone astray, let us return this Yom Kippur: return to truth, return to trust, return to one another, to ourselves, and to God.

1. Sissela Bok, *Lying, Moral Choice in Public and Private Life* (New York: Vintage Books, 1999), 31.

2. Bok, xxvii-xxviii.

3. Bok, 6-8.

4. Bok, 33 ff. Augustine's works on the subject are called "On Lying" and "Against Lying."

5. Baba Mezia 23b-24a. This is discussed in Louis Jacobs, *Jewish Values* (Hartmore House, 1960), 151-52.

6. Baba Mezia 2a.

7. Sanhedrin 97a. The original story is also reprinted in C. G. Montefiore and H. Loewe, *A Rabbinic Anthology* (Schocken, 1974), 398-399, #1090; and in H. N. Bialik and Y. H. Ravnitzky, *The Book of Legends* , translated by William G. Braude, (Schocken, 1992), 701, #126.

8. The retold story is in Molly Cone, *Who Knows Ten?* (UAHC, 1965), and in Steven M. Rosman, *Sidrah Stories* (UAHC, 1989), 141-44.

Strangers and Citizens, Fences and Security

Kol Nidre 5764
October 5, 2003

You know the Hebrew prayer, the *Ashamnu*, which we read this evening: an alphabetical acrostic, using the sequence of first letters of words to form an alphabet with an embedded message. The *Ashamnu* says that we have sinned: from Aleph to Tav, or (in English) from A to Z. Clearly, we sin in both languages, and—to their credit—the translators and editors of our prayer book have created an acrostic prayer in English to capture the style—if not the literal meaning—of the *Ashamnu* prayer.

Tonight I want to go right to the end of the English alphabet to talk about what we in the business might call the "x-sin": xenophobia. We may joke about this word, for it seems a stretch in the context of a prayer, but tonight I believe there are few sins more immediate and more pressing upon our society and upon our lives as Jews than xenophobia: the fear of strangers.

The two passages we read tomorrow from the Torah are linked by their focus on the *ger*, the stranger, or resident alien, in our midst. Tomorrow morning, we will see in Deuteronomy the powerful image of the entire community standing together before God: men, women, children, and "even the stranger in your camp" as they enter into the covenant with God (Deut. 29:10). These *gerim*, or strangers, are not Israelites, but they are participants in the covenant between God and the Jewish people.

The afternoon Torah portion that we read from Leviticus expands on the position of the *ger*, the stranger, in the Jewish community: "When strangers live with you in your land, you must not oppress them. The strangers who live with you shall be to you like citizens; you shall love them as yourself, for you were strangers in the land of Egypt" (Lev. 19:33-34).

Thus as Jews, we are commanded repeatedly and clearly to treat strangers fairly, to consider them citizens, to love them as ourselves. This is a theme—an essential and seminal teaching. We must treat strangers as our own people because we were strangers in the land of Egypt. With direct knowledge of what it is like to be "strangers in the land," the authors of these texts and subsequent commentators understood how easy it is to take advantage of a minority group, and they applied an ethical imperative that still speaks to us today.

How much we need reminding of that imperative today in America, in the land of Israel, and in our own lives. We are a nation still recovering from the trauma of tragedy, a nation at war, a nation plagued by fear of terrorism. In these days we have compromised our imperative of welcoming the stranger, and we have let our suspicion of others sabotage our value of being a haven to the oppressed of the world.

Like so many of your grandparents, my grandparents came to these shores not just to escape the pogroms of Europe, but in search of freedom and better lives. They survived the difficult voyage to become strangers in a new land that adopted them—more or less willingly—and that they, in turn, eagerly embraced. I think of them and their enormous loyalty to America, which gave them a new life and new hope, as I reflect on the many immigrants who helped to build and continue to strengthen our nation today. I am proud that Temple Sinai's history includes commitment to the Sanctuary Movement in the 1980s as well as providing job opportunities on our staff. We have worked around issues of communication and reached out across linguistic barriers because it is the right thing—the Jewish thing—to do.

Today our nation, however—in the name of patriotism—is suspicious of innocent immigrants who seek what our grandparents sought: freedom and a better life.

In the wake of September 11, Congress—at the urging of the Administration—passed the USA PATRIOT ACT to allow the indefinite detention of immigrants and other non-citizens. Our government did not need to show that these people are terrorists when it imprisoned more than 1,200 men of Middle Eastern and South Asian descent and refused to disclose their identity, location, and the reason for their detention, or when it sought to question an additional 8,000 men who are lawfully in the United States.[1]

Now we can treat U.S. citizens as "enemy combatants," detaining them in military facilities without charges, without access to legal counsel, without judicial review.

Now the Justice Department is seeking to expand its powers through the Domestic Security Enhancement Act, "PATRIOT ACT 2," which would provide for summary deportations without charges or evidence if the Attorney General suspects that the immigrant may be a risk to national security.[2]

Many of you know much, much more about these laws than I do. What I know is that these are laws not of patriotism but of nativism. They are laws not of protection but of suspicion. They are laws that tear at our nation's commitment to welcome the stranger and replace that welcome with mistrust. These laws have compromised the civil liberties of thousands of legal residents and immigrants, and they have created new fears and suspicions.

As Americans, we must be concerned about civil rights; we must be concerned with the legal protection of the accused—and the unaccused; we must be concerned with public suspicion turning into harassment.

And today—as Jews—we must listen to the words of Torah: "When strangers live with you, you must not oppress them. ... Love them as yourself, for you were strangers in the land of Egypt." Today, we are commanded to know the heart of the stranger.

How much security is enough?

What is its human cost?

When does our quest for national security destroy the values that have built our nation?

At Temple Sinai we have studied civil rights and national security through our most recent Zwerdling Shabbaton program and understand many of the issues that confront our nation and confront each of us. I am proud that our Reform Movement is the first Jewish organization to take a stand on these issues, and I hope our congregation's Critical Issues Committee will provide leadership. Let us raise our voices on behalf of the innocent strangers in our midst and their families who suffer with them.

These are frightening times for us as Americans and as Jews, and these are terrible times for Israelis. We all want a secure Israel: as Jews, as Zionists, as Americans, as people of good will. We all want peace in the Jewish state. There must be an end to the terrorism of yesterday and the many incidents before it.

I believe that the only way to achieve a peaceful and secure Israel is through a two-state solution. And I see that an expanded American role is the only way to achieve the peace that we desire and desperately need.

No less do the majority of Israelis want peace through the same two-state solution, but how can they find it when they are under siege?

No less than America does Israel need to welcome the stranger, to protect the stranger's rights, to treat the stranger fairly. Essential to the Zionist dream of a democratic Jewish state is a state that places paramount importance on human rights. Yet how can we work to establish these human rights, and protect the rights of the stranger, in the face of terrorism? Has the Zionist dream turned into a nightmare?

As we know, the Israelis are constructing a fence to mark the border between Israel and its Palestinian neighbors. The fence serves two purposes: It is for security, and it is a symbol of the authority that Israel must maintain. The struggle now is to determine who will be inside this fence and who will be outside this fence.

Would that this fence might keep a sense of well-being—*shalom*—inside, and terrorism outside.

Would that this fence would say to those Jews who have settled illegally in the West Bank : "Know that you are outside the border."

Would that this fence would keep weapons out and permit people to enter to find work or medical treatment.

Would that this fence were a temporary measure to establish security today and create good neighbors tomorrow. That is my hope. Yet I know that no fence can do all this, that no Israeli border can possibly provide all the security Israel so desperately needs. No fence will keep out all the terrorists.

Israel's needs speak to us especially today, on the thirtieth anniversary of the Yom Kippur War, a grim reminder—especially yesterday and today—of Israel's constant need for security and its struggle for peace. How well I remember that terrible news: the shock and dismay we all felt. A newly ordained rabbi, I was leading Yom Kippur services for the University of Cincinnati Hillel when word reached us of the attack. How our prayers that day were filled with anguish and fear! And, indeed, Yom Kippur has never been the same!

This day for me, since then, comes not just as the Day of Atonement, but as a day that reminds us of our unity as a people and our links to Israel. On this day especially we remember that our fate is linked inextricably with the fate of Israel, that as Jews we must look to Israel for support and be Israel's support as well.

We can and must support Israel through programs of our Temple

Sinai ARZA chapter, national ARZA, and the Jewish Federation, and by advocating on behalf of Israel. We can support Israel with our contributions. This year I urge you to support Israel with a visit, joining with many other American Jews who will be traveling to Israel in the coming weeks and months. Join us on our Temple Sinai trip this December, or go another time. Just *go*. Support Israel with your dollars, yes, but this year support Israel with your feet.

Israel must have peace and security. Israel must have our support. Israel must renew the Zionist dream. Writing in the Israeli press and in the American *Forward* newspaper, Avraham Burg shared his own anguish at what has become of the Zionist dream. No one could be a stronger Zionist: Burg served as speaker of the Israeli Knesset from 1999 to 2003 and is a former chair of the Jewish Agency for Israel. Yet he writes:

> "It turns out that the 2,000-year struggle for Jewish survival comes down to a state of settlements, run by an amoral clique of corrupt lawbreakers who are deaf both to their citizens and to their enemies. A state lacking justice cannot survive. ... Even if the Arabs lower their heads and swallow their shame and anger forever, it won't work. .... We have grown accustomed to ignoring the suffering of the women at the roadblocks. ... The children of Palestinians ... spill their own blood ... because they have children and parents at home who are hungry and humiliated."[3]

This grim assessment calls out to us to embrace a value that Israel must hold dear: Listen to the voice of the stranger.

Can our brothers and sisters in Israel hear that anguish? Of course they can, and they must, as they heard in the official Or Commission Report released last month. This Israeli government commission courageously investigated the events and the causes of the current Palestinian Intifada, which began in October 2000. The Commission pointed out, "The behavior of the Arab sector leadership contributed to the depth of the events and their force," and also stated that "government handling of the Arab sector has been primarily neglectful and discriminatory. ... The state did not do enough or try hard enough to create equality for its Arab citizens or to uproot discriminatory or unjust phenomena."

Both terrorism and abuse must stop.

The only hope, in my mind, is working to build pockets of understanding and caring, working to create a new generation of leaders who are sensitive to the security needs of Israel and the human needs of the Palestinians. I have shared with you in the past my sabbatical experiences with *Shatil*—neighborhood and community development— and civil rights organizations in Israel. I know what a difference they can make.

The voice of the stranger must be heard in Israel just as it must be heard in America. Certainly Israel must be guided by Torah: "When strangers reside with you in your land, you shall not wrong them. The strangers who reside with you shall be to you as your citizens; you shall love them as yourself, for you were strangers in the land of Egypt."

Can Israel treat strangers as citizens? It always has striven for that goal. Can Israel love the strangers in their midst? It has no choice but to work for it. Can Israel be restored as a light to the nations and a society of peace, justice, and equality? That is Israel's destiny, and we must work with Israel to achieve it.

This is a vision that falls somewhere between optimistic and messianic in its hopefulness. There are many tasks to accomplish, many leaders to find, many challenges to overcome before this is even thinkable . . . and many changes to effect that are not in our control.

Yet we must remain hopeful, for that is our task. Clearly we cannot hope for peace without understanding, nor is it possible to achieve a democratic society in Israel without justice. Still we ask, "Who will bring the peace? Who will be able to make the breakthrough?"

For centuries the Jewish people has waited for the Messiah to solve the problems of this world and provide us with hope for the future. Especially in difficult times, we have waited and watched for the Messiah.

One rabbi said that the Messiah would come disguised as a beggar. The Messiah would not come until everyone who passes her reaches out a hand to help.

Still other rabbis said that the Messiah would appear as a Gentile, to remind us that God speaks through all human beings.

One rabbi related that the Messiah would be found at the main gate of Rome (for the rabbis, this was the gate of the enemy). What was he doing there? Sitting among the beggars and changing their bandages, one by one.

When will the Messiah come?

When will peace come to all?

When will we learn to love the stranger?

When will we put aside our suspicions for a moment and worry about people *and* security?

"When will the Messiah come?" Rabbi Joshua asked the Messiah, and the Messiah answered, "Today," but he meant, "Today, if you would only hearken to my voice."[4]

Our task, as Jews, is to listen to the voice, to recognize our sin of xenophobia, to reach out to the strangers in our midst. We must listen to that sacred voice and to our own hearts, and find peace and security and the strength to work for a new day.

1. "Surveillance under the USA Patriot Act," www.aclu.org..
2. ACLU Fact Sheet on Patriot Act II, March 28, 2003, *ibid.*
3. Avraham Burg, "A Failed Israeli Society Collapses While Its Leaders Remain Silent," *Forward*, August 29, 2003.
4. Sanhedrin 98a; see C.G. Montefiore and H. Loewe, *A Rabbinic Anthology*, 583; and Louis I. Newman, *The Talmudic Anthology*, 279.

Showing Up, Belonging, Caring

Yom Kippur Morning 5764
October 6, 2003

I often quote Woody Allen to the Confirmation class: "Eighty percent of success is showing up."

Yom Kippur should be a *10* on the "showing up" scale. We'd like to think that everyone shows up for Yom Kippur (although not everyone does, of course). We'd like to think that the holiest day of the year reaches out to almost every Jew: to show up, to fast, to repent. We'd like to know that there is at least one Jewish occasion (why not the most important day?) that summons the entire community.

Most likely, that one Jewish occasion is not Yom Kippur, despite our expectations and despite the many people we see here today. The most recent National Jewish Population Survey, released just last month, found that only 59% of Jews fast on Yom Kippur, while 77% attend a Passover Seder. Clearly: Jews like to eat more than they like to fast. So what else is new?

But what about showing up? The Torah portion we read this morning describes a covenant ceremony that places paramount importance on showing up. The text begins, "You stand this day, all of you, before Adonai your God—your ... elders and officials, all the men of Israel, your children, your wives, even the stranger in your camp ... to enter into the covenant of Adonai Your God" (Deut. 29:9-11).Moses then continues: "I make this covenant, with its sanctions, not with you alone, but ... [also] with those who are not with us here this day" (Deut. 29:13-14).

Now, if everyone in the Jewish community were there, from the highest to the lowest, who was missing? What did Moses mean when he said, "Those who are not with us here this day"?

The rabbis of the Midrash had an answer, of course. They said that the phrase refers to those who were *spiritually* present, the souls of all future generations of Jews.[1] The twelfth century French commentator Bekhor Shor added that this phrase also refers to converts to Judaism, proselytes who would cast their lot with the Jewish people in the succeeding centuries.[2]

Who didn't show up? The people who were not born yet or who had not yet decided to join the Jewish people. In other words, to the rabbis of the Midrash, all the Jews were present and the covenant was binding on succeeding generations—all of *us*.

This is a curious idea for us hardheaded moderns. *We* were present at Sinai? *We* were obligated by that generation?

These same questions were posed by Isaac Abravanel, in fifteenth century Spain. He asked, "Who gave the generation of the wilderness which stood at the foot of Mt. Sinai the power of obligating all those who would arise after them?"[3] Abravanel, of course, answers his own question: "There is no doubt that if a man receives a loan from another that the duty of repayment falls on him and his descendants. Just as the children inherit their parents' property, so they inherit their debts. Even though the children were not alive when the debt was incurred, they are still responsible for repaying it."[4]

Writing during the Spanish Inquisition, Abravanel also said, "Though they and their descendants would do all in their power to assimilate, they would not succeed. They would still be called Jews against their own will and would be accused of Judaizing in secret and be burnt at the stake for it."[5]

How powerfully Abravanel's words resonate with us post-Holocaust Jews, especially with the words of the Kol Nidre prayer still echoing in our ears, emphasizing the religious vows we cannot keep.

There are Jews who show up, and there are Jews who do not. There are Jews who accept their Judaism, and there are Jews who deny it. There are Jews who cling to their Jewish heritage, and there are Jews who distance themselves from it. There are Jews who feel their Judaism in their heart but don't do anything about it (Cardiac Jews), those who feel their Judaism only in their stomachs (Gastronomic Jews), and those who deny their Judaism altogether. Early in my career as a rabbi, I realized that my concern and energy must be focused on those Jews who do show up—you—but in the spirit of confession, I must tell you that I continue to worry about those who do not.

On this day of the great ingathering of our people, when we read about the eternal covenant incumbent on all Jews, I especially worry about the Jews who are missing, "who are not with us this day." Where are they? How can we reach them? How can we get them to stand with us?

In addition to the National Jewish Population Study, the American Jewish Identity Survey by Egon Mayer also was released recently. The number of Jewish children who say they have no religion has gone up, while the number of Jews who embrace Judaism has gone down. There are more people with Jewish parents than we thought and a smaller and smaller number of them who embrace—or even accept—their Judaism. We all know these people. They are our friends and neighbors. We can gently share with them what our Judaism means to us and set a positive example.

Most striking to me is how few Jews belong to a synagogue. In the most recent study, only 46% of self-identified Jews belong to a congregation. In some cities and in smaller communities, the percentage is much higher, and in other cities, such as Washington, it is much lower. Who isn't showing up in synagogues? More than half of the Jewish community. They ignore or reject or repress or perhaps are ignorant of the emotions and motivations that bring us together here today.

I am not talking about the people who are too old or too sick to go out. I am not talking even about the few of our congregants who may think that some meeting they have today is more important than Yom Kippur. I think they're absolutely wrong, of course, but I'm not talking about them.

No. I am talking about the more than 50% of Jews in America who have nothing to do with the Jewish community. For it is not as if the Jews who do not belong to synagogues connect to the Jewish community in other ways. Some do, but the overwhelming majority does not. Only half as many Jews belong to a Jewish community center or another Jewish organization. Most of the unaffiliated have no formal contact with the Jewish world at all.

I believe in personal responsibility. Just as everyone should have a doctor and a dentist, every Jew should have a synagogue and a rabbi. Just as every citizen should pay taxes and vote, every Jew should choose a synagogue and attend it.

As I have said before, from this bimah and elsewhere, I believe that the low rate of synagogue affiliation is the shame of the Jewish community. I believe the low rate of synagogue affiliation among Jews is a greater threat to Jewish survival than any other warning we may hear. Meaningful and committed synagogue affiliation strengthens the individual, the family, the congregation, and the Jewish community.

What does it mean to belong to a congregation? There are many paths to the door and many misunderstandings. Some think that the Temple is there to give out tickets for the High Holy Days—catering to the "Revolving Door Jew" who comes in for Rosh Hashanah and goes out for Yom Kippur, never to be seen again until next Rosh Hashanah. Some think that the Temple is there just to educate their children, and they leave once their children graduate from high school—or earlier.

Some think the Temple is there to raise money for itself. When I spoke to my cousin in Arizona last week, his first question was whether or not we achieved our "goal" on Rosh Hashanah. At first I didn't understand what he meant: a High Holy Day appeal. As it turned out, his most significant Jewish memory of the High Holy Days is not hearing the shofar or Kol Nidre or standing beside his parents in the synagogue. His memory is that the doors of his childhood synagogue were locked each year while the president of the congregation made an appeal for more funding, and one year, my cousin—a child then—had to go to the bathroom and was not allowed to leave. I was sad for him, and I simply said that at Temple Sinai, our appeals on the High Holy Days are not for money.

Our goal on the High Holy Days is to enrich and ennoble and to change people's lives. Our appeal is for commitment to Judaism and the synagogue. Temple Sinai is not a health club, where people pay for a workout or a massage. Temple Sinai is not a Jewish community center, where people come and go for an occasional course, or to meet other Jews, or to swim in a Jewish setting.

The sign at our front door tells one and all that Temple Sinai is a *kehilah kedoshah*, a holy congregation, a sacred community that is dedicated to practicing Judaism, teaching Judaism, and living Judaism, with all the ethical imperatives that our religion demands of us. We live or we die as a congregation based on the commitment of our members. We flourish or we fail based not on the number of cars in our parking lot or bodies at our services, but on the strength of the covenant that binds us together.

Yes, our congregation is a place of worship and education and a building to which people come to meet other Jews. But our congregation is so much more than that. Our synagogue is a house of worship and celebration, where people experience the peak moments in their lives surrounded by those whom they love. Our synagogue is a sanctuary of comfort, where we capture the essence of our lives and comfort the mourners in our midst. Our synagogue is a center of commitment where together we pursue justice, strengthened by numbers, to repair our world. Our synagogue is a house of assembly where we reach out to one another and mark significant events in the Jewish history we share, the holidays we celebrate, the texts we study together. It is a sacred community where we grow together and rejoice together and seek God together.

A woman once introduced herself to me as "a paying, but not a praying Jew." It was important to her that she belong to a synagogue, having fled a German Jewish community that was destroyed after she left. But services? "No, thank you. They don't do anything for me." I realized soon enough that she was not being hostile, but honest, and would do her share. I convinced her to be the bulletin editor for a few years, which never required her to attend a service. Just as there are many ways to be a Jew, there are many ways to be an active and contributing member of a congregation. Our synagogue needs many kinds of commitments.

We each need to think of ourselves as "a member for life of Temple Sinai," for this is *your* Jewish life. Membership in Temple Sinai is the communal life we build, the spiritual life we seek, the life of mitzvot we support, the life of study we promote, the life of justice that sustains us all. Temple Sinai unites us in a cradle-to-grave covenant, a sacred thread that binds us to one another and to our congregation.

Our sin this Yom Kippur is *not* not showing up; our sin is not caring enough. Our sin is taking our congregation for granted. Our sin is squeezing the education and the succor and the positive experiences of Judaism that our synagogue offers into a little corner of our very busy lives instead of making it an essential background of our lives. Our sin is in forgetting who we are, in not appreciating the importance of this congregation in our lives. Our sin is in failing to understand the profound significance of the Jewish community that we build here, how it enriches all of us and strengthens our lives. Our sin is in not accepting responsibility, keeping our hands in our pockets instead of reaching out to others. Our sin is in failing to provide the best example for the next generation of Jews, most of whom love being here until some pre-adolescent moment in their lives, when they think it is time to challenge us.

We have good intentions, most of us, like the poor woman who found an egg. She gathered her children around her and told them, "Now we have nothing more to worry about! We will not eat this egg, but I will ask our neighbor to put the egg under her hen. Then we will have a chick, and soon we will have many chicks and eggs. But we will not eat all the eggs or the chickens; we will sell them to buy a calf. The calf will grow into a cow, and we will have milk. Soon we will have calves and cows, and I will sell some of them to buy a field. Then we will have chickens and eggs, cows and calves and fields, and all our needs will be met!"

Just then, as she was speaking, the egg fell out of her hands and broke.[6]

So it is with us. The High Holy Days arrive, and we are filled with hope and expectations. We want to do better in the coming year, and we make our plans. But the days slip by, and our resolve weakens. Our thoughts don't lead to action, and we are back where we started.

May this year be different: May our good intentions grow and lead us to one another. May they deepen our commitment to the covenant we share and to the congregation that brings us together and links us to our God. May we reach out together to one another and to the missing in our midst. May we realize that just showing up is never really enough.

1. *Tanhuma Nitzavim* 3, cited in Jeffrey Tigay, *JPS Torah Commentary*, Deuteronomy, 278; 398 n.27.
2. Jeffrey Tigay, *JPS Torah Commentary*, Deuteronomy, 278; note on 29:14.
3. Nehama Leibowitz, *Studies in Devarim, Deuteronomy* (Jerusalem, 1980), 298. Also cited in Gunther Plaut, UAHC *Torah Commentary*, 1542.
4. Leibowitz, 299.
5. Leibowitz, 302.
6. S. Y. Agnon, *Days of Awe*, 22-23.

Finding Our Place

Erev Rosh Hashanah 5765
September 15, 2004

Sometimes we see things a bit differently from the pulpit, and occasionally we see a drama unfolding before our very eyes. One scene that we see repeatedly involves a couple who come to the service after it has begun. One of them walks in first and finds a seat. A few minutes later, the other one arrives, having parked the car, but she cannot find her husband, who is already seated in the congregation. She looks one way and then the other, but she is looking from the wrong angle, and she cannot spot him. If it takes more than a minute or two, I can almost feel the frustration and then relief as she spots him and sits down next to him. We are in the business of reuniting families and friends, so it is tempting to intervene during the search process (a discreet signal might be enough; at least a mental message), but these couples and families almost always find their way together again, or—to put it differently—she finds her place in the congregation.

This evening, as each of us has arrived, separately or with our family or friends, we have found our places in the sanctuary. On this eve of the New Year, we ask ourselves the larger version of this question: What is our place in the sanctuary? With whom do we sit? Before Whom do we stand?

Our sanctuary does not have reserved seats, purposefully, so our place may change from service to service, from holiday to holiday. The founders of Temple Sinai rejected the practice of reserved seats on the High Holy Days because they believed in the democracy of the synagogue. They felt strongly that where an individual worshipped should not depend on how much support they gave to the congregation, nor on how long their family had been members, as was the practice in many congregations and still is in some. We are all equal before God, our founders believed, and we believe it as well. So our worshippers arrive early (indeed, some too early) to claim their favorite seats in the sanctuary.

The freedom to sit is linked to the freedom to worship, and the freedom we Jews have found on these shores for the last 350 years. These are freedoms we cherish, freedoms we celebrate this year together as we examine the history of American Judaism. The 23 Jewish souls fleeing from Recife, Brazil, sought freedom to worship and to begin their Jewish lives anew as they landed in New Amsterdam. Their numbers grew to 200 or so Jewish pioneers in Colonial America who sought safe haven on these shores. By the eve of the American Revolution, their numbers had grown to almost 2,000. They composed a prayer for the congregation they established in New York City: "As Thou hast granted to these thirteen states of America everlasting freedom ... so mayst Thou bring us forth once again from bondage into freedom."[1] These earliest American Jews came to this land seeking freedom, freedoms we take for granted today: freedom to worship, freedom to practice their Judaism, as our American founders established what some of them called "free exercise and enjoyment of religious profession and worship to all mankind."[2] The Hebrew Congregation in Newport, Rhode Island, wrote to George Washington in 1790 to praise the new government for "generously affording to all liberty of conscience and immunities of citizenship" and thanked God "for all of the blessings of civil and religious liberty" that Jews enjoyed. They wrote, and Washington quoted their words in his reply, that the new U.S. government "gives to bigotry no sanction, to persecution no assistance."[3]

The freedom that the first American Jews sought and found on these shores was a source of concern for some Jews, of course. Congregation Mikveh Israel in Philadelphia reported back to their supporters in Amsterdam: "In this country ... everybody does as he pleases. ... The *Kahal* [or, community] has no authority to restrain or punish anyone, except ... denying them synagogue honors." One immigrant wrote to her parents in Hamburg in 1791: Here "anyone can do what he wants. There is no rabbi in all of America to excommunicate anyone."[4]

Today we have rabbis, we rarely practice excommunication (but beware), and we cherish above all the freedom we have as American Jews. But are there limits to that freedom? Does the freedom extend from doing as much Judaism as you want—to doing nothing? Do we have freedom to hurt the Jewish community, such as the Jews for Jesus campaign currently under way in Washington? Does this freedom have any boundaries at all? Do we have standards about the people we welcome into our Jewish community: those who want to be Jewish or associate themselves with Judaism; those who are married or related to

Jews; those who want to learn about Judaism. Are there people who should not be part of our community? Can we say that we do not consider anyone to be part of us? Or has our freedom given way to license, so that there are no boundaries at all?

Once it was easy to know who was a Jew. Jews wore certain clothes, didn't eat certain foods, scrupulously followed certain laws, and lived close to their synagogues. Today, we don't all look Jewish, we don't all eat Jewish, we don't live among Jews, and we certainly don't all pray Jewish—or at least very often. When I ask, "What is our place?" perhaps I am afraid to ask the real question, "Do we have a place?"

Certainly for many Jews there is no place for Judaism in their lives. Far more than half of the American Jewish community today does not belong to a synagogue, nor in all probability, to any institution of Jewish life. Probably two thirds of the Jews in America have no Jewish place in their lives. I am not the first to express concern about Jewish survival. In 1845, one Jewish physician in New York wrote, "Desperate diseases require desperate remedies," lest the Jewish name in America become "a matter of history, but not of reality." In South Carolina, another wrote in his diary in 1833, "A synagogue as it exists ... will not be found in the U.S. fifty years hence."[5] While the prediction of this twenty-year-old makes us smile, let our smile not be smug or self-satisfied. For there are still far too many Jews who never set foot inside a synagogue from year to year, who are for all purposes lost to the Jewish community.

Have no doubt that the enduring institution of Jewish life is the synagogue. This is the place that Jews gather, meet one another, and meet God. It is the place where Jewish values are studied and put into practice. It is the place of Jewish learning for every generation. It is the crucible of Jewish culture and Jewish life. I rejoice in seeing our seats filled this Rosh Hashanah, but I cannot help but worry about the many Jews who are not in a synagogue to welcome the New Year. What is their place? Where do they meet their people? We do not force anyone into our building, but we must do more to encourage the unaffiliated to find a place for themselves in the Jewish community. Some, to be sure, have consciously decided to plan their Jewish lives outside of the Jewish community. But many, I have no doubt, are not here because they just didn't get around to it. They need encouragement, and we must be willing to reach out and help them enrich their Jewish lives. We must remember our own place and share it this year with others whom we know: our neighbors, co-workers, friends, family who have not yet found a congregation and a place for themselves in the Jewish community.

The seats we sit in this evening as we welcome the New Year remind us of the value of community. We sit with one another, gathered as a large *kehilah*, or congregation, to worship, to remember our commitments, to reflect on our shortcomings, and—above all, for the purpose of this sermon—to reestablish our connection to our people. Many people comment to me about the "large crowds" on the High Holy Days. Some of the early twentieth century Jewish immigrants wrote back to their families in Europe of the strange style of American synagogue architecture: "They build synagogues here in the New World that expand! They have so many people on Rosh Hashanah and Yom Kippur, and so few the rest of the year. It is a godless land where synagogues are showcases."[6]

To this day we make jokes about "Revolving Door Jews," in for Rosh Hashanah and out for Yom Kippur. I don't see this as a description of our congregation, where so many people are involved in study and worship, communal activities, and committee work on a regular basis. You might think that the sanctuary is full of strange faces on the High Holy Days, but it is not. Some people say that even though they have been a member of the congregation for years, they don't know anyone on Rosh Hashanah. While that certainly may be true, most of the people here are also here throughout the year: to learn or be with their children, to participate in one program or another. While the congregation has changed—and grown—over the last two decades, the noble core remains intact. And I certainly recognize most of the faces we see these Days of Awe.

But as our congregation has grown, I ask: How has each of us grown? Has our core—our Jewish core—remained intact? Have we grown in Jewish knowledge? In Jewish commitment? Have we grown in our ability to pray? In our dedication to Jewish causes? Have we remained faithful to Judaism as the core of our being? Do we remain committed to building and maintaining a vibrant Jewish community here in Washington and in America? We come here today to find strength for that sacred work, seeking renewal for the Judaism in our lives and in the life of our community.

In Washington, and at Temple Sinai, it has become too easy to be

Jewishly anonymous. Most of us learned long ago how to act so that we do not stand out, so they will ask someone else to volunteer for a job we might not want to do. We learned how to be one of the "faces in the crowd," and unfortunately the High Holy Days reinforces that feeling of anomie and alienation. Before you leave this service, as you are waiting for the lines to clear, take a moment to introduce yourself to the people around you. The Rosh Hashanah liturgy reminds us that we are all in this together, and this evening and tomorrow we have a special opportunity to get to meet some members of the congregation you might otherwise miss. Don't forget that they have chosen to sit in the same part of the sanctuary.

Many centuries ago, there was a nobleman who sought to create a legacy for the people of his town. He decided to build a synagogue and kept the plans secret until the building was completed. When the synagogue was opened for the first time, all the townspeople marveled at the building's beauty. Someone noticed, however, that there were no lamps. "How," they asked, "will the synagogue be lighted?" The nobleman pointed to brackets that were throughout the building, on the walls. Then he gave each family a lamp that they were to bring with them every time they came to the synagogue. "Each time you are not here," he said, "that part of the synagogue will be unlit. This will remind you that whenever you fail to come, especially when the community needs you, some part of God's house will be dark."[7]

We need to bring our lamps when we come to the synagogue: our lamps of commitment and caring, our lamps for study and worship, our lamps of building a sacred community that we all share in. My first congregation was the only one in Topeka, Kansas. Partly because of its isolation, everyone was on the lookout for new Jewish individuals and families moving to town. It seemed that everyone knew when a new colleague had decided to move there. Often, because they were concerned about Jewish life in the community, I had met them as well. How we reached out to people to join our congregation! How pleased we were to welcome a new Jewish soul or family! How much we need to learn from such communities about reaching out and bringing people in and building a shared community that benefits all of us.

Today we often focus instead on who used to be Jewish. While we feel some sense of pride that there are Jewish roots in the families of both John Kerry and Wesley Clark,[8] we need to remind ourselves that

Judaism has totally disappeared from both of these families. We need to ask ourselves, will Judaism remain in our family? How strong will that Judaism be?

The answer to this question is that Jewish survival depends on building communities, and communities depend on congregations. That is the message of the 350 years of Jewish life in America, and that is the message of our own congregation, as well. In a score of different ways, we build community, we create the opportunity to be Jewish with one another. We reach out with study and prayer and concerts and marches and cooking breakfast for homeless men and visiting sick children and collecting coats and hats and creating a home in Sinai House for people who would not have it. We do it together, just as we sit together this evening and throughout these Days of Awe. We are such a diverse congregation, we must remember this New Year what it is that unites us as a community: a commitment to Jewish values that we share.

It is not enough to know where we sit. We must also know before Whom we stand. "Whom" has a capital W in this phrase that is written in Hebrew over many arks in many synagogues throughout the world. "*Da lifnei mi attah omeid*, Know before Whom you stand" is inscribed over the ark because it reminds us that the synagogue is not just a gathering place, but a place with a purpose, not just a house of the people, but God's house as well. These High Holy Days are infused with much "God-talk," in our prayers, in our presence here, even in our greetings: "May you be written for a good year." Who is doing the writing?

There are some who would say that we write ourselves into the book. After all, our prayer book tells us that our own deeds dictate our future. As Jews, we believe in free will, that we ourselves determine whether our lives are filled with good or evil. On Yom Kippur we will read from Deuteronomy: "See, I have set before you . . . life or death, blessing or curse; choose life, that you and your descendants may live" (Deut. 30:15, 19). Who is deciding and writing? Before Whom do we stand? What do we believe as 21st century American Jews? We are experts at interpretation, at finding metaphors, at redefining. We live in the theological shadow of Mordecai Kaplan, who taught us that Judaism is really a civilization, that we should worry less about God and more about the Jewish people. We are comfortable—perhaps most comfortable—with religious naturalism, an interpretation of Judaism growing out of Kaplan's teachings. It teaches us that we do not need to believe in miracles or the supernatural to be believing, practicing, good Jews. We can believe in God as the forces of good in the world, the still small voice of conscience inside us, the creative forces in nature.

Still, we are accountable before this redefined God—just as we are accountable to a more personal God whom we encounter in our lives and to whom we might pray. My guess is that we do not think about God much during our everyday lives, except for the peak experiences. Yet we come here to welcome the New Year with God on our minds.

What does God expect of us, however we conceive of God for ourselves? Once the Jewish answer was easy: fulfilling 613 mitzvot was the center of the Jewish life. Shabbat observance, *kashrut* or dietary laws, and worship all centered on what God expects of us. Today we have redefined these and other commandments to be our links to the Jewish people rather than to God. And we have redefined the good that we do in the most general terms. We have recast our pursuit of social justice to become community service. Instead of wanting our children to be good Jews, we want them to be good people. Instead of focusing on the Jewish values inherent in mitzvot, we seek the universal principles that everyone can agree upon. We have taken the message of the Hebrew prophet that inspired Jews for generations and made of it universal statements. What does God expect of you? asked the prophet Micah. He answered with words that everyone can take stock in: do justly, love mercy, walk humbly with your God. But do we do these today because God expects them of us or because we just feel good when we do them?

Our prayer book tells us the message of these days and links our actions to God's expectations: Repentance, prayer, and *tzedakah* change God's mind and grant us life.

I hope you remember the story of the man who forgot where he put his clothes when he got undressed each night. To solve his problem, he devised a system. He wrote on a slip of paper each article of clothing and its location, and he left the slips of paper on his bedside table. In the morning, he got up and saw that his shirt was on the hook, his pants in the closet. The system worked, and each morning he was able to pull himself together, or at least get dressed. But one morning, as he stood with the slips of paper in his hand, he began to weep. "I know where my clothes are, but where am I?"

We come here today wanting to know where we are. We come here today looking for our place, looking for the people among whom we sit, looking for the One before Whom we stand. May our search be successful, and our year be sweet.

1. Jonathan D. Sarna, *American Judaism* (Yale, 2004), 36.
2. Sarna, 36. the quote is from New York, 1777.
3. Sarna, 38-39.
4. Sarna, 45.
5. Sarna, 75.
6. Sarna, 175 ff.
7. Story courtesy of Rabbi Mindy Portnoy.
8. John Kerry and Wesley Clark were both contenders for the Democratic nomination for President in 2004; each had a Jewish parent or grandparent.

Mending and Miracles

Yom Kippur Morning 5765
September 25, 2004

Back in the good old days, when people used to repair their shoes, shoemakers (cobblers) would walk through the town, knocking on doors and ask if people had any shoes to mend. People would hand their shoes to the cobbler who would repair them on the spot. Once, in a town called Berditchev, in Russia, the town cobbler was making his rounds just before Yom Kippur. He came to the home of Rabbi Levi Yitzchak and asked the rabbi, "Have you something to mend?" Rabbi Levi Yitzchak was overcome with grief and said, "*Weh ist mir*, woe is me, for Yom Kippur is almost here, and I still have not mended myself!"[1]

Today we ask ourselves, "How can I mend *my* life?" Yom Kippur comes to help us mend our spirits and our Jewish lives. It gives us the opportunity to focus our attention on our deeds and our misdeeds. It provides us with the rituals and structure of worship and fasting to mend our souls and our spirits. We can only mend ourselves effectively, however, if we do it with intention and sincerity.

This is the same message we heard in Second Isaiah in this morning's Haftarah. The people ask God, "When we fast, why do You pay no heed? Why, when we afflict ourselves, do You take no notice?" God answers, "Because on your fast day you pursue your own affairs, while you oppress all your workers! Because your fasting leads only to strife and discord, while you strike with a cruel fist! Such a way of fasting on this day will not help you to be heard on high" (Isa. 58:3-4).

God says: You cannot blindly follow the law without changing your heart. You cannot expect a simple fast to make a difference in your life or in the world. You cannot expect to reach Me just by going through empty rituals, just by fulfilling prescribed obligations. God continues: "Is this what you call a fast, a day acceptable to the Eternal? No, *this* is the fast I have chosen: to unlock the shackles of injustice, to loosen the ropes of the yoke, to let the oppressed go free, and to tear every yoke apart. Surely it is to share your bread with the hungry, and to bring the homeless poor into your house; when you see the naked, to cover them" (Isa. 58:5-7).

Second Isaiah, like other biblical prophets, rails against performing meaningless rituals and thinking that they will make up for the injustice we find everywhere in our society. He says that your fast will mean nothing if you do not pursue justice in your life. The prophet Amos speaks for God, saying, "I loathe, I spurn your festivals. … If you bring me offerings, I will not accept them. … Spare Me the sound of your hymns. … But let justice well up like waters, and righteousness as a mighty stream" (Amos 5:21-24).

What are we to make of these pronouncements, we who are gathered in prayer and observance, we who are fasting and offering prayers and hymns? We are, after all, the good Jews, the ones who came to the service and are observing Yom Kippur.

The answer is that the rituals are not enough. They are not enough to change us, nor are they enough to change our world. They are not enough to reach God, nor are they enough to reach our souls. To accomplish the real goal of Yom Kippur, we must look at our actions for the last year and not just vow to better our lives, but to actively seek justice and pursue righteousness. Fasting and coming to a service are not enough.

Last May, as our nation observed the fiftieth anniversary of the landmark Supreme Court decision, *Brown v. Board of Education*, I understood this distinction in a new way. After all the ceremonies, after all the pundits and preachers and presidential candidates, I had my own reflections on Topeka. When we lived there in the mid-1970s, twenty years after the Brown decision, the city still was not integrated. We lived in West Topeka, and almost all of the small black population lived in East Topeka. It was as if there were two cities, for we rarely saw members of the black community anywhere around town. Neither the city's workforce nor its institutions nor its cultural events were integrated. Now the case has been reopened, and we know that despite the landmark decision, despite the celebration, despite the work of many dedicated individuals and groups, the city is still not integrated. There are still two Topekas, as there are two Washingtons and two Chicagos and two Detroits. More than a single court decision, more than words and rituals, more than courage is necessary to achieve justice. There is so much mending to do.

So it is in Russia, as Sherry and I saw this summer. After centuries of czarist anti-Semitism that many of our grandparents escaped; after

Stalinist oppression and cruelty; after years of post-Stalinist refusal to permit Jewish life or emigration, the Jewish community is free to be Jewish again. The leaders of the Progressive Jewish congregations we visited in Moscow and St. Petersburg are capitalizing (you should pardon the expression!) on this new freedom; they are working tirelessly to reach out to their communities, and they are committed to seeing them flourish.

Yet in Moscow that Shabbat, everyone in the congregation was elderly, and in St. Petersburg they have such a very long way to go in their Jewish learning and understanding. The middle-aged and younger people in that congregation know nothing of Jewish religious life. While we rejoice in their new freedom to learn and practice their Judaism, it is practically overwhelming to think about how very far they must go and the obstacles they must overcome, to build a community that cares and shares like the ones in which we live. There is so much mending to do.

We take so much for granted: the opportunity to learn and remember our Judaism, the privilege to celebrate Jewish holidays, the right to gather as a Jewish community. Our struggle is not to overcome oppression but simply to make a little time for Judaism, to choose it when it conflicts with soccer or lacrosse practice. Our struggle is not to be allowed to celebrate our holidays, but to celebrate them with meaning. Our struggle is not to be permitted to learn Hebrew, but to take it seriously. Our freedom as Jews also has meant that we are free to ignore our Judaism, free to think of it as one more extracurricular activity, free to walk away from it because it is just not interesting enough compared to instant messaging and everything else that competes for our attention.

Coming to the Temple is not enough. Coming to the religious school classroom is not enough. Coming to the sanctuary is not enough. We need to understand what is going on. We need to concentrate. We need to take it seriously. We need to see how it fits into our lives, determine who we are, how we live, how our values are shaped. We, too, have a lot of mending to do.

On the first day of religious school the teacher in one classroom I visited was smiling proudly. She was pleased because when the time came to collect *tzedakah*, or righteous giving, every child in her class had brought a contribution. All the children were smiling. I smiled, too.

Every week, in every classroom, we collect *tzedakah*, as do most religious schools in America. Why?

We want to teach our children about the importance of *tzedakah* and the value of generosity. We want our children to grow up with this value and pass it along to others. Many families practice *tzedakah* at the beginning of Shabbat and every holiday. Some families work together to integrate *tzedakah* into family celebrations, such as bar or bat mitzvah. But how many of us really think about the *tzedakah* that we fulfill? Or is it a ritual we do without consideration?

Once our people gave *tzedakah* because it was considered a fundamental religious act: giving *tzedakah* and behaving righteously were central to Jewish life. Our High Holy Day prayer book tells us that *tzedakah*, along with repentance and prayer, are powerful enough to change God's mind during these Days of Awe. We give *tzedakah*—and many still think of it this way—because God expects it of us. We give it as a way of bringing goodness into the world. We give it not out of compassion, but out of a sense of justice. We give it not for what it might bring us, but for what it can bring the world. We recognize that every Jew is responsible for *tzedakah*, even the ones who are recipients of communal funds. We understand, with Maimonides, that the highest forms of *tzedakah* are anonymous gifts and the very highest is giving a person the opportunity to become independent.

I have fond memories of the way that I learned about *tzedakah* when I was growing up. In Jewish stores, of course, there was always a *pushke* or two, a box for contributions to a particular cause. Now we have a penny exchange at the cash register or an empty cup for tips.

And when I was growing up, I learned that every family had its own favorite charity. When something good happened to the family, like a new baby or a graduation, or when something bad happened, like illness or death, friends and neighbors would know what organization the family was committed to, and they would make a contribution to mark the occasion. Righteous giving, *tzedakah*, was a meaningful and public part of the life of each family.

Not any more. Today, when I ask a bereaved family if they would like memorial contributions to go to a particular charity, they most often do not have one in mind. Many want to support medical research for the disease that took their loved one or the hospice that treated them with such compassion. This saddens me, I must tell you, for I think of the life of a person as more than the cause of their death, more than the time that they were sick. I want to know what this person lived for, not what she died of.

I want all of our people to be committed enough to at least one cause that they work for it, support it, and share their resources with it until it becomes *their* cause. We can have many causes, many opportunities for *tzedakah*, but too many of us simply give by default because we are badgered by the requests in the mail and dinnertime phone calls.

Judaism teaches us that it is not just what we give, but how we give that matters. Let us recapture the spirit of *tzedakah*, link it to Jewish values that speak to us, recognize how it can mend us and our spirits, and make it an essential part of our lives.

Making righteous giving a central Jewish theme of our lives will redefine what has come to be seen by too many as a tax deduction rather than a religious act. Making righteous giving central to our lives is a way of finding our place in the Jewish community, of making this year better, of instilling new meaning into deeds that may have lost their Jewish component.

One of the miracles of Jewish life in America, especially in the twentieth century, has been the development of Jewish charities. Many studies have demonstrated that Jews are the most generous of ethnic or religious groups, and the success of scores of Jewish institutions and causes demonstrates the Jewish commitment to generosity. My fear is not that Jews are less generous, but that our giving is no longer linked to the values that have guided our people, that it is seen more as a path to acceptance in the community and less as religious obligation.

My concern is that it is too easy for our children to put the coins their parents give them into the envelope without thinking, too easy for us to write a check, too easy for us to click on "donate now." My concern is that it is so easy that we have lost the intent, the context, the reason for what we are doing. We have separated the act of giving from the understanding that what we are doing is righteous giving, a Jewish responsibility.

In her book, *Rambam's Ladder*, Julie Salamon explores the levels of *tzedakah* delineated by Maimonides.[2] The levels of charity depend on the attitude of the giver, not on the amount. The lowest rung on the ladder is to give begrudgingly, or as Salamon writes, "You can kill the soul of a person by giving him an insincere smile while administering your bounty."[3] The second level is to give less than is proper, but to do so cheerfully. Next is to hand money to the poor after being asked. How many of us wait to be asked when we know the need is present? Next is handing money to the poor before being asked, but risk making the recipient feel shame. Above these are levels of anonymity: allowing your name to be known, giving to people you do not know, or total anonymity. The highest level is the gift of self-reliance: giving someone a loan or gift or work so that he will never have to rely on others again. All of these levels are based not on how *much* one gives, but on *how* one gives. What matters most is our motivation, our values, our understanding.

Would that we might mirror that religious school class, each of us giving with a genuine smile. Would that each of us would give out of a sense of Jewish responsibility, seeking justice and righteousness. Would that each of us would grow this year in our commitment to *tzedakah*, understanding it as a religious obligation and not just kindness to others. Giving, as important as it is, is not enough. We must give with the proper motivation and understanding.

You may remember the story of the rich man who fell asleep during a Shabbat morning service. He woke up during the Torah reading just in time to hear the verses instructing the Israelites to place twelve loaves of challah on a table in the Tabernacle in the wilderness. He thought that God was speaking directly to him, asking him to bring twelve loaves of challah.

The request seemed a little odd, but the man took it seriously, and when he prepared his challah the next Friday, he baked twelve extra loaves and brought them to the synagogue. He decided that the only proper place to leave them was in the ark with the Torah scrolls. He went into the empty sanctuary, opened the ark, arranged the loaves, thanked God for instructing him about what to do, and left.

No sooner had the man left the building than the *shammas*, the janitor, arrived to clean the sanctuary. As he dusted the seats, he prayed, "God, I am so poor. My family has nothing to eat for Shabbat. Unless You can perform a miracle, God, we all will starve!" As he spoke, the *shammas* opened the ark, and there were twelve loaves of challah!

"God," he said, "I had no idea You worked so quickly." He took the twelve loaves home to share with his family.

Minutes later, the rich man returned to the synagogue, curious about whether or not God ate the challah. He went into the sanctuary, opened the ark, and saw that the challah was gone. "You really did eat my challah," the man said to God. "I'll bring twelve more loaves next Friday."

And so the following week the rich man brought twelve more loaves and left them in the ark. Soon afterward, the *shammas* arrived, and as he cleaned the sanctuary, he spoke to God: "I don't know how to say this, God, but we are out of food again. Those twelve loaves were wonderful. We ate seven, sold four, and gave one to *tzedakah*. But now nothing is left. We need another miracle." With that, he opened the ark and found twelve more loaves. "Thank You, God. This is wonderful."

This challah exchange became a weekly ritual that continued for many years. Like many rituals, neither man gave it much thought after a while. But one day, the rabbi was in the sanctuary when the rich man brought the challah. He saw him place the loaves in the ark, and the rabbi saw the *shammas* take them out. The rabbi called the two men together and told them what they had been doing.

"I see," said the rich man sadly. "God doesn't really eat challah."

"I understand," said the *shammas*. "God hasn't been baking challah for me after all."

Both of them were afraid that now God would no longer be present in their lives.

The rabbi asked them to look at their hands. "Your hands," he said to the rich man, "are the hands of God, giving food to the poor. And your hands," the rabbi said to the poor man, "are also the hands of God, receiving gifts from the rich. So, you see, God can still be present in your lives. Continue baking and continue taking. Your hands are the hands of God."[4]

There is so much mending to do in our broken world. May our hands be the hands of God, giving and receiving goodness. May our hands be the hands of God, reaching out to others—here in our own community, in Russia, in communities around the world—to strengthen them. May our hands be the hands of God, pursuing justice, pointing the way to opportunity for others. May our hands and our hearts be one, sharing our bread with the hungry, making our fast today work for righteousness, giving courage to the afflicted.

---

1. S.Y. Agnon, *Days of Awe*, 26. From *Zikhron la-Rishonim*.
2. Julie Salamon, *Rambam's Ladder*, (New York: Workman Publishing, 2003).
3. Salamon, 34.
4. Lawrence Kushner, *Invisible Lines of Connection*, 55-59. The story is attributed to Zalman Schachter Shalomi.

Resurrection and Renewal

Erev Rosh Hashanah 5766
October 3, 2005

Rabbi Joshua ben Levi lived in the land of Israel in the third century of the Common Era. He said that if you see a friend whom you have not seen in twelve months, you are supposed to say a special blessing.[1] As we gather this Rosh Hashanah, some of us have not seen some of our "Temple friends" since the last High Holy Days, and it is more than twelve months since last Yom Kippur. So I invite you (and you don't need to feel guilty, in case you haven't been here a lot) to repeat the blessing after me: *Baruch atah Adonai m'chayeih hameitim.*

The translation of this blessing is "Blessed are You, Adonai, who revives the dead."

Inviting you to recite a blessing that has been controversial in Reform liturgy and the subject of great discussion for centuries is a bit manipulative on my part.

What did Rabbi Joshua ben Levi mean? Did he believe that people die when we do not see them? Have they died in our lives? Did he really invite us to believe in the resurrection of the dead? Or was he simply guiding us in what to say when we see friends after many months? And why say that?

This simple blessing, at the end of the traditional *Gevurot* prayer at almost every Jewish service, has had several versions over the years. The early Reform rabbis pointed out that "modern" Jews do not believe in bodily resurrection, so they changed the language of this prayer. You may remember *noteia b'tocheinu chayyei olam,* "Who has implanted within us eternal life" from the *Union Prayer Book,* or *m'chayeih hakol,* "Blessed are You, the Source of life," in *Gates of Prayer.*

Are these differences minor? Yes, they are so minor that most people probably would not notice them. But the changes are based on what we believe, which is not minor. Do we Reform Jews believe that the dead return to life? When the surviving widow says at the grave of her husband, "I will see you soon!" what are we to understand? Are we speaking in metaphors, or do we really believe that the dead live on—and might return to us some day?

What if I were to tell you that a belief in the resurrection of the dead has been a core belief in Judaism for centuries? (It's true.) What if I were to tell you that the belief in resurrection is not in our prayers by accident, but by design? A belief in resurrection is one of the thirteen articles of Jewish faith articulated by Moses Maimonides, whose work and life we will be studying together this year. He wrote, "I believe with perfect faith that the dead will be brought back to life when God wills it to happen."

While some detractors accused him of not being faithful enough, Maimonides called this belief "a cardinal point of our religion, universally acknowledged by our people, incorporated in our prayers" and said there was "no other interpretation than the literal."[2]

But what of us? Do we believe in resurrection? Can we be good Jews if we do not? What does it mean to us? What difference does it make?

As a rabbi, I am frequently asked what Jews believe about an afterlife.

The simple answer is that different Jews have different beliefs.

Some Jews believe, with the rabbis of the Mishnah and Talmud, that this world is only the vestibule—the entryway or passage—for the world to come.[3] They believe that by fulfilling *mitzvot*—Jewish obligations or commandments—we will earn or merit life in heaven.

Some Jews believe that our lives are examined by God after we die to see if we performed enough *mitzvot* to enter heaven. In his classic story, "Bontshe the Silent," Y. L. Peretz describes the courtroom where the defense attorney and prosecutor confront one another before God, the Judge. There are other midrashic stories of examination or trial, with some individuals going instead to *Sheol*, or purgatory.[4] Thus life continues even after death.

There are many ways to believe in resurrection. This summer, bird watchers and the scientific community were excited by a sighting of an ivory-billed woodpecker, thought to have been extinct in the United States since 1944. Confirmed sightings have given new hope to ornithologists and naturalists alike. Writing in *Science* magazine last June, editor Donald Kennedy ended his editorial on the ivory bill with the words, "*Baruch mechayei Hametim*, Blessed is the One who gives life to the dead."[5]

In the year just ending, the Angel of Death (to use the Jewish metaphor) visited two members of our congregation—worshipping with us this Rosh Hashanah—and was pushed away. One of them suffered cardiac arrest but was kept alive by CPR and paramedics and is now healthy and back at work. *Baruch atah Adonai m'chayeih hameitim.* The other suffered a head injury, a trauma that shut down her heart and lungs, the parts of our body we so often take for granted. Now, after many treatments and operations, she is mending well and back at school. *Baruch atah Adonai m'chayeih hameitim.*

What of the person we have not seen for a year? Were we afraid she had died, and now we are relieved that she is still alive? Rabbi Joshua explains himself by quoting Psalm 31: "I am put out of mind, like the dead; I am like an object given up for lost" (Ps. 31:13).

Are the dead ever out of our thoughts, however? Are they ever given up for lost?

Rather, I believe that Rabbi Joshua is teaching us that seeing is believing. If we do not see someone for a year, we have lost touch with them, and we must mark their return into our lives. The intersection of their lives with ours is cause for a blessing, and the blessing is for the renewal of the relationship, not unlike the renewal of life in resurrection.

Tomorrow morning, we will read another story of life and death, the *Akeda*, or the binding of Isaac. Last month someone asked me a question I have heard many times before: "With all the wonderful stories in the Torah, why do we read this horrible story about child sacrifice?" There are many answers to that question, and we rabbis give a different answer each year. They are called sermons.

Some of you may be aware of the shocking midrash in which Abraham really *does* sacrifice Isaac. The angel cries out a minute too late, the knife comes down, and Isaac is gone. Read Genesis carefully, and you will see that Isaac disappears at the end of the story. As we will hear tomorrow morning: "Abraham then returned to his servants, and they departed together for Beer-sheba" (Gen. 22:19)—without Isaac! Isaac does not reappear until years later, a long time for midrash writers to work with. Some rabbis speculated that Isaac had gone off to study in a yeshivah; others said that Isaac died and was reborn.

Here is the scene they created: When Isaac heard the angel call out, "Do not raise your hand against the boy," Isaac gave thanks and recited the blessing, *"Baruch atah Adonai, m'chayeih hameitim."* Others said that the knife actually touched Isaac's throat, and at that moment he died or saw the light of God or was seized by panic, and uttered the words of the blessing, *"Baruch atah Adonai, m'chayeih hameitim."*[6] Either way, they concluded that Isaac himself was the author of this blessing, praising God for giving us new life.

There is another rabbinic tradition that Satan tried to stop the attempted sacrifice. (I bet you thought we Jews didn't believe in Satan, either. The rabbis believed enough to write about him.) In this tradition, Satan bet God that Abraham would not follow through on God's demand. When Abraham began his journey, Satan went along in various disguises. First he tried to dissuade Abraham; then he tried to convince Isaac to flee. Finally, Satan turned himself into a stream across their path. Abraham and Isaac waded deeper and deeper into the water. When the water came up to Abraham's neck, he looked up and said to God, "You asked me to do this! You told me we had a relationship! What happens if we drown?" God then dried up the stream and they continued on their journey. Perhaps at that point, too, Isaac might have said, *"Baruch atah Adonai, m'chayeih hameitim."*

We have been too close to floods and life and death these past weeks, too close to near sacrifices.[7] As we looked to the Gulf Coast, we saw destruction and devastation such as we have never seen before. One woman, eventually evacuated to New Iberia, Louisiana, said, "For days I sat on the roof of my house watching dead bodies floating by. I am so glad to be alive!" Even from this distance, we have seen so much death, so much suffering. What sense can we make of this tragedy as we enter this New Year?

We have seen so much of death that it is very hard to imagine new life. Can these cities, desolate and polluted, be brought back to life? Can the shattered lives of so many people and families be restored? With all the help that so many people are giving, with all the funds, with all the encouragement: can new life overtake death of the spirit? How can this happen?

This can happen only if we rebuild faith. While we speak about rebuilding homes and businesses and schools, rebuilding cities and towns, what we really need to rebuild is faith: faith in our society that has failed so many, faith in our government that has failed so many, faith in humanity in the light of the looting, graft, and corruption. It was not just the Gulf Coast communities that suffered, not just their hopes that died with the hurricane. Part of us has died as well. For we all have lost faith, we all have felt that it could be us in harm's way. We all have felt that we, too, could be suffering the total loss of these storms and floods. We empathize with our own congregants whose families are there, who attend school there, who have a part of their lives on the Gulf Coast.

We also have lost our sense of confidence in a society—our society— that put so many people at risk, failed to heed warnings, was found wanting to protect life and health in the most basic way. While I will speak on this theme further on Yom Kippur morning, the question we must ask ourselves tonight is whether we can regain the faith and the necessary confidence to see these communities reborn. We, in our relative comfort, from this great distance, can try to empathize with those whose homes and lives and work were blown away. Can we help them say in their own words, *Baruch atah Adonai, m'chayeih hameitim?* To utter those words takes faith and confidence. Partly through our caring and our outreach, I know that many in Mississippi and Louisiana have found the faith they needed. Through the equipment and household goods we have sent to disabled people in Mississippi, through the backpacks our Confirmation class assembled for evacuated children in Louisiana, through the assistance we sent as a congregation to many projects and funds, we have helped to create new faith and confidence.

Listen to the words of Isaiah that we will read as our Haftarah on Yom Kippur: "Your people shall rebuild the ancient ruins, and lay the foundations for ages to come. You shall be called 'Repairer of the breach, Restorer of streets to dwell in'" (Is. 58:12).

We read these words of Second Isaiah with new meaning this year. Originally written around 530 B.C.E., they tell us of the feelings of the Israelites who were exiled to Babylonia in 586 B.C.E. and then permitted to return some 50 years later when the Persians defeated the Babylonians. They returned to a desolated Jerusalem, and the rebuilding went more slowly than hoped. Here the prophet explains that it is not just the physical act of rebuilding, but the spiritual rebuilding that is necessary. The people must also remove the chains of oppression and bring God into their lives. Then will they repair the breach, restore the streets, and lay the foundations for ages to come.

We Jews have a particularly significant message to offer to the world at this particular moment in history, for we have witnessed so much desolation. We have seen our capital, Jerusalem, destroyed by the Babylonians and rebuilt; destroyed again by the Romans and rebuilt. We have seen our villages and cities throughout Europe pillaged by the hatred of pogroms. We have seen our synagogues torched and our cemeteries desecrated. We have seen our sacred books and scrolls forbidden and burned. Over and over again, we have seen our religion attacked and our most precious objects shattered. We have returned to find our towns and cities, our synagogues and academies, destroyed. We have sought faith to rebuild and found these words of Isaiah a source of hope for our people. We have rebuilt so many of our houses and synagogues and communities over the centuries that these memories of rebuilding and rebirth have sustained us and can sustain others. We have returned to witness the destruction of our communities and worked to give our people new life. We have seen the resurrection of the people of Israel over and over again.

Perhaps that is why Rabbi Joshua ben Levi said—prophetically—that if you see someone whom you haven't seen in a year you praise God who revives the dead. We have seen so many dead and seen so much brought back to life. This blessing speaks to us especially on Rosh Hashanah, for the New Year comes with new hope for each of us. Just as Rabbi Joshua understood death and resurrection metaphorically, so we see that this is a season of new life for each of us. All year long, we are constantly being reborn. Our bodies are made up of cells that are constantly dying and being replaced. Our tongues, for example, contain 500,000 taste cells, and each night as we sleep, more than 14,000 are replaced.

Each morning, we are renewed and restored when we awake, and Jewish tradition prescribes that we recite—even before getting out of bed—"*Modeh ani l'fanecha...* I offer my thanks before You, who has graciously restored my soul to me."[8] Does our prayer upon waking mean that we believe that we die each night and are resurrected each morning? Of course not, but it uses this imagery to help us to understand the miracle of life and the importance of waking restored. Just as our sleep renews our bodies, so awakening—and this blessing—restores our spirits. Just as we are supposed to thank God for restoring us each morning, so we thank God each year for the life we have and seek renewal in the coming year.

We have so much to teach and so much to learn this year. Confronted by images of death and desolation, we must be thankful for the safety of our homes and community. Confronted by our history of destruction, we must help others seek the courage to rebuild. Confronted by the fragility of life itself, we must enter the New Year with gratitude and renewed hope. Confronted by the loss of faith of so many, we must find new strength in a new year. *Baruch atah Adonai, m'chayeih hameitim,* We praise You, Adonai, who renews all life.

1. Babylonian Talmud: Berachot 58b.
2. "Treatise on Resurrection" (*Ma'amar Tehiyat Ha-Metim*) in Jacob S. Minkin, *The Teachings of Maimonides*, 402.
3. *Avot* 4:16
4. *Mishnah Sanhedrin* 11:1,2
5. *Science*, 3 June 2005, 1377.
6. Shalom Spiegel, *The Last Trial*, 28ff., especially 30-33.
7. Hurricanes Katrina and Rita struck the Gulf Coast states in August and September 2005. The storms and the flooding that followed caused thousands of deaths and billions of dollars in property damage.
8. In full: "I offer my thanks before You, living and established Ruler, who has graciously returned my soul to me; Your faith is great."

Is the Bible True?

Rosh Hashanah Morning 5766
October 4, 2005

Three times in our service this morning we have read, "*Hayom harat olam*. This is the day of the world's birth." We teach this idea in our religious school: that Rosh Hashanah is the birthday of the world. We talk about the Jewish birthday party for the world. We tell stories about it to our young children, and I often weave this theme into our Tot Shabbat and Shalom Shabbat services.

Do Jews really think that the world was created on one day—or in six days, as Genesis tells us? Where does this myth come from, and how do we understand it?

The ancient rabbis (about 2,000 years ago) were discussing in what months various biblical events might have occurred. One of these rabbis, Eliezer, said that in Tishri (this month) the world was created; also during Tishri, Abraham and Jacob were born, Joseph left prison, and our ancestors in Egypt were released from slavery, six months before they actually left the country. He obviously liked the fall.

Another rabbi, Joshua, said that the world was created in Nisan, in the spring.

Each brought arguments in support of their positions. Rabbi Joshua pointed out that the creation story says, "Let the earth bring forth grasses and trees bearing fruit." This must be in the spring, not in the fall.

Rabbi Eliezer argued that the trees are full of fruit in the fall, not in the spring.[1]

The argument continued and was never really resolved, but Rabbi Eliezer seems to have won the debate. Based on his statement, we have the traditional prayer—found in the earliest Jewish prayer books—that the world was created in Tishri, on Rosh Hashanah.[2] *Hayom harat olam*: This is the day of the world's birth.

I find this connection between Rosh Hashanah and creation charming and poetic, but I do not believe it.

So if I do not believe the world was created on Rosh Hashanah, or in six days, you might ask, "What do I believe about the rest of the

Bible? What are we modern Reform Jews to make of the Bible 'stories'? If one is not true, are they all false?

With evolution under attack, with school districts battling about the teaching of science, and with faculty, administrators, school boards, textbook publishers, and the public all at one another's throats: where do we stand?

For thirty years I have been teaching the play *Inherit the Wind* in Confirmation class, discussing the issues of the consequences of a literal interpretation of the Bible and the conflict between science and religion.

While *Inherit the Wind* is based on the 1925 Scopes trial, the stage directions set the time as "Not too long ago," and the playwrights (prophetically) tell us: "It might have been yesterday. It could be tomorrow."[3] At one turning point in the play, Matthew Harrison Brady, the character based on William Jennings Bryan, is called to the witness stand to testify on the Bible. He reports that a "fine Biblical scholar, Bishop Usher, has determined for us the exact date and hour of the Creation. ... It is not an opinion. It is literal fact . . . he determined that the Lord began the Creation on the 23rd of October in the Year 4004 B.C. at 9 a.m."[4] It seems he agreed with Rabbi Eliezer.

The controversy rages, and in August President Bush offered his opinion that "both sides ought to be properly taught." It is as if the clock has been turned back eighty years, and the scientific discoveries and advances of the last 150 years offer just one alternative way of understanding our world. Evolution is just a theory, some say, and there are many theories we could study—ignoring what the word "theory" really means in this context.

Why are we still having this debate? Why are Creationism and Intelligent Design still considered viable options? What is the real conflict?

It is about whether or not the Bible is true. It is about our belief in religion and how we view the world. It is a controversy that dates back to Moses Maimonides in the twelfth century, who tried to reconcile Aristotelian science with the Bible.

I consider the Creation story in Genesis to be literature, a great legend created by skillful writers to teach us a lesson. I do not think the authors of Genesis were trying to explain precisely how the world operates, as scientists do; I believe they were trying to make sense of the world around them and extract lessons for their lives. The editor of the Torah included two different creation stories, in Genesis chapters 1 and 2, respectively, each with different details and very different styles. He included both, we believe, because both were popular, or sacred, or deemed worthy of inclusion. It obviously did not bother him that they were different accounts. The message was that the world is good, that the gift of life is sacred, that God is the Source of life. If we view them as literature, the details are less important than the messages they impart.

I always am intrigued by contemporary Reform Jews who feel they must explain and justify the details of biblical stories. Not distinguishing between literature and history, they are caught up trying to "rescue" the story from those who would deny its truthfulness. People have told me about how the winds and tides at the Sea of Reeds could have made the waters part. They have "interpreted" the days of the Creation story as thousands of years for each day and attempted to reconcile the discrepancies in the Noah story. For me these stories are legends with a message. Some are parables; we know that many have similar versions in nearby cultures. Other stories are simply delightful. They contain messages of lasting significance. We view them as part of our sacred literature because of the guidance they carry for us and their place in Scripture. But that does not make them true.

For me the Hebrew Bible is an anthology of stories and legends, laws, ethical commandments, history, poetry, and teachings of wise and committed people. As we study these books seriously, we learn that we need to compare some passages to others from neighboring cultures, while some passages convey such a clarion call to justice that their meaning is immediately clear. Some of the laws we find troubling, as the ancient rabbis did 2,000 years ago. Some of them define who we are as Jews in covenant with God. But does our Jewish identity or our relationship with God depend on the truth of these stories? Absolutely not.

Indeed, a modern critical reading of these stories leads us to find them interesting, but not true. We should know them (as educated people and as educated Jews), appreciate them, analyze them as literature, study their origins, and extract the message they have for us. But we should not accept them as factual.

For years I have enjoyed telling stories to young children. I hope they find my stories entertaining, and when they have a message, I hope they understand it. I want them to learn about our cultural heritage, and I want them to appreciate the value that is being conveyed by the story. Sometimes a child will say, "I like that story! Is it true?" I have learned to say, "No, it is not true, but it's a great story, isn't it!" If they are a little older, I add, "The point of the story is important, and something that you should remember, but the story is not true."

Those who fight for inclusion of Creationism or Intelligent Design in school curricula do not share much in common with me. Their faith relies on the truth of the Bible and on the accounts of creation that I view as fiction, which is why my perspective is so threatening to them. My faith relies on God and the moral and ethical teachings of Scripture.

Our daily service does contain a prayer about God the Creator: not the Creator in six days, mind you, but the One who creates light and darkness, who ordains peace and fashions all things. What is meaningful to me is that there is a Creator who cares about us and has filled the earth with goodness and order. There is so much wisdom to take from this story that (for me) to spend energy discussing whether or not it is true misses the point. I do not base my faith on the truth of the Bible, so I am not troubled if science has disproved the details of a biblical story or if literary criticism shows the contradictions in the text.

For me, there is no significant conflict between religion and science.

While both science and religion seek to explain the world, they take different approaches and arrive at different conclusions. They operate in separate realms and have dissimilar goals.

Science describes the world. It investigates and analyzes how the world functions and creates models to help us understand.

Religion may begin by looking at the world, but religion is a search for the values that guide our lives.

The realm of science is "is."

The realm of religion is "ought."

Logically speaking, we cannot deduce "ought" from "is." Science describes bird migrations and earthquakes and chemical reactions, but it does so without passing judgment on any of these physical events.

Religion, on the other hand, may describe events but always points to an inherent value:

Creation tells us the world is basically good.

The exodus tells us to cherish our freedom, but to remember the plight of the slave.

The miracle at the Sea of Reeds teaches us that God protects us.

I want us to feel passionately about the values we find in the Bible, both in the stories and in the laws.

We might ask, "Did Jacob really have a dream about a ladder to heaven?" Instead we should ask, "What are *our* dreams? Can we find God's presence in our own places? Can we find a sacred place in our own lives that we might consecrate, as Jacob did? Are there links to God that we may not have explored?"

When the Torah teaches us not to oppress our neighbor, or to use fair weights and measures, or to pay our employees without delay, we can use that teaching to apply even more widely these rules of fairness.

And so here we are, on Rosh Hashanah, the presumed birthday of the world. What is the message that our liturgy takes from this legend that we read at the sounding of the shofar? Hear our prayer:

> This is the day of the world's birth. This day all creatures stand
> before You in judgment, whether as children or as servants.
> As we are Your children, show us a parent's compassion; as we
> are servants, we look to You for mercy: shed the light of Your
> judgment upon us, O holy and awesome God.[5]

The prayer reminds us of our relationship with God as parent and master. The prayer states that God provides for us and cares for us, and by saying the prayer, we acknowledge our dependence on God. On these Days of Awe, in particular, we recognize that the food we eat, the water we drink, the shelter we have, are all from God.

This is an odd view of the world for us moderns, we who provide so much for ourselves. Or is it?

This Rosh Hashanah, we have seen so many people whose lives have been transformed in the few hours of a storm.[6] What a powerful reminder that everything we have, all the creature comforts we know, even the water we drink (that sustains our lives) can disappear in a moment.

Can this reminder also lead us to gratitude? Can it lead us to recognize that all we have is lent to us? Can it guide us to acknowledge that we stand before God, as all creatures do? This is the message of Rosh Hashanah, an especially powerful message this year.

Most of us never worry about these issues. We worry about real estate taxes going up; we worry about our careers; we worry about fitting another sport into our schedule. We worry about getting on the right team, or in the right office, but not enough about doing the right thing. We worry, almost all of us, about not having enough time. But we don't worry enough about how we use the time we have. We may worry about keeping current with movies or books, but we do not worry about keeping current with God. Until this week, when the calendar forces us to think differently, to recognize where we fit in: with our families, with all our relationships, with Judaism, with God.

Most of us reject the notion of our dependence on God. We distance ourselves from those who say, "God will provide." We know we must provide for ourselves, take control of our own fates.

But when we reject our dependence on God, where does that leave us? What remains of our relationship with God?

Does our relationship with God hinge on our understanding the Bible as true? Must we accept the creation as factual to realize our dependence on God? Must we believe in the literal truth of the exodus to understand that we are part of the Jewish people, with a particular past, future, and destiny? Not at all. We have, instead, Rosh Hashanah and Yom Kippur to tell us who we are, where we are, before Whom we stand, and where we are headed. We have a magnificent Bible with legends that teach us significant values and laws that guide our lives. Let us use these days and these stories well. Let us restore our faith and commitment together.

---

1. Babylonian Talmud, Rosh Hashanah 10b-11a.
2. Lawrence A Hoffman, *Gates of Understanding, II.*,189, n. 209. The prayer is first found in Seder Rav Amram Gaon, 9th century, the first Jewish prayer book.
3. Jerome Lawrence and Robert E. Lee, *Inherit the Wind*, introductory note.
4. Lawrence and Lee, 85.
5. *Gates of Repentance*, 143; "in judgment" is omitted in the prayer book translation, but added here.
6. The devasting Hurricanes Katrina and Rita struck the Gulf Coast states in August and September 2005.

Hiding From Responsibility

Yom Kippur Morning 5766
October 13, 2005

A man had the opportunity to visit both heaven and hell. First, he went to hell and found people seated around tables that were overflowing with delicious-looking food. But no one was eating; they were all sitting and looking longingly at the food. Why? The man saw that strapped to each person's arm was a long stick that prevented them from bending their arms and rendered them unable to eat the food in front of them. This was their punishment: to be eternally tantalized and hungry and unable to eat.

In heaven, the man found a similar scene. The people also were seated at tables covered with delicious food. They, too, had sticks attached to their arms so they could not bend their elbows. But in heaven—instead of sadness—there was joy. People were eating! The man went up to one of the people and told her what he had just seen in hell. He wondered what the difference was. The woman explained: "Here in heaven, we feed each other."

The Haftarah we have just read, designated for this service in the Talmud 1500 years ago, also presents us with people who are not eating; they are fasting, as most of us are. Second Isaiah chastises the people for appealing to God with an "empty" fast. The people fasted, as if they were repenting or trying to repent, but they still tended to their businesses and they still oppressed their workers. "Is this the fast that God desires?" asks the prophet. Is God moved by people who starve their bodies if they continue to act unjustly?

No, says Isaiah, it is the wrong fast, an empty gesture. Rather, this is the kind of fast that God desires:

To unlock the shackles of injustice . . .
To let the oppressed go free . . .
Surely it is: to share your bread with the hungry
To bring the homeless poor into your house
When you see the naked, to cover them,
Never hiding yourself from your kin (Is. 58:6-7).

Each year this Haftarah reading puts our fasting in a new light. It tells us that we must not engage in empty rituals, but that we must seek justice as the true repentance for our sins. Isaiah tells us we must raise our voices like a shofar and cry aloud without holding back when we see injustice. That is a powerful message for this day and this year.

There are many ways that we and our fellow Americans responded to the hurricanes we witnessed in these past weeks. We sympathized with those who have lost so much. Some of us focused on global warming; some of us concentrated on the inadequacy of our government's response. Some of us found positive hope in the enormous generosity of Americans. We all studied this tragedy from different perspectives. What all of us saw, however, was the face of poverty in the people who were left behind.

Have no doubt about it: In all the counties and parishes affected by Hurricane Katrina, almost a quarter of the children were poor before the hurricane, and among black children, almost half were poor. Forty percent of the black children in New Orleans lived in households without cars, compared with four percent of white children.[1] The families you and I saw on television in the wake of Hurricane Katrina did not stay in New Orleans because they were stubborn or did not know any better. They remained because they could not afford to leave, because they had no way to leave, and—often—because they had nowhere to go. More than one-quarter of the children in Louisiana and Mississippi are poor; and before we distance ourselves from these facts, I remind you that almost one-third of the children in Washington, D.C are poor, as well. These are shameful facts for the richest nation in the world, and for our city, with its towering level of education and income.

We need to work to loosen the yoke of poverty and let these oppressed go free. We lead sheltered lives here inside the Beltway, here in Upper Northwest, Chevy Chase, and Bethesda. We rarely venture across the Anacostia River to see that nearby face of poverty. We read the statistics, and many of us do work to alleviate poverty, but how often do we actually see the faces of the poor? Hurricanes Katrina and Rita blew in our faces the stark and timely reminders of the oppression of poverty in our nation. Let them be reminders of the oppression of poverty right here in our own city, clearly one of the richest and the poorest places in the land. On this day of fasting, when most of us will feel a slight tinge of hunger, we need to remind ourselves how many in our midst feel that hunger every day and cannot break their fast, for it knows no end.

Isaiah tells us to share our bread with the hungry and to bring the homeless poor into our house. Last Sunday we walked for Sinai House. It was inspiring to see so many children and parents—700 registered walkers—participating in our annual walk to support our efforts to give families with children a fresh start. We provide them with subsidized housing, help with education and finding jobs, help with childcare and putting the lives of their families back in order. For thirteen years our congregation has steadfastly provided this assistance —all for just four families at a time. Our efforts are worthy, but we know they are a drop in the bucket.

More than 30,000 poor children live in the District of Columbia: a staggering number that can make us feel helpless about making a difference! Yet we do not feel helpless (or at least we do not let our feelings of helplessness overwhelm us) as we work together to help these four families and then—when they move out to self-sufficiency—four more families, and on it goes. I am reminded of the midrash about how we will recognize the Messiah. He will be in the most crowded part of the city, among the poor and sick, changing their bandages one by one by one. So are we helping families: one by one.

Yet even that is not enough unless we also can change policy. Let us begin with the shortage of affordable housing that forces so many to live in squalor. On Sunday, many of us signed petitions sponsored by our Social Action Committee in favor of affordable housing resolutions in the District and in Montgomery County, measures that would go a long way toward expanding the stock of this housing in our community.

Some years ago our Sinai House board learned that we could help our residents even more effectively by utilizing Section 8 vouchers. This federal program serves two million poor households by making up the difference between what these people can pay for rent and what their housing would cost. In Washington, D.C., for example, people earning the minimum wage would end up paying 118 % of their income for the least expensive two-bedroom apartment. These vouchers bridge the gap between what people can afford and what their housing costs, and these vouchers work. Both tenants and property owners like them, and both political parties support them.

Yet there is not enough money to support the program, and

80,000 vouchers have been eliminated for this year with a total of 450,000 families in danger of being dropped over the next five years.[2] The voucher program is in jeopardy of being changed dramatically by the Department of Housing and Urban Development. We need this program to make Sinai House work, as do thousands of other housing programs like ours across the country. If anything, we need more vouchers, more programs, and shorter waiting lists to obtain the vouchers and other assistance. We can hear Isaiah's words ringing today: "Take the homeless poor into your house." We need to raise our voices, as Isaiah instructs us, to ensure that this program grows to meet the overwhelming needs of the poor throughout our land.

Isaiah says, "Never hide from your kin." Isaiah calls to us not to hide from our kin or our responsibility. This same word—*titalem*—appears in Deuteronomy: "If you see your fellow's ox or sheep gone astray, you must take it back to him. Do not hide [from your responsibility]. ... Do the same with his garment, with anything that your fellow loses and you find: you must not hide. ... If you see his animal fallen on the road, do not hide. You must help him raise it" (Deut. 22:1, 3, 4).

Titalem is translated as "ignore," "remain indifferent," or "withdraw yourself," but it really means "to hide." That's what we all do, isn't it, as we pass the beggar on the street? We hide. We hide from our responsibilities to others, we hide from other people, we hide from Isaiah's imperatives, we hide from our Jewish obligations, we hide from God.

Yom Kippur comes to summon us out of hiding.

Adam and Eve hid from God after they ate from the fruit and heard God walking in the garden. God called out to Adam, "*Ayeka*, Where are you?" (Gen. 3:8-9) So God calls out to us each Yom Kippur, "*Ayeka*, Where are you?" God calls out to us to come out of our hiding, to assume responsibility, to face up to our shortcomings, to acknowledge our sins.

Jonah hid from responsibility, too, as we will read this afternoon. God told Jonah to go at once to Nineveh and proclaim judgment upon it. But Jonah fled from serving God. He went to the port of Yafo and boarded a ship in the other direction. Jonah understood his responsibility, but he hid from God and from what he knew he needed to do.

How often do we hide from what we need to do: to make sure that the poor, who have lost so much, still have an opportunity, still have hope, still have a hold on life. Isaiah tells us that we should raise our voice and let it resound like a shofar, but too often we keep silent.

Some of us, of course, do not have a voice that is heard by our very own government. We live in the District of Columbia and live without representation, a travesty of justice. We live among 570,000 other American citizens who also have no voice in our national government. I am proud that our congregation has initiated a resolution that will be voted upon at the Reform Movement biennial next month calling for voting rights for the District of Columbia. Temple Sinai's Social Action Committee and Board of Trustees led the way and called on other area congregations to join us in bringing this resolution to the Union for Reform Judaism. Believe it or not, this resolution came to the Reform Movement biennial meeting once before several years ago, and it was voted down. So I am asking you—including those of you who live in Maryland and Virginia—to raise your voices and contact your friends in other Reform congregations around the country. Tell them to look for this resolution, to endorse it, and to vote for it. Explain to them that those who live in Washington, D.C., do not have any representatives in Congress. Believe me, based on my own experience, I think you will be surprised at how many do not know this. Share with them your outrage at this travesty of justice.

We need to raise our Jewish voices, as well, at the World Zionist Congress next June. We need to make a clear statement to the world Jewish community that there is more than one kind of Jew, that religious freedom is a Jewish value, that Reform Judaism is a valid and legitimate expression of Judaism. We must do this by registering for the World Zionist Congress elections now online or by mail and then by voting for the ARZA Reform slate. There are forms on the table in the lobby. Take them for yourselves and for others. Do not hide from the form or lose it when you get home. Fill it out, pay your $7, send it in, and vote when you receive your ballot. Our goal is to register 1,000 individuals from Temple Sinai over the next several weeks.

Registering and voting for the ARZA slate in this election is the only way that we can make our statement that we Reform Jews must be recognized in Israel, that we care about Israel, that Rabbi Portnoy and Rabbi Potter and I are real rabbis, that our congregation is really a holy congregation, that what we practice is authentic Judaism. This is how we must and can demand our legitimate place among the Jewish people. For too long the tyranny of the Orthodox rabbinate has denied our validity and our existence; for too long have they have kept support from our congregations and schools in Israel; for too long have they have suppressed and denied our authentic expression and interpretation of Judaism at every turn. We must raise our voices, as Isaiah instructs us, and proclaim that God demands justice.

We need, finally, to raise our Jewish voices on behalf of the victims of genocide in Darfur. I am proud that the banner on the front of our building reminds all the travelers on Military Road day after day about this issue of conscience. I am proud that our congregation leads others in placing these banners on the synagogues and churches throughout the Washington area. I am proud that we remind our city of this human tragedy. We Jews know genocide too well. We have suffered along with the other victims of hatred and ethnic cleansing in Rwanda and Bosnia and now in Darfur province of Sudan. We must be the voice of conscience and cry aloud that this tragedy must stop. We must not hide from our responsibilities as Jews and as citizens of the world to call for an end to these attacks and for the beginning of support and comfort for the victims. Like Isaiah, we must remind our nation and its leaders of this disaster and become the conscience that calls for justice.

Justice is elusive. Sometimes it hides from us. But we must not hide from it. It is, as the Torah portion this morning teaches us, not too baffling, nor is it beyond reach. It is not in the heavens, but here on earth. It is as close to us as our own city and as far away as Africa. It is very close to us, in our mouths and in our hearts, and we must look for it and then find it. We must lift our voices and cry like a shofar to unlock the shackles of injustice and let the oppressed go free, to share our bread with the hungry, to reach out to the homeless poor, never to hide from what we must do. Then our light will burst through like the dawn and we will repair what is broken in our world.

---

1. Statistics from Children's Defense Fund.
2. Center on Budget and Policy Priorities, "President's Budget Would Restore Some Rental Vouchers..."2/24/05.

Starting at the Back:
Confronting Our Shortcomings

Kol Nidre 5767
October 1, 2006

You may remember the story of the rabbi who was overcome with remorse one Yom Kippur eve. During the Kol Nidre service, she suddenly threw herself down on the bimah in front of the Ark and cried out, "Source of Mercy, how well I know my weaknesses and shortcomings! I am here to lead this congregation, but I have fallen short. I throw myself down before You, Holy One, for I know that I am a nothing."

Everyone was startled by this interruption in the service, of course, especially the cantor. At first he did not know what to do, but then he, too, walked before the Ark, threw himself down, and began to wail, "Creator of the universe, I, too, am not strong enough for the task of Yom Kippur. I know the words, I know the music, but I cannot direct my heart to You enough. I have failed. God of forgiveness, I—too—am a nothing."

The congregation was stunned. Suddenly, from the back of the sanctuary, the shammes (or head usher) ran up to the bimah and threw himself down before the Ark and began his plea, "I feel so inadequate for this task of serving You, especially on this holiest day of the year. I am just one of the people, a servant in Your house. I am a nothing."

So there were the three of them, lying face down before the Ark, when the rabbi turned to the cantor, pointed to the shammes, and said, "Look at him. Look who thinks he's a nothing!"

Our Kol Nidre service may not be so dramatic, but like these leaders of the congregation, each of us is called on Yom Kippur to stand before God, to approach the Almighty, to find the humility and remorse we need to begin our atonement.

How do we do it? How do we change our lives from indifference to caring, from sin to forgiveness, from denial to acknowledgment, from arrogance to humility?

As with many jokes, there is an element of truth in this story.

The rabbi and the cantor are expected to serve as role models of repentance on the High Holy Days, and our liturgy tells us exactly how. Our Kol Nidre service begins each year not with the lighting of the candles, not with an upbeat *"L'shanah tovah,"* not even with the Kol Nidre itself, but with a personal prayer from the rabbi before the open Ark: "Sovereign of the universe, in awe and humility I have come to stand before You to pray with Your people Israel and on their behalf. Who is fit for such a task?"[1]

The cantor chants a parallel prayer, *Hineni,* at the beginning of our Erev Rosh Hashanah service: "Behold me, of little merit, trembling and afraid, as I stand before You to plead for Your people. O gracious God … accept my petition and that of my people."[2]

Both of these prayers come from a tradition dating back to the Middle Ages, when the leader of the congregation's worship began the service with a meditation acknowledging personal inadequacy and asking for God's help. Our Reform tradition includes these two deeply personal prayers, designed to guide congregants toward their own introspection and repentance at the beginning of the Erev Rosh Hashanah and Kol Nidre services.

How do we prepare ourselves to pray? Most of us look for our favorite seats: Are they available? Can we see the rabbi? Can we see the cantor and choir? Can we hear? Will the sun be in our eyes? Is there a draft? Where are our friends sitting? We go and wish them a *Shanah Tovah.* Perhaps we look at the service sheet.

What else should we do? One Chasidic rebbe was asked by a follower, "What do you do before praying?" He answered, "I pray that I may be able to pray properly."[3]

Most of us either do not recognize or have lost sight of the importance of preparing to pray, and we need to be reminded, as Rabbi Potter taught us on Rosh Hashanah Eve. As difficult as it is, as alien as that is to most of us modern Jews, we are here this evening to pray. We are here to look at our lives, to see where we have fallen short, to reestablish our relationships with God and with the Jewish people.

It is easier to succeed at these tasks if we practice them regularly. Most of us do not practice enough; if we did, we would need a larger sanctuary! So the pressure is on: We have only tonight and tomorrow to accomplish unique and important tasks, and we need all the help we can get.

Unlike any other prayer, the *Hineni* prayer—the cantor's public meditation—was traditionally sung by the cantor as he (or she) entered from the back of the sanctuary. The first part of the Rosh Hashanah service was led by someone else, and now it was the cantor's turn to lead the congregation in prayer. As he walked up to the bimah, the cantor chanted, "Here I am, of little merit, trembling and afraid, as I come before You to plead for Your people." The music and the words rise to represent the gravity and responsibility of leading the congregation.

The cantor may know the words and the music, but is the cantor personally adequate for the task? This prayer reminds us that even the best among us fall short of our promise. And if our leaders whom we regard as exemplars fall short, how much more so do all of us fail to achieve our potential!

Those of us who lead this congregation—the clergy, the staff, and the volunteers—work very hard to prepare for the High Holy Days. We learn the words; we learn the music; we write messages and sermons; we invite the readers and polish the *rimonim*; we tend to the details of safety and security and tickets and parking; we prepare and rehearse.

Most importantly, we must prepare our hearts to humble ourselves before God and other human beings, to restore and renew our lives and strengthen ourselves for the tasks of daily living that lie ahead. The *Hineni* prayer of the cantor on Rosh Hashanah and the rabbi's prayer this evening come to remind us of the most difficult preparations we must undertake.

How can we prepare ourselves for these tasks? How can we find repentance and forgiveness so that we can begin again, with a clean slate, to shape ourselves into the kind of ethical, moral, thoughtful people we know we should be?

In his book, *No Future Without Forgiveness*, Archbishop Desmond Tutu describes the work of the Truth and Reconciliation Commission in South Africa, which he chaired from 1996 to 1998. The monumental task facing post-Apartheid South Africa was restoring this broken nation and helping it face its future. Today is here to remind us that we, too, are broken and must face our future. As Archbishop Tutu writes, we all need to become forgiving, repentant, reconciling, and reconciled.[4]

For Jews, this is what Yom Kippur is about: It is the Day of Truth, the Day of Reconciliation, the Day of Forgiveness. It is the day of restoring ourselves with one another and with our God.

First we must begin with the truth: Where have we fallen short?

Where have we been neglectful? Where have we been less than we could be? Our prayer book enumerates many sins and symbolically tells us that we have sinned from *Aleph* to *Tav*, from A to Z, or Zed, as they would say in South Africa. Once we encounter the truth about ourselves this past year, we can begin the difficult work of seeking forgiveness from those we have hurt and reconciliation with those who have turned away. Tutu says that the most difficult words in any language are "I am sorry." They are difficult to say to our spouse, to our child, our parent, our partner, our friend. They make us vulnerable, for we never know if these words will be accepted and where they will lead. Today is the day to say these words, for today is the day of forgiveness.

For most of us, our sins are sins of omission: what we should have done and did not do. Sabbaths and holidays we ignored; study we should have undertaken; injustices we should have decried; *tzedakah* we should have given.

Let me begin, then, with my own confession.

I am sorry that too often I do not demand enough from you. I want you to be comfortable in your Judaism; I want you to feel good about your synagogue; I want you to find strength and comfort in the way you live your Jewish life.

I am sorry that for too many years I have fallen short in telling you what to do; I know that I have focused on the positive and not been sufficiently prescriptive. I might teach you how you *could* celebrate Shabbat, but I stop short of telling you that is what you *should* do. I teach you *how* to study Torah, but I don't tell you that you *should* study Torah. I present opportunities for social action and charity, but I have tried not to make you feel guilty when you do not act on them. I am, perhaps, what Alexander Pope called a "soft" clergyman: a cushion who "never mentions Hell to ears polite."[5]

My punishment is to face daily the dismal state of observance in our congregation. It is not just that so few congregants gather here every Friday evening for our beautiful Shabbat service. I know that people are tired on Friday evening, that many would rather have dinner with family or friends.

But how many even mark Shabbat with candles and Kiddush? How many mark this weekly passage of time and try not to miss it? I am afraid to ask.

How many feel Shabbat is important enough not to accept other engagements on Friday evening? I am afraid to ask.

Many of us are deeply involved pursuing social justice: in our work, as volunteers, in our political lives. How many of us, however, are called to repair the world *as Jews*? How many of us know the sacred texts that lie behind the good deeds we pursue? I am afraid to ask.

I know that many of us read Jewish books and articles and find enrichment in the little study that we do. Yet how many of us take the time for regular study, beyond the occasional book we read with a Jewish theme? I am afraid to ask.

I should not be afraid to ask. Too often I have been flexible when I should have been demanding, forgiving when I should have been guilt-provoking, patient when I should have been insistent. Too rarely have I led—and pushed—more people to greater Jewish observance and commitment. I am committed to doing better in the coming year, and I seek your forgiveness.

All of us fall short. All of us fail to use our power and position consistently for good; all of us too frequently take the easy way, the less painful and demanding way. And all of us can do better.

The great American Conservative rabbi, Milton Steinberg, preached a famous sermon, "Only Human—The Eternal Alibi." Rabbi Steinberg related this scene: A child had committed some slight annoyance. His father lost his temper and struck the child. Immediately the father was ashamed and apologized to the child, saying, "I'm only human."[6] What this father meant is that to be human is to be weak.

As humans we take the easy path and do not do what we know we should do; we miss the mark of what we could and should be. We turn to meanness, dishonesty, and cowardice. How often we use the excuse of being "only human" for all our own misdeeds. Milton Steinberg teaches us that in reality being human is the basis for every noble, honest, and brave act: being humane and humanitarian.

We should not think of ourselves as "only human," but as gloriously human, recognizing and acknowledging the greatness of being human that is within each of us and then letting that greatness guide our lives. Being human leads us to justice, mercy, humility, and love of others. These are all uniquely human traits, and only we humans can achieve them.

Being "only human" is the basic message of Yom Kippur. We come to the synagogue on Kol Nidre night with two messages in our pockets. In one pocket we read, "I am but dust and ashes." Or, as the rabbi and cantor and shammes said, "I am a nothing." I am flawed; I have fallen short; I am prone to weakness. In our other pocket, however, is the message: "The world was created for my sake." As the Psalmist writes, "I am but little lower than the angels" (Ps. 8:6). I am capable of greatness. I am created in God's image.

How do we achieve the greatness that is within us as humans?

How do we each approach these Days of Awe?

How do we each find our own way to stand before God?

Like the cantor singing *Hineni*, we start at the back and work our way up to the front. We begin by recognizing where we have fallen short, by acknowledging our flaws and our shortcomings, by admitting our inadequacies. For all of us are less than we could be, all of us filled with regrets, all of us broken and imperfect. Our tasks on this day are to admit our shortcomings and to resolve to do better in the days and year ahead. We must forgive ourselves and one another and repent of our failures: in our Jewish lives, in our professional lives, in our family lives. And then we must ensure that we do not repeat these shortcomings and failures.

Many say that Moses was the greatest Jew who ever lived. He had the closest relationship with God and knew God face to face. Moses shaped the Jewish people, leading them courageously from bondage to freedom, to a covenantal relationship with God, to a way of life that has lasted for 3,500 years. We also know that Moses had a temper, and when he lost his temper, there were consequences. Coming down Mount Sinai, holding the tablets of the Ten Commandments, he saw the golden calf and the people dancing around it. Moses "hurled the tablets from his hands and shattered them at the foot of the mountain" (Exod. 32:19-20). In his rage, he broke the most precious gift from God to the Jewish people!

Have you ever wondered what happened to the broken tablets? Broken and imperfect, they were still a gift from God and therefore sacred. One midrash tells us that the broken tablets were placed inside the holy ark with the second set of tablets because both were sacred. The set that was intact told the Israelites how to approach perfection; the broken tablets reminded them that no one—not even Moses—is perfect. All of us—even though we are broken, even though we are imperfect—are worthy of being in God's presence. All of us are broken. All of us stand before the Ark.

Our task today is to see where we are broken, where we have failed. Our task today is to repair the breaks in our lives, to make ourselves whole, to achieve the greatness that is within us as we stand in God's presence.

1. *Gates of Repentance*, 247.
2. *Gates of Repentance*, 19.
3. *The Hasidic Anthology*, ed. Louis I. Newman, 332. *Gates of Prayer*, 3, #2. The story is about the Tsanzer Rebbe, Chayim Halberstam, 1793-1876.
4. Desmond Mpilo Tutu, *No Future Without Forgiveness* (Image/Doubleday, 1999), 165.
5. "Moral Essay IV, To Richard Boyle, Earl of Burlington," ll. 149-150, in *Selected Poetry and Prose*, 210.
6. Milton Steinberg, *Only Human – The Eternal Alibi*, edited by Bernard Mandelbaum (New York, 1963), 3-6.

Strangers in Our Midst

Yom Kippur Morning 5768
September 22, 2007

You may remember the story of the man who approached a poor person on the street. Moved by this stranger's condition, the man reached into his pocket to give him some money. It was then that he realized that he had left his wallet at home. Now he was standing right in front of the poor stranger and had nothing to give him. What was he to do? He reached out his hand and took the poor man's hand in his. "Please forgive me," he said. "I have nothing to give you today, nothing to help you with." The stranger responded: "No need to apologize. You have reached out to me, and I thank you for this handshake. With your hand you have given me dignity and shown me that you care."[1]

This Yom Kippur we ask: Are our hands extended in welcome? Do they reach out to others? Or do we keep them in our pockets? How do we respond to the stranger in our midst?

These are questions we ask ourselves on Yom Kippur, for we will read in the Torah this afternoon that holiness is defined by how we treat the stranger:

> When strangers reside with you in your land, you shall not wrong them. The strangers who reside with you shall be to you as your citizens; you shall love each one as yourself, for you were strangers in the land of Egypt: I the Eternal One am your God.[2]

Thirty-six times in the Torah we are commanded not to oppress the *ger*, or stranger.[3] Because he lives with us, we are obligated to respect him and treat him well—in this text, *like one of us*. Commandments to protect the widow and orphan were common in many Near Eastern cultures. What set the Torah apart was this concern for the stranger. Again and again we read, "for you were strangers in the land of Egypt." We empathize with the downtrodden; we uniquely appreciate the plight of the stranger; our concern is not only with the rights of the stranger, but with the feelings of the stranger as well.

The rabbis of the Talmud also discuss the different ways we might wrong the stranger. The Bible, they point out, refers to verbal wrongs, but there are monetary wrongs as well. Sometimes different wrongs can overlap. The rabbis say we must not go into a store and pretend to show interest in purchasing an item we do not intend to buy. Our words mislead the merchant and thus wrong him.

With the stranger in our midst, we must not say, "Remember your life before you joined our community, how needy you were." We must not shame our neighbor, for that is as if we have shed his blood.[4]

The Talmud tells us how carefully we must watch our words when we speak to strangers: "Do not taunt your neighbor with the blemish you yourself have" (for we were strangers in the Land of Egypt). The Talmud continues with a proverb: "If there is a case of hanging in a man's family record, do not say to him, 'Hang up this fish for me.'"[5]

Contrast this sensitivity with the great national debate in our nation today on how to treat the strangers in our own midst: the resident aliens, the guest workers, the legal immigrants and the undocumented.

Why are we so focused on this issue? Because of security concerns? Economic concerns? Ongoing nativism? Concerns about health? Can there be any question about the just and proper course for our nation?

Our government is still deadlocked on the issue of immigration reform.

- In 2005 the House of Representatives passed legislation criminalizing undocumented immigrants living in the United States and making it more difficult for legal permanent residents to obtain citizenship. The Senate did not pass this bill.
- In 2006 the Senate passed a comprehensive immigration bill creating paths to citizenship for undocumented workers but putting in place stringent English language and civic requirements. The House did not pass this bill.

In fact, the only legislation to be put into law called for the construction of a 700-mile fence along the U.S.-Mexico border.

George Washington declared, "The bosom of America is open to receive ... the oppressed and persecuted of all nations and religions."[6] Nevertheless, there is deep fear of immigrants in our nation today. Because there is fear in our land, at no time has the voice of our Jewish community been needed more. When thousands are languishing in detention and all our government can do is build a fence to keep people out, we must raise our voice like a shofar and proclaim what is right.

Welcoming is not just what we do in our synagogues and our homes. Welcoming is what we must do in our nation.

As a nation, we are suspicious of the strangers in our midst. At worst, we are concerned they may be terrorists, or at best that they may take the place of "true Americans" in the job market. Rather than delighting in the values and new perspectives that newcomers bring to our land, we worry that they will overrun us. Legislation right here in the Washington suburbs abolishing day laborer centers and keeping immigrant children out of school tells us how worried and afraid many of our neighbors are about illegal immigration and the perceived need for control.

We Jews come from a different perspective. Particularly as American Jews we are comfortable in welcoming the stranger, for most of us are well aware that our parents, grandparents, or great-grandparents were strangers—immigrants—themselves. The first Jewish immigrants to these shores, now more than 350 years ago, were immigrants fleeing from hostility, yet they established themselves and made significant contributions to this nation. In 2005, a broad cross-section of the Jewish community supported "A Jewish Vision for the Future of American Immigration and Refugee Policy," developed by the Hebrew Immigrant Aid Society, or HIAS, the advocates of Jewish immigrants since the nineteenth century and supporters of all immigrants to these shores on behalf of the Jewish community.[7]

Have no doubt that in troubling times like these for immigrants, the Jewish community calls out for fair treatment, due process, generous policies, and caring services for those who seek refuge on our shores. As Jews our history begins with the command to understand the plight of the stranger, as we read today, and continues with the values of *hesed*, or kindness; the importance of hospitality; and redeeming the captive. Our Reform Movement has spoken out on the issue of immigration policy often. We have championed the rights of refugees, urged fair and generous immigration policies, promoted inclusive naturalization and citizenship paths, and demanded due process for citizens and non-citizens alike.

As a Jewish community, and as a congregation, we must work to put our values into action and raise our voices like a shofar on behalf of the strangers in our midst. We must reach out our hands in welcome and in support.

These Jewish values also have an impact in Israel, as we all know. Founded in fulfillment of the Zionist dream, Israel was the realization of the ingathering of the exiles of our people from throughout the Diaspora. The Israeli Declaration of Independence, in 1948, stated that the State of Israel would be open for all Jewish immigration and for the ingathering of Jewish exiles. The Law of Return, passed in 1950, guaranteed that every Jew has the right to immigrate to Israel.

But what about non-Jews? We all rejoiced in Israel's initial welcoming of the refugees from Sudan—more than 1,000 of them, including 300 from Darfur. This reminded us—from our safe and comfortable distance—of Israel's welcoming of the 400 Vietnamese boat people in 1977 and refugees from Thailand after that. It reminded us of the "Good Fence" through which Arab neighbors seeking medical help would pass to Israel for life-saving treatment, even during war.

When the Israeli government announced that it would return Sudanese refugees to Egypt, therefore, many of us were profoundly disappointed, and there was an outcry of protest in Israel. The Prime Minister sought to distinguish between refugees of the genocide in Darfur and economic refugees simply seeking a better life in Israel.

The Minister of Justice took issue with this, asserting that "Israel has an obligation to assist the refugees who fled tyranny."[8]

Remembering our Torah portion, "The stranger who resides with you shall be to you as one of your citizens," we expect the Jewish homeland to welcome refugees of any background. As Rabbi Yisrael Lau, the former Chief Rabbi of Israel put it, "As Jews, we cannot turn our heads from the suffering of another nation."[9] When the dust settled, Israel announced that it intended to grant citizenship to several hundred refugees from Darfur, doing its part to help this humanitarian crisis for the world.

Some ask, "Why not more?"

We must consider the magnitude of the problem that confronts Israel as it struggles with this difficult issue. Between two and four million Sudanese now are living in Egypt, with a mere 12,000 having been granted refugee status. It is not surprising that many of these refugees would want to cross the border into Israel. Reports of their mistreatment in Egypt abound, and more than 1,000 Sudanese already live in Israel, working in the hotel and other industries.

At the same time, we must remember that Israel has absorbed one-quarter of its current population over the past twenty years, with nearly 100,000 refugees from Ethiopia, as Rabbi Michael Boyden points out.[10] At the same time, Israel is dealing with more than 125,000 illegal foreign workers, all in a country of just seven million people, approximately the same population as Virginia, in a land that is smaller than New Jersey and one-fifth the size of Virginia.

As Jews, we want Israel to do its share and to be a model of compassion for the rest of the world. A model of caring it must be, but clearly Israel cannot accept all the African nationals who would want to live there.

How much we want Israel to be faithful to our ethical imperatives! We need the Jewish state to be a Jewish homeland *and* an exemplar of morality. We need it to be a place that welcomes Jews, as it has been, when no one else wants them; and we want it to be a place that welcomes non-Jews, particularly when no one else wants them. When the two principles conflict, we want Israel to find a course between its Jewish mandate and its ethical imperative.

This potential conflict has been a challenge since the founding of the Jewish state. My Talmud teacher in Jerusalem, Yehoshua Amir, gave a sermon in 1949, on the second Yom Kippur after the establishment of Israel, about the High Priest's three-part Yom Kippur confession, as described in Leviticus, which we will read about this afternoon.

First the High Priest reaches out his hands on the head of a bull and confesses the failures of himself and his family. Then he confesses a second time for all the other *kohanim*, or priests. Then he confesses a third time, on behalf of all the House of Israel, the Jewish people.

In his Yom Kippur sermon, Dr. Amir pointed out that now that Israel had become a state, a fourth confession, for all the world, was necessary. Now that the Zionist dream was a reality, Israel had a responsibility to its non-Jewish citizens. Israel would have to concern itself with the plight of "strangers" in its midst, Professor Amir said, and become a voice of morality in the world.[11]

As Israel prepares for its 60th anniversary, these issues loom large.

How can the Jewish state remain a homeland and haven and also deal fairly with the strangers in its midst? How do we reach out our hands this Yom Kippur? In confession? In welcoming?

May our own confessions this day bring us closer to God, closer to one another, closer to our responsibilities to all people. May we strengthen ourselves and find the strength to help others.

1. Simon Certner, *101 Jewish Stories for Schools, Clubs, and Camps,* 113.
2. Leviticus 19:33-34. The translation is from the URJ Torah Commentary, revised edition.
3. Babylonian Talmud: Baba Mezia 59b; Rabbi Eliezer the Great states that some count 46 occurrences of this commandment.
4. Baba Mezia 58b.
5. Baba Mezia 59b.
6. General George Washington in a letter to the members of the Volunteer Association and other Inhabitants of the Kingdom of Ireland who have lately arrived in the City of New York, December 2, 1783. *The Writings of George Washington,* ed. John C. Fitzpatrick, vol. 27, 254 .
7. Available at www.hias.org.
8. *Human Rights Information Paper,* August 2007, "Sudanese in Israel: The Current Situation," Jacob Blaustein Institute for the Advancement of Human Rights, American Jewish Committee.
9. *Human Rights Information Paper.*
10. HUCAlum listserv posting 31 August 2007.
11. Cited in Michael Marmur High Holy Day Ideas, 5768.

Sacred Journeys Together

Rosh Hashanah Morning 5770
September 19, 2009

When the new rabbi arrived, everyone was eager to hear his first sermon. Many people came for the first Shabbat and liked what he said. More people came the second week, but they were a bit surprised that he gave exactly the same sermon. There was some murmuring within the congregation: Maybe he was really pressed for time, even overwhelmed by his new position. The third week came, and he gave the same sermon yet again!

At this point, the president of the congregation began receiving phone calls, so she made an appointment to meet with the rabbi privately. She didn't want to criticize, she said, but many members wanted to know why he had given the exact same sermon three weeks in a row.

The rabbi explained that he had observed the congregation in the days that followed his first sermon. While many people had told him how much they liked the sermon, no one had taken the message to heart. No one had changed, so far as he could tell. Their values were still the same. So, he told her, he just had to keep repeating the same message until people really heard it and made it part of their lives.

So it is that I speak again to you this morning about why it is so important to me personally that you understand—in your hearts and in your minds—that your membership in Temple Sinai is membership in a sacred community that we must build together: together with one another and together with your clergy.

We read this morning that Abraham and Isaac left their servants behind and headed up the mountain. Abraham said, "The boy and I will go up there; we will worship and will return to you." They took what they needed, and "the two walked off together" (Gen. 22:6).

We don't know what Abraham and Isaac each thought they might find on this journey, and the rabbis of the Midrash have spun many stories. We do know, however, that Abraham saw it as a sacred journey, and the innocent Isaac went along.

How easy it is to forget that *our* lives are also sacred journeys!

We, too, must traverse many challenges: in our families, with our

225

health, in our careers. Today, we gather to put all of this into perspective. Today, we gather to see and appreciate that our lives are sacred journeys that we take together.

As your rabbi, this is my belief that I want you to embrace: that active participation in our Jewish community transforms our everyday lives into sacred journeys.

When Abraham and Isaac went up the mountain, the text says: *Veyeilchu shneihem yachdav,* "The two of them walked together" (Gen. 22:8).

"The two of them" tells us that being Jewish is not a solitary act. We have no tradition of monastic retreats or solitary spiritual quests. For us, it is crystal clear: Life is with people.

To recite the *Kaddish* or perform a *brit milah,* tradition tells us to have a *minyan.* To study texts, we must find ourselves a partner or a group. To live our lives, we must have a community: witnesses for a *ketubah,* a free loan society, a burial society.

Building community is a sacred responsibility that falls to each of us. To support one another in crisis, to be present, to inspire the next generation: all these bring God's presence into our midst.

Birth, coming of age, illness, death: we often think of these as personal—even private—matters.

People tell me they are uncomfortable attending a bar mitzvah service or Confirmation unless they are actually invited, or visiting someone who is sick unless they know them really well, or calling a new neighbor and inviting them to a Shabbat service. Yet these are the moments when we most feel the need for support. These are the points on our journey when we most need one another.

A baby-naming at a Shabbat Service, a bar or bat mitzvah, Confirmation: these events are not just for the child, not just for the family, not just for the friends. They are important markers for our community—opportunities to welcome, to take pride, to celebrate and rejoice with one another.

Too many of us are alone in our Judaism. This saddens me, for it tears at the fabric of what we should be and could be as a congregation: rejoicing with one another, caring for one another, journeying together on life's path.

Vayeilchu: "They walked."

Judaism is not static, but moving and continuous. We value and respect tradition, but we do not venerate it. Nor, as Reform Jews, do we follow it blindly, whether it is the hour at which we worship or the melody we love. We seek meaning in our traditions, customs, and practices, and we need them to bring us closer to God.

It is surprising to me how tenaciously some people hold on to their old ways.

In one town, people noticed that Shlomo stood up at the same time during each service. Nobody knew why he stood up, but he seemed to know about Jewish tradition; so, after a few weeks, everyone in the congregation stood up at that point, too. It became a tradition in that synagogue to stand at that point in the service.

Until the new rabbi came. He didn't understand; that wasn't what he had always done. When he asked, everyone said, "Ask Shlomo," and so he did. Shlomo explained that his back was weak and every now and then he had to stretch, and strangely enough, it always seemed to come at the same point in the service. Soon, everyone else had begun stretching then too.

Sometimes we all need a break to stretch: to view the Judaism we practice or the customs we follow, and examine if and how they work for us.

As we walk our sacred paths, we cannot just lift our feet up and down; we must propel ourselves forward.

As I think about life at Temple Sinai, I see many members—too many—who just move their feet up and down in place, but they do not come any closer. Some come here because they want to educate their children, but they do not want to learn themselves. Some say they would like to be more involved, but they never take that critical step forward.

I see committees and projects that are struggling for committed members to help them in their work of supporting Israel or reaching out to interfaith couples or building the archives, but no one steps forward.

Our congregation is blessed with many devoted lay leaders and volunteers who give generously of their time and their expertise to support the work of Temple Sinai. Yet I cannot help but think of those hundreds more whose lives would be so enhanced by engaging in the sacred work of our congregation.

How much we need you to step forward and join our common journey!

How much you need to step forward: to join us and enrich your journey.

And there are others who do not even step in our door.

I have said before and I tell you again: It is the shame of our Washington Jewish community that the rate of synagogue affiliation is so low: probably about one in three.

I understand that we live in an age of fee-for-service. We are accustomed to à la carte menus, to paying for what we get and not getting anything we do not pay for. You want the deluxe package? You'll have to pay for it!

It is easy to make the leap. People say, "We don't come to the Temple often enough to justify paying dues."

This mindset describes an economic relationship: I pay and I get.

Belonging to a synagogue, however, is a sacred relationship, not an economic one.

Our primary task at Temple Sinai is to build a sacred community. That responsibility extends beyond classes and worship and celebrating milestones. Our most important purpose is to create a sacred community: a whole that is more valuable than the sum of its parts.

What I witnessed in the small towns I have served as a rabbi were Jewish communities that take nothing for granted. The arrival of a new Jewish family is celebrated by all. Both old-timers and last year's newcomers reach out immediately and persistently. Each individual is valued for what he can bring to the congregation, what she can contribute to the future of Jewish life in the community.

We, too, must reach out to the unaffiliated and uninvolved among us and bring them into our tent. We must show them what it means to be part of a sacred community. We also must continue to reach out to our own members who are less involved and hear what they need and want from us, as we have done in our long-range planning initiative.

We must reach out as Abraham reached out, sitting at the entrance of his tent, rushing to greet strangers, welcoming them into his home. We are working on this, but we need more than a smile and a handshake (or fist-bump) at the door. We need more than a phone call.

We need to get to know one another, to bring someone new to a service or a program. And we need to reach out to those in our midst:

checking on a homebound neighbor, working together on a social action project. For we are all walking the path together, each of us with our own stride and at our own pace.

Yachdav: "The two of them walked on *together.*"

Abraham and Isaac were father and son, but what links us?

Many of you tell me—sometimes with amusement, sometimes with pride—that until you saw one of your colleagues or neighbors at services you didn't know that person belonged to Temple Sinai! It is very special and pleasing to discover that bond.

Consider our bonds.

Clearly we are not all Jewish, for we have many non-Jews in our families and in our congregation who contribute immensely to the life of the Temple. They are integral to Temple Sinai and in many ways they make us who we are: a sacred community of Jews and those who live with Jews and those who choose to join themselves to our congregation and join us on our sacred journey.

Geography, vocation, and education do not unite us. Temple Sinai always has been and still is a metropolitan congregation; our members come from near and very far. We represent many diverse backgrounds and professions, although we do have more than our fair share of lawyers.

What, then, brings us "together"?

Each of us needs companions with whom we can walk up God's mountain. Adults need friends just as children need friends.

Yes, we make friends in school, soccer, our neighborhoods, our offices.

Here at Temple Sinai, however, we work together not to win a game or fix the street or improve SAT scores.

Here, we share a commitment to repairing our broken world. Here, we commit ourselves to the eternal values of pursuing peace, seeking justice, celebrating and sanctifying the most important moments in our individual and collective lives.

Here, we look not just to the immediate future or the distant future, but to the eternal future.

And though we may not recognize or acknowledge it, here we share a desire to find God in our midst.

This is our sacred community, and we must build it together. The rabbis and the cantor cannot do it for you, nor can we do it alone.

We must step forward to share our Jewish lives with one another, within our nursery and religious school classes, through our adult support groups, through our worship services, and through the peak moments—from the heights of joy to the depths of despair. We must seek ways to connect, ways to affirm one another, ways to help one another find the meaning that we all seek in our lives. This is how we sanctify each act and sanctify our lives.

When this works, as I have been privileged to witness it working many times at Temple Sinai, we are blessed with an appreciation of what a sacred community can be.

We understand why 2,000 years ago the great rabbi Hillel said: "Do not separate yourself from the community."[1] We understand why 1,000 years later Rashi pointed out that one should not pull back when the community is experiencing difficulties so that "one can be united with it when it experiences joy."

We need the community and the community needs us.

And so:

I want to leave you understanding that Temple Sinai represents an unbroken and unbreakable link with the Jewish people, committed to eternal values, participants in the covenant with God.

I want to leave you believing that Temple Sinai is your Jewish home, your connection to Jewish life here and throughout the world.

I want to leave you feeling that Temple Sinai can help you find answers to the questions of how to live a life of meaning and purpose.

I want to leave you knowing that your membership in the congregation binds you and your lives to one another, that it can show you the way and put you on the path to the Eternal.

May we walk forward, together, on our sacred journey.

---

1. Avot 2:4.

Kol Nidre: Seeking the Sacred

Kol Nidre 5770
September 27, 2009

Why does this night draw us here? What is so compelling about hearing and saying the Kol Nidre?

We can trace its history back to the ninth century Common Era, when it first appeared in the prayer book of Rav Amram Gaon, even as he called it "a foolish custom."[1] Over the years many rabbis objected to including it in the Yom Kippur Eve service, and our own Reform Movement left it out of our prayer books until 1978, when the editors included it in *Gates of Repentance*. In the Middle Ages, Kol Nidre was used to justify the accusation that Jews were untrustworthy because they could be released from all their obligations—so their enemies thought—just by uttering this simple formula.

Kol Nidre is not a prayer, but a legal declaration to absolve us from unkept vows. Its words are "archaic and technical,"[2] as one commentator noted, and clearly not spiritual. How has this legal declaration become the focal point of the holiest day of our year?

If it is not the words or the message, perhaps it is the music that speaks to our hearts, that pulls our minds to focus on the awesomeness of this holy night. Perhaps it is the idea that we stand before God to be judged, seeking to encounter our shortcomings. Perhaps it is our realization that the year is turning—that we are each moving forward with so many promises we have made still unfulfilled.

What we can say with certainty is that our people transformed this legal formula into one of the most moving moments of our High Holy Days. With solemnity and drama we chant these words and find profound meaning in these moments.

How does this happen? Where does the power of Kol Nidre come from?

We stand before the open ark, with witnesses from the congregation holding our Torah scrolls to remind us that we are joined together as a congregation in our commitments and our responsibilities. The words remind us that we have failed to live up to our promises: to God and to one another. The music captures our profound regret and the seriousness of the moment.

How can we know if it's working? How can we know if Kol Nidre is turning us back to God and to our people? The archaic and legal language of Kol Nidre was transformed into a moving and deeply personal prayer. Can we be transformed into better Jews and people?

On Rosh Hashanah, I spoke about my belief that active participation in our Jewish community—reaching out to each other—transforms our everyday lives into sacred journeys. Tonight—Kol Nidre—I want to speak to you about reaching inward. How can we take the bits and pieces of ordinary existence and transform them into a life of meaning, a holy life?

Our sin is that too often we take the sacred and make it ordinary.

A few years ago the *Wall Street Journal* reported on a trend. The headline read, "You don't have to be Jewish to want a bar mitzvah," and the story featured a young woman who told her parents that she wanted a bat mitzvah. She said she "found the singing inspiring and offered to learn Hebrew. She also said she wanted a big party. Her parents thought the request was unusual since the family is Methodist."[3] Her parents hosted a lavish party for 125 friends. The girl was satisfied and told the reporter, "I wanted to be Jewish so I could have a bat mitzvah. Having the party fulfilled that."

When I share this story with our Confirmation students, they are usually indignant. Some say, "How could she have a party if she didn't do the work?" Others say, "She isn't Jewish!" And some say, "She misses the point. Bat mitzvah is not about the party. It is about accepting responsibility as a Jew." Those students receive a broad smile and a special blessing from me.

I often find myself explaining that the bar mitzvah is at the service. Just about all our Temple Sinai families understand and express very well the meaning and significance of the day—at least to me—but, sadly, others do not understand. How many people take a sacred milestone and turn it into a secular event like any other party? How many people transform the holy into the ordinary? Dancing the hora doesn't sanctify the marriage or the bar mitzvah. We reduce so much in our lives, shortening messages to fit Twitter, abbreviating even "Oh my God!"—words once spoken only with reverence—to OMG.

With Kol Nidre we do just the opposite: on one night each year, we take a legal formula and transform it into a deeply moving and sanctified moment.

Years ago, when I lived in Jerusalem, I took my laundry each week to an Orthodox woman in my neighborhood. One week, as I dropped off my laundry, I said, "I will see you next week," and she answered, *Im yirtze haShem*, "God willing." I smiled and probably chuckled as I repeated the phrase, *"Im yirtze haShem."*

She was insulted. She snapped at me, "You never know what God will deal us. One day my husband was alive, and the next day he was gone. Now this is what I do so I can survive. We owe every day to God above." That put me in my place. I had turned the sacredness of her speech into something ordinary.

This is our sin, and we are all guilty: converting the sacred to the secular.

It is so easy to minimalize Judaism and God, narrowing our vision and trivializing our religion. The *Washington Post* reported the struggle of Facebook users to describe their "Religious Views" in 100 characters or less. One subscriber said, "It's Facebook. The whole point is to keep it light and playful … But a question like that kind of makes you think."[4]

I would hope we can all still think.

We spend so much of our lives focused on the light and playful and superficial. How much we need the reminder that there is so much more.

Once our Jewish world was filled with organizations that were guided by Jewish values. We put Torah at the center, and we looked out for one another. Today the "corporate model" has overtaken Jewish values. Our local Jewish Federation has a CEO. Our Reform Movement has a "marketing department." *Tzedakah*, or righteous giving, has given way to "development." If language reveals values, then it seems that our Jewish community is no longer different from a theater company, museum, or an orchestra.

And how often do we take the sacred act of giving *tzedakah* and transform it into a focus on what is deductible? How often have we taken our sacred responsibilities as Jews and turned them into secular ends?

Sadly, many of us view our Judaism as a leisure-time activity that must compete with all the other leisure pursuits in our lives. "How can our daughter continue religious school when she lives for soccer?" We weigh and compare membership in our synagogue with memberships in a museum or a club, overlooking the fact that only one of these memberships is central to who we are as human beings, and only one of them is sacred. How easy it is for us to lose sight of the sacred.

In our day of converting the sacred to the secular, why does this night draw us here? Why do these holy days draw us here?

I believe that we are desperate to capture a sense of the sacred in our lives. We yearn for holy moments.

As your rabbi these 25 years, I have been privileged to help you find and feel those sacred moments in your lives. I have seen parents (despite being consumed with worry as the bat mitzvah date approached) moved to tears as their child is called to the Torah. I have sat with you and prayed with you at the bedside of your husband or wife or parent or child. I have witnessed how you have been comforted in your mourning by the outpouring of love and generosity of your friends and your congregation. I have seen the profound joy on your faces under the *huppah.* Together, we have walked through times that have shaken us all to our roots, moments when we have cried out for meaning, for understanding of how a loving God can let tragedy occur.

As your rabbi, it is my *zechut,* my privilege—shared with my clergy colleagues—but also my responsibility to help you find this meaning and sacredness in your life. As I prepare my remarks to speak to each bar or bat mitzvah, as I shape a eulogy from what I know or learn about a person, this is my great honor: to identify and add insight and celebrate what makes the life of that person—whether 13 or 93—a sacred journey.

It is my privilege—and my responsibility—to contemplate and help you understand how our lives are guided and motivated by the values of our tradition. How can our stories, our texts, our commandments transform the ordinary into the sacred? How can Judaism help us consecrate our lives?

Why are we drawn here tonight? To pray? To participate in an ancient ritual? To see our friends? To feel guilty? To be moved? To examine our lives? We owe it to ourselves to reflect on our reasons.

Many of us come to pray, even though we may be unsure how to pray. Prayer is difficult. Prayer takes practice and discipline. We pray partly in Hebrew, a barrier for many of us.

Most importantly, real prayer forces us to be honest with ourselves, to strip away our defenses before God. Prayer requires us to turn to the God before Whom we stand. We who follow intellectual professions are at a disadvantage, because prayer is not an intellectual exercise. It is an exercise of the spirit. It requires us to use another part of our brain.

In our very intellectual and cerebral congregation, I see a new yearning to engage in prayer, to engage with God. Our long-range planning survey and many comments reveal that there are many of you who seek new meaning in your worship, who crave a personal relationship with God.

This is a challenge for us as Liberal Jews. We wrestle with this. In last Sunday's *New York Times Magazine*, Zev Chafets quoted my colleague Marc Gellman: "Our people don't get emotional in public. The only time I can recall really serious praying was after 9/11."[5] At a memorial service in his synagogue, Rabbi Gellman saw what he calls "transcendent davening," as there was in ours. What is more usual, as Rabbi Gellman says, is the reaction of Mr. Golden, an atheist. His son, writer Harry Golden, asked his father why he went to services every Saturday. He answered, "My friend Garfinkle goes to talk to God, and I go to talk to Garfinkle."[6]

Why are we here? Maybe we came to talk to Garfinkle, but perhaps we also want to be able to talk to God. I am convinced that more of us are looking for moments of holiness in our lives—even if we do not realize it. I am convinced that we seek to step out of time for a few minutes, to be totally focused on what is really important to us. We seek those "peak experiences," as Maslow called them. In our own ways, many of us are yearning for the sacred to help us find meaning in our lives. We are seeking to experience holiness.

Our tradition teaches us a few techniques, and we have had a "spirituality circle" in our congregation exploring what might work for some of us. We fast on Yom Kippur to feel closer to God. Some of us find that the melodies, others find that the words, bring us closer to God. Some of us have found it through intensive and extended communal learning, as in our adult bar and bat mitzvah classes. Some of us find that stepping out of time for Shabbat brings us closer to God.

I want to leave you understanding that there is no one single road or path for everyone. What is necessary, however, is that you are open and willing to begin your journey.

As I approach retirement, I cannot help but wonder where my own journey will take me. How will I find sacredness? How will I handle this transition? Will I age gracefully, as I have seen so many of you do? Will I continue to find meaning in my days and years? Will I still be able to number my days and find wisdom, as the Psalmist tells us, still find holiness in my life? These are questions all of us ask as we journey from stage to stage, seeking the sacred

I am always excited when I see a rainbow. Usually it is incomplete and just lasts a few moments. Some people see it as a natural phenomenon relating to physics: rain refracting sunlight. Others think of a rainbow as a political symbol, representing many racial backgrounds or varied sexual identities.

At the end of our wonderful Temple Sinai tour of Israel last February, we saw a magnificent rainbow. It gave us the opportunity to say the blessing for seeing a rainbow:

> *Baruch attah Adonai, eloheinu melech ha-olam zocheir hab'rit, v'ne-eman biv'rito, v'kayam b'ma-amaro.* We praise You, Eternal God, Sovereign of the universe: true to Your word, You remember Your covenant with creation.[7]

Say that blessing and you move beyond the science, you move beyond the great diversity of humankind; you are moved to see God's relationship to all of us.

How can we recapture that relationship in our lives, that relationship that we have too often forgotten or ignored or pushed aside?

How can we find holiness? How can we experience the sacred?

We need to prepare. We need to open ourselves up. We need to make room for holiness, to let it into our crowded lives. Kol Nidre comes to help us reflect on our shortcomings, to acknowledge how far we have strayed from holiness, and to embrace the sacred in our lives.

There is a story about Israel Baal Shem Tov, known as the Besht, the founder of Chasidism in the 18th century. One High Holy Days, he approached his synagogue but did not enter. His puzzled followers asked him what was wrong. He said that there was no room for him. There were many people in that shul, but there clearly was room for him, too. What could he mean? He continued:

You have filled this room with your selfishness. You are each too filled with yourselves and your own importance and your own needs. You have no room in your thoughts for anyone else. What room have you left for God? There is no room for God in God's own house! And there is no room for me."[8]

Yom Kippur is the day to make room in our thoughts for God and for one another. It is the day to examine our lives and seek holiness. It is the day to leave behind our broken promises and begin anew. It is the day to transform our ordinary acts into sacred deeds. May the words of our mouths and the yearnings of our hearts find favor before God, who is our Redeemer.

1. Max Arzt, *Justice and Mercy: Commentary on the Liturgy of the New Year and the Day of Atonement* (1963), 204.
2. Arzt, 201.
3. Elizabeth Bernstein, "You Don't Have to Be Jewish to Want a Bar Mitzvah," *Wall Street Journal*, 1/14/04.
4. "Soul Searching on Facebook," *Washington Post*, August 30, 2009.
5. Zev Chafets, "Is there a Right way to Pray?" *New York Times Magazine*, September 20, 2009, 45.
6. Chafets, 45.
7. *On the Doorposts of Your House* (1994), 27.
8. Adapted from Chasidic folklore. Published in Steven M. Rosman, *Sidrah Stories* (UAHC, 1989), 79-81.

Pursuing Justice and Holiness

Yom Kippur Morning 5770
September 28, 2009

In 1965, Rabbi Abraham Joshua Heschel was one of the leaders of the now-famous civil rights march in Selma, Alabama. A reporter pulled him aside and asked why he was marching and not praying. "I am praying," Heschel replied, "with my feet."[1]

Later, reflecting on that day, Heschel wrote, "I felt a sense of the Holy in what I was doing. ... Even without words our march was worship."[2] Still later, he would add:

> I felt again that Jewish religious institutions have ... missed a great opportunity ... to interpret a civil-rights movement in terms of Judaism. The vast number of Jews ... are totally unaware of what the movement means in terms of the prophetic traditions.[3]

This is our situation today: we work for justice, we work to repair our world, we engage in social action and *tikkun olam*, but we fail to understand how it is driven by our Jewish values and texts.

To me "social action" and "*tikkun olam*"—repairing the world—carry special meaning. They describe the good we do in our community and in our world as Jews and as a congregation. They embody prophetic Judaism come alive: religious motivation that reflects a Jewish understanding of the values that lead us. In my mind, social action and *tikkun olam* are different from "community service," the contributions we also should all make as citizens in our society.

Temple Sinai has a distinguished role in the history of social action and prophetic Judaism. My predecessors Rabbis Balfour Brickner and especially Eugene Lipman developed and shaped the concept of Jewish social action for our Reform Movement and for the wider Jewish and religious communities. They worked with giants from our congregation such as Arthur Goldberg, Joseph L. Rauh, Robert Nathan, and Rabbi Richard Hirsch, and their work today is carried on by my inspiring colleague Rabbi David Saperstein and many others at Temple Sinai. We stand on their shoulders. Their commitment echoes in the work of scores of members of our congregation today who serve and lead our nation in so many areas of pursuing justice, repairing our world, and working to establish the sacred values taught by our prophets.

How does prophetic Judaism lead us to justice? How does repairing our world lead us to holiness?

Listen to the words of Second Isaiah from our Haftarah this morning:

> This is the fast I look for: to unlock the shackles of injustice, to undo the fetters of bondage, to let the oppressed go free, and to break every cruel chain, to share your bread with the hungry, and to bring the homeless poor into your house (Isa. 58:6-7).

We give meaning to our fasts and substance to our rituals—we add holiness to our lives—by helping others among our people and in our community. We must raise our voices like a shofar, Second Isaiah tells us, to reach out to the afflicted in our midst.

These goals are not controversial. None of us would disagree with this anonymous author. We are motivated to help our neighbors, improve our world, reach out to those who need us. We teach these values in our nursery school and religious school, we require projects of our bar and bat mitzvah students, and many of our adults devote much of their time to acts of loving kindness. We accept these precepts and act on them.

I want to leave you understanding that these acts alone are not enough.

We do so many good deeds, help so many people, but I want us to do it as a Jewish community. I want you to feel called by the summons of these words in Isaiah. I want you to understand that we must act not just out of the goodness of our hearts, but because that is our Jewish responsibility.

The contemporary Judaism most of us practice and believe has a universal message, reminding us that all people are children of God. Most of us think that while we Jews may observe our religion a bit differently from our neighbors—we celebrate Yom Kippur and read prayers in Hebrew, for example—we are all basically people. As humanitarians, we need to put prejudice aside, treasure everyone's gifts and background, and welcome one another into the great human family. Our children learn they must recognize value in each human being. Most of us were raised with these concepts; we embrace them and pass them on to our children. We are gratified to share these humanist principles with other religions and with non-religious people, as well. Who could object to them?

That's not enough for me, nor should it be enough for us.

I want for us to pursue our social justice with the words of Isaiah and Micah and Hillel ringing in our ears. I want for us to see that our efforts to repair the world are our obligation, not just a nice thing to do.

I know a rabbi who always raises his voice when he says "*v'tzivanu*" ("you have commanded us") in a blessing. Here is how he would say the social action blessing created by our Reform Movement:

*Baruch Attah Adonai Eloheinu Melech ha-olam asher kid'shanu b'mitzvotav **v'tzivanu** lirdof tzedek.* Praised are You, Adonai our God, Sovereign of the universe, who hallows us with Your mitzvot and **commands us** to pursue justice.

Reciting these words as we engage in an act of *tikkun olam* consecrates our act by reminding us that we are fulfilling a religious obligation. It establishes a context for what we are doing and demonstrates that we understand we are engaging in holiness, as Heschel would teach us.

To pursue justice, we also must go beyond helping others. We must work to change the society that creates the problem. We can collect food for the hungry, toiletries for the homeless, coats and school supplies for the disadvantaged. Unless our goal is to help all people move out of poverty, however, we have not completed our task.

We create miracles all year long at Sinai House, but where were we when the housing vouchers that so many poor people depend upon were being cut back? We can roll up our sleeves and repair houses and serve dinners to homeless people, but we also must work for justice in our legislatures and in Congress. Second Isaiah does not tell us just to feed the hungry. He insists that we also break the shackles of injustice.

As we make our choices and decisions, we must be guided by Jewish texts and values. Health care reform can be viewed in many ways, for example. From an economic perspective: How many people can we afford to include? It can be viewed from a pragmatic perspective: Which system will work best? It can be viewed from a humanitarian perspective: What do we owe to all our citizens? Is it right that so many people—one-fifth of our population—do not have adequate health insurance?

How would Second Isaiah view health care reform? How do I view it?

From a Jewish perspective.

Rabbi Gail Labovitz teaches us that there are two verses in the Torah that can help us develop a Jewish view on healing and health care. In Exodus (21:19) one person injures another. The assailant must pay the victim for his medical costs, and "he shall certainly heal him." The rabbis of the Talmud understood this passage as the basis for the responsibility of all healers to help the sick and injured.

Commenting on this verse in the 13th century, Nachmanides emphasizes, "Do not say that God caused the illness so God must be the Healer. Here is a commandment to heal, and it is just as important as saving a life."[4]

Rabbi Labovitz also cites Deuteronomy 22:2, which teaches us that one who finds lost property must return it to the owner. The text says, "He must return it to him." The rabbis of the Talmud applied this verse to doctors, who are obligated to return the health of their patient as something that was lost.

Our obligation as Jews is to choose healing. We are taught that we should not live in a town without a doctor and that a community has a responsibility to provide medical care to the needy. The Talmud presents the example of a healer named Abba. He had a box for coins in his rooms so people could pay anonymously, and those who could not pay would not be ashamed. This ideal is modified by Rabbi Eliezer Waldenberg, in a 1985 responsum, who concluded that doctors should not be compelled to treat patients without being paid; therefore, he said, the community must compensate doctors for patients who cannot pay.

Caring for the sick is a community responsibility that we all must share. These Jewish values are rooted in biblical times, developed in rabbinic literature, and form the basis of our contemporary Jewish understanding of the importance of health care in our society.

Temple Sinai is more than a political party, more than a lobbying or advocacy group. We are a *kehilla kedosha*—a holy congregation—motivated to act by our tradition, our texts, and those who came before us. Only when we know and understand this can we truly find our voice as a prophetic community to act and to advocate in the true spirit of *tikkun olam*, repairing the world.

The difference between community service and *tikkun olam* is like the difference between charity and *tzedakah*. Both involve giving and raising money for worthwhile causes. Charity comes from the heart, and the word itself derives from the Latin word for "heart." We give charity because we are compassionate and our hearts are moved by the suffering of others.

Tzedakah, on the other hand, is righteous giving, rooted in the word for justice, *tzedek*. We give *tzedakah* because we are commanded to pursue justice and because we are obligated to counteract oppression. We will read in our Torah portion this afternoon: "Leave the gleanings and the fallen fruit for the poor and the stranger. ... Do not pervert justice ... but judge fairly. ... You must have honest scales. ... You shall love the stranger as yourself" (Lev. 19:9-10, 15, 34, 36). We give *tzedakah* not only out of compassion but because giving *tzedakah* is the right thing to do. It is truly "righteous giving." Giving it makes us feel good, but it also gives meaning to our lives and makes us holy.

Abraham Joshua Heschel prayed with his feet. We too must pray with our feet and pray with our hands. We must study our texts and identify our values, and then we must pursue justice. We must defend the widow and the orphan, befriend the stranger, ensure fair treatment for all, and not stand idly while our neighbor bleeds. We must find the strength to fight for these causes and reach out to so many in our midst. We know that, as Rabbi Tarfon taught, it is not up to us to complete the work, but neither are we free to avoid it.

We must continue to pray with our hands and our feet, we must walk and work together to help repair our broken world, and we will find holiness if we seek justice and righteousness together.

---

1. Edward K. Kaplan, *Spiritual Radical* (New Haven: 2007), 225. Also Ruth Messinger, 2009 Baccalaureate Address at Stanford University.
2. Kaplan, 225.
3. Susannah Heschel, ed., *Moral Grandeur and Spiritual Audacity* (New York, 1966), xxiii-xxiv.
4. See Berachot 60a, Baba Kama 85a and Nachmanides *Torat Ha-Adam*. Cited by Rabbi Gail Labovitz in a conference call for rabbis, August 19, 2009.

Purim-Torah Messages

For generations Jews have used Purim as an opportunity to exploit their sense of humor. Rabbis and others have written spoofs, parodies, and Purim-Torah, the "study" of sacred texts in ways that are anything but serious. With so many traditions under attack in our world today, the custom of Purim-Torah, with its tongue-in-cheek interpretations of obscure passages and points of law, continues to remind us of the value of making fun on Purim—of ourselves and even our Jewish texts.

1986

Once, the wise people of Chelm were debating what to put on their Purim banner. The Chelmites had decided to make a banner for each Jewish holiday, and each banner would display a symbol to represent the most important idea of the holiday. For Rosh Hashanah they had a shofar, for Hanukah a menorah. But for Purim, a great debate arose. One faction insisted the best symbol for Purim was the gragger, or noisemaker. Only on Purim do we have noisemakers.

No, said the advocates of the hamantasch. The gragger speaks to our ears but the hamantasch speaks to our stomachs and souls. Whether we think of the shape as a reminder of Haman's pocket or ear or hat is unimportant. But we can't have Purim celebrations without hamantaschen. Graggers are used just during the Megillah reading; hamantaschen are eaten all day on Purim and up to Pesach.

Now, both sides had advocates who felt deeply about the issue. As the debate continued, the people of Chelm realized that the Purim banner was a dangerous issue confronting their city. "We must find a solution to our problem," said the mayor. The town council went into emergency session and spent several days and nights pondering the problem. An election would not work because the town was evenly split, and a different symbol was ruled out because that would make *everyone* unhappy.

"We must reach a compromise that will make everyone happy," said the wise rabbi. So they decided to create a new symbol—a gragger in the shape of a hamantasch. "What will we call it?" asked the people. The town council decided on "graggertasch." Everyone was happy and soon the artists began making the banner.

Everyone was pleased, that is, until they tried to decide on the color for the inside of the graggertasch. "Blue, for the prune filling." "Prune? Black, for poppy seeds." "But the best filling is orange apricots!" And so the debate began anew. . . .

244

1987

You may know that there is a long tradition of adding to the Book of Esther. While our tradition has frequently created midrashim to embellish many stories within our Bible, the Book of Esther has always been particularly attractive to midrash writers. In fact, an entire Additions to the Book of Esther is found in the Apocrypha, a collection of works, such as Maccabees, included in Greek translations but omitted from the Hebrew Bible. Additions to the Book of Esther, which is integrated into the biblical text of Esther, provides much sought-after material lacking from the biblical book: The mention of God, a prayer of Mordecai on behalf of the doomed Jewish people, and other Jewish elements transform the otherwise secular fairy tale into a religious book that was more pleasing to the third century B.C.E. authors.

The following expanded translation was recently unearthed among documents presumed to have been shredded:

"In the sixth year of the reign of King Ahasuerus (which means 'Teflon' in Judaeo-Persian), a crisis developed. One of the King's advisers offered to pay 10,000 talents of silver through a secret bank account, as had Haman three years earlier (Esther 3:9). Ahasuerus forgot about the offer, as he often forgot about state matters.

"One sleepless night, however, he asked that the state history be read to him (6:1-2). The King did not read very much, preferring more lively entertainment. But this night, fortuitously, he wanted the chronicles read to him.

"We can imagine his surprise and consternation when he learned of this offer to pay a large sum to the royal treasury through secret channels. Indeed, it was a story of intrigue and questionable loyalty, and the King was mightily upset that he had forgotten—or had never known—about the matter.

"Not knowing what else to do, the King at once prayed for guidance: 'God-who-has-been-expelled-from-the-classroom, I turn to you in prayer and supplication. Lead me to the right; tell me what to do in my confusion. Amen.'

"Just then, the King's most trusted advisors appeared in the outer chamber. Summoning them to his bedside, he asked: 'What should be done for a man whom the King desires to honor?' (6:6) 'Raise him high, so all may see him,' they answered.

"Presuming their words to be sent by God, the King did as they suggested. He placed them in a starship named 'Shaddai' (known by its Persian acronym, SDI*) that they might find favor in the eyes of all. Thus, no one ever found out which advisors might have known about the secret money. The King was, in his own eyes, rescued from the crisis, and the time was transformed from one of grief and anxiety to one of relief and calm" (9:22).

---

*During the presidency of Ronald Reagan, the acronym SDI referred to a controversial anti-missile project known as the Strategic Defense Initiative.

1989

For many years, scholars have debated the relative merits of the latke and the hamantasch in an attempt to determine the most authentic Jewish food. Recent events, however, point to a third food that wins over both. It is more authentic, better suited to the holiday, biblically ordained, and more wholesome and nutritious than either latkes or hamantaschen: pizza.

Most people think pizza comes from Italy (except for New York or Chicago pizza), but this is not so. Pizza, as I will demonstrate, is an ancient dish, and its name is derived from biblical Hebrew. More than that, pizza is a food that historically has had special qualities: It is a redemptive food that saves its eaters from danger.

A quick look in a biblical dictionary will prove these points. The word *patzah* occurs 15 times in the Hebrew Bible and has two related meanings. The first is to open wide, especially one's mouth. This is a clear reference to pizza, which must be eaten with a wide-open mouth to accommodate the width of a slice and to avoid burning the roof of one's mouth.

The second meaning, which finds its way into modern Hebrew, is to deliver, rescue, or save. Psalm 144:11 reads, *"P'tzeni: Rescue me and deliver me from the hands of strangers, whose mouths speak lies."* Clearly, this is a quotation from Queen Esther, part of her prayer in preparation for the banquet she prepared for Ahasuerus and Haman. This is apparently one of the misplaced verses of the Bible, lost for centuries in the Book of Psalms and only recently discovered by biblical critics.

The reason Esther used this particular word was the nature of the food she was preparing. It had long been customary in Persian Jewish circles to serve pizza at "deliverance banquets." These were feasts arranged to intercede with enemies on behalf of one's people.

"Deliverance banquets," not surprisingly, were delivered by people on very speedy donkeys.

The original food goes all the way back to patriarchal times. You may remember the story of the three messenger-angels who came to visit Abraham and Sarah (Gen. 18). Abraham, with his characteristic hospitality, invited the strangers into his tent as he, Sarah, and their servants hurriedly prepared a meal for their distinguished visitors. For centuries, scholars have been troubled with the issue of what Abraham served. The text clearly shows Abraham violating Jewish dietary laws: He prepared a dish with flour cakes (thought to be *pita*, but obviously pizza), veal, and dairy products. How could Abraham and Sarah not have known better than to mix milk and meat? The answer is obvious: Based on recent textual insights, we have learned that the food was a special kind of pizza.

Similarly, scholars have wondered about the menu of Esther's deliverance feast. You will remember that she prepared not one banquet but two. Until now, the biblical text has been silent on what food was served, but the recent discovery of this lost verse proves beyond all doubt that it was pizza, the redemptive food—the combination of cheese and flour cakes—that Esther served her distinguished guests. On the first night, in the ancient tradition of Sarah and Abraham, Esther prepared veal pizza. But as she was about to serve it, one of her servants informed her of the dietary law, so she needed a last-minute substitution. On the second night, as she placed the cheese pizza in front of the King and Haman, she uttered the words from Psalm 144: "Rescue me, save me from the hands of strangers, whose mouths speak lies, whose oaths are false." That, of course, was the turning point of the story.

We must restore pizza to its rightful place as the Jewish food *par excellence*. It is, after all, far more nutritious than hamantaschen and a better source of protein. It is lower in cholesterol than (some) latkes. Unlike the latke and the hamantaschen, it is mentioned in the Bible and derives from an ancient tradition of welcoming guests. And it is a good food with redemptive qualities.

1990

Last year, before Purim, I proved conclusively that pizza was not only an important Jewish food, but that Esther served pizza to King Ahasuerus and Haman, thereby establishing it as the Purim food *par excellence.*

As convincing as my arguments were, I must report to you that my conclusion was wrong. Recent documentary evidence has emerged to demonstrate that it isn't pizza but poppy seeds that are the central food of Purim.

You may have realized, in the recent spate of articles about the Dead Sea Scrolls, that every book in the Bible is represented in those documents except Esther. For some strange reason, which scholars have yet to adduce, the Book of Esther has been suppressed among the corpus of documents in the Dead Sea Scrolls until now. Not only has this spectacular release of the Dead Sea Scrolls edition of Esther focused scholarly attention on the text; it has also answered numerous questions heretofore unresolved.

For many years scholars have wondered: What did the guests eat at the seven-day party that King Ahasuerus threw (1:5)? When Esther was taken into the palace to prepare for her tryout as queen, what were her rations (2:9)? Why did the two courtiers, Bigthan and Teresh, become angry with the King and plot to do away with him (2:21)? When Esther and her maidens led the Jewish community in a fast, what did they eat for the three days (4:15)? What did Esther serve at the wine feast that she prepared for Ahasuerus and Haman (5:6, 7:1)? As the Jews celebrated their salvation, what did they serve (9:17)?

Bigthan and Teresh were plotting to overthrow the King, it turns out, because of the mandatory drug-testing program that the King had just approved. "Who does he think he is?" they asked. "Here he is carousing for days on end and then coming at us with a holier-than-thou attitude? It must be Haman behind this wicked scheme. We will show him by making sure that the drug tests fail." Because of their background in chemistry, the two knew that the tests could be inaccurate if the subjects ate poppy seeds prior to the compulsory tests. The poppy seeds would make every test positive. As a result, Bigthan and Teresh urged everyone in the King's court to eat large amounts of poppy seeds. If all the drug tests were positive, they reasoned, all the tests would be invalidated, and the plan would be shown to be as ridiculous as it was.

So the campaign began: Everyone was to eat poppy seeds. That time of Ahasuerus's reign became called the "Pop Period." People began to eat not only poppy seeds, but in their enthusiasm they consumed large amounts of popcorn and popovers and pappadoms. Hunger for Pop foods spread from the King's court to the King's harem (now referred to as Pop-tarts). And so it was done.

Eventually, it was poppy seeds that all the partygoers ate, that Esther took as her rations while preparing to try out for queen. It was poppy seeds that sustained Esther and her maidens as she fasted on behalf of the Jewish people, and it was poppy seeds that she served at her feast for Ahasuerus and Haman. So what could be more appropriate for the Jews to serve on their days of feasting when danger had passed but poppy seeds, the source of the entire story?

You may know that the tradition to drink on Purim stems back to a saying of Raba quoted in the Talmud (Megillah 7b). He said, "It is one's duty to mellow oneself on Purim until one cannot tell the difference between 'cursed is Haman' and 'blessed is Mordecai.'" Raba knew how to add up the numerical equivalents of Hebrew letters and recognized that the two phrases in Hebrew "blessed is Mordecai" and "cursed is Haman" both add up to 502 in Gematriya. Talmudic scholars have always assumed that the term "to mellow oneself" referred to the use of wine. But not so. In fact, if you look carefully at the text, you will see the words "to mellow oneself with poppy seeds" also adds up to 502, the exact same number as the other two phrases. From Bigthan and Teresh to Raba the Talmudic sage, the poppy seed tradition was somehow lost. But let it be renewed.

Raba also said that a Purim feast that begins in the evening must continue into the morning. The other rabbis repeated this saying 40 times to get it straight. So let it be with us. But you must come in costume. You must wear something outrageous on Saturday night and a costume for a Purim character on Sunday morning. If you are bashful, wear part of a costume. This year we are doubling our Purim fun and excitement with something for everyone. So mark your calendars now and start scrounging for a costume and collecting poppy seeds. Some people are already scraping off their challahs on Friday nights.

1991

You may have wondered why a piece of pizza is called a "slice," instead of a "wedge." Slicing, after all, refers to objects that are long and narrow, such as slicing bread or cucumbers. What we do to a pizza is to cut it, not slice it.

The answer to this weighty question goes back many years to a community debate among the wise men and women of Chelm about the nature of Purim foods. They were discussing the proper names for Purim delicacies and discovered a disagreement. What many people had been calling *hamantaschen* was corrected by the community's Hebrew teacher who told them the proper name was *oznei-haman*. "Proper, schmopper," exclaimed the mayor. "I've been calling them *hamantaschen* for years, and no one has corrected me yet."

Soon the community found itself deeply divided. The Hebraists all rallied to the defense of the Hebrew teacher and wrote placards and signs proclaiming the correctness of *oznei-haman* (ears of Haman). The Yiddishists, on the other hand, paraded in favor of *hamantaschen* (Haman's pockets) as the name that most Jews knew and loved. The divisions over this Purim pastry so polarized the community that the town council of Chelm declared an emergency session to determine which name was correct. After hearing arguments from both sides, they decided that neither name was correct and that a third name must be sought. It wasn't just that they were afraid to alienate half the town's population. They pointed out that both of the other names were misleading. Neither ears nor pockets were really always triangular, and they could easily think of people's ears and people's pockets that were a variety of shapes. While ears and pockets were of many shapes, hamantaschen were always triangular. So they decided to call the pastries hamantriangles, or *sh'lish-haman*.

The new name met with immediate success. The Hebrew teacher was pleased that a new Hebrew word was introduced to the community. The leaders of the Yiddish circles were also mathematicians, and they were pleased with the geometric elegance of the new name. The rabbi, who happened to be a professor of theology, pointed out that the three-sided pastries with their new name really stood for God, Torah, and Israel. And the members of the Committee to Preserve Interfaith Relations were delighted to point out that while many faith groups had their Trinity, the Jews also had their *sh'lish-haman*.

The new name was so successful and proved to be such a unifying influence in the community, that soon anything that was triangular was referred to as a *sh'lish*. Even the Lithuanian Jews of Chelm, who normally spurned such trends, referred to *sh'lish*. It came out as *slece*, however, as their dialect didn't distinguish between "sh" and "s."

It was about this time that one of the leaders of the Lithuanian community in Chelm decided to open a pizza restaurant. She knew of pizza's biblical origins and its well-established associations with the Book of Esther, having read my essay on the subject in translation. But she also knew that pizza's popularity and tastiness would make her restaurant a success and possibly make her a rich woman. In particular, her innovation was to offer pizza in individual servings, wedge-shaped pieces that she would sell to busy Chelmites on the run.

As she was trying to decide what to call these pieces, she noticed that they were largely triangular, the shape of the *sh'lish-haman*. So she began her advertising campaign by inviting people to pick up a *sh'lish* of pizza. Only because she was Lithuanian, she called it a "slece of pizza." A printer's error changed "slece" to "slice." (In Hebrew the two words are spelled virtually the same.) And from that grew the common expressions "to pick up a slice of pizza." Soon the name caught on and was used around the world, in tribute to the Lithuanian Chelmite restaurateur.

1992

For generations and generations, students of the Bible have thought that the Book of Esther was about how the Jews were saved. Recent studies, however, reveal that the book is really a story of sexual harassment. For many years, feminists have considered Vashti—who stood up to the ever-inebriated Ahasuerus—a role model.

Vashti knew sexual harassment when she saw it, and she knew how to fight it. She blew the whistle so loudly that she is remembered and admired to this very day, even though she doesn't speak a word in the entire Book of Esther. By refusing to appear before the King, Vashti "committed an offense not only against Your Majesty but also against all the officials and against all the peoples in all the provinces of King Ahasuerus. For the Queen's behavior will make all wives despise their husbands, as they reflect . . . that she would not appear" (1:16-17). How easy it is to make the victim into the evildoer.

The true demon of the story—and the great harasser of his day—is Haman, of course. We can easily overlook Haman's behavior toward women, for we focus on how filled with hatred and enmity he was. But a quick look at Chapter 7, the turning point of the story, will prove my point.

Scholars always have wondered what went on in the palace the night of Queen Esther's feast. After Esther disclosed that Haman had been the adversary and enemy, the King stormed into the garden, "while Haman remained to plead with Queen Esther for his life ...." As the King returned from the garden, "Haman was falling on the couch on which Esther reclined. 'Does he mean', cried the King, 'to ravish the Queen in my own palace?' No sooner did these words leave the King's lips than Haman's face was covered (7:7-8)."

Why was Haman's face covered? The Oxford Annotated Bible suggests that Haman fell as a suppliant at Esther's feet, but we know better. The footnote explains that the face of a doomed person was covered in Greco-Roman times. We now know that Haman was hiding from tabloid photographers.

With what did Haman cover his face? With a bit of Esther's gown that he tore off. This tearing also has been overlooked by most scholars, but it is central to the story. The Hebrew word for tearing is *p-r-m*, the real root of the name of the holiday: Purim.

Unfortunately, both the Book of Esther and the holiday of Purim have been subjected to one cover-up after another. Not only has the sexual harassment theme been so cleverly disguised by later editors that it is all but lost; the linguistic root of *Purim* has been overshadowed by the spurious etymology of casting lots (*pur*). Not until this year, with the release of the secret contents of some very old and tattered scrolls, have we been able to recapture the original Purim theme and derivation of the word itself.

But how could this authentic message of the Book of Esther be overlooked for so long? And how do these characters relate to each other? Who is guilty of harassment and who of entrapment? And how can we possibly sort out all these conflicting claims?

For the answers to these questions, you must come to Café Shushan on the Saturday before Purim, where Rabbi Portnoy and I will debate these issues. And come to the Megillah reading on Wednesday night and hear the sanitized version.

1993

Scholars have been perplexed for years about Mordecai. Although he is a central figure in the Book of Esther, we know little about him. The text says his family had been carried into exile in Babylon, but what about him? What was his profession? What kind of person was he? We can answer these questions only by carefully examining our text and then reading analytically between the lines.

First, we need to understand the setting: It was a time of change in the kingdom. Ahasuerus had accepted the resignation of his Queen, leaving a power vacuum and creating anxiety among his advisers as to how the next period of his administration would progress. Who would find favor with the King, and who would not? Who would be admitted into the inner circle, and who would remain on the periphery? Who would make policy, and who would be forced to live under it?

It is at this transitional moment that we find Mordecai lingering around the palace and the gate of the city. According to the book of Esther: "Every single day Mordecai would walk about in front of the court" (2:11) and "at that time, Mordecai was sitting in the palace gate" (2:21). Obviously waiting for "the call," Mordecai was eager to secure his place in the new administration. Not wanting to appear obtrusive, he merely pretended to be curious about how his cousin Esther was doing in the queenship competition. Quite clearly, however, Mordecai was looking out for himself. He wanted to be available but not appear to be too available. That is how the story opens.

Mordecai's profession can be discerned from the text as well. We read at the end of the Book of Esther: "Mordecai recorded these events. And he sent dispatches to all Jews throughout the provinces of King Ahasuerus, near and far" (9:20). Whether Mordecai was a PR person, speechwriter, spin doctor, or spokesperson is not as important as the fact that he clearly made his living by communicating—he was known for his sound bites. He had a reputation for this, and Esther felt comfortable relating Mordecai's report of a treasonous plot against the King (2:22).

Mordecai, moreover, knew how to get his message across, even when he was outside the palace and Esther inside. The turning point of our story is the series of messages between Mordecai and Esther (4:6-17), including Mordecai's brilliant formulation to the Queen: "Do not imagine that you, of all the Jews, will escape with your life by being in the King's palace" (4:13). Mordecai obviously knew how to write, was one of the great communicators of his day, and could move even heads of state to action.

But how high can an adviser go, even one who writes well and has good connections? Will he get "the call"? Will his fortunes change? Will he move from the palace gate to the very center of power? Can he find restitution for the ill treatment he may have received?

In fact, Mordecai is compensated twice for his suffering, but in most unusual ways. The first time, Haman is commanded to take royal garb, place it upon Mordecai, and parade Mordecai on the King's horse, proclaiming: "This is what is done for the man whom the King desires to honor" (6:11). Later, after the downfall of Haman, Mordecai is elevated to second-in-command, taking Haman's place (8:2), and is entitled to wear "royal robes of blue and white, a magnificent crown of gold, and a mantle of fine linen and purple wool." The power that Mordecai garnered for himself was one thing; his royal attire, however, seems to exceed the normal perquisites of his office.

Only recently have some scholars begun to consider Mordecai as an early messianic figure. His role in saving the Jews, his royal garb, his place of power at the palace: all point in this direction. Indeed, some in the Lubavitch movement have been most eager to prove that the current Lubavitcher Rebbe is a direct descendent of Mordecai, a figure of a "saving king" in the Bible.

Understanding the character of Mordecai, then, is central to our understanding of Jewish life and Jewish history. A lobbyist at the palace gate, a public relations practitioner and right-hand man to leaders, Mordecai went on to greatness in his own right. The text tells us that instead of just speaking for others, he came to speak on his own behalf as well. As he rose to power, he came to wear royal garments and be associated with the messianic aspirations of his people.

Today, the streets of Jerusalem are filled with banners displaying a photo of the Lubavitcher Rebbe and the words "Welcome the King Messiah;" the *New York Times* has extensively covered the messiah's possible presence in Crown Heights. But bear in mind that the origins of this campaign go back to Mordecai, the Jewish wordsmith and lobbyist who made good. Who do you suppose wrote the book?

1994

For years, we've taught and been taught that the story of the Book of Esther is the story of how the Jewish people was saved.

This is simply not so. Though the Book of Esther recalls the planned destruction and ultimate deliverance of the Jewish people—and though there are elements of palace intrigue, power, and sexual politics—the story is really about information.

If you look carefully at the text, you can see that again and again the story spotlights the sending of messages and the sharing of information. King Ahasuerus's greatest challenge is how to communicate with his subjects, who are spread over half the world. Mordecai's greatest challenge from outside the palace is how to communicate with Esther, who is inside the palace. Haman's greatest challenge is keeping his messages from being intercepted. You might think these issues are immaterial. In fact, they are all elements of the dominant theme. I will demonstrate my case.

When Ahasuerus issues his edict for the destruction of the Jews, the text tells us "the King's scribes were summoned and a decree was issued ... to every province in its own script and to every people in its own language" (3:12), Later, verse 14 tells us that the text of the document was to be "publicly displayed to all peoples." Ahasuerus knew well that the mails and other information delivery systems were clogged, especially because his kingdom included several different countries with different peoples speaking a variety of languages.

We not only have the problem of the King communicating with all of his subjects, but the problem of getting messages into and out of the palace. We all carry the picture of Mordecai sitting outside the palace gates with messages being sent from Esther to Mordecai and back again (4:8, 12). Getting the word out and getting the word from person to person was the most vexing problem that the kingdom faced.

But solving the problem was less difficult than many anticipated and easier for us to understand. In Chapter 9 the original edict is reversed, and "the King's scribes were summoned ... and letters were written, at Mordecai's dictation ... to every province in its own script and to every people in its own language" (8:9). How were they sent? Scholars have puzzled over this issue for centuries because the text is unclear.

Chapter 8 tells us that "letters were dispatched by mounted couriers, riding steeds *ha-achasht'ranim, b'nei haramachim*." Since this is the only time these words are used in the Bible, scholars have had to guess what they mean. One translation is horses that are "used in the King's service, bred of the royal stud." Scholars have long recognized that the first word (which resembles "Ahasuerus") is a Persian loan word. Only recently, based on new archaeological discoveries, scholars have finally determined that this word means "facsimile" in Persian.

Thus the method of dissemination of these important letters was by facsimile, not horse and rider. Ahasuerus had discovered a more effective method for getting the word out. He knew the great importance of being a successful communicator. He understood that via the palace fax he could reach thousands of people and spread the word with extraordinary dispatch.

B'nei haramachim refers to children of the information superhighway. It refers to how we accept new modes of communication. The text reflects the great urgency with which these messages must be communicated. Previous messages had been sent in various languages by riders, but now that the Jews had to be saved, extraordinary speed was necessary.

It will come as a surprise to some readers that fax transmissions date back to Biblical times, but as Esther and Mordecai themselves would have pointed out: Where there's a will, there's a way.

1995

We often are astonished by the way in which life imitates art. I myself rejoice when the words of the Bible anticipate actual events.

Take the story of Queen Vashti in the Book of Esther, for example. We learned that Vashti was summoned "to display her beauty to the peoples and the officials, for she was a beautiful woman" (Esther 1:11).

You know the rest of the story: Vashti refused, the King was incensed, a new queen was sought, Esther was chosen, the Jewish people were saved.

We often ignore, however, the intricacies of the beginning of the story and therefore miss much of the real message and relevance of these immortal verses.

Let us begin with the character of Vashti, a heroine for many feminist readers of the Bible, but still long misunderstood. Recent studies have shown that her name, taken from the Persian, really means "physician." Court records from the reign of Xerxes indicate that during his reign, one of his queens served as his surgeon general. Putting these facts together, we conclude that Vashti served as surgeon general for the realms of Persia and Media.

Surely you remember that the Bible tells us that during the time Ahasuerus hosted a banquet for seven days, with no drinking restrictions, Vashti also held a banquet for the women in the royal palace. Perhaps you wondered, as I did, why the women's banquet was separate.

The answer is that it was not a banquet at all, but a weeklong conference called by Queen Vashti, the surgeon general, on the topic of sex education in the schools of the kingdom. The conference was attended by experts in many fields; it was there that Queen Vashti made something of a slip of the tongue—a comment heard throughout the kingdom. That is the real meaning of Verse 1:18, "This very day the ladies of Persia and Media, who have heard of the Queen's behavior, will cite it to all your Majesty's officials, and there will be no end of scorn and provocation!" When King Ahasuerus summoned Vashti, then, it was neither to look at her nor display her, but to rebuke her. Queen Vashti believed she had done nothing wrong, so she refused to appear.

The King's advisors tried to decide what to do next. They did not want to appear benighted or seem to be taking aim at the surgeon general (Queen). So they devised a new strategy, a "Contract with the Kingdom."*

Our text says they suggested, "If it please Your Majesty, let a royal edict be issued by you, and let it be written into the laws of Persia and Media so that it cannot be abrogated, that Vashti shall never enter the presence of King Ahasuerus" (1:19). The phrase *d'var malchut* ("royal edict") has been translated many ways. Quite clearly the intent is that this was a royal contract, a statement of agreement between the King and all the Provinces.

The royal contract did not stop with the banishment of Vashti. A new queen would be sought and when she was crowned, the King would not only give a great banquet but proclaim a remission of taxes for the provinces (2:18).

The King's very cunning advisors made sure that the new Queen's presence was celebrated by a tax cut as well as block grants to the states and provinces to underwrite some of the programs that were being cut from the kingdom's budget. The text continues: Ahasuerus "distributed gifts as befits a King."

You may think that this is only a remarkable coincidence. In fact, it demonstrates how the events of our day can be foretold by Scripture. What really was missing in the realm of King Ahasuerus were family values.

That was what was on the mind of Queen Vashti in organizing her conference. That was what was on the mind of Mordecai, who had reared and cared for his uncle's daughter as her foster father. That was even what was on the mind of Haman's wife and ten sons, who were hard-pressed to maintain their loyalty to the evil Haman.

It was the quest for family values that would give rise to this "contract with the realm,"* and through it these advisors would attempt to bring their own version of light and truth to the people of Persia and Media.

---

*The "Contract with America" was a campaign-defining document released by the Republican Party during the 1994 Congressional elections.

1997

Some people think the Macarena originated in Latin America and was brought, via cruise ships, to the United States. Here this simple dance has found its way into bar and bat mitzvahs, weddings, and even the most American of institutions: national political conventions. Few people realize, however, that the Macarena actually has its origins in ancient Shushan, in the Purim story that we read in the Book of Esther each year.

You remember that at the end of the book, we are told that the Jews "enjoyed relief from their foes" and that the month of *Adar* had been transformed "from one of grief and mourning to one of festive joy. They were to observe them as days of feasting and merrymaking" (Esther 9:22). The feasting the Jews in Shushan could figure out on their own, but the merrymaking presented them with something of a puzzle. How could they distinguish this rejoicing from other rejoicing, such as the King's great banquet mentioned in the first chapter?

Clearly they needed a dance specifically designed to commemorate this wonderful saving of our people. The name that they called this dance came from two words related to the Purim story: *makah*, or smiting, because Haman had attempted to smite the Jewish people; and *rinah*, or rejoicing, as the Jews were commanded to do at the end of the story. Indeed, the text tells us that this month was transformed from a time of grief to one of joy, from a time of fear that our people would be smitten to one of rejoicing.

So it is not surprising that the name chosen for this new dance, based on this verse, was a dance in which they turned from smiting to rejoicing, *makah-rinah*. The dance was not to be done by couples, of course, for it was a polygamous society. How could the King possibly dance with all of his wives at once? It needed to be a group dance, for the Jewish community also did not have men and women dancing together.

The motions of the dance were designed to commemorate the incidents of the Purim story, as recorded on the scroll and in the Book of Esther. The dancer begins by reaching out his or her arms, as Esther reached out to the King, not knowing whether or not he would accept her plea. The hand is turned up, as the King extended the golden scepter to Esther when she appeared in his court (5:2). The hands are placed on the shoulders, reminding us of the courage that Mordecai gave to Esther, charging her to go to the King and plead for her people (4:8). The hands are put at the back of the head, reminding us of how Mordecai refused to bow down to Haman and held his head erect (3:2). The hands are placed on the hips to remind us of the journey of Mordecai through the city upon the King's horse led by Haman. The wiggling, of course, reminds us of the movements of the horseback ride that humiliated Haman and honored Mordecai for his loyalty.

With all of these moves accomplished, the dancer then turns, a central theme of the Purim story. Some scholars argue that the turning in the *makah-rinah* represents the turning point in the story when the King realized that Haman was disloyal and a threat to the Queen and her people (7:5-7). Other scholars, however, refer to the verse at the end of the story, saying that the month had been turned from one of grief and mourning to one of festive joy (9:22). There have been others who have linked the turning to the King's turning from Vashti to Esther or the Jews' turning from oppressed to exalted. But turn we must, whether it is based on one point in the story or another, and then the cycle begins anew.

There are undoubtedly some who will be surprised to learn that the Macarena is really of biblical origins and not from this hemisphere. But there are those of us who feel that there are far more resources within the Bible than any of us ever imagined, and to get at them, all you need to do, as one rabbi said, is to turn the Torah over and over again, for everything is in it (Avot 5:22).

1998

For centuries, readers and critics have speculated about Haman's official position in the Court of Ahasuerus.

When Haman is first introduced (Esther 3:1), the text recounts, "Sometime afterward, King Ahasuerus promoted Haman. ... he advanced him and seated him higher than any of his fellow officials." On the basis of this passage, many students of the Book of Esther assume that Haman was second in command to Ahasuerus, much like Joseph was to Pharaoh. And, indeed, the Anchor Bible translates this verse as "advancing him and making him the Prime Minister."

A careful reading of the text, however, reveals that Haman was in a very different position. After all, a prime minister never would plot to do away with an entire people! A prime minister would not be wealthy enough to "pay 10,000 talents of silver for deposit in the royal treasury" (3:9). Haman brags to his friends and his wife about his great wealth and his new position (5:11). Exactly what was that position?

Our answer lies in Chapter 7, in the fateful encounter between Esther, Haman, and King Ahasuerus. As you will recall, Esther had invited the King and Haman to dinner, and then she invited them back again a second night. When the King asked Esther what she desired, she responded that she and her people were about to be destroyed. "Who is the one who dared to do this?" asked the King. And in the climatic verse, Esther exclaimed, "The adversary and enemy is this evil Haman!"

Here we must note that the text continues in Hebrew: ". . . and Haman *niv'at* before the King and Queen." Most translations render this phrase as "Haman cringed in terror before the King and Queen" or "Haman stood aghast before the King and Queen."

Such a reaction, however, does not conform with Haman's character; therefore, the word must be a misprint. The inversion of two letters reveals the true meaning of the phrase: Haman was the *teva*, the special prosecutor, in the court.

Once we grasp and accept this emendation, we certainly can understand how the real story had been suppressed over the centuries. King Ahasuerus had been under attack in some quarters for engaging in obvious sexual harassment. Had he not, after all, summarily ordered his wife "to appear to display her beauty to the peoples and the officials" (1:11)? And when she refused, had he not fired her, removing her from her position as his wife?

Persia was in a general uproar at the time. Rumors had spread about improper investments in the 127 provinces and the kingdom of Ahasuerus.

Many of the eunuchs, moreover, were engaging in a rebellion to protest working conditions: They were expected to guard the women who flocked to Shushan to audition for the queenship. "Who does he think he is?" asked the eunuchs. "And who knows what sorts of activities are occurring within the walls of the royal palace?"

Selecting a new queen, after all, had been a long and arduous process. Each of the women scheduled to try out for the part required twelve months' preparation: six months with oil and six months with perfumes. Furthermore, the text explicitly states, "She would go (to the King) in the evening and leave in the morning for a second harem" (2:14). This was too much for the eunuchs responsible for the harems; they blew the whistle.

At the same time, the women of the kingdom were sick and tired of seeing their sisters being used and exploited. Clearly, the time had come for a change, and the laws of the kingdom that prohibited such exploitation needed to be enforced, even if the King were the miscreant. There were so many rumors and innuendoes rampant about shameful activities within the royal household.

Thus it came to pass that as a result of public pressure an independent counsel was appointed to look into the entire matter. In order for this to work, of course, the incumbent had to have broad powers to investigate, to seek the truth, to prosecute if necessary, to get to the bottom of what was really happening.

So we should not be surprised that Haman, who was appointed as the special prosecutor in the court of Ahasuerus, should be elevated to a position higher than any of his colleagues. Nor should we be surprised that the King, wishing to curry favor with this newly appointed person, would place him at his right hand and attempt to win his favor. Nor should we be surprised that Esther would invite—and that Haman would accept—an invitation to dinner that would lead to his downfall.

The moral of this story? Those who are filled with hatred eventually get deposed.

1999

Now that e-mail has come to Temple Sinai (please: not too many messages too fast), we may justifiably rejoice in our office's entry onto the information superhighway. On the other hand, as the great preacher Ecclesiastes pointed out, "There is nothing new under the sun."

In fact, there is significant evidence to prove that the Purim characters we all know and love had access to computers. You may think that this is preposterous because, as we all know, the computer is a 20th century invention. But is it impossible?

Never forget that there are hidden meanings in Scripture. Indeed, a recent book on the secret code of the Hebrew Bible is only the latest in a long series of explications of the Bible that demonstrate its hidden and secret meanings.

We all recognize that the Book of Esther is written in exaggerated and fanciful language and set in an ancient period. What we may not realize is that in changing the setting of this book, the authors carefully and subtly disguised the computer references in the text.

How else could the official edict have gone out "to the governors of every province, to the officials of every people … in its own script and in its own language" (3:12)?

How else—other than through e-mail—could Esther, who was inside the palace and Mordecai, who was outside the palace, have communicated with each other?

How else could Mordecai have recorded these events "and sent dispatches to all the Jews throughout the provinces of King Ahasuerus, near and far" (9:20) except by means of a broadcast e-mail? Heaven knows they did not have radios!

You may think that these wide-ranging communications were accomplished by bicycle couriers and messengers, as the text implies. You may think that there is no compelling evidence that computers were employed in the extensive kingdom of Ahasuerus. You are wrong. There is hard evidence, a "smoking computer," as it were.

In the beginning of Chapter 6 of the Book of Esther, we are told that King Ahasuerus was unable to sleep and ordered the archives to be read to him, for the King was only semi-literate. Sitting groggily before his monitor at midnight, he was scrolling mindlessly through his archived files looking at the icons when someone entered his room.

Our translation says that Ahasuerus asked, "Who is in the court?" (6:4). The original text actually should be translated, "Who called a Judge?"

It is the original Hebrew of this phrase that is particularly noteworthy: *mi kara shofet*. If you write this phrase in Hebrew, you will see immediately what actually appeared on the King's screen: "Microsoft." Remember, however, that Ahasuerus was not a great reader and that the text appeared without vowels. No wonder it has taken us centuries to sort out what really happened that night!

To sum up: King Ahasuerus was searching the archives of his computer when the Microsoft logo appeared; the King's exclamation was misunderstood by his recorder, who was transcribing his every word for inclusion in the kingdom's archives; and the Jews almost paid with their lives.

If you doubt this interpretation of the story, consider this fact. The numerical values of the letters in the Hebrew phrase, "Who called the Judge?" when added to the numerical values of the letters in the word *Purim*, total 1,032. In *gematria* (the study of hidden meanings in the numerical values of Hebrew words), this is almost exactly the numerical equivalent of the phrase "the tip of the scepter."

The text tells us (5:2) that Esther touches the tip of the scepter as a sign that she found favor in the King's presence. What do they know?

It is clear that the scepter was not really a scepter but the joystick of the King's computer. He invited all visitors in his court to play computer games with him; that was the way he showed he had the common touch.

There can be no doubt that the Kingdom of Ahasuerus was networked and the populace computer literate. As Ecclesiastes said, "There is nothing new under the sun."

2000

The people who brought us the religious rating system for movies have turned their attention to the Bible. They realized that our culture could be polluted not just by what appeared on the silver screen, but also by what might be read in religious institutions and at home. They have boycotted Disney; they have initiated censorship in libraries; now they have turned their attention to the Bible itself. One book that has captured their attention in particular has been the Book of Esther. "After all," they pointed out, "there were those who didn't feel that Esther should be included in the Bible in the first place." So they studied and probed and combed through the text carefully.

I regret to inform you of these serious objections that have been raised to the Book of Esther in recent days by religious leaders of some considerable repute:

1. Anti-family values: King Ahasuerus's advisors tell him that Queen Vashti's behavior will make all wives despise their husbands (1:17). Clearly the beginning of the story is a bad example for the preservation of family values.

2. Sexual harassment: Queen Vashti is ordered to appear wearing her royal diadem "to display her beauty to the peoples and the officials" (1:11). Clearly the King is using her for his own purposes, and there are even those who say she is summoned to appear wearing *only* her royal crown.

3. Misogyny, or hatred of women: the King orders that beautiful young virgins be sought, supplied with cosmetics, and that a beauty contest will ensue to choose the new Queen (2:2ff.).

4. Idolatry: Mordecai is ordered to kneel or bow low before Haman, and refuses (3:2).

5. Corruption and bribery: Haman offers to pay 10,000 talents

of silver for the destruction of the Jews, and the offer is accepted (3:9).

6. Drug use: King Ahasuerus hosts a seven-day-long banquet, where the rule for drinking was "no restrictions!" (1:7-8). When the Jews' fate was sealed, the King and Haman sit down to drink (3:15).

7. Violence: A gallows is erected for the purpose of hanging Mordecai (5:14); it is later used to hang Haman (7:9).

8. Sexually explicit material: From the beginning of the book, reference is made to the eunuchs attending the King and Queen (1:10). It cannot be described further here.

9. Violence: The revenge of the Jews on their enemies is described in some detail (9:5 ff), setting a terrible example for subsequent generations.

10. Adultery: Haman is caught lying on Esther's couch (7:8), clearly exemplifying the wrong values for readers of all ages.

Truth be told, these ten objectionable passages are just the beginning of the end of the Book of Esther. The story is filled with explicit material, violence, the disintegration of the family (Esther, after all, has neither father nor mother, and Mordecai has a bizarre relationship to his cousin and adopted daughter, Esther.) This is a book, moreover, wherein women do not know their place, where men do not know their place, wherein no one knows his/her place, and which is politically incorrect in the extreme.

These recent censors have discovered these objectionable passages and have concluded in community after community that to let our children read this book would be to pollute their minds. To make this book the center of a ritual, a service, or even (heaven forbid) a holiday, would be blasphemous. "Can there be any greater purpose than to protect our children from illicit materials?" they asked.

Consequently, they have set out to expunge the Book of Esther from the Bible and to cancel all Purim celebrations in any community where they might hold a majority on the school board, the power commission, the water authority, the boxing commission, or other places of political power.

What I find most disappointing about these backward-thinking people is that they miss the point. There is room for both a children's version of the story of Esther and an adult version.

The only way that we can fight back and preserve the holiday of Purim for all generations, is to make sure that we have enough adults at our Purim service every year. We need more than just the parents of young children to be at the service. We need people with grown children, people without children, people with positions of power and influence in our congregation and our community to join together to cheer Esther and Mordecai, to drown out the name of Haman. They need to appreciate the nuances of this Book and the messages it has for every generation.

Don't let them take it away from us! Join us for the Purim service and Megillah reading. This is, after all, an adult book with adult themes, and we must protect our children from those who would take this story away from them.

2001

Most people think that the "chad" is a modern invention relating to punch card ballots.* This is not so. Indeed, there is considerable evidence that the chad is of biblical origins, and investigating the use of this word in the Book of Esther can further our understanding of the authentic meaning of the story.

The word *chad* occurs in the Bible in Ezekiel 33:30, as a version of *echad*, meaning "one." The *aleph* drops away, as it does frequently in Rabbinic Hebrew, leaving the one-syllable word, pronounced with a guttural "ch," as in "loch" (never as in "chop"). As we will see, the two words are interchangeable in biblical Hebrew.

The word *chad* also means "sharp," as in Ezekiel 5:1, Psalm 57:5, and Isaiah 49:2, referring to a sharp knife, a blade, a sharp tongue or mouth. Clearly what is implied here is the instrument used for punch-card ballots and the sharp words that follow upon elections.

In order to understand the subtleties of the text, however, we need to put these two meanings of the word together.

When we do, we understand that the Book of Esther is not about the Jewish Queen finding her identity and saving her people. No, the Book of Esther is about the contest between Haman and Mordecai for the office of Prime Minister.

The word *echad* occurs four times in the Book of Esther. And, as I will demonstrate, each time this word is used, it refers to the protrusion from the punch card ballots in the election for Prime Minister.

Esther 3:8 Haman says to King Ahasuerus: "There is a *chad* people, scattered and dispersed among the other peoples ... in your realm, whose laws are different from those of any other people and who do not obey the king's laws; and it is not in Your Majesty's interest to tolerate them." Clearly Haman here is referring to the Jewish people, the clan of Mordecai, his opponent in the forthcoming election. Haman here is stating that the Jewish people ***stick out***.

Esther 3:13 "Accordingly, written instructions were dispatched by couriers to all the King's provinces to destroy, massacre, and exterminate all the Jews, young and old, children and women, on a *chad* day, on the thirteenth day ... of the month of Adar, and to plunder their possessions." This prescribed day of reckoning for the Jewish people, in Haman's decree, issued by King Ahasuerus, was a day that would **stand out** for the Jews.

Esther 7:9 King Ahasuerus learns that Haman is about to engage in illegal election practices by destroying the other candidate's voters: an entire people. The King is enraged at this presumptive act; Haman pleads for his life with Queen Esther; and just then Harbonah, the *chad* of the eunuchs attending the King reveals that Haman has erected at his house a stake for Mordecai. Harbonah courageously speaks out at this critical moment in the story, thereby **standing out** from all the other of the King's attendants.

Esther 8:11-12 The King has permitted the Jews of every city to assemble and fight for their lives ... on *chad* day in all the provinces of King Ahasuerus, namely, on the thirteenth day of Adar. Clearly the day **stands out** for the Jewish people, as it does for all the people of the realm of King Ahasuerus. The dire fate of the Jews throughout the kingdom is happily averted, and the tables are turned. Haman, once the aggressor, is now put on the defensive. The Jewish people is saved, Mordecai wins the election for Prime Minister, and justice is done.

As I have demonstrated, the word *chad* means to stand out, or stick out, a clear reference to the punch card ballots that were used for Prime Minister elections in biblical times. While we may not have strong archaeological evidence, the textual evidence I have demonstrated above is clear.

Thus this linguistic analysis forces us to rethink our understanding of the Book of Esther.

The focus of the story is really the election of Prime Minister for the entire realm of King Ahasuerus: 127 provinces from India to Ethiopia; the primary characters of the book, of course, are Haman and Mordecai.

It is most unfortunate that the focus of the book was shifted to Queen Esther by misguided feminist editors at the time that the biblical text was completed. Indeed, this tampering with the text—compared to the original intent of the story—turned the ancient rabbis against the book, almost leading them to remove it from the biblical canon. Prescient rabbis, with foresight about future election and punch card ballot issues, led some of the religious leaders to press for inclusion of the Book of Esther in the Bible.

Today, unfortunately, the original meaning of the book is all but forgotten, and there are even those feminist critics who look to the book for a glimmer of hope that Esther and Vashti, Esther's predecessor as queen, might serve as examples of strong women characters in the Bible. All this misses the core point of the story, an election drama if ever there was one.

When the election was over and Mordecai became Prime Minister and Haman was punished for attempting to rig the election, a victory song was written: *"Chad Mi Yodea?"* or "Who knows the Chad?" It was—and is—a merry song, with all participants joining in as they count from one to twelve. Over time, this song became disassociated from Purim and bumped to the Passover Seder, where it is still an important element in the celebration.

I hope my insightful analysis of the biblical origins of the chad and the real meaning of the Book of Esther can be brought to light again for all Jews to appreciate.

---

*"Hanging chads" became noteworthy during the contested 2000 Presidential election when many of Florida's incompletely punched ballots were not counted by tabulating machines.

2002

For many generations Bible readers and scholars alike have wondered about the party that Queen Esther gave for King Ahasuerus and Haman. You remember that the Queen, with considerable trepidation, comes to the King, who asks her, "What troubles you, Queen Esther? And what is your request? Even to half the kingdom, it shall be granted you" (5:3). The Queen answers, "Let your majesty and Haman come today to the feast that I have prepared" (5:4).

But why this sudden dinner party? What was the occasion? Certainly it was important, for Haman boasted to his wife and friends, "Queen Esther gave a feast, and besides the King she did not have anyone but me. And tomorrow, too, I am invited along with the King" (5:12).

Recent textual studies that I have undertaken have demonstrated that the purpose of Queen Esther's dinners was to celebrate her fiftieth birthday. Some may find this surprising. They have thought that Queen Esther was young. They have thought this because over the years so many children have dressed up as Queen Esther on Purim. They have thought it because she is described as being "shapely and beautiful" (2:7). They have thought it because the text tells us that when her parents died Mordecai, her uncle, had adopted her as his own daughter.

But nowhere does it say how old Mordecai was or how old Esther was.

The proof that Esther was celebrating her fiftieth birthday, however, comes not from the silence of not knowing how old she was, but from the text itself. As often happens in the biblical text, a word is misplaced—in this case the word *chamishim*, or fifty. In chapter 5:14 the word appears, with Haman's wife and friends saying to him, "Let a stake be put up, fifty cubits high. ... " Clearly the word "fifty" slipped down from the previous verse, "Queen Esther gave a fiftieth birthday feast," and a discreet scribe years ago moved the word to indicate the height of the gallows rather than the age of the Queen.

There are those who think that the age of the Queen was supposed to remain a secret, just as other things in her background were confidential. After all, "Mordecai had told her not to reveal her people or her kindred" (2:10). Indeed the word for "kindred" really means her age, but biblical translators wanted to make a secret of the fact that her age itself was secret.

Perhaps Mordecai was concerned about age discrimination in the palace, especially in the beauty pageant. Mordecai, as a caring uncle and foster father, wanted nothing but the best for his niece, and he saw that there might be those who would be concerned about a Queen in her forties.

In the climactic scene in the book, Esther says that all that she requests is her life and her people. King Ahasuerus asks, "Who would dare to threaten the Queen?" Esther answers, "Haman." For some reason, the mortified Haman is found by the King "lying prostrate on the couch on which Esther reclined" (7:8).

I've always wondered about this scene. Quite clearly Haman is begging for forgiveness, but why is Queen Esther lying down? Now I understand it. She is tired from her fiftieth birthday party and is lying on a special "fiftieth couch." After all, the word "fifty" appears in the next verse (7:9), obviously misplaced by another scribal error that moved it to a new location.

So there you have it. Esther and Mordecai attempt to keep her age a secret, fearing age discrimination. Queen Esther plans a private fiftieth birthday party, as demonstrated by the text. As part of the birthday party, she lies down on a special fiftieth birthday couch, an integral part of the story.

Clearly the story is about Queen Esther saving the Jewish people, but it is also about her coming of age. She had reached the age of "giving counsel" (as the Rabbis would later say), a significant milestone in anyone's life. And she wanted to have an important celebration to mark this milestone.

Congregations have fiftieth birthdays too, just like Queen Esther. Temple Sinai's fiftieth birthday party is on Saturday night, February 23, just before Purim. There will be delicious food (fit for a Queen and King), great music, and lots of excitement.

We are also celebrating the burning of the mortgage on our building, the tenth anniversary of our nursery school, and the life-changing success of Sinai House. What an opportunity! It only comes once every fifty years, so don't miss out. And be sure to send a separate check supporting Sinai House with your response. This year, more than ever, we need to celebrate. Remember the Yiddish proverb, "There are so many Hamans, but just one Purim."

2003

Once there was a young girl named Esther. Orphaned at a young age, she was reared by her cousin Mordecai and his wife, Invisible. Esther was not an easy child to rear, truth be told, and she caused great concern to her noble cousins. She was frivolous and unfocussed and didn't seem to care about very much. She was into make-up in a big way and seemingly addicted to instant messaging. Most of the time she just wanted to "hang" with her friends, a phrase Mordecai and Invisible found most alarming and distasteful in their Shushan community. Esther did not like religious school, went grudgingly, and couldn't wait for it to be over. At the same time she couldn't wait for her bat mitzvah, because she would get to wear a lot of make-up, be with her friends, and have a blast of a party.

Mordecai and Invisible were most concerned about Esther's "attitude" and lack of direction. "Where will her values come from? What will become of her?" they asked one another. And most of all they asked, "Will there be Jewish life after bat mitzvah?"

Mordecai and Invisible admired Queen Vashti, because she was able to balance her career as a physicist with her palace responsibilities. She was a cutting-edge scientist who somehow managed to put up with her buffoon of a husband. Then one night, as you know, he got drunk again, and Vashti found herself deposed, still a good scientist, but no longer the Queen.

Immediately young Esther wanted to take Vashti's place. She wasn't so interested in the authority that the queen might wield. All her friends were interested, too, and Esther wanted to be with them. She had heard, moreover, that there was a lot of make-up in the palace and real make-up experts to show you how to use it. What more could a young girl ask for?

"When will she grow up?" Mordecai and Invisible asked each other. "What's a nice Jewish girl doing putting on make-up in the palace?" But the more Invisible and Mordecai worried about their cousin, the more set in her ways she became.

You can imagine how surprised Mordecai and Invisible were when (as the story says) "Esther was taken to King Ahasuerus, in his palace. ... The King loved Esther more than all the other women, and she won his grace and favor; so he set a royal diadem on her head and made her Queen instead of Vashti" (Esther 2:16-17).

Mordecai and Invisible wondered, "What will happen next? Will she rise to the position? Will she get beyond make-up and instant messaging? Will she remember who she is? Will there be Jewish life after bat mitzvah?"

Fortunately for our story, there was an unhappy crisis. Haman threatened all the Jews, and this gave Mordecai the opportunity to remind Esther that: (1) She needed to do something serious for once in her life. (2) She needed to appeal to the King and plead for her people. (3) "Do not imagine that you, of all the Jews, will escape with your life by being in the King's palace" (4:13). and (4) "And who knows, perhaps you have attained to royal position for just such a crisis" (4:14).

This was quite a wake-up call for Esther, who simply had been enjoying palace life until then. She had first wondered, "Won't this just blow away?" But Mordecai was direct in saying, "If you keep silent in this crisis, relief and deliverance will come to the Jews from another quarter, while you and your father's house will perish" (4:14).

What would she do? First she decided to give up food, fasting for three days, along with her maidens, and asking all the Jews to do the same. Then she gave up instant messaging. Then she even gave up make-up. Then, with her head clear and her values restored, she appeared before the King and asked him to join her for a game of Ultimate Frisbee and bring Haman along as well.

When Esther and the King met again on the next day, she took a deep breath and told the King that what she really wanted was her life, and the life of her people, and Jewish life after bat mitzvah.

"Jewish?" said the King. "But I thought you were Persian, with a name like Esther." "I changed my name," said Esther, "from Hadassah, because we thought it sounded better, you know, more acceptable in the palace." The King was dumbfounded and not very bright, but at least he remembered that he loved Esther, and he knew that she was loyal to him. The King turned on Haman, the evil one, and saw to it that Haman would "hang" with his friends. Moreover, he purged that phrase out of the language of Shushan for many centuries ... until quite recently, in fact.

Esther, for her part, went on to college and graduate school, pursued a career as a historian of science, and wrote her dissertation on significant Jewish figures in the scientific life of the kingdom. Eventually Mordecai and Invisible stopped worrying about Esther and realized that since she taught religious school and volunteered at her synagogue, there was, indeed, Jewish life for her after bat mitzvah.

2004

There have been many people over the years who have looked to the Bible for answers to their problems. Many have found wisdom, and many have thought that by looking at the codes embedded in the Bible, they would find not only guidance for life but also answers to contemporary problems. In recent years there have been several books that have elaborated on the biblical "codes" which can be broken by interpreting the Hebrew letters or their numeric equivalents.

With this in mind I turned to the Bible for help in solving the mystery of the missing weapons of mass destruction.* I thought it was reasonable to look in the Hebrew Bible for the "WMDs" since Hebrew (as we all know) is a language based on roots of three letters. Perhaps there would be a hidden message in the biblical text that would solve this mystery that has confounded our nation and much of the world.

The first problem was what letters in Hebrew related to "WMD." This is no small matter, since there is no "W" in Hebrew. While there is no exact equivalent, the "W" of course looks just like the Hebrew letter *shin*. When you realize this, and you realize that the Hebrew word *shin mem dalet* means "destroy," it appears we are on to something.

Where, you may ask, does this word appear most often in the Bible? Of course, it is in the Book of Esther, where Haman plots to destroy all the Jewish people (Esther 3:6); and in three parallel passages there are written instructions issued by the King to destroy, massacre, and exterminate the Jews (Esther 3:13, 7:4 and 8:11). But this still does not answer where we can find the clue for the missing weapons of mass destruction.

There is a fifth occurrence of the word "destroy" in Esther 4:8, "he also gave him the written text of the law that had been proclaimed in Shushan for their destruction." The word "written text" in our translation is *patshegen*, a word that occurs only once in the Hebrew Bible. The word is clearly not a Hebrew word but borrowed from

Aramaic, a cognate language with Hebrew at the latter biblical period. But curiously enough, a similar word, *parshegen*, occurs in the Book of Ezra (7:11). Truth be told, we have no idea what these words mean. But we do know one thing: that the biblical authors or scribes weren't quite sure how to spell the word because they spelled it two different ways in two different books. Let's look at the word carefully, and if we do, we see that the word that is supposed to be there is really "pentagon," a word we all know and understand. Indeed, "pentagon" has been camouflaged in the biblical text to conceal the real meaning of these words in our day. By changing one letter, the biblical authors have diverted our attention from the real solution to this biblical puzzle; they have changed "pentagon" into a "handwritten copy." Today we can change the word back to its original form, read the verse as it was intended, and solve the biblical puzzle: "He sent the Pentagon word of the presence of weapons of mass destruction."

Moral: You can never be too careful or too scrupulous when searching for the truth.

---

*The primary purpose articulated by the Bush administration for invading Iraq in 2003 was to find and destroy Saddam Hussein's purported cache of weapons of mass destruction, or WMD. Investigations later determined that Iraq's WMD program had been abandoned years earlier.

2005

Q: What is "Purim-Torah"?
A: A parody based on a Jewish text in honor of the joyous holiday of Purim.
A: You're supposed to be happy in the month of Adar, especially on Purim, so we try to be funny.
A: We make fun on Purim— of ourselves, even of Jewish texts.
A: Jews are supposed to believe in humor, especially on Purim.

Mordecai had this message delivered to Esther: "Do not imagine that you, of all the Jews, will escape with your life by being in the King's palace. On the contrary, if you keep silent in this crisis, relief and deliverance will come to the Jews from another quarter. ... And who knows, perhaps you have attained a royal position for just such a crisis" (Esther 4:13-14).

This is a crucial turning point in the story, so we should look at these verses very carefully. Esther is reluctant to help her people. Mordecai is somewhere between insistent and intense. He is looking for any way to fight the King's edict and save his (and Esther's) people.

For generations, people have wondered what Mordecai means by "another quarter." Some commentators wondered if this is a veiled reference to God, who is otherwise absent from the story and the entire book (in case you hadn't noticed) and speculate that Mordecai is predicting a *deus ex machina* conclusion to the story.

What Mordecai is really complaining about is his vision of the future—where it seems that only children celebrate Purim.

He foresaw that adults would consider Purim a holiday of Pediatric Judaism, the fifth Jewish movement. If they don't have children to bring to the Temple, they just stay home. "What a pity!" says Mordecai, because it is the adults, not the children, who will be able to save the Jewish people. Too many adults, Mordecai predicts, will practice

Vicarious Judaism, the sixth Jewish movement. They will believe they are Jewishly involved because they send their children to the Temple, but they forget to go themselves. Some drop off their children on Sunday mornings and do not venture into the building; others send their children with other people and keep an even greater distance.

Mordecai states that relief (*revach*) will come to the Jews from another quarter. The Hebrew word *revach* occurs only this one time in the entire Hebrew Bible. This leads some of us to think that maybe it is a copying error, an opportunity to emend the text. All we have to do is to change the vowels and the word becomes *ruach:* spirit or enthusiasm.

Then the meaning of Mordecai's statement becomes clear: "If you keep silent in this crisis, the Jews will find new enthusiasm for this story and this holiday." Mordecai thus predicts that at some point adults will say, "It's time for us to have a part of Purim. It's high time we, too, celebrate." After all, this is an X-rated story, full of intrigue, sexual harassment, drunken orgies, and general ridiculousness. The children can have their version and their celebration, of course. But we need to let the adults celebrate, too—with enthusiasm and spirit and spirits, as the Rabbis prescribed.

At Temple Sinai, we will follow Mordecai's insistent command.

We also will gather to find deliverance from the _____ crisis of the day. Take your choice: Social Security, apathy, values, Jewish indifference, taxes, traffic, anthrax. Join us as we celebrate the lost adult holiday, Purim.

2007

As a former high school and college debater, I have long been interested in the origin of debate. There are those who trace debate back to the Roman Senate, clearly a forum for the exchange of ideas. Others trace debate back to the Greek philosophers, who engaged in dialogue, and through dialogue, found truth and understanding. In the Jewish world, there are those who trace debate back to the rabbis of the Talmud, who argued over points of law. Others see the origins of debate in the story of Moses, who presented his case before Pharaoh, tangling with the royal courtiers and magicians.

They are all wrong. The truth is that debate began in the court of Ahasuerus, told in the Purim story in the Book of Esther. The proof is clear.

So many people who have read the first chapter of Esther have wondered how the King could give a banquet that lasted seven days (1:5). The Hebrew word here, *mishteh*, comes from the word "to drink," so we know right away that it was not a food banquet. But could there be a seven-day drinking orgy? Hardly. There must be a deeper meaning, and I am pleased to report that I have found it. The seven-day event was a debate tournament. The text specifically states that there were representatives from the 127 provinces of the kingdom, which extended from India to Ethiopia. A separate tournament was hosted by Queen Vashti for the women (1:9) because coeducational debate had not yet found acceptance in the kingdom. There were judges and experts present, for the text clearly tells us, "The King consulted the sages learned in procedure" (1:13).

Perhaps you are thinking that you learned that the King hosted a drinking feast, and that is what the text seems to say. In the Bible, however, we always must look beneath the surface to more nuanced meanings. Sometimes these meanings can be found in the letters themselves. Using the time-honored Jewish practice of *gematria*, we can assign a numerical value to each letter. By adding the letter values, we learn the numerical value of each word and find some of the hidden meanings.

The letters of *mishteh* add up to 745. Add the word *diyun*, or debate, equaling 60, to make 805. Now take the Hebrew words *l'hitvakeach Purim*, "to argue a Purim debate." They, too add up to 805. Could this be a coincidence? Absolutely not! To the contrary, this proves that the banquet (*mishteh*) was really a Purim debate tournament.

In the modern period, this tradition has been transformed into a latke-hamantasch debate, originating at (why am I not surprised?) the University of Chicago Hillel Foundation more than 60 years ago. While the tradition there may be to mark this annual event on the Tuesday before Thanksgiving, they are clearly wrong; as I have just proved, it is a Purim tradition and should be marked as such.

This year we are bringing this noble tradition to Washington (the capital, as Shushan was the capital). The first Latke-Hamantasch Debate at Temple Sinai will decide which delicacy is the ultimate Jewish food.

Don't forget the ancient Jewish proverb: The proof is in the hamantasch. Be happy. It's the month of Adar.

2008

For centuries, biblical scholars and rabbis of all sorts have wondered about Esther's feast, as described in the Purim story. First Esther risks her life and appears before the King without being summoned. She asks him to come to a banquet she has prepared, along with Haman (Esther 5:1-4).

When the King and Haman arrive and the King asks her what she wants, she says only, "Please come to another banquet I have prepared for tomorrow night" (5:7-8).

As the narrative suspense increases, readers and scholars alike have wondered for centuries what Esther served at this famous banquet. While many Jewish holidays have specific foods associated with them, Purim has only a dessert: hamantaschen (Haman's pockets or [in Hebrew] Haman's ears). We doubt that Esther served these for dessert; but more importantly, what was the main course?

We Jews have always felt that the text tells us the story. One rabbi 2000 years ago wrote, "Turn the text over and over, for all knowledge is within it" (Avot 5:22).

There are many ways to analyze a biblical text. Scholars have used concordances for many years; some trace words in other cognate Semitic languages, such as Syriac and Akkadian, to determine how a rare word in the biblical Hebrew text may have come from another language. For really tough cases, we resort to numerology, adding up the numerical equivalents of particular words that we suspect have a hidden meaning in the very letters.

This is what I have done to determine the menu of the *mishteh* or "banquet." The simple meaning of the word is that it was a drinking feast, but we can hardly imagine that Queen Esther would have invited the King and Haman to a cocktail party and not served any food. But can we recapture the ancient menu and use it in our contemporary Purim celebrations in the 21st century?

I have good news as we ponder this weighty question. Scholars have recently discovered an original text of the heretofore-lost Talmudic tractate called Baba Meiseh that contains a fascinating and enlightening discussion of the Purim story.

In Baba Meiseh, Rabbi Sheylah asks: "What is *mishteh*? Scripture refers to it as the banquet that Esther served, but what did she serve?"

Rabbi Shikur answered: "*Mishteh* means a drinking party. How do we know that she served food at all?"

Rabbi Chacham: "Surely you can't drink without eating. And no Jewish hostess would invite people over without something to eat."

Rabbi Sheylah: "But what was the menu? What did she serve?"

Rabbi Chacham: "Let us look to the letters of the words themselves. The letters of Purim add up to 336. I once visited my colleague, Rabbi Mordecai, who had a special interest in Purim because of his name. He said that there were those who said that Esther served cheese, but others said it could not have been for she knew that the King was lactose-intolerant. There were those who said that she served peanut butter squares. But it could not be, for she knew that Haman had a nut allergy, and Esther did not want to confront him yet.

Rabbi Mordecai continued: "Surely she served chicken, a staple in many Jewish recipes. There are those that say that Esther was a vegetarian, but it was not so. How do we know? The letters of chicken, *ofe*, add up to 156. The difference between 156 and 336 is 180, a magical number in Jewish lore. 180 is 18 times 10, or ten lives. Surely this is a reference to the ten sons of Haman who were killed later in the story (9:7-9). A better proof-text you cannot find: Ten times life foreshadows the end of the story and confirms the chicken menu."

Rabbi Sheylah: "What kind of chicken? What was the recipe?"

Rabbi Chacham: "Once again we must look to the letters and their value for hidden meaning. The letters of *mishteh* add up to 745." He continued in the name of Rabbi Mordecai: "Clearly she served chicken fingers, for the letters of "fingers," or *etzabaot*, add up to 569. The difference of 176 (*kuf, ayin, vav*) is a Hebrew abbreviation for offerings of lesser or higher value. This phrase refers to offerings in the days of the ancient Tabernacle, where Israelites who could afford to bring more gave larger offerings, and those who could not brought smaller offerings— thus, the invention of the graduated income tax and synagogue dues system. Esther served chicken tenders because they were convenient and every non-vegetarian enjoys them still. They also conveyed a hidden message: Each of us should support the community according to our means. It is a value ahead of its time—and a delicious Purim treat."

I can hardly contain my excitement in knowing that the menu for Esther's feast was chicken fingers. This year we are serving chicken fingers (and vegetarian alternatives) at our Purim dinner in commemoration of this discovery. Join us also for a Latke-Hamantasch Debate. The debate last year was wildly successful, and by popular demand we have continued it this year. Have a new ritual once and it is an innovation. Have it twice and it is a tradition.

2009

For many generations, Megillah readers and listeners have wondered what Esther served at the feast she prepared for King Ahasuerus and Haman.

You may remember that Queen Esther invited them to a feast and as soon as they arrived and asked Esther what she wanted, she replied that she wanted them to come to the feast the next day. Why the double invitation? If Esther wanted to invite them for the next day, why didn't she do that the first time? The answer is clear and will be understood by anyone who has prepared a large feast: caterer failure.

While there are some who say that the feast was really a drinking party, pointing to the fact that it is called a wine feast, *mishteh yayin*, the truth is that there must have been food served. After all, no Jewish host or hostess would invite people over simply to drink wine without having some very special food, especially for a King and a Prime Minister.

The question persists, then: What did Esther serve?

Answers to these deep questions often are found within the text itself. Through the magic of *gematria*, we can discern the menu for the feast. In using *gematria*, we determine the numerical value of each letter in the Hebrew alphabet and see where our journey takes us.

In this case, we begin with the holiday of Purim, which has the numerical value of 336. In the part of the Esther narrative that is often overlooked, we read that the ten sons of Haman are hung, in part as reprisal for Haman's attempted destruction of the Jewish community.

- We multiply these ten sons by their lives that were taken (or *chai*/18) and come up with 180, an important and significant number in the context of the Purim story.
- By subtracting 180 from 336 we are left with the number 156, which certainly must have special significance of some sort in the Purim story.

Its significance is, of course, the source of sustenance for Esther, the food she served at the royal feast. You may want to think of it this way: when we remove the elements of death from the Purim story, what is left that sustains life? What Esther served—the main dish—the pièce de résistance of the feast—is tied closely to the climax of the story, when Esther reveals her identity, acknowledges her Judaism, and explains how Haman has betrayed the King, the Queen, and the Jewish people.

It is no coincidence that the Hebrew word *ofe*, or chicken, has the numeric value of 156. Certainly Bible commentators and archaeologists alike have long speculated that it was chicken that Queen Esther served at the royal feast, and this excursion into *gematria* surely proves the point.

Why, you might ask, did Esther first invite the King and Haman to her feast and then when they showed up say that all she wanted to do was to invite them for the next day? The answer is that at the last minute Esther lost her chicken purveyor, identified by some scholars as Pollo Shushan. Suddenly, the source of the main entrée went out of business, requiring Queen Esther to reschedule and regroup. She understood that she could not have a feast with just wine but that she needed food—good food—to provide to the King and to Haman. It took her another day to find another chicken supplier, one who would be able to meet the high standards of the palace community, and we understand from the outcome of the story that the chicken purveyor provided just what was needed. There are those commentators who say that the name of the holiday—Purim—is based on the multiple **purveyors** that Esther sought.

Something similar has happened at Temple Sinai. The chicken purveyor that we have used for Tot Shabbat and Shalom Shabbat for many years recently folded his tent and moved on. In our quest for the perfect entrée, we have scoured the metropolitan area, spoken with our congregants, designed and distributed feedback forms, and our quest continues. Unlike Queen Esther, we are unable to delay a day and really must have our chicken (and our vegetarian alternatives) on the day that people come to worship. So our quest for the perfect food—the perfect entrée—continues.

Do not delay. Mark your calendar now, and bring your sense of humor. While you may have misplaced it in these dark hours, I know it's there somewhere. We all need Purim every year, and this year it's especially important.

2010

To this day, no one really understands what the word "Purim" means. You probably learned in Sunday School that the word means "lots," referring to the lots that Haman cast to determine the date on which the Jews would be destroyed (Esther 3:7 and 9:24). Like so many other things that you learned in Sunday School, however, there is more to it.

In fact, scholars simply do not know. As Hayyim Schauss points out in his classic *Guide to Jewish Holy Days:* "The origin of Purim cannot be stated with certainty" (p. 252). In a note, Schauss explains: "The meaning that the name 'Purim' originally had is also obscure to this day. The explanation that the Book of Esther gives for the name was conceived in later times. For a festival must acquire its name from the essence of the day, not from an unimportant incident. Of what importance is it that Haman decreed the day through the throwing of lots? The various explanations offered by Jewish and Christian scholars for the name Purim are mere hypotheses and none of them wholly satisfactory."

Over the years, scholars have speculated that "pur" was related to *purah* (wine-press), or *parur* (pot), or *parar* (to split or divide). All of these are wrong and have been discredited.

Until now, that is. For here I reveal the true hidden meaning of "pur." How was I able to discover this hidden meaning?

One day I was studying the famous saying of the first century Rabbi Ben Bag Bag, referring to Torah: "Turn it and turn it, for everything is in it. Reflect on it and grow old and gray with it. Don't turn from it, for nothing is better than it" (Avot 5:22). (I study this portion often because I identify with the gray part.)

This time I took the first command literally. I wrote out the word פור and turned it upside down. You need to try this now. This Hebrew word written upside down, according to the prescription of Ben Bag Bag, becomes the English word "GIL."

In order to understand the hidden meaning, however, one needs to understand the English "GIL" as transliterated Hebrew. In Hebrew, *gil* (גּיל) means "age." This interpretive technique follows Ben Bag Bag: "Turn it and turn it." In other words, when we turn the word *pur* twice, we come up with *gil*, or "age."

Age is indeed a central theme of the Book of Esther, as we all know. The King Ahasuerus banishes his long-time (older) Queen Vashti and seeks not just a new queen, but a beautiful YOUNG maiden as the new queen. Shamelessly, the King throws off his life partner for a young virgin, seeking only YOUTHFUL replacements. It is our good fortune—and we thank God—that Esther came from a good family and was wise beyond her years.

A parallel plot, often overlooked, is revealed when Haman's wife, Zeresh, tells him, along with his trusted advisors, "If Mordecai ... is of Jewish stock, you will not overcome him; you will fall before him to your ruin" (6:13). Haman, of course, ignores the wise counsel of his mature wife and goes off on his own, making a pass for the YOUNG Esther. Some people never learn.

Clearly the message of the Purim story is to respect age and not chase after youth, especially if you are an old king who has trouble setting limits. I am so pleased that I discovered this hidden meaning before I retired, so I could share it with you. And how meaningful that the key was provided by Ben Bag Bag, who instructs us to "grow old and gray with it."

So be sure to read parts of this bulletin upside down, or in the mirror, to look for hidden meanings and solutions to everyday problems. You never know what you will find.

Scholarly Writings

C. D. Ginsburg and the Shapira Affair: A Nineteenth-Century Dead Sea Scroll Controversy

British Library Journal
Vol. 21, No. 1, Spring 1995
Reprinted with permission.

In July 1883, Moses Wilhelm Shapira, a well-known Jerusalem dealer in antiquities and ancient manuscripts, offered to sell a scroll of Deuteronomy to the British Museum, one of his regular customers. Thus began one of the most celebrated incidents in the history of biblical scholarship, a saga that continues more than a century later.[1] The Deuteronomy scroll offered by Shapira was written in the same ancient Canaanite Hebrew script (also called Palaeo-Hebrew or Phoenician) that appears on the Mesha or Moabite Stone. This particular palaeography, coupled with significant differences between this text and the standard biblical text, made the fifteen fragments of this scroll extremely interesting to Victorian Bible scholars. The possibility that an original or (at least) very ancient manuscript of Deuteronomy had been discovered generated great public interest.

Upon his arrival in London, Shapira first visited Sir Walter Besant, secretary of the Palestine Exploration Fund. As Besant recounted later in his *Autobiography*, "a certain Shapira, a Polish Jew converted to Christianity but not to good works, came to England and called upon me mysteriously. He had with him, he said, a document which would simply make students of the Bible and Hebrew scholars reconsider their ways; it would throw a flood of light upon the Pentateuch; . . . It was nothing less than a contemporary copy of the book of Deuteronomy written on parchment."[2] On 26 July 1883, Besant gathered a group of experts to view a manuscript that might have been written by Moses himself. Besant invited, among others, Christian David Ginsburg, the biblical and Masoretic scholar; Edward A. Bond, Principal Librarian of the British Museum; Captain Claude Conder; Professor Aldis Wright; and artist William Simpson. Ginsburg was asked to examine and evaluate the manuscript on behalf of the British Museum and to report his findings to Bond. In fact, Ginsburg did much more than that over the next month. He published a transcription of the scroll in the weekly journal *Athenæum*, helping to promote considerable public interest in it.[3] While Ginsburg performed his examination and review, some fragments were placed on display at the British Museum amid widespread publicity. Even the Prime Minister, William Gladstone, a friend of Ginsburg and a supporter of his research, came to view them. The *Jewish Chronicle* referred to the scroll as the "New Version of Deuteronomy."[4] Scholars came from Europe, including the French scholar and diplomat, Charles Clermont-Ganneau.

Finally, on 22 August, Ginsburg reported to Bond, "The MS of Deuteronomy which Mr. Shapira submitted to us for examination is a forgery."[5] The next day Shapira wrote a desperate letter to Ginsburg: " . . . you have made a fool of me by publishing and exhibiting them [the fragments], that you believe them to be false. I do not think that I will be able to survive this shame. Although I am not yet convince [*sic*] that the MS. is a forgery unless M. Ganneau did it. I will leave London in a day or two for Berlin."[6] Shapira disappeared for more than six months, and on 9 March 1884, he committed suicide in Rotterdam. The Shapira fragments also have disappeared, but the incident has remained one of the great scholarly controversies of all time. Ginsburg was portrayed as saving the British people considerable money and embarrassment, especially when word emerged that Shapira had earlier offered the scroll to German scholars who had rejected it.

In the 1950s, after the discovery of the Dead Sea Scrolls, there was renewed interest in the Shapira fragments. The American scholar Menahem Mansoor suggested that the Shapira Deuteronomy scroll might have been authentic, for Shapira had claimed the scroll was discovered near the Wadi Arnon on the east side of the Dead Sea. Mansoor's research was featured in the *New York Times* in August 1956 and later presented in a paper at a meeting of the Society of Biblical Literature in December 1956.[7] Mansoor's hypothesis was attacked by a number of biblical scholars at the time and defended by others.

Was Shapira guilty of fraud? Was he the "impudent forger" himself? Was Shapira misguided or was he sufficiently knowledgeable to pass judgement? How certain was he of the authenticity of the scroll? What were his motives? What risks was he taking? As for Ginsburg, why did he wait to release his verdict? If the scroll was a clear and clumsy forgery, why did he not recognize it immediately? Was he simply evaluating a suspicious document, or were other factors at work? The scroll fragments are still missing and presumably destroyed, so no new evidence is likely to come from them.[8] New evidence has emerged however, from contemporary accounts and letters. By studying Shapira's background and the relationships among Shapira, Ginsburg, the British Museum, and Charles Clermont-Ganneau, we may be able to understand better this fascinating incident in biblical and literary scholarship. Through a clearer appreciation of the individuals involved, we can cast some new light on the Shapira scroll incident.

At the time of Ginsburg's death, 7 March 1914, *The Times* retold the story of how "One of the most interesting incidents in Dr Ginsburg's career was his exposure in August, 1883, of the fraudulent Shapira manuscript of part of the Book of Deuteronomy."[9] The 1914 account is noteworthy because of several details:

The Manuscript . . . was offered to the British Museum for £10,000 [*sic*], but Dr. Ginsburg pronounced it to be a clumsy forgery, the work, probably, of four or five hands. Shapira committed suicide in the following year, and Dr. Ginsburg afterwards bought the manuscript for a few shillings at Sotheby's. . . .

Shapira had himself, in 1877, sold some [synagogue scrolls] to the British Museum and among other similarities it was found that the width of these slips corresponded exactly with the height of the slips on the forged manuscript.

Dr. Ginsburg thought that the person who compiled the text was not acquainted with the archaic characters in which it was written, and dictated it to amanuenses who reproduced faults of pronunciation that showed that the author was a Jew of Northern Europe.

To give the document an appearance of antiquity the Moabite Stone was used as a guide by both author and scribes. As it was expressed in a leading article in *The Times* of August 27, 1883, "The scribes have copied, with a very suspicious fidelity, the writing and the arrangement of works for which the stone furnishes an example."[10]

In 1914, then, the incident still was cited as an example of how Ginsburg saved the British people from public expense and embarrassment. Shapira was certainly remembered as a swindler and purveyor of fraudulent manuscripts. An 1883 *Punch* cartoon depicted Ginsburg and Shapira, in front of the British Museum "Showing, in very fanciful portraiture, how Detective Ginsburg actually did Mr. Sharp-eye-ra out of his skin."[11]

Up to 1883, however, Shapira had not been considered a swindler or a disreputable dealer in fraudulent antiquities. Facts are limited, and some sources are suspect. Nevertheless, we do know that M. W. Shapira was a dealer in antiquities and manuscripts in Jerusalem and that he had been a major supplier to the British Museum.[12] An autobiographical novel by Shapira's daughter, Myriam Harry, provides one portrait of the man, his work, and this incident. Certainly *La petite Fille de Jérusalem* (published in English as *The Little Daughter of Jerusalem*) is not an impartial and reliable source, but other sources verify Shapira's claim to be a "Correspondent to the British Museum."[13] Shapira's position as a reputable supplier of manuscripts is described by J. Leveen in his supplement to G. Margoliouth's *Catalogue of the Hebrew and Samaritan Manuscripts in the British Museum*. Leveen writes:

> With the appearance of the ill-fated bookseller W. M. [*sic*] Shapira, a third chapter opens in the history of the Hebrew collection . . . Shapira travelled extensively though the east and tapped previously unexploited sources, with the result that the Hebrew collection was enriched by nearly three hundred manuscripts between 1877 and 1882 . . . [T]he collection of 145 volumes acquired from Shapira in July 1882, . . . at one stroke raised the Karaite section of the Hebrew manuscripts to one of outstanding importance, only surpassed by the Firkovich collection in Leningrad . . . If the death of Shapira in 1884 dried up a fruitful source, the expansion of the Hebrew collection still went on, although manuscripts were not bought in such large numbers as from Shapira.[14]

By 1883, then, Shapira's place as a regular supplier of books and manuscripts to the British Museum was well established and recognized. Shapira wrote two articles for *Athenæum* in July 1882 describing the Karaite manuscripts he was selling to the British Museum.[15] He understood their importance to biblical scholarship and praised Ginsburg's work on the Masorah (the history of the text of the Hebrew Bible).[16] In 1881, Shapira had written on the Jerusalem Siloam inscription and also had tangled in *Athenæum* with both A. Neubauer and A. H. Sayce about the Siloam inscription, its palaeography and grammar.[17]

The Karaite manuscripts were of interest to Ginsburg, who had written a history of the Karaites early in his career.[18] In addition, Ginsburg wrote a descriptive review of one of these new acquisitions in *Athenæum* in March 1883.[19] In an introduction to six Karaite Bible manuscripts in 1889, Reinhart Hoerning also links Ginsburg and Shapira. Hoerning describes the manuscript collection purchased "in July, 1882, from the late M. W. Shapira, the well-known antiquarian bookseller of Jerusalem." The collection, Hoerning states, "raises the library of the British Museum to one of the vast storehouses of information concerning the history and literature of this curious and powerful sect."[20] Ginsburg's involvement is evident when Hoerning notes "his special thanks . . . to Dr. Ginsburg, not only for kindly aid in the revision of the proof sheets, but also instruction in the Masorah."[21] Presumably, in reading the proofs, Ginsburg did not object to this description of Shapira; Hoerning dedicates the volume to "his master and friend Professor Franz Delitzsch and Dr. Christian D. Ginsburg."[22]

The relationship between Ginsburg and Shapira dated back to at least to January 1872, when Ginsburg went on an expedition to Moab. He wrote in his journal on the 24th of that month, "I also saw another inscription of a similar character but of a much older date and therefore of greater importance. This Mr. Shapira possess [*sic*] and has kindly promised me a square."[23] Two days later Ginsburg wrote:

> I saw in the window of Mr. Shapira a bookseller and a dealer in antiquities a fragment of an old stone with an inscription which at cursory glance looked almost exactly [like] a piece of the Moabite Stone and I at first sight took it to be so. He then told me that he had more pieces and that he had only obtained them last night . . . Most impatiently I returned to Mr. Shapira and on my examining them more closely, I found that they were pieces of quite a different stone.[24]

Hoerning confirms that the relationship between Ginsburg and Shapira continued during the years 1877–82, when Shapira was helping the British Museum build its Hebrew manuscript collection. Thus, by the time Shapira came to London with his Deuteronomy manuscript and Ginsburg was asked to evaluate it, the two men had known each other and engaged in collaborative scholarly pursuits for more than eleven years.

To understand better Shapira's role in this episode, we should look at the letters he wrote to Hermann Strack on 9 May 1883 and to Edward A. Bond on 28 August 1883.[25] In a ten-page letter to Strack, Shapira describes "a curious manuscript written in old Hebrew on [sic] phoenician letters upon small strips of embalmed leather and [which] seems to be a short unorthodoxical book of the last speech of Moses in the plains of Moab."[26] Shapira describes his encounter with Bedouins in July 1878 when he heard the story of scrolls having been discovered several years before in caves above the Arnon River in Moab. These scrolls had been found by Arabs in the late 1860's, well before Shapira's trip to the east side of the Dead Sea with Professor Almgeitz in 1875.[27]

Shapira openly speculates on the scroll's authenticity. He explains to Strack that he had prepared a transcription and sent it to a Professor Schlottmann on 24 September 1878, five years earlier. Schlottmann had rebuked Shapira, stating, "How I dare to call this forgery the Old Test[ament]? Could I suppose even for a moment that it is older than our unquestionable genuine Ten Commandments?"[28] In response to Schlottmann's judgement, Shapira first asked himself, " . . . if it is by all means a forgery, who could have been such a learned and artful forger? And for what purpose? As the money I paid for the manuscripts was not worth the speaking of."[29] Shapira speculates the date of the manuscript to be " . . . judging from the form of the letters . . . an early time, as between the date of the Mesa stone and the Siloam inscription, or about the sixth century B. C. But one must be very cautious . . . the date may be very late. The question will of course be for scholars to decide."[30] At first Shapira concludes the letter by stating that Strack will "be better able to find the faults and virtues of it than I. I will also ask pardon for all my daring suggestions, and ask [you] to give me some candid opinion about it."[31] Yet then he adds a postscript: "Dr. Schroeder . . . German Counsul in Beiruth, is now here [in Jerusalem] and has seen a strip and thinks that the manuscript is unquestionable [sic] a genuine one, his chief proves [*sic*] are the beautiful Phoenician writing as well as the pure grammatical Hebrew and the outward look of it."[32] These are hardly the arguments of a conniving swindler, a forger, or someone pressing a sale of a questionable manuscript. On the contrary, Shapira goes out of his way to point out some of the problems in the manuscript, to raise different viewpoints, and to describe the flaws in the document.

Strack gave his reply in a letter to the *Times* on 31 August 1883:

> In the month of May last I received from Mr. Shapira, then at Jerusalem, a long communication concerning his codex [*sic*]. In my answer of the twenty-seventh I declared that it was not worth his while to bring such an evident forgery to Europe. At the end of June, or in the beginning of July, however . . . Mr. Shapira came to Berlin to see me and show me his manuscript. After a short examination of it, I repeated my former verdict . . . .[33]

Strack's immediate judgement (without having seen the manuscript) must have been difficult for Shapira, harking back to an incident in which Moabite pottery he had sold to Germany in 1873 was discovered to be forged.

Shapira's letter of 28 August 1883 to Edward A. Bond, following their July meeting at the British Museum, was written from Amsterdam. Shapira begs Bond for reconsideration of the manuscript and urges further examination of it by scholars from several different backgrounds. He writes, "The sin of believing in a false document is not much greater than disbelieving the truth. The tendency of showing great scholarship by detecting a forgery is rather great in our age."[34] Shapira reviews the arguments Ginsburg published in his report and answers many of them. He concludes by stating, ". . . I am not convinced that the manuscripts are false. Nevertheless, I do not wish to sell it [*sic*] even if the buyer should take the risk for himself (I have such offers.)"[35]

What about Schroeder, who had seen one of the scroll fragments? He not only judged them to be genuine but offered to buy them, an offer Shapira declined. Encouraged by this positive judgement, Shapira took the scroll fragments to Berlin in late June or early July to show to Strack, who remained unconvinced.[36] On the same trip, the persistent Shapira took the scroll fragments to Halle and Leipzig, where he met with Hermann Guthe on 30 June to show him the manuscript.[37] Guthe reports that he had personally met Shapira in Jerusalem in the spring and summer of 1881, and that Shapira came to see him in Leipzig to obtain his expert opinion of the manuscript.[38] With Guthe's publication of his monograph on the scroll fragments, completed on 14 August 1883, the Shapira manuscript officially achieved published scholarly recognition.[39]

Shapira then returned to Berlin, seeking further expert opinions and offering the scroll for sale to the Berlin Royal Library. On 10 July he presented the scroll to a group of scholars convened and hosted by Richard Lepsius, an Egyptologist who was the Keeper of the Royal Library, Berlin. This group of scholars also included August Dillmann, Eduard Sachau, Adolf Ermann, Schrader, and Moritz Steinschneider. In ninety minutes they reached their decision: the manuscript was a "clever and impudent forgery."[40] They refused to purchase the manuscript for the Royal Library.

Shapira next went to London, and thus began the notorious conclusion to his odyssey. Meeting with Walter Besant, secretary of the Palestine Exploration Fund, on Friday, 20 July, Shapira "informed the Secretary that he had brought to England a manuscript, which if genuine would be certainly considered of inestimable value, being nothing less than a text of the Book of Deuteronomy, written on sheepskin, in characters closely resembling those of the Moabite Stone, and with many and most important variations. He [Shapira] refused to show the documents to the Secretary, but offered to do so if Captain [Claude] Conder were also invited to be present." There was then a second meeting: "On Tuesday, the 24th he returned, and, in the presence of Captain Conder and Mr. Walter Besant, he produced the manuscript, and with it an account in writing of the manner in which he acquired it."[41]

By that second meeting between Besant and Shapira, Besant already had invited (on Monday, 23 July) a group of scholars to see the manuscript:

Palestine Exploration Fund, 1 Adam Street, 23 July 1883

Mr. Shapira of Jerusalem has brought to England an Old Hebrew Manuscript apparently of great antiquity containing the text of Deuteronomy with many important variations. He will bring the manuscript to this office on Thursday next the twenty-sixth . . . at 12 A. M. and will be very glad if you can meet him in order to see it.[42]

The group included Walter Besant, E. A. Bond, E. Budge, Mr. Bullen, Captain Claude Conder, Rev. C. D. Ginsburg, Professor Lewis Hayter, William Simpson (an artist with the *Illustrated London News*, who served on the P. E. F. Executive Committee), and Professor Aldis Wright of Oxford University. Perhaps there were ten people present, according to an eyewitness account of the meeting by William Simpson, who kept a journal and described the meeting six months after it occurred.[43] In his journal, Simpson gives a colourful account:

> Mr. Shapira produced a small glazed bag–the small "carpet-bag" of the period, from which he drew forth the pieces of very dark looking leather, and threw them in a very jaunty manner on the table, round which we all stood. With them were some fragments of Hebrew MSS., one of which was rolled up in a rude way, and suggested from its shape and colour the unsmoked half of a gigantic cigar, which I suggested must have been left by Og, King of Bashan . . . as the letters on the Deuteronomy MS were not very distinct, Shapira produced a bottle of spirits of wine and a hair pencil, and he washed them over with this so that the characters could be more clearly seen. To any one accustomed to precious documents, the rude way Shapira handled and rubbed these pretended old fragments was, had one believed them to be real, a sight to make one shiver. The grand performance of Shapira, however, was when one of the gentlemen put a question about the leather, and Shapira to show him what it was like, tore off a fragment nearly an inch in diameter and held it out in his hand. This he really did to a document he declared to be as old as 900 B.C. – Mr. Bullen was standing beside me, and I whispered in his ear, "See there is a precious fragment worth at least five hundred pounds torn off." – This estimate was of course based on Shapira's valuation of a million for the whole. At one time the bottle of spirits of wine tumbled on the table, and made a great mess — the MS. getting a full share of it. Of course nothing could be settled regarding the claims of the manuscript at such a meeting, and it was finally decided that

Dr. Ginsburg should take them in charge and keep them in the British Museum, while he inspected them. Dr. Ginsburg carried them off, — and the documents while I write are still in the Museum.

William Simpson 23 January 1884

Certainly Simpson is a trifle cavalier in his description of the 26 July meeting. According to Walter Besant's recollection, Simpson's comment about the value of the leather fragment Shapira tore off was made after most of the scholars had departed, with only Simpson, Besant, and Claude Conder in the room. Besant records that after stating, "I suppose it is worth five hundred pounds," Simpson " . . . chuckled and went his way. Simpson entertained a low view of the worthy Shapira, Christian convert."[44] Besant's view of Shapira was not much higher. Besant introduces the incident in his *Autobiography* by referring to "a certain Shapira, a Polish Jew converted to Christianity but not to good works," reflecting a bias that both Besant and Simpson may have shared.[45]

A week after the 26 July meeting at the Palestine Exploration Fund offices the first reports of the Shapira Deuteronomy manuscript appeared in the press. The *Times* of Friday, 3 August, carried the first report of "Fifteen leather slips" being offered to the British Museum; on the same day the *Jewish Chronicle* carried a "new version of Deuteronomy."[46] Ginsburg published the first translation of the manuscript the following Wednesday, 8 August; the first account of the origin of the scroll appeared in the *Jewish Chronicle* the following Friday; and the first of three articles appeared in *Athenæum* the next day.[47] The articles in *Athenæum* contained the new version of the Decalogue, in Hebrew and English, as well as a commentary. Ginsburg wrote, "In the next issue I hope to give the other portions of the text in their proper sequences, commencing with the beginning of Deuteronomy." The commentary in the *Athenæum* article is followed by a letter of 7 August 1883 from Shapira describing the history of the scroll and his acquisition of it.

In his second installment in *Athenæum*, on 18 August 1883, Ginsburg treats the manuscript as potentially legitimate, giving only a few textual notes at the end of his presentation of the manuscript's Hebrew text and a translation of the beginning of Deuteronomy.[48] In the last of the three articles, on 25 August 1883, Ginsburg comments, "I have designedly abstained from making any remark or calling attention to any anomalies in the Hebrew text, as my report, which is to appear next week, will contain a full account of all the peculiarities of the MS. And the conclusion I have arrived at about its genuineness."[49] Through these three articles in such a respected journal as *Athenæum*, Ginsburg lent an aura of credence to the manuscript and claimed he was an impartial judge. Since Ginsburg saved the numerous press accounts, which appeared daily in newspapers throughout England, it may be safe to assume that he relished the controversy he was nurturing.[50]

Shapira's letter to Ginsburg of 7 August describing the origin of the scroll and how he came to possess it was, in fact, the third in the course of a week. On 2 August he had written complaining that Ginsburg had failed to keep an appointment with him, and on the 6th, from his room at the Cannon Street Hotel, he had sent him a long defense of the charges against him concerning the Moabite pottery.[51]

Ginsburg's reticence regarding the scroll's genuineness was noticed by William Simpson, who made an undated entry in his journal:

> From that meeting [26 July] the pieces of leather . . . were removed to the British Museum, where Dr. Ginsburg has since been busily engaged transcribing the characters into their Hebrew equivalents, and also in translating the whole into English. This is now nearly completed and will be presented to the Trustees of the Museum. Dr. Ginsburg has been very reticent while so engaged, and has not expressed any opinion as to the genuineness of the manuscript; but he is understood to be making a report on it for the Trustees, to guide them as to whether they should enter into negotiations with Mr. Shapira for the purchase of the document. In this report Dr. Ginsburg will have to express his notions regarding its authenticity, and consequently all interested in Biblical matters are waiting anxiously to learn what such an authority will have to say, and whether the learned Dr. will date them 800 B. C. or 1800 A. D. The pieces of skin have become very much darker since they were first exhibited at the Office of the Palestine Exploration Fund. On the few parts of the leather where the characters could be easily seen they have now become so darkened that it is with difficulty they can be made out.[52]

Coupled with Ginsburg's reluctance in passing judgement on the scroll and his presentation of it as potentially authentic is his clear wish to encourage publicity about the fragments. His own publication of the text, translation and "comment" in *Athenœum* led to subsequent articles in the *Times*, the *Academy*, and a host of newspapers throughout England.[53] Nowhere in all this publicity is mention made of Shapira's visit to Europe, the judgement of German scholars, or Shapira's offer to sell the scroll to the Royal Library in Berlin. Through mid-August, the many newspaper accounts reveal that Ginsburg did much to publicize the manuscript and keep public interest stimulated. As Ginsburg took his time formulating his verdict, public excitement grew. Heightening the suspense, Ginsburg published his transcriptions and translations of the manuscript over a period of three weeks without ever indicating his evaluation of the scroll.

A subplot of this drama began to unfold on 15 August when the French diplomat and archaeologist, Charles Clermont-Ganneau, arrived in London to view the Shapira manuscript. Clermont-Ganneau had reason to be very interested in the Shapira manuscript; it was he who had proved that Moabite pottery pieces which Shapira had sold earlier to the German government were forgeries. Shapira viewed Clermont-Ganneau as an enemy, as he was portrayed in *The Little Daughter of Jerusalem*, the autobiographical novel by Shapira's daughter. One recalls that after Ginsburg's verdict was published, Shapira wrote him the distraught letter (23 August 1883) quoted at greater length above, stating, "I do not think that I will be able to survive this shame. Although I am yet not convince [*sic*] that the MS. is a forgery unless M. Ganneau did it . . . ."[54] While many commentators have noted this historical connection, none has pointed out the connection between Clermont-Ganneau and Ginsburg. Both were deeply interested in and published versions of the Moabite Stone, a great archaeological find of the nineteenth century. The inscription on this stele provided the prototype for early Semitic writing and was similar to the early Hebrew or Phoenician script on the Shapira manuscript. But the similarities between the discovery and publication of the Moabite Stone and the Shapira manuscript go beyond the form of the letters.[55]

The Moabite Stone was discovered originally by the Rev. F. Klein of the Church Missionary Society in 1868. As word passed among German and English archaeologists, Clermont-Ganneau, then at the French Consulate in Jerusalem, saw the importance of making a "squeeze" or impression of the stone. He also was determined to outbid the representatives of the other countries and obtain the stone for France. Ginsburg describes, in his commentary on the Moabite Stone, how Clermont-Ganneau, recognizing the great importance of this find, acted "with more enthusiasm than discretion" and "employed several agents to obtain squeezes, and even the Stone itself." By offering a large sum for the stone, Ganneau created "too great a temptation and a bait for the different chiefs, each one of whom naturally wished to obtain the prize . . . The Moabites . . . sooner than give it up, put a fire under it and threw cold water on it, and so broke it, and then distributed the bits among the different families. . . ."[56] Summarizing the events surrounding the discovery of the Moabite Stone, Ginsburg further notes:

> . . . the very oldest Semitic lapidary record of importance yet discovered, which had defied the corroding powers of more than 2,500 years, was at last broken up, through the unwise measures adopted by a young French *savant* [i.e. Clermont-Ganneau], who, in spite of knowing that others were first in the field bidding for it, was determined to outbid them, in order to secure it for his own nation.[57]

Throughout the introduction to his work on the Moabite Stone, Ginsburg makes several disparaging comments about Clermont-Ganneau and accuses him of acting irresponsibly. Eventually, the Moabite Stone did end up in Paris, and a squeeze copy of it is in the British Museum.

Just as Clermont-Ganneau was successful in obtaining the Moabite Stone for France, he did not hesitate to become involved in new archaeological controversies. He took particular interest in archaeological forgeries and published a number of studies on them. So when he arrived uninvited at the British Museum requesting to view the Shapira Deuteronomy manuscript, his interest was probably unwelcome. Was he there to steal the scroll for France, as he did the Moabite Stone? Was he there to discredit Shapira again, as he had with the Moabite potteries? Was he there to upstage Ginsburg and demonstrate his superior scholarship in detecting forgeries?

In a long letter to the *Times* of 21 August 1883, Clermont-Ganneau describes his mission to the British Museum:

> I reached London on Wednesday last, entrusted by the Minister of Public Instruction in France with a special mission to examine Mr. Shapira's manuscripts, at present deposited in the British Museum, and which have, for some time past, excited such great interest in England.[58]

Clermont-Ganneau describes his background in the matter, implying his expectation to be welcomed and included in the investigation of the manuscript:

> My studies of the stone of Mesha, or "Moabite Stone," which I conveyed to the Louvre, and reconstructed in its entirety, my decisive disclosures with regard to the fabrication of spurious Moabite potteries purchased by Germany, and my labours in connection with Semitic inscriptions generally, gave me, I ventured to think, some authority upon the question; and caused me to hope that the favour would be shown to me, which was accorded to other scholars, and to persons of distinction, of making me acquainted with these documents; which, if they should prove to be authentic, would unquestionably be of incalculable value.[59]

Clermont-Ganneau admits that he "entertained in advance most serious doubts" of the authenticity of the Deuteronomy manuscript, and that he came to London "in order to settle these doubts. But I thought it my duty to pronounce no opinion until I had seen the originals."[60] He continues his narrative:

> As soon as I had arrived I went to the British Museum, where my learned and obliging friend, Dr. S. Birch, was kind enough to introduce me to Dr. Ginsburg, whom I found in the Manuscript Department, engaged in studying the fragments, in company with Mr. Shapira. Dr. Ginsburg was good enough to allow me to glance at two or three of the fragments which were before him, and postponed until the next day but one (Friday), a more extended examination. He showed, however, some degree of

hesitation; and finally expressed himself as uncertain whether it would be convenient or not to submit the fragments to me. It was agreed that I should have a decisive answer on Friday. I fancied that Dr. Ginsburg feared some encroachment on my part, in the matter of the priority of publication of a text which he has deciphered with a zeal, which I am happy to acknowledge, and which he has had the honour of first laying before the public.[61]

Through this very letter, of course, Clermont-Ganneau has done just that: encroached on Ginsburg's control of the announcement of his verdict on the scroll. Just as Clermont-Ganneau states that he was "ready to bind myself to refrain from . . . publishing anything whatsoever on the contents of the fragments," he has done that very thing. He continues:

On Friday, I went again to the British Museum, and Mr. Bond, the principal librarian informed me, in the presence of my distinguished friend Mr. Newton, that he could not, to his great regret, submit the fragments to me; their owner, Mr. Shapira, having expressly refused his consent. There was nothing to be said against this. The owner was free to act as he pleased. It was his strict right, but it is also my right to record publicly this refusal, quite personal to me; and this, to some extent is the cause of this communication. I leave to public opinion the business of explaining this refusal . . . In these circumstances, the object of my mission became difficult to attain, and I almost despaired of it.

Clermont-Ganneau persisted in his mission and based his conclusions on the "hasty inspection of two or three pieces" he had handled on his first visit and "the examination of two fragments" on public display. On Friday and Saturday, Clermont-Ganneau stood with "the crowd of the curious pressing round these venerable relics" to reach his scholarly conclusion:

The fragments are the work of a modern forger. . . . I am able to show, with the documents before me, how the forger went to work. He took one of those large synagogue rolls of leather, containing the Pentateuch, written in the square Hebrew character, and perhaps dating back two or three centuries, rolls which Mr. Shapira must be well acquainted with, for he deals in them. . . . The forger then cut off the lower edge of this roll—that which offered him the widest surface. He obtained in this way some narrow strips of leather with an appearance of comparative antiquity, which was still further heightened by the use of the proper chemical agents. On these strips of leather he wrote with ink, making use of the alphabet of the Moabite stone, and introducing such "various readings" as fancy dictated, the passages from Deuteronomy which have been deciphered and translated by Mr. Ginsburg, with patience and learning worthy of better employment. — Clermont-Ganneau Aug. 18[62]

As Ginsburg is patiently deciphering, transcribing, translating, editing, and publishing this manuscript, Clermont-Ganneau is able to come to this quick and immediate conclusion, having been denied the opportunity to view the manuscript directly and then only a portion of it in the public display cases. He was denied access on Friday, 17 August, and spent Friday and Saturday doing his best to examine the manuscript. He wrote his letter on Saturday, 18 August, and it was published on Tuesday, 21 August.

Ginsburg's drawing of the text from part of Shapira's Deuteronomy manuscript (by courtesy of the Trustees of the British Museum, Add.41294, fol. 35).

In the same issue of the *Times*, Claude Conder of the Palestine Exploration Fund writes, "I have no hesitation in concluding that the supposed fragments of Deuteronomy were deliberate forgeries." As Ginsburg was working patiently to release his verdict, how distressing it must have been for him to have a scholarly opinion appear before his officially solicited judgement. This was especially true since Ginsburg's previous encounter with Clermont-Ganneau concerned which country would control the Moabite Stone: England, France, or Germany. Now the issue was who would control deciding the authenticity of the Shapira manuscript, and how embarrassing it would be if England purchased this manuscript when Germany had regarded it as a forgery.

On the other hand, one might ask: What took Ginsburg so long? And why did Strack and the other German scholars not share their impressions of the manuscript with their counterparts in England earlier, while the manuscript was first under consideration? In response to the second question, we have something of an explanation from Hermann Strack in his letter to the *Times*.[63] In response to the first question, we can turn to a letter that Ginsburg wrote to his daughter Ethel just after the Shapira incident, on 3 September 1883, from the British Museum:

> . . . The excitement about the MS. has by no means ceased. You will probably have heard that last Saturday the Spectator the Saturday Review and other periodicals had still articles on the subject.
>
> I do not think that the month which I spent on the MS. is time thrown away though it is a forgery and though the deciphering of it has nearly blinded me. Though I was sure the first week of my examination that it was a forgery yet the extraordinary cleverness and skill displayed in the production of it as well as the fact that a company were engaged in it made it absolutely necessary thoroughly to make it out, to translate it and to publish it before I gave the verdict and before publishing the Report. By so doing I made it impossible for this clever band of rogues to practice any more impositions.
>
> Mr. Shapira has disappeared and the ms. is still here. I do wish you would come up to town to see it for it is so wonderfully clever. If I could afford it I would give £200 for it. There is such a demand for my Report that the British Museum have decided to reprint it with the original and my translation . . . [64]

From this letter we can see the great pride Ginsburg took in the notoriety that the entire incident brought him. We also see Ginsburg's own explanation about the timing of his report, and a clear statement that he, too, recognized that the manuscript was a forgery from the beginning. His explanation, however, is not compelling. If the manuscript was clearly a forgery, why did he spend a month working on it, when he was busy producing his volumes on the Masorah, his magnum opus? Given that deciphering the manuscript was difficult and taxing on his eyes, why did he bother to "make it out, translate it, and publish it" rather than just presenting his scholarly opinion that the work was a forgery? Clearly Ginsburg saw the opportunity to create public interest in this manuscript and to establish himself as the defender of the British people from fraud and forgery.

PUNCH, OR THE LONDON CHARIVARI.

PUNCH'S FANCY PORTRAITS.—NO. 152.

MR. SHARP-EYE-RA.

SHOWING, IN VERY FANCIFUL PORTRAITURE, HOW DETECTIVE GINSBURG
ACTUALLY DID MR. SHARP-EYE-RA OUT OF HIS SKIN.

The British journal Punch published this cartoon shortly after Ginsburg declared the Shapira manuscript a forgery.

Magnifying the public interest in the manuscript also served to popularize Ginsburg's fields of scholarly interest, biblical studies and archaeology. Creating a public event served the interests of the Palestine Exploration Fund, the British Museum, and Ginsburg himself. Symbolically it established British scholarship in this field.[65] All of these reasons are more compelling than Ginsburg's statement that he "made it impossible for this clever band of rogues to practice any more impositions."

Ginsburg's comment to his daughter about desiring to purchase the manuscript is curious. Shapira's last letter to Ginsburg, on 23 August, states that Shapira will leave London in a day or two for Berlin. Five days later, Shapira wrote a long letter from Amsterdam to Edward A. Bond, the Principal Librarian of the British Museum, asking for reconsideration of Ginsburg's decision.[66] When Shapira left London, he left the manuscript behind, as Ginsburg wrote his daughter. Ginsburg's desire to purchase the manuscript is not surprising, even though he had just declared it a forgery. Ginsburg was a collector of Bible manuscripts, and he found this one intriguing and "so wonderfully clever." What is surprising is the £200 price he mentions.

Less than two years later, in July 1885, the British Museum would sell the manuscript at Sotheby's for £10 5s. to the bookseller Bernard Quaritch. Notice of the manuscript appeared in the 1887 Quaritch catalogue:

> BIBLE. The most original MS. of Deuteronomy, from the hand of Moses . . . as discovered by the late Mr. Shapira, and valued at £1,000,000; 15 separate fragments . . . written in the primeval Hebrew character on strips of blackened leather, £25.
>
> Ante Christum 1500 –A. D. 1880[67]

The description of the manuscript establishes both the identity of the scroll and its symbolic value to England: "These are the famous fragments which Dr. Ginsburg so painfully deciphered and published in the Times, and which led the religious world of England to sing halleluiahs. The scoffing atheists of Germany and France had refused to acknowledge them genuine."[68] The following year Quaritch exhibited the unsold manuscript at the 1887 exhibition of Anglo-Judaica.[69] The manuscript may have been acquired subsequently by Sir Charles

Nicholson, as A. D. Crown suggests, and has since disappeared, perhaps destroyed in the fire in Nicholson's home near London in 1899.[70] Given Ginsburg's own interest in the manuscript and its inexpensive price in both 1885 and 1886, it is surprising that he did not purchase it himself. His quotation of the £200 price to his daughter, moreover, does not fit the facts. Perhaps Ginsburg was concerned about the appearance of impropriety in purchasing a manuscript he had declared to be a forgery.

The manuscript remained famous for some years after Ginsburg's verdict was released, and the entire incident was one of the most celebrated scholarly controversies of the nineteenth century. By examining the historical context, we can see that Ginsburg did more than simply expose a forgery. The entire episode symbolized the scholarly competence of the British and their approach to biblical archaeology and documents. The British emerged triumphantly as careful and thorough investigators, not bested by the French nor by the Germans. Thus did an 1883 encounter between two East European-born Christian converts, Shapira and Ginsburg, destroy one man and establish the other as a guardian of the reputation and the resources of the British people.[71]

---

1. Most basic primary source documents are collected in British Library, Add. MS. 41294, "Papers Relative to M. W. Shapira's Forged MS. of Deuteronomy (A. D. 1883 – 1884)" [a Xerox reproduction of these papers is also held in the Oriental and India Office Collections, Or. MS. 14706]; and in Or. MS. 14705, "Documents connected with the Shapira Ms. of Deuteronomy, Moabite Pottery, etc." The latter is a photographic reproduction of an original dossier, or album, comprised of press-clippings, articles, and manuscript notes assembled by William Simpson, London, 1884. (The photographic reproduction of the album was kindly donated to the British Library in 1992 by the Valmadonna Trust, London, which holds the original.) Other contemporary accounts of the incident are contained in: "The Shapira Manuscripts," *Palestine Exploration Fund Quarterly Statement*, Oct. 1883, pp. 195 – 209; Hermann Guthe, *Fragmente einer Lederhandschrift enthaltend Mose's letzte Rede an die Kinder Israel* (Leipzig, 1883); Franz Delitzsch, "Schapira's Pseudo-Deuteronomium," *Allgemeine Lutherische Kirchenzeitung* (Leipzig), 7 Sept. 1883 (cf. pp. 844 - 6, 869 – 71, 893 – 4, and 914 – 16); C. Clermont-Ganneau, in *Revue politique et littéraire*, xxxii, no. 13 (29 Sept. 1883), and in his *Les fraudes archéologiques en Palestine* (Paris, 1885), ch. iii-iv; *Autobiography of Sir Walter Besant* (New York, 1902, reprinted 1971), pp. 161 – 7; and A. C. R. Carter, "Shapira, the Bible Forger," in his *Let Me Tell You . . .* (London, 1940), pp. 216 – 19.

A second group of publications followed reports, in 1956, of the investigation of Menahem Mansoor as reported in the *New York Times* (13 Aug. 1956) and the London *Jewish Chronicle* (28 Dec. 1956). Mansoor's research is presented best in his article, "The Case of Shapira's Dead Sea (Deuteronomy) Scrolls of 1883," in *Transactions of the Wisconsin Academy of Sciences, Arts and Letters*, xlvii (1958), pp. 183 – 225; Mansoor concludes that "neither the internal nor the external evidence . . . supports the idea of a forgery" and that "there is justification . . . for a re-examination of the case" (p. 225). Mansoor's conclusion is attacked by M. H. Goshen-Gottstein in "The Shapira Forgery and the Qumran Scrolls," *Journal of Jewish Studies*, vii (1956), pp. 187 – 93, and in "The Qumran Scrolls and the Shapira Forgery," *Haaretz*, 28 Dec. 1956 (in Hebrew); and by Oskar K. Rabinowicz, "The Shapira Forgery Mystery," *Jewish Quarterly Review*, N. S., xlvii (1956 – 7), pp. 170 – 83. Mansoor is supported by J. L. Teicher, "The Genuineness of the Shapira Manuscripts," *Times Literary Supplement*, 22 Mar. 1957. See also the *Jewish Chronicle* (London) for 15 Feb. and 9 and 16 Aug. of 1957.

Additional studies of the incident include: John Marco Allegro, *The Shapira Affair* (Garden City, New York, 1965); O. K. Rabinowicz, "The Shapira Scroll: A Nineteenth-Century Forgery," *Jewish Quarterly Review*, lvi (1965/6), pp. 1 – 21; A. D. Crown, "The Fate of the Shapira Scroll," *Revue de Qumran*, vii (1970), pp. 421 – 3; Neil Asher Silberman, "One Million Pounds Sterling: the Rise and Fall of Moses Wilhelm Shapira, 1883 – 1885," in his *Digging for God and Country: Exploration, Archeology, and the Secret Struggle for the Holy Land, 1799 – 1917* (New York, 1982), pp. 131 – 46; Menahem Mansoor, *The Dead Sea Scrolls: A Textbook and Study Guide*, 2nd edn. (Grand Rapids, Michigan, 1983), ch. xxv, pp. 215 – 24; Colette Sirat, "Les Fragments Shapira," *Revue des études juives*, cxliii (1984), pp. 95 – 111; and most recently Hendrik Budde, "Die Affäre um die 'Moabitischen Althertuemer,'" in Hendrik Budde and Mordechay Lewy, *Von Halle nach Jerusalem: Halle – ein Zentrum der Palästinakunde im 18. und 19. Jahrhundert* (Halle, 1994), pp. 106 – 17, esp. item V/24.

[*BRITISH LIBRARY JOURNAL* EDITOR'S NOTE: Some shorter accounts are found in the *Revue des études juives*, vii (1884), p. 316; J. Jacobs, "Shapira, M. W.," *The Jewish Encyclopedia*, vol. xi (New York and London, 1905), pp. 232 – 3; F. F. Bruce, "Shapira Fragments," *Encyclopaedia Judaica*, Vol. xiv (Jerusalem, 1972), cols. 1301 – 2; S. Fisch, *Shapira the Forger and the Midrash Haggadol* (Leeds, [c. 1961], mimeograph), pp. 1 – 3; H. Rabinowicz, "The Shapira Manuscript Mystery," *Jewish Chronicle* (London), 13 Mar. 1964, pp. 9 and 50; Albert van der Heide, "De Shapira-affaire," *Alef Beet: Tijdschrift van de Vereniging tot Bevordering van Kennis van Hebreeuws*, iv, no. 2 (1994), pp. 28 – 31; idem, "Vijftien reepjes leer maakten Wilhelm Moses Shapira kapot," *Nieuw Israelitisch Weekblad* (4 Mar. 1994); and N. A. Silberman, *The Hidden Scrolls: Christianity, Judaism, and the War for the Dead Sea Scrolls* (London, 1995), pp. 36 – 9. Various newspaper accounts are cited in a number of the studies.

There are several fictionalized accounts of the affair. Firstly, there is the autobiographical novel by Shapira's daughter, Myriam Harry [Perrault-Harry],

La petite Fille de Jérusalem (Paris, 1914), first published in English translation in 1911; see also the supplement by Yaakov Asya, "Parashat Shapira," in his Hebrew translation of Harry's novel entitled *Bat Yerushalayim ha-ketanah*. Harry's second book, *La Conquête de Jérusalem* (Paris, 1903), also contains material relating to the affair; cf. the English translation, *The Conquest of Jerusalem* (London, 1905), pp. 118 – 19 and 164 – 73. The Israeli historical novel by Shulamit Lapid, *Keheres ha-nishbar* [*As a Broken Vessel*] (Jerusalem, 1984), is based on the Shapira affair.

There have also been several television and radio programmes on the Shapira affair in Israel and Canada, including a film produced in 1980 by Kastel Enterprises in Tel-Aviv (on which correspondence was conducted with Quaritch in London), and more recently for CBC Radio, Toronto, in 1992, edited by Margaret Horsfield. Thanks are due to Mr. Nicholas Poole-Wilson of Bernard Quaritch Ltd. for making available his "Shapira correspondence" file, based on regular queries to Quaritch over the years. According to Mr. Poole-Wilson, hope never fades at Quaritch that the fragments will still turn up, in a drawer or behind a wall.

It is worth noting, finally, that Theodor Gaster, in a memoir of his father Moses Gaster, recounts that his father possessed a "roll of leather inscribed with a portion of Deuteronomy in characters very much like those of the Dead Sea Scrolls. (My father thought it might be part of the notorious Shapira frauds, but my recollection is that the script was very different and that the column was a narrow, vertical one, and not written longitudinally, as were those fabrications.)" See "Theodor's Memoir," appended to Moses Gaster, *Memoirs*, ed. Bertha Gaster (London, 1990; printed privately), p. 111; the memoir was first published as the "Prolegomenon" to Moses Gaster's *Studies and texts in folklore, magic, medieval romance, Hebrew apocrypha and Samaritan archaeology*, vol. i (New York, 1971). Theodor Gaster does not record the subsequent fate of this particular "roll of leather" in his father's library, which was kept in their dining-room cupboard. Most of Gaster's Hebrew manuscripts were acquired, before and after his death, by the British Museum and the John Rylands Library in Manchester, but the whereabouts of this possible "Shapira scroll" is unknown.]

2. *Autobiography of Sir Walter Besant* (New York, 1971), p. 161.
3. *Athenæum*, no. 2911 (11 Aug. 1883), p. 178; no. 2912 (18 Aug. 1883), p. 206; no. 2913 (25 Aug. 1883), p. 242.
4. *Jewish Chronicle* (London), 3 Aug. 1883, p. 13.
5. *The Times*, 22 Aug. 1883.
6. Letter of M. W. Shapira to C. D. Ginsburg, 23 Aug. 1883 (BL, Add. MS. 41294, document F).
7. John Hillaby, "American Revives Bible Scroll Case", *New York Times* (13 Aug. 1956), p. 1. See also the subsequent article, "Scholars Dispute Scrolls' Validity," *New York Times* (28 Dec. 1956), p. 14.
8. For a description of the history of the Shapira scroll after 1883, and a possible solution to its disappearance, see A. D. Crown, cited above.
9. *The Times*, 9 Mar. 1914.

10. Ibid., 6.

11. *Punch*, 8 Sept. 1883: Punch's Fancy Portraits, no. 152.

12. *BRITISH LIBRARY JOURNAL* EDITOR'S NOTE: A survey of the various Hebrew manuscript collections assembled by Shapira is provided by Benjamin Richler in his *Guide to Hebrew Manuscript Collections* (Jerusalem, 1994), p. 175. On Shapira's earlier and "uncontested" Hebrew manuscript offerings to the British Museum, see his own handwritten "List of Hebrew Manuscripts mostly from Saana in Arabia [Yemen]", *c.* 1880, 28 ff., preserved in the Department of [Western] Manuscripts, British Library, as Add. MS. 41293 [a Xerox reproduction of this list is also in the Oriental and India Office Collections, Or. MS. 14707]; H. Derenbourg, "Les Manuscrits judaïques entrés au British Museum de 1887 à 1890 [nos. Or. 11 – Or. 4117]," *Revue des études juives*, xxiii (1891), pp. 99 – 116, 279 – 301 ("les manuscrits hébreux, provenant de Schapira," Or. 1451 – 1490; "ceux qui ont été apportés de San "à par lui et d'autres," Or. 2210 – 2230; "le magnifique fonds karaïte acheté à Schapira," Or. 2459 – 2602); J. Leveen's introduction to the index volume of G. Margoliouth, *Catalogue of the Hebrew and Samaritan Manuscripts in the British Museum*, part iv (London, 1935; reprinted 1977), pp. viii – ix; H. M. Rabinowicz, *Jewish Literary Treasures of England and America* (New York and London, 1962), pp. 19 – 22; and D. Rowland Smith, "Genizah collections in The British Library," in D. Rowland Smith and P. S. Salinger (eds.), *Hebrew Studies*, British Library Occasional Papers, xiii (London, 1991), pp. 21 – 2.

On Shapira's Karaite manuscripts acquired by the Museum, see Reinhart Hoerning, *British Museum Karaite Manuscripts: Descriptions and Collation of Six Karaite Manuscripts of portions of the Hebrew Bible in Arabic Characters . . .* (London, 1889), and on these same manuscripts see also now Geoffrey Khan, *Karaite Bible Manuscripts from the Cairo Genizah* (Cambridge, 1990), esp. p. ix; Derenbourg, op. cit.; S. Poznański, "Die Qirqisāni-Handschriften im British Museum," in *Festschrift zum achtzigsten Geburtstage Moritz Steinschneider's* [*Tehilah le-Moshe*] (Leipzig, 1896), pp. 195 – 218, and G. Margoliouth's review in *Zeitschrift für hebräische Bibliographie*, ii (1897), pp. 99 – 100; H. Ben-Shammai, "Some Judaeo-Arabic Karaite Fragments in the British Museum Collection," *Bulletin of the School of Oriental and African Studies*, xxxviii (London, 1975), pp. 126 – 32. See also [R. Hoerning], "Karaitic MSS." [List of Karaite Manuscripts in the British Museum], unpublished handlist, *c.* 1885, held in the Hebrew Section of the British Library; Poznański's "[List of Karaite Manuscripts in the] British Museum," among his handwritten location lists preserved in the Poznański Archive in the Jewish National and University Library, Jerusalem; and G. Tamani, "Repertorio dei manoscritti ebraici caraiti," *Henoch: Studi storicofilologici sull'ebraismo*, i (Turin, 1979), p. 277. (None of the latter three works makes reference to Shapira as provenance of specific MSS.) For lists (of Shapira's manuscripts) held in the Staatsbibliothek, Berlin, see M. Steinschneider, *Verzeichnis der hebräischen Handschriften* [in the Royal Library] (Berlin, 1878 – 97), vol. i, p. v, and nos. 176 and 176^b , and Richler, op. cit.

Among the Hebrew collections which Shapira helped build was that of

Adolf Sutro in San Francisco, on which see the published catalogue by W. M. Brinner, *Sutro Library Hebraica* (San Francisco, 1966), pp. iii – iv, and also S. Roubin [Rubin], *Sefer Torah katuv be-yad rabi Mosheh ben Maimun: A Scroll of the law supposed to have been written by Maimonides* (San Francisco, 1894), p. 13. See also Roubin's typescript *Catalogue of the Hebrew and Arabic Manuscripts in the Sutro Library* (San Francisco, 1894); the unpublished catalogue by Ephraim Deinard, *Reshimat Kitve yad me-'otsar ha-sefarim shel hagevir ha-śar ha-'adon Adolf Sutro [Catalogue of the old Hebrew and Arabic Manuscripts of the Library of the Hon. Adolph Sutro]* (San Francisco, 1897); and another unpublished catalogue, prepared under the Work Projects Administration, by J. Saloman, J. Friedman, and J. J. Davidson, *Catalogue of the Hebrew and Arabic Manuscripts in the Sutro Library* (San Francisco, 1938 – 41). On the Sutro collection and its catalogues, see Louis I. Newman, "Solomon Roubin and Ephraim Deinard, cataloguers of the Hebraica in the Sutro Library in San Francisco," in W. J. Fischel (ed.), *Semitic and Oriental Studies: a volume presented to William Popper* (Berkeley and Los Angeles, 1951), pp. 355 – 64. There is also an unpublished (?) report on this collection by G. A. Kohut, "Description of the Hebrew-Arabic Manuscripts at the Sutro Library, San Francisco, California," Dallas, s. a. (*c.* 1898), 2 pp. (now held in the Oriental and India Office Collections of the British Library, Or. MS. 14700). On Deinard and the Sutro collection, see also Simcha Berkowitz, *Ephraim Deinard (1846 – 1930): A Transitional Figure*, M. A. thesis, Columbia University, New York, 1964, pp. 43 – 4 and 58; on Deinard and Shapira, and in particular for Deinard's view of the Shapira affair, see Deinard's *Zikhronot bat 'ami [Memoirs of Jewish life in Russia]* (St. Louis, 1920), pp. 133 – 42.

13. The novel was published in English, under the same pseudonym, as *The Little Daughter of Jerusalem* (New York: E. P. Dutton, 1919). On Shapira's status as a British Museum correspondent, see John Marco Allegro, *The Shapira Affair* (New York, 1965), p. 17, and the editor's note above.

14. Leveen, op. cit. Leveen, although reversing Shapira's initials, confirms (p. ix, n. 1) that "It was this bookseller who offered to the Museum fragments of the Pentateuch on leather purporting to be of extreme antiquity, but afterward discovered to be forgeries."

15. *Athenæum*, no. 2855 (15 July 1882), p. 80; no. 2856 (22 July 1882), pp. 113-114.

16. Ibid., 2 July 1882, p. 114.

17. Ibid., no. 2805 (30 July 1881), p. 144; no. 2806 (6 Aug. 1881), p. 176; no. 2807 (13 Aug. 1881), p. 208.

18. C. D. Ginsburg, "The Karaites: Their History and Literature," in *Proceedings of the Literary and Philosophical Society of Liverpool*, xvi (1861 – 2), pp. 155 – 70. (This essay was also listed among other works by Ginsburg in *The Moabite Stone* [London, 1871] as available directly from the publisher, Reeves and Turner [i.e., as a separate off-print].)

19. *Athenæum*, no. 2892 (31 Mar. 1883), p. 409.

20. Reinhart Hoerning, *British Museum Karaite Manuscripts: Descriptions and Collation of Six Karaite Manuscripts*, p. v.

21. Ibid., p. xii.

22. Ibid., dedication page (unpaginated).

23. C. D. Ginsburg, "Journal of an Expedition to Moab, 1872" (BL, Add. MS. 41291), p. 13.

24. Ibid., p. 18.

25. M. W. Shapira, letter to Hermann Strack, Jerusalem, 9 May 1883 (BL, Add. MS. 41294, document B), and M. W. Shapira, letter to Edward A. Bond, Amsterdam, 28 Aug. 1883 (BL, Add. MS. 41294, document H).

26. Shapira to Strack; Jerusalem, 9 May 1883, p. 1.

27. Ibid., p. 2.

28. Ibid., p. 4.

29. Ibid., p. 5.

30. Ibid., pp. 9 – 10.

31. Ibid., p. 10.

32. Ibid.

33. Hermann L. Strack, letter to the *Times*, 4 Sept. 1883, p. 6.

34. Shapira to Edward A. Bond, Amsterdam, 28 Aug. 1883, p. 1.

35. Ibid., pp. 11 – 12.

36. Hermann L. Strack, letter to the *Times*, 4 Sept. 1883, p. 6.

37. Hermann Guthe, *Fragmente einer Lederhandschrift*, p. 1.

38. Ibid.

39. Neil Asher Silberman, *Digging for God and Country*, p. 139.

40. Strack, letter to the *Times*, 4 Sep. 1883, p. 6. See also "Report from Berlin," *Times*, 28 Aug. 1883; and Allegro, *The Shapira Affair*, p. 46. The unsigned "Report from Berlin" in the *Times* states that "This committee consisted of Professor Dillmann, of the Hebrew Chair; Professor Sachau, the distinguished Orientalist; Professor Schrader, the celebrated Assyriologist; Professor Ermann, another Hebrew scholar; and Dr. Schneider [*sic*], who in the years between 1852 and 1860, compiled the valuable catalogue of Hebrew books, &c., in the Bodleian Library at Oxford," as well as "Professor Lepsius, the famous Egyptologist, who is keeper of the Royal Library." Strack refers to those present at the meeting as "several other scholars (Professor Dillman [*sic*], Professor Sachau, &c.)." Allegro (p. 46) enumerates this "high-powered body of scholars" as Professors Richard Lepsius, August Dillmann, Eduard Sachau, Adolf Ermann, and Dr. Moritz Steinschneider. The *Times* report incorrectly refers to Moritz Steinschneider as "Dr. Schneider," but is it is unclear whether the "Prof. Schrader" mentioned is the same as Prof. Schroeder, who had declared the manuscript genuine and offered to purchase it. Strack, in his letter to the *Times*, states that "Nothing of this was then made public, because no one in Berlin for a moment supposed that the codex in question would be the object of further discussion," implying that Schroeder was not present.

The *Times*'s "Report from Berlin" similarly cites no dissenting opinion: " . . . they unanimously pronounced the alleged codex to be a clever and impudent forgery . . . so satisfied were the committee with the general internal evidence . . . that they deemed it unnecessary to call for further proof." The committee, according to this account, did not share completely their verdict with Shapira: "the committee deemed that it was not at all incumbent upon them to demonstrate a negative, and therefore told the expectant Mr. Shapira that they were disinclined to enter into a bargain with him. They were quite willing, it is true, to buy his wares, though only as an example of what could really be done in the way of literary fabrication."

41. "The Shapira Manuscripts," *Palestine Exploration Fund Quarterly Statement*, Oct. 1883, p. 195.
42. Invitation sent by Besant (in BL, Add. MS. 41294.
43. This is BL, Or. MS. 14705, the album (or rather photographic reproduction thereof) referred to above, in n. 1. The meeting is also described in a letter from Besant to Ginsburg, 2 Jan. 1884 (BL, Add. MS. 41294, document G). See also *Autobiography of Sir Walter Besant* (New York, 1902), pp. 161 – 4; and Allegro, *The Shapira Affair*, pp. 48 – 51.
44. *Autobiography of Sir Walter Besant*, p. 162.
45. Ibid., p. 161.
46. *Times*, 3 Aug. 1883; *Jewish Chronicle* (London), 3 Aug. 1883, p. 13.
47. *Times*, 8 Aug. 1883, p. 11; *Jewish Chronicle*, 10 Aug. 1883, p. 10; *Athenæum*, no. 2911 (11 Aug. 1883), p. 178.
48. *Athenæum*, no. 2912 (18 Aug. 1883), p. 206.
49. *Athenæum*, no. 2913 (25 Aug. 1883), pp. 242 – 4; the quotation is on p. 244.
50. Over forty contemporary newspaper accounts of the incident, from English and European newspapers and journals, are included in Add. MS. 41294, "Papers relative to M. W. Shapira's forged MS. of Deuteronomy," given to the British Library by Ginsburg.
51. Ibid., Documents D and E.
52. BL, Or. MS. 14705; separate undated note by William Simpson.
53. *The Academy*, no. 588 (11 Aug. 1883), pp. 99 – 100. See also n. 49, above.
54. M. W. Shapira to C. D. Ginsburg, London, 23 Aug. 1883 (BL, Add. MS. 41294, document F).
55. On the Moabite Stone, see now H. Budde, "Die Affäre um die 'Moabitischen Althertümer'", in *Von Halle nach Jerusalem*, cited in n. 1, and G. Lehrer-Jacobson, *Fakes and Forgeries from Collections in Israel*, exhibition catalogue of the Eretz Israel Museum (Tel-Aviv, 1989), pp. 12 ff.
56. C. D. Ginsburg, *The Moabite Stone: A Facsimile of the Original Inscription, with an English Translation, and a Historical and Critical Commentary*, 2nd edn. (London, 1871), p. 10.
57. Ibid., p. 10.
58. Letter to the *Times* by Clermont-Ganneau, dated 18 August. The letter appeared in the *Times*, 21 Aug. 1883, p. 8.
59. Ibid.
60. Ibid.
61. Ibid.
62. Ibid.
63. Strack writes, as stated above, that "Nothing of this was then made public,

because no one in Berlin for a moment supposed that the codex in question would be the object of further discussion" (letter to the *Times*, 4 Sept. 1883, p. 6). In writing this letter on 31 August, Strack seems unaware of Guthe's publication about the manuscript, or chooses to ignore it.

64. BL, Add. MS. 57486, document H.

65. On this point see also Allegro, *The Shapira Affair*, especially ch. 10, pp. 74 ff.

66. Shapira to Ginsburg (Add. MS. 41294, document F); Shapira to Edward A. Bond (Add. MS. 41294, document H).

67. Bernard Quaritch, *A General Catalogue of Books offered to the public at the affixed prices* (London, 1887), vol. iii, p. 3192, lot no. 32270. The description corresponds with the Sotheby sale catalogue, "The Schapira [*sic*] Manuscripts, no. 302, Deuteronomy in Hebrew, 7 numbered and 8 unnumbered fragments, *written on leather.*" A copy of the latter description appears in Harry Rabinowicz, "The Shapira Manuscript Mystery," *Jewish Chronicle* (London), 13 Mar. 1964, p. 9. One notes that the Quaritch catalogue does not refer to the manuscript outright as a forgery.

68. Quaritch, op. cit. The Quaritch description fails to mention that the "famous fragments" were declared a forgery by Ginsburg. One interpretation of the phrase "led the religious world of England to sing halleluiahs" is that Ginsburg's evaluation and judgement preserved the authenticity of the authorized text of Deuteronomy. The Shapira manuscript, after all, represented a conflicting version of the book and challenged the received biblical text. In addition, Ginsburg's verdict saved the British people world embarrassment by not accepting as authentic a manuscript that European authorities had declared a forgery. But the last sentence of the Quaritch 1887 description implies that the British religious community accepted what the "scoffing atheists" of Germany and France "had refused to acknowledge [as] genuine." In fact, Ginsburg, Clermont-Ganneau, and Strack all came to the same conclusion: that the scroll was a forgery. Perhaps Quaritch himself was not convinced and thought that the scroll might be authentic and have religious relevance.

69. J. Jacobs and L. Wolf (compilers), *Catalogue of the Anglo-Jewish Historical Exhibition, Royal Albert Hall, London, 1887* (London, 1888), p. 136, no. 2091.

70. See A. D. Crown, "The Fate of the Shapira Scroll," and also Harry Rabinowicz, "The Shapira Manuscript Mystery," both cited above.

71. For assistance and encouragement in conducting the research for this essay I thank Brad Sabin Hill, Head, Hebrew Section, The British Library; Dr. David Patterson, Director, Oxford Centre for Postgraduate Hebrew Studies, under whose auspices much of the research was conducted; the staff of the Bodleian Library, Oxford; and Dr. Michael Grunberger and Peggy Pearlstein of the Hebraic Section, Library of Congress, Washington, D. C. I also thank Dr. Marc Lee Raphael for his research assistance and editorial advice, and above all, Dr. Sherry Levy-Reiner for her scrupulous editorial care and acumen, and her continuing support of this research in so many ways.

The Uses of Masorah in Public Scripture Reading

Delivered at the International Organization
for Masoretic Studies
Society of Biblical Literature
July 23, 2003

A few years ago a young woman preparing for her bat mitzvah had a special request: She was prepared to chant the Hebrew text of her Haftarah, but—contrary to our congregation's custom—she did not want to read the English translation. Her reading included Hosea 2:4, " . . . let her put away her harlotry from her face and her adultery from between her breasts. Else I will strip her naked and leave her as on the day she was born." These were difficult words for a twelve-year-old girl to read in front of her friends and family, so I granted her permission to read the Hebrew and to skip reading the translation.

This student did not realize that there was a long-standing tradition of avoiding embarrassment in public Scripture reading: substituting euphemisms for objectionable words; and a few passages that the rabbinic tradition prescribed should be read but not translated. In addition, of course, there are other passages where the text is emended, or *Tikkune Soferim*, and hundreds of passages where variant readings have been preserved in *Qere/Ketiv* variants. Together with five passages called *Itture Sopherim*, or the Omission of the Scribes, and *Kethiv ve-la Qere*, or words written but not read, we can gain insight into how the ancient rabbis and the Masoretes not only safeguarded the text, but also protected the sanctity of Scripture reading and the dignity of the congregation.

Today I will examine some of the history of Scripture reading and the effect of some Masoretic phenomena upon the public reading of Scripture. The biblical and rabbinic tradition of Scripture reading begins with Nehemiah 8. The Israelites who returned to the Land of Israel from their exile in Babylonia were ignorant of the Bible and Jewish practice. Ezra sought to restore the literacy of the people:

[He] assembled them in the square before the Water Gate and

"brought the Torah (or Teaching) before the congregation, men and women and all who could listen with understanding. . . . Ezra opened the scroll in the sight of all the people," [with others assisting him] "They read from the scroll of the Teaching of God, distinctly [translating it] and giving the sense; so they understood the reading" (Neh. 8:1,2, 5, 8).

The public reading of Scripture had a profound effect on the people: The people wept as they heard the words (Neh. 8: 9). The reading ritual was so successful that the people were moved to rediscover their Jewish observance, celebrate the holiday of Sukkot, as prescribed by the reading, and return to their biblical roots.

But what really happened that day in the square before the Water Gate? Did the people understand the Hebrew text of the Bible? Did they know what they were listening to? The ancient rabbis of the Talmud and Midrash understood this verse to say that there were four elements of the public Scripture reading. "They read from the scroll" refers to Scripture reading in the Hebrew original; "distinctly" refers to a translation or *Targum*; "they gave the sense" refers to the division of the verses; "so that they [the people] understood the reading" refers to the accentuation of the verses; while others say that "understood the reading" refers to the masorot (BT Nedarim 37b).

Another understanding of this verse from Nehemiah leads us to believe that Scripture was read with three people standing together: a *baal kore*, or Torah reader, who read or chanted the Hebrew text; a *meturgeman*, who translated (probably a verse at a time) into the vernacular Aramaic; and a *darshan*, or commentator, who provided midrashic and other commentary.[1] Ben Zion Wacholder points out that during the Mishnaic period (ending 220 C.E.), the Hebrew readers were laymen, while the translators were professionals. Wacholder argues that they did not use a written *Targum*, but provided a verse by verse translation, interspersed with the Torah reading. Clearly this translation was necessary because "the people as a whole were not adequately familiar with the Hebrew of the Bible."[2]

The Mishnah attests to this practice in tractate Megillah: "One who reads in the Torah may not read fewer than three verses; he may not read to the translator more than one verse [from the Torah] or [from the Prophets], three verses . . . " (M. Megillah 4:4). In a further Talmudic comment on this practice, Rabbi Ulla said that the one who reads from the Torah should not prompt the translator so that people should not say that the translation is written in the Torah scroll. Similarly, the reader opens the scroll, finds the place, rolls the scroll together and recites the blessing with the scroll closed, then opens the scroll to read, so that people will not think that the blessing is contained in the scroll.[3]

The final paragraph in Mishnah Megillah is of particular interest to us:

> The story of Reuben is read in synagogue but not translated. The story of Tamar is read and translated. The first account of the incident of the Golden Calf is both read and translated, the second is read but not translated. The blessing of the Priests is read but not translated. The stories of David and Amnon are read but not translated. The portion of the chariot is not read as a Haftarah. . . . The portion "Make known to Jerusalem" is not read as a Haftarah (Mishnah Megillah 4:10).

In commenting on this mishnah, the Talmudic rabbis noted that some portions of scripture are both read and translated, some are read but not translated, and some are neither read nor translated.[4]

The verses that are not translated are left in the Hebrew to preserve the dignity of the congregation, to not embarrass the listeners, cast aspersions on biblical characters, or introduce a controversial theological issue.

The story of Reuben, Genesis 35:22, is the first of the five examples: "while Israel stayed in that land, Reuben went and lay with Bilhah, his father's concubine; and Israel found out." Clearly Reuben's act of incest reflects badly on Jacob's first-born son, as Jacob recalled in his deathbed testament: "Reuben, you are my first-born . . . unstable as water, you shall excel no longer; for when you mounted your father's bed, you brought disgrace—my couch he mounted!" (Gen. 49:4). The verse Genesis 35:22 is also interesting from a Masoretic point of view because it presents a double set of (*Madinchae-Ma'arvei*) conflicting accentuation marks and a break within the verse, complete with a *petuchah* gap. The verse, after the internal break, concludes: "Now the sons of Jacob were twelve in number."

There are four additional sections that the Mishnah prescribes are to be read and not translated:

- The second account of the Golden Calf, Exodus 32:21-25, because, according to the Talmud, "a man should always be careful in wording his answers." This section contains the verse singled out by the Talmudic rabbis, Aaron's explanation to Moses that the people gave Aaron their gold, " . . . and I hurled it into the fire and out came this calf!" (Exod. 32:24) Rashi notes that Aaron's response is theologically dangerous, as if to say that the idolatrous calf had powers of its own (BT Megillah 25b).

- The priestly blessing, because it contains the word *yisa*, or lifted up. Rashi reads this as objectionable because its particularistic theology may be subject to misinterpretation.

- The story of David, II Samuel 11:2-17, the story of David's liaison with Bathsheba, and

- The story of Amnon, II Samuel 13:1-4, the story of Amnon's rape of his sister Tamar. Both these stories are, according to the Mishnah, to be read but not translated, presumably out of respect to the reputation of the characters. The Talmud, however, states that these stories are to be neither read nor translated. According to some commentators, the Talmud text should read consistently with the Mishnah, that they *are* to be read but not translated.

We might expect that the Masoretes, recognizing the Talmudic law on not translating the text out of respect to the congregation, marked these verses. In fact, however, the rabbinic instruction on reading but not translating these verses was never included into the Masoretic notes. There is no mention of them in any Masoretic index or list, and we might say that the rabbinic instruction was dropped by the Masoretes and lost. In a way this is not surprising, because these instructions are not really related to the biblical text, but to the public reading of the text. The rabbis of the Talmud, on the other hand, even provided a mnemonic device (REBDN=Reuben, Egel, Beracha, David, Amnon) so that readers could remember which sections are not to be translated. While there are many comments on the priestly blessing contained in contemporary Bible commentaries, as well as the other passages, I found none referring to the Talmudic interdiction on translating the blessing.

As far as I can determine, there is no note on the prohibition to translate contained in any of the major bilingual Torah or Bible editions, nor in any critical editions of the Hebrew Bible. The rabbinic practice of not translating these verses has not been transmitted.

The Talmud continues the section in Tractate Megillah 25b with a list of euphemisms that should be employed in reading the biblical text: "Our Rabbis taught: Wherever an indelicate expression is written in the text, we substitute a more polite one in reading" (Soncino, p 154). The rabbis provide examples:

- Instead of *yishgalenah*, he shall ravish her, we read, *yishkavenah*, he shall lie with her.
- Instead of *b'ofalim*, we read *b'tahorim*, a less objectionable word for hemorrhoids.
- Instead of *harei yonim, divyonim*, dove's dung.
- Instead of *chareyhem* and *sheneyhem*, excrement and urine, we read *tzoatam* and *meimei raglehem*, the water of their feet.
- Instead of *lamachraot*, latrines, we read *lemotzaot*, or "outhouses."

In this Talmudic passage, Rav Nachman is quoted that "*kol litznuta asira bar militznuta d'avodat kochavim*, All sneering is forbidden except the ridiculing of idols." The term *litznuta* has been translated as "gibing," "sneering," or "scoffing," with evident reference to obscenity.[5]

These substitutions, based on the Talmudic passage Megillah 25b, have given rise to *Qere-Kethiv* variants and Masoretic notes about them. In his work, *Biblical Text in the Making*, Robert Gordis lists 16 citations in his list #2, "Guide Against Obscenity," with the introduction, "Where the text reads a word which might be too coarse when read in the Synagogue, the Reader is enjoined to substitute one of milder force."[6] Gordis notes that:

> This category of the *Kethib-Qere*, . . . is very ancient. The changes . . . presuppose a period when the Hebrew language, with all its nuances and idioms, was still well-known by the broad masses of the people. Hence, their origin must lie in a period preceding the penetration of Aramaic into the Jewish community and its replacement of Hebrew as the spoken language of the masses.[7]

The Masoretes noted these examples and compiled them in Masoretic lists,[8] as noted by Christian David Ginsburg in his *Introduction to the Massoretico-Critical Edition of the Hebrew Bible*:

> In accordance with this [Talmudic] rule, not only does the Massorah duly register these stigmatized expressions, but all the MSS. of the Bible with the Massorah and every edition of the Massoretic text give in every instance the authoritative substitute as the official reading in the margin and furnish the consonants of the text itself with the vowel-signs which belong to the marginal reading. These, however, are simply typical examples and we shall see in the sequel that this principle was applied by the authoritative redactors of the Sacred Scriptures far more extensively to remove indelicate expressions and anthropomorphisms.[9]

While not necessarily noted in this way, most of the Bible editions likely to be used for synagogue reading noted the *Kethib-Qere* substitutions in these instances.[10] It is noteworthy that the Talmudic rabbis felt the need to act as censors for the biblical text. In most cases, these changes are bowdlerisms, named after Thomas Bowdler (1754-1825), who published an expurgated edition of Shakespeare's works. They are problematic for those who are troubled by censorship, and also compromise the integrity of the biblical text. The rabbinic discussion in Megillah 25b focuses on the nature of some of the words that are changed in reading, but it does not raise the issue of changing the words of the Bible for the sake of politeness. The rabbis see these changes in a midrashic context, substituting words to seek new meanings in the text, but without really altering the biblical text. It appears that they perceived the written text as permanent, while they accepted alternative readings to preserve the dignity of the congregation.

There are three additional categories of textual changes that are significant to note:

- *Tikkune Sopherim*, the Emendations of the Scribes: These eighteen passages have been emended for theological reasons, according to the lists contained in rabbinic literature and the Massorah. As Ginsburg puts it, "the editorial principle [is] that indelicate expressions and anthropomorphisms are to be removed" in these "passages altered in harmony with this canon."[11] In the example given by Kelley, Mynatt, and Crawford, Genesis 18:22, the presumed original text, "Adonai stood before Abraham" was emended to read, "Abraham stood before Adonai." The alteration removes the irreverent picture that God stood before Abraham, ready to serve him.[12] There are several lists of these passages in various midarashic sources, beginning with the Mechilta, most of which are incomplete. The complete list is given in Ginsburg's Massorah,[13] among others. As interesting as these passages are, they really do not have an impact on the public reading of Scripture, since the original text is not offered in the text. Israel Yeivin points out that some modern scholars contend that the original text showed the received reading, and the *Tikkune Sopherim* "represents midrashic interpretation, not text history." Other modern scholars contend that these corrections were indeed made by the scribes to avoid irreverent expressions.[14]

- *Kethiv ve-la Qere*, Words written but not read: The Talmud passage Nedarim 37b-38a lists five texts where a word is written in the biblical text but omitted in public reading. These are noted in several contemporary printed Bible editions with the word in question printed without vowels and a textual note that the word is to be written but not read.[15]

- *Qere ve-la Kethiv*, Words read but not written: The same Talmud passage lists seven passages with minor variations. These, too, are noted in several contemporary printed Bible editions.

Itture Sopherim and *Mikra Sopherim* are also mentioned in Talmud Nedarim 37b-38a. *Mikra Sopherim* refers to the words *Eretz, Shamayim,* and *mitzrayim*, whose proper reading might change in pausal form. Gaonic commentary suggests that since these changes are not indicated in the consonantal text, the Sopherim needed to teach it. Yeivin points out that these unexplained references have no evidence to help us understand them. *Itture Sopherim* are five instances where an expected *vav* conjunction is not in the text. The question pertaining to these passages is: Why did the scribes not employ a *Kethib-Qere* system to mark these texts?[16]

These latter four categories of textual changes provide us with only the corrected text, clearly well established by Talmudic times, since they are mentioned in Nedarim 37b-38a. The Talmudic text there states that they are all "*halachah* from Moses at Sinai." The Talmudic notes to this phrase explain: "thus they are read" (Rashi) and "thus Moses received them at Sinai and transmitted (*masar*) them to Israel" (Tosafot). Quite clearly, this designation is to establish the authenticity of the changes. The Talmudic rabbis employed this phrase to designate textual elements that they thought might be called into question, such as accentuation marks. Ginsburg explains it as the rabbis stating that the changes are "according to a very ancient tradition."[17] We should understand them not as a historical statement but as the rabbis' way of reinforcing that it is part of the received text of Scripture.

The largest category of these variations is the *Kethiv-Qere* variants noted throughout the Hebrew Bible. Printed Bible editions vary in how these variants are presented, yet they are the most common and significant ones for Scripture readers. We need to educate Scripture readers, teachers, and tutors about these variants, how they are presented in the biblical text, and how they are to be read.

Readers of Hebrew scripture today participate in a very ancient tradition, going back to the days of Ezra and Nehemiah. Done properly, the text should be able to instruct and move the congregation, maintain fidelity to the text, and keep alive textual traditions that date back to the time of the Mishnah, two thousand years ago. The Masoretic notes and apparatus have preserved the text and maintained a tradition of accurate reading. Even in light of this tradition of precision, the Masoretes, and the rabbis before them, still valued the dignity of the congregation. They were prepared to offer alternative words, even to suppress readings, to avoid obscenity and irreverent readings that would embarrass the congregation. They substituted euphemisms and emendations, thereby changing the text that they labored so hard to preserve.

1. See Ben Zion Wacholder, "A History of the Sabbatical Readings of Scripture of the 'Triennial Cycle,'" Prolegomenon to Jacob Mann, *The Bible as Read and Preached in the Old Synagogue*, vol. I., (New York, Ktav, 1971), p. xiv.-xv. Wacholder cites BT Megillah 3a.
2. Wacholder, pp. xix-xx.
3. BT Megillah 32a. (Soncino, pp. 192-3)

4. BT Megillah 25a (Soncino, pp. 151-2) In his Talmudic commentary, the Vilna Gaon omits the words, "and some are neither read nor translated." (Soncino, p. 151, n. 13)

5. So the note in the Soncino edition, p. 154.

6. *The Biblical Text in the Making, A Study of the Kethib-Qere*, Augmented edition, (New York, Ktav, 1971), p. 86.

7. Ibid., Prolegomenon, p. XVIII.

8. Cf. Christian David Ginsburg, *The Massorah*, Vol. II., p. 416, Letter 'ayin, ¶722; Vol. II., p. 607, Letter Shin, ¶138.

9. With a prolegomenon by Harry M. Orlinsky, (New York, Ktav, 1966), pp. 346-7.

10. I have checked the *Soncino Chumash* (ed. A. Cohen), *Pentateuch and Haftorahs*, ed. J. Hertz, Koren Bible edition, *Biblia Hebraica Leningradensia* (ed. A. Dotan), Jewish Publication Society *Tanach* and JPS *Torah Commentary*, U.A.H.C. *The Torah, A Modern Commentary* (ed. W.G. Plaut), and Rabbinical Assembly *Etz Chayim*(ed. D. Lieber)

11. Ginsburg, *Introduction*, p. 347.

12. Page H. Kelley, Daniel S. Mynatt, and Timothy G. Crawford, *The Masorah of Biblia Hebraica Stuttgartensia* (Grand Rapids, Michigan, Eerdmans, 1998), p. 38.

13. *The Massorah*, vol. II., p. 710, ¶206.

14. Israel Yeivin, *Introduction to the Tiberian Masorah*, translated and edited by E. J. Revell, *Masoretic Studies #5* (Scholars Press, 1980), p. 50.

15. See, for instance, *Biblia Hebraica Leningradensia* and Jewish Publication Society *Tanach* on II Kings 5:18; and the Artscroll Ruth on 3:12.

16. See Yeivin, pp. 51-2, and Kelley, et. al., p. 40.

17. Ginsburg, *Introduction*, p. 308.

From *Oxford Dictionary of National Biography*
Edited by Colin Matthew and Brian Harrison (2004) 1064w

"Christian David Ginsburg"

By permission of Oxford University Press.

Ginsburg, Christian David (1821 – 1914), Bible scholar and missionary, was born on 25 December 1921 in Warsaw, Poland, to Baruch Ginsburgh (or Güntzberg). Little is known about his Jewish family of birth. Family tradition maintains that his parents lived in Spain before migrating to Warsaw before Ginsburg's birth; that an ancestor was in the court of the Spanish monarchs Ferdinand and Isabella; and that his mother was English. One older brother is mentioned in an account of his conversion to Christianity.

In Poland, Ginsburg pursued Bible studies and was a cotton spinner, working at Ozorkow for some years. On 7 October 1845 he married Teiszer Mala Berkewicz according to Jewish rites; they had one child. After several years of contact with the Warsaw mission of the London Society for Promoting Christianity Amongst the Jews, Ginsburg was baptized by the Reverend F. W. Becker on 3 October 1846 and took the name "Christian." Leaving his wife and child behind, he travelled to England under the auspices of the London Society and moved into the London Society's Operative Jewish Converts' Institution. He applied, unsuccessfully, in 1849 to its Hebrew College (opened in 1840), but enrolled instead in July 1850 (on probation) in the Jews' College in London, the British Society [non-Anglican] missionary school (founded 1847). There he studied a curriculum based on Bible, Hebrew and Greek that was designed to prepare students to become missionaries. He studied with Benjamin Davidson, the first principal of the college and the first missionary employed by the British Society, and he established what became a lifelong friendship with Isaac Salkinson, later a missionary in Vienna and a translator into Hebrew of the New Testament and of the works of Shakespeare and Milton.

After completing his course, Ginsburg was in 1853 appointed a missionary for the British Society in London, and in 1857 he was transferred to Liverpool. In the same year he also published his first book, a translation and commentary on the Song of Songs. In 1858, he became a naturalized British subject. It is not clear what happened to his first wife, but on 9 October he married Margaret Ryley *née* Crosfield, the daughter of William Crosfield, a Liverpool sugar refiner. His wife's family, who were Quakers, actively supported the work of the British Society and promoted his own scholarship. There were two children: Benedict William Ginsburg, born in October 1859, and Ethel Margaret. In 1867 Margaret died, and in the following year Ginsburg married Emilie, *née* Hausburg, daughter of F. Leopold Hausburg of Woolton. They had three daughters: Emilie Catherine, Hildegarde Beatrice, and Sybil Gwendolyn.

Ginsburg's scholarly interests grew and deepened. In 1861, he published his translation and commentary on Ecclesiastes. He became an active member of the Literary and Philosophical Society of Liverpool, giving papers and publishing articles in their *Proceedings*, including histories of the Karaites in 1862 and of the Kabballah in 1865. In February 1863 he was awarded an honorary LLD degree from the University of Glasgow. In 1863, Ginsburg retired from missionary work because of his health and in order to devote his full energy to his scholarship. In 1864, he published a history of the Essenes, a Jewish ascetic sect in the "Second Temple" period, and joined the committee of the British Society. In 1867, he published an annotated translation of Jacob ben Chayim's *Introduction to the Rabbinic Bible* and of Elias Levita's *Masoret Ha-Masoret*. In 1870, he was invited to be one of the original members of the Old Testament Revision Company, and he subsequently moved to a new home at Binfield, Berkshire, to be closer to his work in London.

In 1870 Ginsburg published a book on the Moabite stone, including a transcription, a translation, and a commentary. The Moabite (or Mesha) stone was a monument of the mid-ninth century B.C., containing an inscription by King Mesha of Moab, which was written in ancient Canaanite letters. In 1872 Ginsburg participated in an expedition to Moab. His most important scholarship, however, focused on his work on the text of the Hebrew Bible and the Massorah. Working with sixty manuscripts, he collected and collated textual variants and notes to prepare his Massoretico-Critical edition of the Hebrew Bible, which was published in 1894 by the Trinitarian Bible Society. In his "Introduction" he described the Massoretic enterprise of counting letters, words, and verses and developing an extensive apparatus of notes to preserve the text. He also collected and collated these Massoretic notes, publishing them in his magnum opus *The Massorah* (4 vols., 1880 - 86), a work of great importance for subsequent Massoretic and biblical scholars. In 1904 Ginsburg was elected editor of the British and Foreign Bible Society's *New Critical Hebrew Bible*, eventually published in 1926. Before his death in 1914 he completed the Pentateuch, the Prophets, and part of the Writings.

Ginsburg was recognized as an authority on biblical and Hebrew matters. In 1883, when the British Museum was offered a manuscript of Deuteronomy written in the same ancient Canaanite script as the Moabite stone, officials asked him to evaluate the fragments. He published the text and translation and then declared the fragments forgeries. In this celebrated incident of the Shapira manuscript, Ginsburg was portrayed as saving the British from financial and scholarly humiliation. Among the first modern Bible critics to recognize and use textual variants and notes, he set the stage for subsequent scholars who have built upon his foundations. Although his work would have benefited more from a critical appreciation of stemmatic types – probing the reliability of independent evidence that one manuscript can bring to another – his careful collation of variants, and his determination to bring these notes, variants, and manuscripts to light, changed the course of biblical scholarship.

Ginsburg also was active in scholarly and political circles. He delighted in social situations and was a member of the Liberal Club, which appointed him to its library committee and which continued to display his portrait. He collected Bibles and engravings, sat as a justice of the peace for Surrey and Middlesex, was a close associate of William Aldis Wright and A. E. Cowley, and was a friend of William E. Gladstone. Ginsburg died at Palmers Green, London, on 7 March 1914, and was buried, after a service in Southgate parish church, at Southgate cemetery, London, on 10 March; he was survived by his wife, Emilie.

-- Fred N. Reiner

In the Congregation
and
the Community

Remarks on the Position of Cantor
to a Special Meeting of Temple Sinai

November 4, 1993

Uppermost in my mind is reminding you that we are one congregation, one community, despite our disagreements. We come from a Jewish tradition of dissent and debate, but only with *derech eretz*—respect for each other and the Jewish values we cherish.

Now I want to rephrase the question, "Should we stop our search?" and ask instead, "Is Temple Sinai ready for a cantor?"

Before I tell you why I believe we are ready for a cantor, I must correct an error being repeated by the Ad Hoc Committee: that I requested rabbinic help or a full-time rabbi. This is not true. I presented the Board with my judgment of the congregation's needs, and I was careful not to recommend a solution. The Board appointed a committee to consider various alternatives. Eventually the Board turned to the long-range report the congregation had approved in May 1987, which recommended a staff including two rabbis and a cantor. Adding a cantor to our staff achieved consensus within the Board last spring and was approved by our congregation.

Yet the question remains: Is Temple Sinai *ready* for a cantor?

What we really are considering tonight is how best to meet a multitude of needs as our congregation grows both in numbers and in its desire to experience Judaism in diverse ways. Our diversity as a congregation has led us to worship in many different modes; now, I believe, we have come to the point where we need someone with particular expertise to guide and develop our musical and liturgical life.

When Temple Sinai's Board was exploring alternatives, I was asked to contact the director of our Rabbinical Placement Commission to discuss the availability of part- and full-time rabbis. Although his job is placing rabbis, his response to my description of Sinai's growth and needs was, "It sounds as if you need a cantor, not a rabbi."

Traditionally, and increasingly in Reform Jewish congregations, a cantor plays an essential leadership role hand-in-hand with the rabbi because we pray through our music. Rabbi Portnoy and I recognize that role, and we welcome the opportunity to have a cantor on our clergy team. We know that Reform Jewish cantors today have particular expertise in developing liturgy, overseeing bar/bat mitzvah preparation, and in ensuring that our children's positive musical experiences in religious school are recreated and reinforced in joyous worship. Temple Sinai needs, on a full-time basis, the liturgical, educational, and musical expertise only a cantor can provide.

I continue to be asked about differences between a cantor and a cantorial soloist, so I will reiterate them.

- A cantor has completed a four-year graduate program that includes a year in Israel and extensive coursework in liturgy, Bible, Hebrew language and grammar. Soloists and cantors both can sing, but cantors can teach Torah and prayers.

- A cantor can guide and lead others who develop liturgies— religious school classes, adult groups—integrating the words and the music.

- A cantor can work with bar/bat mitzvah students—whether they are chanting or reading—helping them understand their portions and coordinating preparations with their families and tutors.

- A cantor is a member of the clergy, invested similarly to a rabbi. Cantors' participation in life cycle events, committee work, and the life of the congregation reflects their status as religious leaders as well as their education. Their contributions are musical, liturgical, educational, and pastoral, originating in their education, background, and personal commitment to the Jewish community.

Is Temple Sinai ready for this: a cantor? Many, many members have expressed to Rabbi Portnoy and to me longings that could be met best by a cantor. Many of our members have grown up with cantors or been exposed to cantors in other synagogues; they know what cantors do and appreciate their contributions. For all of these reasons, Rabbi Portnoy and I believe Temple Sinai is ready for a cantor.

Had we asked years ago, "Is Temple Sinai ready for a woman rabbi?" the answer probably would have been "Some are and some aren't."

A vigorous congregation—like a maturing individual—evolves and takes stock of itself periodically; a vital congregation accepts change that is presented soundly and sensitively. I see Temple Sinai as that kind of congregation: a community able and willing to grow numerically and emotionally and embrace diversity, a congregation on the cutting edge of our Reform Movement, a congregation that will welcome a cantor who can lead us to a deeper appreciation of our liturgical and musical heritage.

For these reasons I urge you to continue our cantorial search.

Invocation

Oklahoma City Bombing Commemoration
sponsored by B'nai B'rith International
United States Capitol
October 13, 1995

Source of comfort and healing:

We gather today to recall the tragedy that shook our nation six months ago, that day of shock and sadness we so vividly remember. We gather today to ask for comfort for the survivors, healing for the broken, solace for families torn asunder. And we gather today to praise the goodness that has emerged from this evil: the generosity of thousands whose hearts were moved; the benevolence of those who rescued and saved and healed; the voluntarism of so many who reached out to the survivors and the bereaved; the human kindness that lent hope to broken lives. Help us to feel the good as we have seen the evil, and grant hope to all whose courage we recognize and praise today. Amen.

Strengthening the Fabric
of Our Jewish Families

Washington Jewish Week
March 20, 1997

At a recent Shabbat dinner in our congregation, I noticed that one of our non-Jewish members was singing the Kiddush. While some of our Jewish members seemed hesitant or unsure of the words, or not singing at all, this member sang the Hebrew very well.

Surely she did not realize the irony of the situation: The Kiddush praises God for setting Jews apart from other peoples, and this member of our congregation, part of "another people," perhaps was trying to demonstrate her solidarity with our (and her) community.

So where does she fit in, exactly? She is rearing Jewish children; she is actively involved in her synagogue; she is committed to preserving and transmitting Judaism to a new generation; and she belongs to no other religious organization. How does she think of herself, and how do we think of her?

Although we never have discussed it, I suspect that she does not want to convert to Judaism. Perhaps she believes it would hurt her parents or siblings; perhaps she has been living without a religious affiliation for so long that this is more comfortable for her.

I know she is committed to Judaism. She is at the Temple frequently, participating in a host of programs. But I did not know that she knew the Kiddush. Does she know what the words mean? Should I tell her?

By teaching our members as a community how to welcome Shabbat, we raise their comfort level and encourage them to welcome Shabbat at home. With this family, we have succeeded. They have been attending these dinners for many years, and they celebrate Shabbat at home. Our member learned the Kiddush in learning how to welcome the Sabbath. How do we, as a congregation and as a community, welcome her?

For 45 years, Temple Sinai has permitted non-Jews to be members of the congregation, as do many Reform congregations. We do not permit non-Jews to lead the congregation in worship or in reciting certain blessings, including the Kiddush. Non-Jews may not have an *aliyah*, though they may accompany a Jewish individual having an *aliyah*; they may not fulfill a mitzvah, such as saying the blessing over the Shabbat candles during a service. For many years, these ritual guidelines seem to have worked well for the regular worship of our congregation.

But what is this congregant's place as a non-Jew among Jews? How can we welcome her, strengthen the Jewish life of her family, and still preserve the religious integrity of our congregation?

To me, her participation makes good sense, because so often it does strengthen the Jewish life of the family. In this time and this place, many Jewish families have non-Jewish members. While conversion is important, and far more than a technicality, it does not work for everyone. Our concern must be strengthening our community and all its members.

A biblical model for this concept is the *ger toshav*, the resident alien. The resident alien is what one traditional source calls a partial proselyte: someone who has not adopted Judaism in its entirety but lives by some of its precepts. In biblical times, the *ger* ate matzah and was prohibited from having leavened products in his home during Passover (Exod. 12:19-20); but he was not allowed to offer the Passover offering without conversion (Exod. 12:48). The *ger toshav* was on the border: keeping some rituals but not permitted to participate in others. They enjoyed equal rights in the courts and were protected from oppression.

We can understand this idea of a "resident alien" from a secular perspective as well. Many in our community are citizens of another country but live among us. They pay taxes but are not permitted to vote. They may make a contribution to our community, but they may be limited by not being part of our political system. These limitations would disappear were they to become naturalized citizens, but they have decided not to do that. They live in a gray area: residing in our midst but not citizens. Do we invite them to picnic on July 4th? Do we permit them to sing "The Star-Spangled Banner"? Do we prohibit them from leading us in singing it?

Similarly, in the Jewish community there are gray areas and black and white areas. We must make judgments about who is a Jew for some ritual purposes, such as marriage or burial in a Jewish cemetery. But in other areas we can afford to be flexible and be guided by our "impressions" that even though someone is not really Jewish, they cast their religious lot with the Jewish people.

Are we willing to follow that biblical model? I hope so, since it may help us to strengthen our community and the fabric of our Jewish families.

Remarks on Intermarriage
to the Temple Sinai Board of Trustees

October 18, 2006

In September, president Jim Jaffe raised the question of whether or not we should seek a third rabbi who would officiate at interfaith marriages. In discussing this with the officers in September and October, Jim pointed out that the time we are adding a rabbi to our staff seemed a logical time to raise this question for Temple Sinai. I was also asked the position of the Reform Jewish Movement on this issue. In discussing the matter, the officers asked me whether I would be comfortable having a rabbi on our staff—or seeking a rabbi—who officiates at mixed marriage ceremonies, which none of our clergy currently does.

I cannot give you a simple yes or no answer because this issue is not about me or my colleagues at Temple Sinai. This question goes to the very essence of our congregation's values. On a practical level, we cannot seek only rabbis who officiate or who do not officiate at interfaith marriages, according to the placement procedures. How candidates view interfaith marriage must be far more important to us than simply whether or not they will officiate.

In these conversations we all recognized that each of us in the leadership of the congregation knows the disappointment of some congregants that their clergy will not officiate at their wedding or at their child's wedding. With the rate of intermarriage in our society about fifty percent, all of us know these issues not only as matters of policy and sociology; we know them because they have arisen in our own families (including mine) and among our friends.

Nobody likes to hear the word *no*. We rabbis and cantors do not like saying no. Indeed, we anguish about these issues on a regular basis. Still, we are called upon to make these decisions and must do so on a regular basis.

Is it a pressing problem at Temple Sinai that our clergy will not officiate at mixed marriage wedding ceremonies? As I noted, we all have been in the position of disappointing some. We also need to recognize, however, that there are congregants who are pleased that the clergy of Temple Sinai abide by these standards and do not officiate at intermarriages. Indeed, for many people this issue is a touchstone for strongly held opinions. To my knowledge, no one has resigned from Temple Sinai during the last twenty years because of our clergy's position. To the contrary, scores of families have joined Temple Sinai because, they say, we are particularly welcoming to intermarried couples and intermarried couples feel comfortable here. In fact, I have heard that we have a reputation in the community of being more welcoming to mixed married couples than other Reform congregations.

Not only has no one resigned, but I must point out to you that for the past twenty years the issue never has risen to the level where I have had a serious conversation with any president or board member about our refusal to officiate. In contrast, we have had serious conversations about other refusals to officiate: Twice the board has discussed our decision not to officiate at the funerals of non-members of the congregation. We have discussed in the ritual committee our requirement that when naming a child at the temple we expect the parents to have committed to rearing the child as a Jew. And we have discussed with the board our decision that the children in our religious school must be raised as Jews and as nothing else; we are not comfortable with children attending our religious school one week and the religious school of a church the next.

What are the current policies of the congregation in this matter? Our ritual policies state clearly that officiation at weddings and funerals is at the discretion of the clergy. When I arrived in 1985, I was told that Temple Sinai also had a building policy that prohibited the officiation of mixed marriage ceremonies within our building. Rabbi Portnoy and I have operated on that assumption since 1985. I also require when I officiate that the wedding couple are either members of the congregation, children of members, or willing to join the congregation at the time of their wedding.

All of our clergy are pleased to meet with interfaith couples to discuss religious issues within their marriage. When they are seeking a Jewish wedding ceremony, we refer interfaith couples from our congregation to colleagues in the community who will officiate at these ceremonies. We inevitably reach out to the young people who have grown up in our congregation, and if they are living in the Washington area, we offer them a complimentary membership in the congregation for the first year after they are married. We are always available to discuss religious or other issues with them and to refer them to community agencies if appropriate. As I have often stated, we are far more concerned with a marriage, which will last for many years, than we are with a fifteen-minute ceremony.

I have preached High Holy Day sermons on these issues at least three times: on Yom Kippur 1988 and 1991, and on Rosh Hashanah morning 2001. In 1991, I said, "I don't apologize for my own decision not to officiate at mixed marriage ceremonies, for I officiate within a context of Jewish law and practice that guides me to that decision. But I do apologize for the mistaken impression that we reject or do not care about these families. We must be a synagogue of open doors, as challenging, threatening, or uncertain as that might be."

These values are based in part on the positions of the Reform Movement and the Reform rabbinate. The authoritative position of the Reform rabbinate came in 1973:

> The Central Conference of American Rabbis, recalling its stand adopted in 1909 that mixed marriage is contrary to the Jewish tradition and should be discouraged, now declares its opposition to participation by its members in any ceremony which solemnizes a mixed marriage. The Central Conference of American Rabbis recognizes that historically its members have held and continue to hold divergent interpretations of Jewish tradition.

The resolution continued by calling on its members to assist in educating children of mixed marriages, providing the opportunity for conversion, and encouraging a creative and consistent cultivation of improvement in the synagogue and the Jewish community. These elements of the Reform Movement's outreach program have been central to our practice and our life at Temple Sinai since the 1970s when the outreach movement was first proposed.

I want you to understand that this is not just a yes-or-no question of officiation. Any discussion of this subject raises the questions of who is a Jew and what do we teach our children about Jewish marriage and Jewish life? At Temple Sinai we have standards, and we are clear about who is Jewish and who is not and their respective roles in the ritual life of our congregation. Over the years we have worked out ways to involve our non-Jewish members appropriately in our ritual life and in a host of activities for the congregation. Certainly we know, recognize, and applaud the deep commitment and strong participation of many of our non-Jewish members. At the same time, we respect their own religious choices, be they in a different religious community or in no religious community. We respect and honor the commitment of those individuals who have chosen to convert to Judaism at the time of their marriage or after. We know how important this decision and this process are for them and for their families. We all must recognize the integrity of their decision to join the Jewish people. Other non-Jewish spouses have considered conversion or taken the course and decided not to convert; we welcome them all.

For decades, Temple Sinai has been characterized by its thoughtful and intelligent investigation of complicated and controversial issues such as Jewish status and mixed marriage. We have not shied away from them, but we have recognized the potential for damaging the relative harmony of our community. In the early 1980s, as Temple Sinai was preparing to search for a successor to Rabbi Eugene Lipman, it went through an extraordinarily difficult period on matters relating to this issue. Rabbi Lipman did not officiate at mixed marriage ceremonies and felt strongly about this matter, as did our first rabbi, Balfour Brickner. Rabbi Harold White, who had been employed part-time at Temple Sinai since the early 1980s, officiated at mixed marriage ceremonies and was widely known in the community to be extremely liberal in his views on officiation. The decision not to continue Rabbi White's relationship with Temple Sinai after Rabbi Lipman's retirement led to a painfully divisive period within the congregation, culminating in an emergency meeting and a congregation-splitting vote not to retain Rabbi White after the conclusion of his contract.

I came to Temple Sinai in 1985 with a mandate to heal, and I quickly recognized that it was of prime importance that the rabbis and clergy should work together as a team. While we need not see eye-to-eye on every issue—and we do not—we nevertheless respect one another's positions and differences. We work together to lead the congregation and to create a sense of community among the clergy, the staff, and the congregation as a whole. I believe it is fair to say that we have achieved this over the years with remarkable success.

Rabbi Portnoy, Rabbi Potter, Cantor Croen, and I understand that when we officiate at a wedding ceremony we are there in two simultaneous roles. We are representatives of the Jewish community; our presence is a clear statement of Jewish religious continuity. Central to the Jewish marriage ceremony we perform is the concept that the couple is being bound "according to the laws of Moses." At the same time, we act as representatives of the state, certified by the secular community to officiate. We have been asked to officiate at weddings where two Jews want only a religious and not a civil ceremony so they would not lose their Social Security or pension benefits. We say no to such requests as well, for that would be breaching our civil responsibilities.

When I was asked by the officers about my feelings about having a rabbi on our staff who would officiate at mixed marriage ceremonies, I told them that I would like to speak with colleagues who had been in that position. I have spoken with a few rabbis, read the Spring 2006 *CCAR Journal* dedicated entirely to the question of interfaith marriage, and read parts of Gary Tobin's 1999 book *Rabbis Talk About Intermarriage*. Gary Tobin points out that "nearly all Jews have an opinion and all Jews have a stake concerning intermarriage," and that "intermarriage is a powerful active force in the consciousness of most rabbis." Here is what I have learned and heard from my colleagues.

- While I know that in some congregations diversity of practice has worked well, I know that in other congregations there have been problems.

- When we come to hire another rabbi, it should be far less important whether or not he or she would officiate at mixed marriage ceremonies than what his or her approach would be. Some rabbis feel passionately about this issue on one side or the other. Some feel that mixed marriage is the greatest threat to Jewish survival and that relationships between Jews and non-Jews should be strongly discouraged. Others feel that officiating at mixed marriage ceremonies is the key to Jewish survival and that they would like to officiate at all the weddings they can and bring these couples into the Jewish community. They may believe that someone who marries a Jew is automatically a member of the Jewish community. I would think that either of these extreme positions would not work at Temple Sinai; both, certainly, would be at odds with the approach of the current clergy and much of our congregation.

- There are many, many issues that a congregation must consider. If a rabbi of Temple Sinai were officiating at mixed marriage ceremonies, under what conditions would we expect him or her to officiate? Would we be comfortable with this rabbi officiating at mixed marriage ceremonies outside the congregation? Would we be comfortable with his or her officiating in churches? Would we be comfortable with his or her officiating on Shabbat or Jewish holidays?

Recognizing that Temple Sinai historically has taken Jewish practice extremely seriously, where would the lines be drawn? And who would draw them?

I learned in my conversations with colleagues that most newly ordained rabbis—and others who would be comfortable in seeking a third-rabbi position in a congregation—would likely follow the lead of the senior rabbi in the congregation. These newly ordained rabbis are not looking to make waves on important issues; they would rather serve and learn from their congregational experiences and their senior colleagues.

The question before us, then, is this: Do we want to embark on a discussion of mixed marriage at Temple Sinai now? Clearly these issues are more complicated and have deeper implications than first meet the eye. Just beneath the surface are passionately held positions. People are understandably hurt when they feel that they or their children are rejected. People feel just as passionately about the need to hold the line to ensure Jewish continuity and survival.

Until now we have been clear on our position about clergy officiation, recognizing that each of us has come to our decision independently. We each regularly examine where we stand and why. At the same time, we also have worked together to craft many parts of temple life to reach out to intermarried couples and non-Jewish family members to ensure that children, parents, and grandparents all feel welcome in our Jewish community.

If the board decides that as a congregation we should examine the issue of rabbinic officiation at mixed marriage and the issues associated with it, I would be pleased to provide guidance and leadership. We already have discussed this in many settings at Temple Sinai, and the conversation can certainly continue and deepen. But I must warn the board that to overturn a fifty-year history of consistency on this issue will be upsetting to many in the congregation. To suddenly make these changes without involving the congregation in a discussion of the larger fractious and potentially divisive issues will seriously threaten the power and strength of the community we labor so hard to build and sustain.

Rabbi's Report
Temple Sinai Annual Meeting

May 26, 2010

The Roman god Janus could look in two directions. He was the god of doors and gates, and we imagine him watching over comings and goings alike. I think of him as having the unique ability to look backward and forward at the same time: a gift very few of us can claim. This evening, in my 25th and final annual report to the congregation, I would like to lead you in looking back at some of the accomplishments of this past quarter century and looking forward at the values that I hope will guide Temple Sinai into the future.

When I came to Temple Sinai in 1985, there were so-called "late" services every Friday evening—typical of American Reform Jewish congregations of the time—and about 25 bar/bat mitzvah services on Saturday morning or afternoon. Shortly after I arrived, I added a monthly Tot Shabbat and participatory dinner as an outreach initiative to families with young children, a group that was missing from our congregation at the time. We invited Robyn Helzner, who was already part of our corps of music leaders, to accompany this service with Rabbi Portnoy or me, and we created a committee of parents to guide us. As the core of participants in Tot Shabbat got older, we added Shalom Shabbat. When we began to engage our middle school religious school classes in leading our service one Friday night per month, we enhanced the 7:30 family service. The students could have a pre-bar/bat mitzvah experience leading a service, and other youngsters could see their peers integrating the Hebrew they were learning with a service. Over time, we also added additional services on Shabbat morning: the lay-led monthly Kehillat Shabbat service and the monthly Simchat Shabbat service. Through this wide array of worship experiences, we have been able to touch various groups within our broader congregational community, helping them create Shabbat here in the synagogue and take it back with them into their homes. And in reaching out to these groups, we have enabled individuals to find common ground and create strong bonds with each other. For several generations of young people, many of whom come to see me when they are home from college or graduate school, the habit of Shabbat worship and a communal Shabbat dinner or lunch started with Temple Sinai's Tot Shabbat.

Once we began attracting families with young children, the number of bar/bat mitzvah students grew from about 25 per year to 80 now. The number of services is important, of course, but more important are the quality of the tutoring process, the accomplishments of the celebrants, and the beauty of the service the young people lead. For me, the year leading up to a bar or bat mitzvah has immeasurable value. As we meet with the students and their family one year out, three months out, six weeks out, and in the week before their *simcha*, we have the great joy of getting to know the young people and their families in considerable depth. We have the incomparable opportunity to link ourselves to them in the context of an event that they will look back on—as they move forward—as a significant moment in their lives and in the lives of their family and community.

Over the years, we also have expanded the number and type of High Holy Day services that we offer and engaged new space and new staff members to support these services. Our celebration of festivals and other holidays has changed many times over the years, but I am pleased that we have enhanced our services particularly on Sukkot, Simchat Torah, Chanukah, and Purim to respond to the changing needs and desires of the congregation and to build traditions of strong participation for these holidays.

Our Adult Education programs also have expanded. In 1985, lifelong learning already was a distinctive hallmark of our congregation: Shabbat morning Torah Study, Sunday morning and Monday evening classes, and a Monday morning Sisterhood class, in addition to special programs. In the past 25 years, we have expanded the reach of all of these educational opportunities and added a regular scholar-in-residence weekend, adult bar/bat mitzvah, two endowed lecture series, and our social justice Zwerdling Shabbaton. Each of the nine adult bar/bat mitzvah classes has continued after their culminating celebration to meet on a monthly basis, and the number of *kallot* has grown over these years as well. Over the past few years, we have added groups for interfaith couples, children of aging parents, parents of young adults who struggle, and women raising Jewish children. This innovative programming speaks to the personal and Jewish needs of members of our congregation who support one another and build strong bonds as well as learn together.

Our nursery school has continued strong since its founding in 1991. It is an institution in its own right, yet it has been an outstanding point of entry for many members of our congregation. I hear repeatedly from our Confirmation class families how important and formative their nursery school experience was. At the same time, we have been able to welcome children and families who have not been part of our nursery school and make them an integral part of the congregation. The nursery school has built community and above all has provided the highest quality early childhood education to hundreds of children who have benefited, along with their families, from the caring and direction of our dedicated staff.

When I arrived at Temple Sinai in 1985, our religious school had 250 students. We had just closed a branch in Gaithersburg that Temple Sinai had opened with the expectation that congregants would be moving to the northern Montgomery County suburbs. Obviously, the locus of our congregation remained in upper Northwest D.C. and the inner Montgomery County suburbs, where most of our people still live. The number of our students grew remarkably, however, so that we now educate more than 600 children in kindergarten through 10th grade. We have three shifts on Sunday morning and evening, plus forty mid-week Hebrew classes in ten time slots. We are beyond capacity again and have just closed the early session to new students for next year.

I take a great deal of pride in the excellent quality of our religious education. Given that we, like every religious school, need to reinvent our curriculum and programming constantly, we have been responsive to students and parents and kept up with the major trends in Reform Jewish education. We have been able to keep our program fresh and vital, to build a faculty that is professional, and to create family education programs that engage parents and students together.

Pursuing social justice always has been one of the hallmarks of Temple Sinai. Some of the modes of social action in the Reform Movement have changed across the country, and we have experienced those changes as well. We still engage a large number of our congregants and many of our religious and nursery school classes in projects of *tikkun olam*, of reaching out to help others in our community. We collect food and other goods on a regular basis and do our part in local organizations to support the homeless, to assist older adults, and to reach out to hospital patients, service personnel, and refugees from the Gulf Coast to Darfur. At the same time, we have been able to engage in a number of policy initiatives, taking stands on the issues of the day. We have spoken out as a congregation on women's rights, reproductive choice, D.C. voting rights, same-sex marriages. We have established Sinai House—a truly model program, supported it throughout our congregation, and celebrated its success.

Over the past 25 years, as the size of the congregation doubled and the religious school almost tripled, the utilization of our building has grown as well. When I arrived in 1985, parts of our building were in significant need of repair. We addressed many of those in our building renovation and expansion in the early 1990s. Now we know that there are many more significant needs that must be addressed in the near future. In addition to a rapidly aging infrastructure, we face inadequate program space, storage space and classroom space for all our activities. This year we continued to borrow program space from Ingleside next door, but we often find ourselves with committee meetings and other activities that cannot be accommodated. We do our best to choose among competing claims for our social hall and other parts of our building all through the year. In short, the building is larger and more usable than it ever has been, but it is still not adequate. It has not kept up with the growing demands and programs of our congregation.

One cannot speak about our building without speaking about money. Our congregation certainly has its own approach to funding and fund-raising, as it has from the very beginning. While we will hear this evening about the financial state of the congregation and approve a new budget, in the long view we have had balanced budgets for the past 25 years and only once have had a surprise excess of expenses over income. Our endowment fund was begun and has grown steadily during my tenure and now exceeds $2 million. We have established the Rimonim Society to encourage members to leave bequests to our synagogue, and that continues to grow. I hear from many rabbinic colleagues that their congregations run at a continuing deficit and they must rely on the largesse of a few contributors to balance the budget each year, but our budget is secure and balanced and watched carefully by a dedicated group of lay leaders and professionals.

Behind the scenes we also have developed several methods of

keeping our cash flow intact, eliminating borrowing and creating a sense of financial stability for Temple Sinai. While these areas are not always ones in which a rabbi is involved, I came to Temple Sinai with a deep commitment to ensuring that the business side of synagogue life was conducted in concert with the spiritual side. To that end, we subject our dues system to constant scrutiny to ensure that no one who wants to participate in the life of our congregation feels excluded.

That is the past. The values on which my vision of Temple Sinai is founded are ones that I hope will continue to be part of this congregation's reality.

Building Community

Temple Sinai pioneered in the development of *kallot* or *chavurot* in the 1960s. We have built community in small groups, through shared interests, neighborhoods, our nursery school, and our religious school. Sometimes it is a struggle to promote and maintain the concept of these smaller groups while also promoting a sense of commitment to the congregation as a whole.

Clearly we need both. We understand that in large congregations such as ours, individuals need to feel a sense of connection on a smaller scale as well as feeling connected to the institution. Communication remains a key to bridging these competing commitments. While the way in which we communicate has changed radically in the past few years, we must continue to seek ways to promote cohesion within our diverse and often overcommitted membership.

The Larger Jewish Community

The values that guide Temple Sinai have inspired our members to participate in the wider Jewish world. Over our history, our congregants have provided—and continue to provide—leadership to the Reform Movement in our region, nationally, and internationally more than any other congregation in the Washington area. Our congregants also have assumed singular leadership positions in the Washington Jewish community and in the social justice arena. In many ways we are a congregation of leaders. We must recognize our place as a national congregation as we continue to accept our leadership responsibilities.

Clearly we are enriched as a congregation by our involvement in our national movement and so many worthy institutions.

Study

For children and for many adults, we are first a house of study. We teach on many levels and in many ways, and we constantly evaluate our educational programs. While our "standard" offerings continue, we must continue to seek new initiatives, such as the family retreat this coming weekend, to engage our members in this highest Jewish value. I have seen how much our congregants want to study, and our challenge is to develop ways to continue to reach them in their busy lives.

Pursuing Justice

Our congregation is filled with members who are deeply committed to the pursuit of justice and the repair of our world. For many, this is an important part of their professional lives and a primary Jewish commitment that leads them to our congregation. We need to continue to build on that commitment, to teach it to our children, and to make it a central principle of our congregational life. We need to advocate for a just society *and* reach out to those in our midst who need our help.

Worship

Many of us find God in this building even as we find our friends and community. Like Jacob wrestling with the angel, we wrestle with how we can find sacred moments in worship and bring holiness into our lives. To create sacred experiences, we need to build regular patterns of worship, help one another understand the liturgy, and—above all—be open to finding God.

For many, the path to God is through the music even more than the words. For others, it is being part of a worshiping community. For still others, the path is through *gemilut chasidim*—righteous acts. For still others, it is through study.

No synagogue can be all things to all people, but Temple Sinai tries to reach its congregants, to challenge them, and to bring them together. Above all, what we need to do is to continue to see Temple Sinai as a sacred community, working together to bring God into our lives through our worship, our study, our righteous acts. How much we need one another in this quest!

Over my 25 years at Temple Sinai I have been blessed to work with many gifted Jewish professionals. My colleagues today at Temple Sinai represent some of the most talented and dedicated members of the Jewish professional community. They share their great gifts with us, day in and day out.

- Rabbi Jessica Oleon has in three years brought enormous energy, enthusiasm, and fresh ideas. She has reached out—especially to our young people—and to every segment of our congregation.

- Jill Stepak in her four years on our professional staff has brought great educational acumen, profound caring, and strength in organization and teaching. Her two colleagues, Diane Zimmerman and Max Socol—who has just joined us to begin our NOAR upper school program—bring a wealth of background and creativity to our religious school.

- Ellen Agler has brought her deep skills of analysis, understanding, and organization to strengthen so many areas of synagogue life. She has been able to reorganize, manage, and sustain our administration, support our building, and enhance all aspects of Temple life.

- Perri Iger-Silversmith in her 20 years here not only has been a profound presence for our younger students but also has built communities with them and their families. She has educated several new generations of learners and had a singular influence on the state of Jewish learning at Temple Sinai and in our community.

- Cantor Laura Croen in her 16 years with us has done far more than bring us beautiful music. She has built a music program that is rich and diverse, and with her enormous caring and pastoral gifts has made a difference in the lives of so many congregants.

- Robyn Helzner has worked at Temple Sinai longer than the 25 years that I have been here. Robyn has guided and nourished so many diverse services and communities and been a partner in our ritual lives. With her remarkable versatility, she has made a unique contribution to the ritual life of our congregation.

- Luis and Dina Tomas have worked at Temple Sinai for 35

years with remarkable devotion. They have cared for so many of us and for our synagogue building. They have built a staff that is remarkable in its dedication and its ability to keep so many programs running so smoothly.

- For these 25 years I have worked side by side with Rabbi Mindy Portnoy. While our styles may be different, we have a superb complementary relationship. For all these years, I have valued her insights and respected her insistence on quality. She has demanding standards and expects all of us to be up to the mark. I appreciate her keen mind and her caring *neshamah*, the soul that leads her to be such an effective pastor.

We have been blessed with so many outstanding lay leaders over these 25 years: presidents and other officers who have given so much to make sure that our congregation is strong and vibrant. We have board members, committee chairs, and a host of volunteers who help make our synagogue what it is, leading our congregation with profound dedication. We will install our board and officers and honor our volunteers on Friday, June 4.

In our office we are fortunate to have a dedicated staff that attends not only to the needs of the office, but to the needs of so many members of the congregation: my own assistant, Marna Barany, who executes her responsibilities so well and also serves as membership coordinator; Linda Katz, Brenda Bergstein, Lili Bender, Robin Berry, Reco Thomas, Anita Greenwald, and our newest addition, Helena Johnson, who has just begun this week. We are all served by each of them, as they seek to meet the needs of both staff and congregants.

Above all, I thank Sherry, who has nurtured me as I have attempted to nurture the congregation; who has cared for me, as my colleagues and I have attempted to care for you; who has taught me with wisdom and insight; and who has shared me with others, as do all our spouses.

You have been an amazing congregation for me to serve these 25 years. You are eager to learn, sensitive to worship, committed to justice, and willing to apply your talents and skills to building a sacred community. May we all go from strength to strength.